Good Practice in Science Teaching

Good Practice in Science Teaching

What research has to say

Second edition

Edited by
Jonathan Osborne and Justin Dillon

 Open University Press

Open University Press
McGraw-Hill Education
McGraw-Hill House
Shoppenhangers Road
Maidenhead
Berkshire
England
SL6 2QL

email: enquiries@openup.co.uk
world wide web: www.openup.co.uk

and Two Penn Plaza, New York, NY 10121-2289, USA

First published 2000
Reprinted 2000, 2003, 2008, 2009
First published in this second edition 2010

A catalogue record of this book is available from the British Library

ISBN-13: 978-0-33-523858-3
ISBN-10: 0-33-523858-0

Library of Congress Cataloging-in-Publication Data
CIP data has been applied for

Fictitous names of companies, products, people, characters and/or data that may be used herein (in case studies or in examples) are not intended to represent any real individual, company, product or event.

Typeset by Aptara Inc., India
Printed in the UK by Bell & Bain Ltd., Glasgow

Mixed Sources
Product group from well-managed
forests and other controlled sources
www.fsc.org Cert no. TT-COC-002769
© 1996 Forest Stewardship Council
FSC

The **McGraw-Hill** Companies

Contents

List of figures

Disclaimer

Every effort has been made to trace and acknowledge ownership of copyright and to clear permission for material reproduced in this book. The publishers will be pleased to make suitable arrangements with any copyright holders whom it has not been possible to contact.

List of tables

Contributors

Philip Adey is Emeritus Professor of Cognition, Science and Education at King's College London. Since the early 1980s he has been one of the leaders of the Cognitive Acceleration projects, including CASE, promoting higher-level thinking in primary and secondary students. His other research interests include the professional development of teachers and the measurement and promotion of creativity in students.

Paul Black worked as a physicist for 20 years before moving to a chair in science education. His interests have moved from curriculum development, to research into learning, and now to research into formative assessment. He has served on projects of the USA National Research Council and as visiting professor at Stanford University, USA. He is Professor Emeritus at King's College London.

Justin Dillon is Professor of Science and Environmental Education and Head of the Science and Technology Education Group at King's College London. He taught science in London schools for 10 years before joining King's in 1989. He has carried out research into children's ideas about science, science teachers' professional development needs and wants, and learning beyond the classroom. He is President of the European Science Education Research Education and an editor of the *International Journal of Science Education*.

Maria Evagorou was a lecturer in science education at King's College London and now holds a post at the University of Nicosia, Cyprus. She worked as an elementary school teacher before undertaking her PhD at King's. Her research focuses on exploring young students' collaborative argumentation within socio-scientific issues, and how online technologies can enhance students' argumentation skills. She has recently received two paper awards: AERA 2008 Graduate Student Paper Award, Science SIG and EdMedia 2008.

John K. Gilbert is a Visiting Professor at King's College London. He has worked as a chemistry teacher, science education researcher, and teacher educator. His research interests are in the roles of models and modelling and of informal learning contexts in science education. He is Editor-in-Chief of the *International Journal of Science Education*.

Melissa Glackin is a lecturer in science education at King's College London. Prior to joining King's, she worked as a biology teacher in London schools and as a project officer for the Field Studies Council. Her research interests are in urban outdoor science teaching and learning.

Christine Harrison is a senior lecturer in science education at King's College London. She worked in London schools for 13 years, which included two stints as Head of Science, before joining King's in 1993. Her research has been focused on assessment for learning and teachers' professional development.

Jill Hohenstein is a Senior Lecturer in Psychology and Education at King's College London. She has worked in both the USA and the UK on research on children's cognitive development. Her current research interests include investigating the ways children can learn about science through language in both formal and informal environments.

Heather King is a visiting research fellow at King's College London. She has worked on a number of international projects studying the nature of learning in informal settings and the varied relationships that exist between museums and schools. Her particular research interests focus on the role and practice of educators employed in museums and other out-of-school contexts.

Alex Manning is a lecturer in science education and Deputy Director of the PGCE at King's College London. Prior to joining King's, she worked as a physics teacher in London schools. Her current research focuses on urban science teachers and departments and she is also interested in initial teacher education and gender issues in science education.

Robin Millar is Salters' Professor of Science Education at the University of York. He taught physics/science in schools in Edinburgh, before moving to York in 1982. His research interests include the role of science in the curriculum, the implications of scientific literacy as a curriculum aim, and the use of diagnostic assessment to clarify and monitor learning goals.

Jonathan Osborne is the California Chair of Science Education at Stanford University, USA. He started his career teaching physics in London schools before joining King's College London in 1985 where he worked until 2008. He has undertaken research into the nature of science and argumentation, attitudes to science and science education for the public understanding of science.

Natasha Serret was a primary school teacher in inner London for six years. She joined King's College London in 2001 as the senior researcher for the primary CASE project and is one of the main authors of *Let's Think Through*

Science! She is currently completing her PhD exploring the relationship between classroom talk and cognitive development.

Shirley Simon is Professor of Education at the Institute of Education, University of London. She began her career as a chemistry teacher before joining King's College London in 1985 where she worked until 2001 as a research fellow and lecturer in science education. Her research interests include teacher professional learning, argumentation in science education and attitudes to science.

Julian Swain was formerly a lecturer in science education at King's College London and taught on the Masters course on assessment. After teaching in London schools, he was involved in a number of national assessment projects such as the Graded Assessment in Science Project. He directed the early versions of the KS3 science National Curriculum assessments. He now acts as an international consultant on educational assessment.

Mary Webb is Senior Lecturer in Information Technology in Education at King's College London. She has taught Biology, Science and ICT in secondary schools and all subjects in primary schools. She has undertaken research and development into pedagogy with new technologies, the use of ICT in science, computer-mediated communication, computer-based modelling and formative assessment.

Introduction

Research matters?

Jonathan Osborne and Justin Dillon

Does research matter to science education? This is the central question that all the contributors to this book attempt to answer. The skill of teaching has been characterized by some as a form of craft knowledge – that is, knowledge which is acquired by practice. As such, it is seen to be dependent on a highly context-specific set of attributes such as the nature of the children, the historical and social context, and the personality of the teacher. Research, it is argued, may inform such practice but its contribution is often marginal and not a feature which can make a significant contribution to improving the quality of either teaching or learning (Lawlor, 1990). In short, good teachers are born not bred.

This volume argues the opposite. First, the view that a mixture of good subject knowledge, pragmatism and ideology is sufficient to ensure excellent and exemplary teaching leaves no space for the teaching of science to progress. Rather, any weaknesses can be ascribed simply to teachers who are deficient in either knowledge or skill. All that is known about what constitutes good practice is essentially already known. The notion that there is a body of research and scholarship that could contribute to the improvement or understanding of practice is greeted with a profound scepticism. This is not to say that teachers do not engage in private reflection on what to teach or how to teach it. However, our view and the view of the contributors to this volume are that if the practice of teaching science is to advance, then there needs to be a public, professional discourse that is informed by more than personal experience. Why do we believe that is the case? The teaching of science requires the teacher to engage with sets of ideas and values about the curriculum, pedagogy and assessment. As Alexander (2004) argues, each of these *enable* teaching, defining, respectively, what is to be taught, how it is to be taught, and how the outcomes are to be measured. Such work takes place in institutions, and in the case of secondary (high school) science, in specialized laboratories, where the work is *formalized* and regulated by local and national policies. Finally, there are features which help us to *locate* and define teaching. For instance, teaching is a cultural act. In the case of science education, it is an attempt to introduce young people to a body of knowledge and practices which are deemed to have significant cultural capital. Then, the teaching of science has a history – both of its successes and its failures – from which we can learn; a history that has also shaped, and will continue to shape, what teachers do. Knowledge of that history is thus an indispensable tool for making sense of both its present state and the future possibilities. In contrast, the pragmatist's view, at its extreme, simply sees exemplary teaching as a requirement for every generation, nay every individual, to reinvent the wheel. In short, the critics' remedies for the failings of educational practice are a recipe for stasis – the ossification of current practice as the epitome of what is best and the denial of hope of a better future. The view taken in this book, in contrast, is that there is a body of scholarship and empirical evidence which can inform and *advance* practice.

This is not to say that teachers cannot learn from each other. Indeed, one of the contributions of research has been to establish that teacher learning and professional development are most effective when teachers come together to form a 'professional learning community' (Bell and Gilbert, 1996; Hoban, 2002). The notion, however, that teachers can learn *only* from each other is akin to arguing that doctors might discover a cure for malaria by watching each other's valiant attempts to treat the symptoms, rather than its cause. Essentially, education, like any profession, requires individuals to stand aside, to study both the minutiae of classroom practice and the broad sweep of both the policy and practice of its institutions, and to ask critical, reflective questions of what they see. In the case of science education, such questions include: Are laboratories necessary for teaching science? What should be the content of a curriculum that meets the needs of all children? How do we interest young children in learning science?

The answers to such questions often demand a level of specialist knowledge which is not accessible to those caught up in the relentless pressures of classroom life. For education is a multi-disciplinary profession, drawing as it does on the more fundamental disciplines of psychology – to inform us about the nature of individuals and the learning process; on philosophy – to inform us about the nature of the science we teach and the aims and values we espouse; on history – as a treasure trove of case studies of how people have dealt with, and responded to similar issues in the past; and last, but not least, on sociology – which informs us about the dynamics of the society in which we are situated and the values and concerns of the interested participants. In short, education is a complex act, informed by many domains of knowledge, imbued with values and an act to which there is more than can be learnt in a lifetime.

Standing at the crossroads of such disciplinary ideas, the task of the academic in education is to sift, to assimilate and to distil the implications for the practice of science education. So, for instance, what are the messages from the evidence collected on the psychology of learning for the teaching of science? What are the implications for pedagogy that follow from constructivist viewpoints? How does evidence from Piagetian-inspired interventions, painstakingly collected, re-orientate our ideas on sequencing and structuring activities for learning science? Or, what does the work of linguists have to say about the nature of scientific language that makes science intrinsically difficult? These are all examples of the kind of questions that academic scholarship in education attempts to address; and all examples of questions which practitioners find difficult to consider for more than a fleeting moment, when engaged in the imperatives of daily life required to navigate the requirements of teaching 5–8 lessons a day and by the relentless drive to achieve improving standards.

Of necessity, research in science education is an investment in belief – a belief that intellectual endeavour and focused study of particular aspects of learning and teaching will result in a better understanding of the predicaments faced by the learner and the teacher. Like any investments, there are winners and losers. But ultimately it is an act of faith that the products of such work will produce tangible improvements. Who could have foretold in 1976, for instance, that the work of Michael Shayer and H. Wylam (1978) investigating the Piagetian levels of the schoolchildren, funded by the Social Sciences Research Council, would ultimately lead to the development of a course which has shown, and continues to show, significant improvements in exam results compared to other schools? Who could have foretold that the work of Rosalind Driver (1983), funded by the Secondary Science Curriculum Review, would lead to a major transformation in our understanding of the conceptual complexities of what it means to learn science? Who could have foretold that the sustained interest in assessment, its function and purpose shown by Paul Black and his colleagues over a period of 20 years would lead to the invaluable insights on the role and function of assessment found in the publication *Inside the Black Box* (Black and Wiliam, 1998)?

Like any profession, there will be products which are mediocre; the PhD theses which languish in some dark and dusty corner; the journal articles that fail to reach the parts that others do. But, we would contend, that this is the price that we have to pay, and *must* pay, if we are to acquire the evidence and understanding to take our knowledge and classroom practice forward, at least a few faltering steps.

Critics point ardently to the weaknesses of such research. In the UK, the Teacher Training Agency (TTA) lecture in 1996 by Professor David Hargreaves notably initiated a debate that still continues. Hargreaves (1996) asked if teaching could be said to be a research-based profession, and concluded that it could not. The problem, he argued, lay in the nature and quality of the outcomes of educational research:

> Given the huge amounts of educational research conducted over the past fifty years or more, there are few areas which have yielded a corpus of research evidence regarded as scientifically sound and as a worthwhile resource to guide professional action.
>
> (Hargreaves 1996, p. 2)

Comparing educational research to that conducted in the field of medicine and the natural sciences, he argued that educational research lacked their cumulative character and too often produced inconclusive or contestable results.

We hope that this volume offers a response to such a critique. Two points need to be made immediately. First, volumes such as this, or the more extensive handbooks on research in science education (Abell and Lederman, 2007; Fraser and Tobin, 1998) would not have been possible 20 or 30 years ago. As a field of enquiry, research on science education has extended both its knowledge and understanding of the nature of problem and some of its remediation. The better examples of this research have been empirically tested in a variety of manners. Second, the comparison with medicine is a flawed analogy. In medicine, the goal is clear – to find ways of improving the health of the patient and its outcome is easily measurable. Either the patient gets better or does not. Education, in contrast, is deeply imbued with values. What constitutes the goal itself is often not a matter of common agreement. For instance, while some teachers might hold the view that it is a knowledge of the concepts of science that matter, others hold these less dear and would prefer to emphasize science as a way of reasoning or way of knowing. Even if we can agree about the goals, often the tools for their measurement lack validity, are unreliable, or both. The English national Key Stage 3 tests given to pupils age 14, for instance, were criticized on both these grounds.

At its very least, what research offers is a vision, informed by evidence, of how practice might be improved. We can imagine no other profession that would attempt to dismantle the links to the research community that offers it new possibilities and improved practice. Doctors would be the first to support continuing medical research; engineers rely on research to provide them with novel materials and techniques; even lawyers, that most-maligned of professions, rely on legal analysts and academics for the advance of their practice. Yet, why so many casual commentators, outside the teaching profession, think that learning and teaching does not warrant research requiring just monitoring of performance remains a source of puzzlement. Is this the measure of the low regard that some politicians and members of the general public have for those who shape the future in our classrooms?

Our contention is that teachers, students and the status of science teaching all have much to gain from research which offers a tool for reflexive examination of practice and its improvements. While some teachers do engage in research on their own practice, it is difficult to keep informed of the ever-growing body of contemporary theory which would help them analyse and interpret the nature of the issues and challenges that confront them daily. Moreover, there must also be a place for the large-scale, academic research project which has the resources and contemporary expertise which can address some of the many challenges that exist within the teaching and learning of science. This book, then, is an attempt to summarize some of that evidence – that which is the most salient at this time.

In this book, we have drawn primarily on a body of expertise that resides in the science education research community at King's College London, asking colleagues to present, wherever possible, the understandings and implications that can be drawn from the wide body of research evidence that exists in their own specialist research interests in science education. Inevitably, in some areas, there is more, and in others, there is less. Perhaps not surprisingly, the 'jam' is unevenly spread but in all cases there has been no shortage. Rather, authors have presented the headlines – essential points for consideration within the limited confines of the space that we have allowed. In these chapters, there are points for consideration

- within the daily round of classroom practice;
- within the department;
- for the wider issues of concern in teaching of science that recurrently surface.

In this, the second edition, all the authors have met and discussed with the editors which issues would be most salient to know for the practising teacher. Each chapter was reviewed by two other authors and discussed at a two-day meeting. We hope, therefore, that this process has contributed to a product which is both comprehensive and communicates clearly what research areas in their separate domains might have to say. Inevitably, each chapter represents a partial view but we believe that in the chapters of this book, there is much of substance that will both inform and challenge the practices of the reader. The evidence and scholarship that are presented are supported by detailed references in the Bibliography at the end of the book together with suggestions for further reading. While the complexity of educational research is such that the nature of the evidence rarely surpasses that seen in Yeats' 'the blue, the dim and the half-light', we hope the reader will find much here that will illuminate many aspects of their practice. In short, that rather than science teaching being a practice which is the cumulation of years of *ad hoc* folk tales, this book will contribute to presenting it as a practice which is supported by a well-established body of evidence that justifies the practices of the classroom teacher.

The original incentive for this book was as a tribute to the research and scholarship of the late Professor Rosalind Driver whose work at the University of Leeds, and then at King's College London, permeates this volume and the work of others. She was one of the most pre-eminent figures in science education of her generation – a major figure on both national and international stages. Not only did she have the respect of science education researchers but, more importantly, that of science teachers. Throughout her professional career, she displayed an enduring passion for science education and took very seriously the responsibility of research in trying to improve our understanding of what is involved in learning and teaching science and, indeed, what might constitute an education in science. With the writing of the second edition, it should also be a tribute perhaps to the contribution that King's College and those who have worked there – Michael Shayer, Philip Adey, Paul Black and many of the authors of this volume – have made. To paraphrase the words of E. M. Forster (1910), its aim is to only connect research and practice so that they live in separation no longer, else robbed of this isolation, both will wither.

1 Science teachers, science teaching

Issues and challenges

Justin Dillon and Alex Manning

Introduction

> *Across the country, the best teachers inspire their pupils with the wonder and excitement of science and engineering. They provide the breeding ground for the scientists, entrepreneurs and technicians of tomorrow. They also make sure our citizens and consumers understand the risks and benefits of modern science. But to do this, teachers require consistent support and access to the best methods and practices*
>
> (Labour Party, 2001, unnumbered).

This chapter focuses on science teachers and science teaching. In doing so, we will refer to challenges raised by our colleagues in the rest of this book who aim to provide 'access to the best methods and practices'. However, any consideration of science teaching needs to take into account three inter-related issues. First, the science curriculum has changed and continues to change in the light of developments in science and technology in the wider world (House of Lords Select Committee on Science and Technology, 2001). Second, the roles and responsibilities of science teachers have changed as the value of science to society has developed and broadened (Dillon, 2002). Third, the training available to science teachers has evolved as a result of major changes in education often instigated for predominantly political purposes (Dillon, 2000). Although the focus of the chapter is predominantly on developments in England, many of the issues are faced by science teachers throughout the world.

The Labour Party's description of what the 'best teachers' do, quoted above, begs the question, what is meant by 'best methods and practices'? There is an implicit assumption in the statement, made by one of the United Kingdom's major political parties, that 'national wealth depends on competing success- fully in international markets' (Laugksch, 2000, p. 84). This argument, which Laugksch describes as a 'macro' level justification for science education, is based on an idea that:

international competitiveness in turn relies *inter alia* upon a vigorous national research and development program in order, first, to maintain or capture ground in the worldwide race for new high-technology products in the case of developed countries and, second, to exploit smaller niche markets in the case of developing countries. Underpinning such a research and development program is a steady supply of scientists, engineers, and technically trained personnel. Only nations whose citizens possess an appropriate level of scientific literacy will be able to sustain this supply.

(2000, p. 84)

Such rhetoric is common among policy-makers worldwide (though challenged by some researchers, see, for example, Osborne and Dillon, 2008, and Chapter 11 in this volume). As recently as December 2008, Lord Grayson, then newly-appointed as the UK's Science Minister, was reported by the BBC as saying: 'Science is fundamental to this country. As we go into this global downturn the importance of maintaining our investment in science has never been greater' (BBC News, 5 December). At a European level, the widely promoted 'Rocard Report', *Science Now: A Renewed Pedagogy for the Future of Europe,* opens with this assertion:

In recent years, many studies have highlighted an alarming decline in young people's interest for key science studies and mathematics. Despite the numerous projects and actions that are being implemented to reverse this trend, the signs of improvement are still modest. Unless more effective action is taken, Europe's longer term capacity to innovate, and the quality of its research will also decline.

(High Level Group on Science Education, 2007, p. 2)

So, in introducing this chapter, we note that science teachers are tasked, throughout the world, with a set of almost Herculean challenges: make science lessons interesting; inspire pupils with wonder and excitement; increase the flow of scientists, entrepreneurs and technicians of tomorrow; and ensure that citizens and consumers understand the risks and benefits of modern science. These external demands help to make science teaching what it is today. This chapter, then, looks at the *habitus* (Bourdieu, 1990) of science teachers – the collection of behaviours, techniques and attitudes which define them and which reflect the influence of culture, politics and society – and at how curriculum, assessment and pedagogy issues continue to present challenges that research might help us to understand better.

Who are science teachers?

Science teachers occupy a unique position in schools. They usually have their own specialist rooms and laboratories; in some countries they may be supported by technicians; and they may, on occasion, wear specialized clothing and use safety equipment. The job entails training students in complex practical skills often dealing with health and safety issues far removed from the experience of teachers of other subjects (Teachernet, 2005). For example, in school science, students are encouraged to use strong acids, fire and scalpels, frequently and with limited first-aid equipment or training.

Science teachers are usually part of a department of either their own discipline or a broader 'Science' grouping. Our experience of teaching in and working with schools, over the years, has led us to recognize that science teachers' allegiance to their specific subject background can be a significant contributor to their identities and thus to their attitude towards the curriculum. Many teachers see themselves as, say, biologists first and science teachers second. This distinction can have implications for how they interpret the curriculum and on how they see their professional development needs (see, also, Chapter 13).

Many countries face a shortage of science teachers, particularly those with a physical science background. In a large-scale survey of mathematics and science teaching in England, Moor et al. found that 44 per cent of science teachers had a degree in biology; 25 per cent had a degree in chemistry and 19 per cent had a degree in physics (Moor et al. 2006, p. 106). The number of science teachers in the 630 departments that responded ranged from two to 24 with a mean of nine teachers (p. 110). Overall, 8 per cent of science teachers were defined as newly qualified teachers (p. 110).

An historical dimension

Throughout many parts of the world, science education has been through a process of almost continual change since the 1960s (see, for example, http://www.nationalacademies.org/rise/backg3a.htm). The most significant changes include the introduction of new courses, such as the Biological Sciences Curriculum Study in the USA and Nuffield Science in the UK; the move towards 'balanced science' (that is, the teaching of biology, chemistry and physics for all students) as opposed to separate sciences or allowing students to opt out of one or more of biology, chemistry or physics; the rise of 'process science' (as opposed to focusing on 'the facts'); the rise of the 'Science for All' and scientific literacy movements; the introduction of a national curriculum or national standards and the associated assessment regimes; and, more recently, the introduction of more vocationally oriented science courses aimed at a broad range of students.

Each innovation has, in some way, challenged existing science teacher pedagogy – the new diplomas being introduced into schools in England being a case in point. Over the years, our view of science has changed (see Chapter 2) as has our view of what learning in science involves (see Chapter 4). The complexity of the relationship between pedagogic change, views of learners and learning, and changes in the representation of science in the curriculum is indicated by this comment by Monk and Dillon:

> Shifting pedagogic perspectives have been the major surface feature of the changes in discourse of science education in the metropolitan countries of the old imperial powers. Generally we have moved from transmission views to more constructivist views. Older views of science as an empirical, inductivist enterprise with access to a knowledge base of an independent reality have been gradually eroded and replaced by newer constructivist views. These are not unitary (Solomon 1994), but multiple. However, they all share a concern for the student's knowledge base as being idiosyncratic and biographical.
>
> (Monk and Dillon, 1995, p. 317)

This gradual erosion of older views of science has come about through curriculum change, the introduction of new courses and through changes to the nature of pre-service and in-service courses. The process of change in science education, since the 1960s, though gradual, has not been one of seamless transition, rather it has involved reconstruction, reversal and high levels of political engagement (Donnelly and Jenkins, 2001). In summary, then, change is not something that is new to science teaching or science teachers, change is ever-present.

Public policy and the science curriculum

Science is still not a hugely popular subject in school, especially in developed countries (Osborne and Collins, 2000; Osborne and Dillon, 2008). Osborne et al. (2003), having reviewed research into pupils' attitudes to science, concluded that school science left a significant number of pupils with negative attitudes towards the subject (see also Chapter 11 in this volume). The UK House of Lords Select Committee on Science and Technology concluded that:

> The science curriculum at 14 to 16 aims to engage all students with science as a preparation for life. At the same time it aims to inspire and prepare some pupils to continue with science post-16. In practice it does neither of these well.
>
> (2001, p. 9)

Although dissatisfaction with school science education was evident in the USA and in the UK even before the launch of the Sputnik satellite in 1957 (Klainin, 1988), the Nuffield Science projects mentioned above, which played a major role in defining science education in the UK in the second half of the twentieth century, owe at least some of their success to what is sometimes termed the post-Sputnik angst (Waring, 1979). However, despite the innovations of the Nuffield era in science education, successive government reports and political commentary have continued to focus on the inadequacy of science education in both primary (elementary) (for example, DES, 1978) and secondary (high) schools (for example, DES, 1979). The criticisms, which, in part, continue today, were partially responsible for the changes in the science curriculum in the 1980s and 1990s. These criticisms have been mirrored in countries such as Australia, Canada and the USA (see, for example, http://www.acer.edu.au/enews/0705_AER51.html).

What, though, is meant by the 'science curriculum'? In the late 1950s, Kerr wrote that '[t]he teaching of general science as an alternative to biology, chemistry and physics has been a controversial topic among science teachers since the Thompson Report of 1918' (1958–59, pp. 156–7). 'General science' was characterized as being of lower status than the separate subjects (see, for example, Goodson, 1985). Since the 1970s, more determined moves were made towards making science 'balanced' across the traditional divisions of biology, chemistry and physics. The rationale was usually expressed in terms of citizenship and living in the modern world (DES, 1985).

In *Beyond 2000*, a critique of science education at the turn of the twenty-first century, Millar and Osborne (1998) picked out what they considered to be the major developments in education, and particularly in science education in England since 1960. First, they identified 'the major curriculum innovation, undertaken by the Nuffield Foundation which ... gave greater emphasis to the role and use of experimental work' (1998, pp. 2002–3). Nuffield Science involved a more experimental, investigative approach to science education pedagogy than had previously been the case (Jenkins, 2004). The Nuffield approach to science education involved an emphasis on practical activities, supported by worksheets, teachers' guides, a network of teachers, examiners, academics and publishers. *Nuffield Combined Science*, first published in 1970, was probably the most influential course. Indeed, Keohane (1986, p. vi) remarked that 'by 1979 ... half the schools in England were using the course wholly or in part'. The 1986 revision of the *Nuffield Combined Science* materials, published as *Nuffield Science 11 to 13*, took into account various changes that had taken place since the first version was published in 1970:

> in that period, school children, schools, science, technology, and society at large have undergone great change. And that is not to mention the great changes in children's expectations of schools and science lessons, in teachers' expectations of children and resources for learning, and in society's expectations of teachers.
>
> (*Nuffield Science 11 to 13*, 1986, p. 2)

The editors and authors of the scheme took into account 'what science lessons in primary schools and for the 13 to 16 age group [would] be like' (*Nuffield Science 11 to 13*, 1986, p. 2). The objectives of the *Nuffield Science 11 to 13* curriculum reflected a view that science education should be relevant to students and should encourage them to act in a 'scientific' manner during lessons (see also Driver, 1983). Acting in a scientific manner, although not actually being a scientist *per se*, involved students developing a critical understanding of the nature of science (Monk and Dillon, 2000) (see also Chapter 2).

Millar and Osborne (1998) also noted another significant development in science education as the introduction of the comprehensive school system in the mid-1960s which led, *inter alia*, to the development of courses 'for the less academic pupil' (p. 2003). This change had enormous implications for science teacher pedagogy. The science curriculum, which traditionally was aimed at preparing future scientists and technicians was inappropriate for the majority of students. The idea of 'Science for all!', first mooted in a public lecture given by James Wilkinson in 1847 (Hurd, 1997), gained ground around this time. Under the broad umbrella of Science, Technology and Society (STS), a range of courses were introduced which aimed to address the needs of girls as well as boys and to provide a more relevant and broader science education for students who would never become scientists (Fensham, 2004; Turner, 2008).

Douglas Roberts (2007a) distinguishes between two 'visions' of scientific literacy: Vision I and Vision II. Vision I 'looks inward at science itself – its products such as laws and theories, and its processes such as hypothesizing and experimenting', whereas Vision II 'looks outward at situations in which science has a role, such as decision-making about socioscientific issues' (Roberts, 2007b, p. 9). A Vision I approach might be appropriate for future scientists whereas a Vision II approach might be better suited for the majority of citizens. The tension between the conflicting visions operates at the level of the curriculum design as well as in the classroom.

Some of the more recent changes in the science curriculum owe something to external political and social factors and, more specifically, to research into girls' under-achievement carried out as long ago as the 1970s and 1980s (see, for example, Head, 1985). At that time, dissatisfaction with the quality of state education in the UK, highlighted by James Callaghan, the Labour Prime Minister in 1976, eventually resulted in the introduction of the National Curriculum by a Conservative government in 1988 (Donnelly and Jenkins, 1999). The National Curriculum was designed, in part, to serve the needs of those who wished to compare schools by ensuring that all schools taught the same content so that their results could be compared more easily than was previously the case. The National Curriculum also addressed the criticisms of those who saw too many girls opting out of the physical sciences at the age of 14 by ensuring that all students studied elements of biology, chemistry and physics (Head, 1985).

With the introduction of the National Curriculum and the concomitant national system of assessment, league tables and parental choice, schools in the 1990s became more competitive (Sinclair et al., 1996) (see also Chapter 10 in this volume). As a result of the general shift in education away from more collegial models of working (such as inter-school collaborations), teachers began to focus more on school improvement in isolation rather than through developing as a 'community of practice' (Lave and Wenger, 1991). The engine for change shifted from an internal personal desire for excellence to an external locus of control within a climate of accountability (such as described by Gewirtz, 2002). Recent initiatives in England, which reflect a desire to put school reform back in the hands of schools, such as the Leading Edge Partnership Programme (see www.ledge.org.uk) and the introduction of Specialist Schools (see http://www.standards.dfes.gov.uk/specialistschools/) may encourage more collaboration to solve shared problems.

Courses developed during the 1980s aimed to increase the emphasis placed on the processes of science (that is, the skills necessary to undertake science experiments) (Jenkins, 2004). Millar and Osborne also noted the influence of the Department of Education and Science policy statement, *Science 5–16* (DES, 1985) which argued that all young people should have a 'broad and balanced' science education (that is, a curriculum containing biology, chemistry and physics throughout the school system) and occupying (for most pupils) 20 per cent of curriculum time from age 14 to 16 (Jenkins, 2004). The introduction, in 1986, of the General Certificate of Secondary Education (GCSE) resulted in a variety of science courses that included all three main sciences intended for all students. This move was not, in our view, universally popular.

Whether science in schools should be separated into biology, chemistry, physics or other science subjects, or whether it should be taught in an integrated, co-ordinated or 'balanced' way, is another issue that has been debated and has implications for the professional development of science teachers. In the UK, there is evidence that more students are being taught separate sciences than has been the case in recent years (Fairbrother and Dillon, 2009) and that the balanced science/separate science debate refuses to go away.

The move towards a model of science education that incorporated studies of the nature of science and of its applications was taken up by the major professional organization for science teachers, the Association for Science Education (ASE). However, their original proposals (ASE, 1979) which promoted more 'attention to the nature of science and studies in environmental science, applied science and the interaction of science and society' (Jennings, 1992, pp. 3–4) proved unpopular with teachers, some of whom did not regard themselves as able to teach socio-scientific issues. Both the ASE and the Royal Society issued policy statements advocating reform in science education (ASE, 1981; Royal Society, 1982).

Since science became one of the three core subjects of the National Curriculum, the nature of science education changed and 'there has been a general acceptance that learning science involves more than simply knowing some facts and ideas about the natural world' (Millar and Osborne, 1998, p. 2003) (for a counter-view, see Hodson, 1990, 1992).

Other key developments not identified explicitly by Millar and Osborne (1998) in their *Beyond 2000* report include moves to make science more multicultural (Reiss, 1993) and attempts to develop a global dimension to science education (Brownlie et al. 2003). The opportunities for the development of a more beneficial relationship between science education and environmental education have also been identified (Dillon and Scott, 2002) (see also Chapter 12 in this volume). Many of these influences and trends in science education need to be understood by science teachers if they are to keep abreast of their subject's place in the curriculum.

Assessment issues

Assessment is the topic of Chapters 9 (formative) and 10 (summative) so we will keep this section rather shorter than the section on the science curriculum. The link between curriculum and assessment is exemplified by the train of events that was set in motion by the introduction of the National Curriculum in England and Wales in 1988/9. In response to some of the criticisms of early versions, the National Curriculum was revised several times. The curriculum was originally divided into more than 20 Attainment Targets. It was progressively reduced to four. The assessment system has also been changed substantially with a return to grades as opposed to levels for examinations at age 16.

Science in the National Curriculum for England and Wales (DoE, 1995) recognized the importance of the inclusion of some education in the epistemological and methodological basis of science by making one of the four Attainment Targets, Scientific Investigation, which was itself divided into three strands:

1. Asking questions, predicting and hypothesizing.
2. Observing, measuring and manipulating variables.
3. Interpreting results and evaluating evidence.

Sc1, as it has become known, was assessed by teachers as part of the overall national system of assessment. The implementation of Sc1 was the cause of more controversy than the content of the curriculum itself. Donnelly et al. (1996, p. 8) point out that:

> [T]he evidence . . . suggests that it was indeed a major change in practice for most science teachers. Despite its origin in a long-established tradition of British science education, Sc1 can be seen as a radical, compulsory form of curriculum development.

The major change was in terms of a shift towards more investigatory practical work than had previously been the case: students were encouraged to undertake experiments in a more exploratory manner (see also Chapter 6). Nevertheless, the evidence from examination boards was that pupils were beginning to achieve standards of work that were not being achieved prior to 1988 (Millar and Osborne, 1998).

Sc1 assessment procedures have also changed as the National Curriculum has been revised with a concomitant necessity for continuing professional development (CPD) for science teachers. The implication is that assessment reform, coupled with curriculum change can drive science teaching in a particular direction. The situation is made more complicated by a recent emphasis on Assessment for Learning (AfL) (QCA, 2007) which incorporates major changes to the way that teachers assess, record and plan lessons (see also Chapter 9 in this volume).

Science teacher pedagogy

Having looked at the influence of the curriculum and the assessment system on science teachers, we turn now to look at science teacher pedagogy itself – the dependent variable. By pedagogy we mean more than teaching. Pedagogy implies the whole philosophy and value system that leads teachers to make the choices they do in what and how to teach. Shymansky et al. writing about their research in Australia describe a 'typical' classroom and science teacher:

> The classroom was a self-contained lecture-laboratory room. The teacher, a middle-aged man with a strong academic background in physical science, was an active graduate student pursuing a masters degree in science education at a local university. He expressed commitment to many constructivist ideas. He was enthusiastic about implementing ideas that he had researched at the university, and valued hands-on/minds-on activities, collaborative problem solving, and communities of learning. However, to some extent he was restricted in his teaching values and intentions by the need to complete the requisite subject matter of the unit of study within an allotted period of time. Nevertheless, within the traditional structure of the science department in his school, his lessons included strategies and activities that promoted knowledge construction and discourse opportunities. He used whole-class discussion for organization of the day's activities, and students frequently worked in small groups to complete experiments, reports, and study guides.
>
> (1997, p. 576)

Although nowadays the 'typical' science teacher might (a) be female and (b) not be studying for a conventional masters degree, and, therefore, would be less aware of the discourse of 'constructivism', there are many characteristics of the description above that would typify a secondary school science lesson in England and many other countries. The crux of the debate about science teachers' pedagogical development relates to the perceived need for teachers to challenge the orthodox 'teaching values and intentions' which manifest themselves in what many would describe as 'traditional science teaching'.

For many teachers, compulsory investigatory work 'by Order' (Donnelly et al., 1996) created the greatest need for a shift in science teacher pedagogy. Teachers had to organize and assess a minimum of investigations (around one or two each term). Although Nuffield Science and later curriculum material attempted to challenge the existing orthodoxy of practical work, the majority of experimental work carried out in schools tended to be confirmatory rather than investigational (Donnelly et al., 1996). However, despite the approach inherent in the National Curriculum documents, commentators (for example, Jenkins, 1992) have argued that little real progress has been made in that school science is not radically different from what went on before the changes. Millar and Osborne, for example, described the science curriculum as being 'a diluted [that is, similar topics but easier] form of the GCE curriculum' (1998, p. 2004). They argued that that the curriculum content was very similar to the O-level courses that preceded the GCSE, which were generally very traditional in their approach and which encouraged traditional science teaching.

Dillon and Osborne (1999, p. 1) argued that there were 'a number of widespread concerns about the capabilities of the extant [science] teaching force to deliver an exciting and engaging experience [to pupils]'. These concerns focused on problems with the recruitment and retention of science teachers (see also Chapter 13). Other issues have also been of concern, for example, the Council for Science and Technology (CST) noted in 2000 that 'a significant number of pupils are negative about the intrinsic and extrinsic merits of science and/or the science curriculum' (CST, 2000, p. 10). This negativity is, in part, a reflection of the ways in which science is taught in schools (Osborne and Collins, 2000).

Keys, reporting on the findings of the Second International Science Study (1982–86), wrote that:

> While the majority of 14 year-olds reported that their teachers normally introduced new material and went over material which had been covered previously at the beginning of each lesson, rather fewer reported that their science teachers summarized what had been taught at the end of each lesson... About half the 14 year-olds reported copying from the blackboard often and half doing so sometimes... Over 90 per cent of the 14 year-olds reported having science tests, about 40 per cent often and 50 per cent sometimes.
>
> (1987, p. 159)

Thus there is little evidence that science teaching, in terms of strategies and tactics, made significant progress during the period from the 1970s to the 1990s when many of today's science teachers were themselves school students. This state of affairs occurred despite the best endeavours of new curricula and new resources which encouraged aspirations of more creative processes that, in the end, were rarely met.

Pedagogical training for beginning teachers

The model that many current pre-service teachers see taught in schools may be little different from what they experienced when they were younger. This lack of alternative models in pre-service education may prove to be a major factor in limiting the professional development of many teachers. Standards applied across the teaching force may neglect the individual biographical element of professional development. Ironically, when placed in teaching practice schools which have teachers with varying styles, our own pre-service students often report tensions in trying to please all the people all the time and, consequently, failing to please anyone.

An approach taken in England and Wales by the then Teacher Training Agency (TTA) strategy involved, *inter alia*, promulgating a series of national standards for teacher training (see, for example, TTA, 1997). Despite the efforts of the TTA (later renamed the Training and Development Agency for Schools (TDA)) to raise the competence of newly-qualified teachers, the evidence suggests that the expertise required to deliver the science curriculum is not fully acquired in initial courses. For example, in a study involving 49 newly-qualified teachers (NQTs) of varying subjects at the end of their first term of teaching, Capel (1998) identified a number of aspects of teaching that the NQTs felt they had not been well prepared for in their initial training. With respect to the issue of teacher individuality, it is critical to point out that Capel also found that: 'the results suggested that the combination of aspects of teaching identified by any one NQT were unique to that individual and resulted from a combination of personal and situational factors' (1998, p. 393). There is substantial evidence from elsewhere in England, Australia and the USA to indicate that pre-service courses only have time to develop sufficient confidence to operate adequately in the classroom and to expose student teachers to a baseline repertoire of essential pedagogic strategies (Luft and Cox, 1998; Mulholland and Wallace, 1999). Teachers entering the profession with this minimum repertoire are in need of continuing teacher development to develop further both in terms of subject knowledge and pedagogic content knowledge (see Chapter 13). In some ways, this has been the case for as long as science has been taught in schools (Kerr, 1963).

As was discussed above, in recent years, science investigations, a particular form of experiment (often involving testing a hypothesis practically) and the legitimate descendant of 'discovery learning', have become widespread (Jones et al., 1992) and mandatory (DoE, 1995). In parallel with a shift towards a more process-based approach to science has come an increased awareness of the need to consider the internal structure of science's epistemology and methodology (Monk et al., 1994). Both of these trends required a change in pedagogy in order to be implemented successfully, in line with the demands of the National Curriculum.

Science education, practical work and the process/content debate

As we discussed earlier, one of the key changes in science education has been the role of practical (experimental) work in schools (see also Chapter 6). We also noted that another related issue is the proportion of time that is spent on acquiring scientific knowledge compared with the time spent on developing skills (the process/content debate). This debate is not new, Jevons, writing at the end of the 1960s, noted that:

> Schoolteachers themselves get very keen on new approaches – which in itself is half the battle won – but their enthusiasm is not untinged with scepticism about the value of pupils finding out for themselves in the laboratory . . . Demands on time mean fewer facts – that is, a lower syllabus content; and that is a price which, in present circumstances, we can afford to go on paying for some time yet as long as we get the right kind of return in the form of minds which are lively and inquiring and not going under in a morass of information.
>
> (1969, p. 147)

Commenting on a recent survey of 510 UK science teachers, NESTA, the National Endowment for Science, Technology and the Arts, said that 'science teachers are resolutely committed to the principle of practical and experiment-based science enquiry learning' (2005, p. 4). Some 84 per cent of their sample considered practical work to be 'very' important with 14 per cent considering it 'quite' important. However, if the defining characteristic of school science is 'the practical', then the characteristics of the practical have changed substantially within our lifetime and within those of many practising science teachers.

Writing in the late 1950s, Kerr stated that there was 'some evidence that teachers of science, particularly in grammar schools, still consider the chief value of their work is associated with the claims made for the study of science as a mental discipline' (1958–59, p. 156). In the 1960s, 1970s and 1980s, experimental work served primarily to demonstrate techniques and to verify theory. In the early 1960s, Kerr, reviewing practical activity in school science, commented that:

> There was a lack of consistency between some kinds of experiments which teachers said they did and the stated value of such experiments. Verification experiments were frequently used but teachers thought their educational value was limited. Tradition and convenience perpetuated outmoded methods. On the other hand, finding out or 'getting-to-know-by-investigation' experiments were infrequently used, especially by the chemists and physicists, although the teachers ranked their educational value high.
>
> (1963, p. 54)

It may well be the case that tradition and convenience perpetuate outmoded methods. Dissatisfaction with the large number of science facts (the 'content') in the curriculum and the emphasis on rote learning have driven debates about science education for many years and prompted new approaches to science education in the mid-to-late 1980s (Hodson, 1990; Donnelly and Jenkins, 2001). This shift occurred partly as a result of an increased focus on the processes of science and how they could be taught and assessed.

Osborne (1993), among others, argued for more thought and discussion in school science and less rote-practical work (see also Gunstone (1991) and Solomon (1991)). Hodson (1990; 1992) criticized poorly planned practical work, describing its use as being 'ill-conceived, muddled and lacking in educational value' (1992, p. 65). The debate (the process/content debate) was not about practical work, *per se*, rather it was more about the relative efficacy of different ways of teaching science. The argument was that if pupils were to learn about how science works, then they needed to develop an understanding of the processes of science (that is, the skills used in doing experiments). As Jevons put it:

> The case for investigational work in the laboratory rests partly on its supposed resemblance to the 'real thing', creativity in research, and the hope that in consequence it will stimulate and foster the right kind of abilities and ways of thought.
>
> (1969, p. 147)

There is some disagreement among science teachers as to whether the amount of science enquiry has changed in recent years: NESTA's survey of 510 UK science teachers, referred to earlier, found that 42 per cent thought that the amount had increased over the preceding ten years while 32 per cent thought the opposite (NESTA, 2005, p. 7). Our perspective, as people who visit schools regularly, is that schools do vary considerably in the nature and the amount of practical work that they carry out, hence the findings of the NESTA survey.

In the same NESTA survey, 99 per cent of their sample of science teachers believed that enquiry learning had a significant (83 per cent – 'very'; 16 per cent – 'a little') impact on student performance and attainment (NESTA, 2005, p. 5). However, views about the role of processes in science education have been contested: some science educators have argued that practical work might help students to understand how scientists work, while others have argued that a process-based approach (that is, an approach that focused on experimental skills) was likely to lead to better understanding of science concepts (Donnelly et al., 1996) (see also Chapter 6).

Final thoughts

We have tried to show that science teachers are made not born, at least in terms of the influence of society's views of science and of the influence of politicians on what is taught and how it is taught. The argument could be made that it is the assessment tail that wags the pedagogy dog. That is, what is assessed and how it is assessed do, in the end, dictate how and what people teach. But the situation is more subtle than that and individual teachers' identities and life histories also influence what they do in the classroom.

We have indicated above how the other chapters in the book provide insight into what is taught, how it is taught, why it is taught, when it is taught and where it is taught. We know a lot about how learners learn and how teachers teach and we hope that in reading the other chapters in this book that you will develop a greater insight into what makes you tick, demonstrate, explain, enthuse and develop.

Further reading

Council for Science and Technology (CST) (2000) *Science Teachers: Supporting and Developing the Profession of Science Teaching in Primary and Secondary Schools.* London: Department of Trade and Industry.

Donnelly, J., Buchan, A., Jenkins, E., Laws, P. and Welford, G. (1996) *Investigations by Order: Policy, Curriculum and Science Teachers' Work Under the Education Reform Act.* Nafferton: Studies in Education.

Layton, D. (1973) *Science for the People: The Origins of the School Science Curriculum in England.* London: Allen and Unwin.

Millar, R. and Osborne, J. (1998) *Beyond 2000: Science Education for the Future.* London: King's College.

Solomon, J. (1991) School laboratory life, in B. E. Woolnough (ed.), *Practical Science.* Milton Keynes: Open University Press, pp. 101–11.

Waring, M. R. H. (1979) *Social Pressures and Curriculum Innovation.* London: Routledge.

2 How science works

What is the nature of scientific reasoning and what do we know about students' understanding?

Jonathan Osborne and Justin Dillon

Introduction – Why science matters

What is science? This question is famously the title of a book by Alan Chalmers (1999) which is now in its third edition since its first printing in 1982. Many would like there to be a simple answer to this question but sadly this is not so. There is, however, considerable agreement about many of the major features of the nature of science – the ones that matter most to the teacher of science. For instance, McComas and Olson (1998) conducted a review of a range of syllabi in the USA and in other countries and found considerable commonality. Osborne et al. (2003) undertook a study in the UK using the Delphi process with leading scientists, science teachers, science communicators, historians, sociologists and philosophers and science educators. This was a three-stage, open-ended questionnaire in which the responses of the participants at each stage were analysed and summarized and fed back after each stage to see if the group could come to any consensus. Despite the well-known disparate views of this community, nine features emerged which the group agreed should be part of the school science curriculum. These were:

- scientific methods and critical testing;
- the relationship between the methods of science and certainty;
- the diversity of scientific thinking;
- the role of hypothesis and prediction;
- the historical development of scientific knowledge;
- the role of creativity in science;
- the relationship between science and questioning;
- the analysis and interpretation of data;
- the role of cooperation and collaboration in the development of scientific knowledge;

A more extensive exploration of the rationale for teaching about how science works can be found in Chapter 3 in this volume.

In this chapter, therefore, we have attempted to set out a contemporary account of how science works. This is an account that is grounded in a mix of scholarship drawn from the work of both philosophers of science and from sociologists of science. We cannot pretend that a chapter like this can do anything other than present the briefest overview of the body of scholarship that has informed the contemporary picture of science. Many will claim that we have oversimplified complex issues and omitted important details and more. We would agree. However, we would respond that the account we offer is the essential elements from which the interested reader can begin pursuing more depth through further reading. To do otherwise would be to produce a book in itself. For others, we hope that it offers sufficient new insights to make them examine the nature of what they do and the messages that might be communicated in the science classroom.

The nature of science has been a subject of debate and study for almost as long as science, as we currently know it, has existed. The sociological study of science began in the 1970s and has added important insights about what scientists do and enhanced our understanding of science as a social practice. Some might ask, why does it matter? After all, what science offers is a body of knowledge consisting of the best explanations that we have about the material world. Why should we waste precious time on discussions about what are essentially philosophical issues? The brief answer to this question is that somebody who only knows *what we know* and who has no sense of *how we know* what we know and how that knowledge relates to other subjects, has no understanding of the manner in which scientific knowledge is created or the intellectual achievement that it represents. Without that knowledge, it is difficult to justify why science is so important to your sceptical student.

Science occupies its position at the curriculum high table as it is part of the cultural capital accumulated by our society. Hence it is considered *so* important that all children must be offered the opportunity to engage with what it has to offer and acquire some of that knowledge. Even an explanation as supposedly as simple as that which sees day and night as caused by a spinning Earth was hard-won knowledge. After all, there are good arguments against the standard and universally accepted explanation. First of all, the Sun does appear to move during the day. Second, if it was spinning, surely when we jumped up, we would not land on the same spot. Finally, if it was spinning once a day, the speed at the Equator would be over a 1000 mph – surely we would be flung off into space? If students in school are not occasionally offered some windows into how this knowledge came to be, so that they can see that science is a rational enterprise where belief is based on the evaluation of evidence (Duschl, 2007), then school science cannot defend itself against the argument that it is simply a 'miscellany of facts' (Cohen, 1952, p. 81) consisting of 'a rhetoric of conclusions' (Schwab, 1962, p. 24). Moreover, a set of facts in science is no more anything of substance than a pile of stones is a house. Indeed without any attempt to explain how we know what we know, school science education in the developed world finds it hard to defend itself against the accusation that it is no better than that offered in traditional societies in that:

> [the] ground for accepting the models proposed by the scientist is often no different from the young African villager's ground for accepting the models propounded by one of his elders. In both cases the propounders are deferred to as the accredited agents of tradition ... For all the apparent up-to-dateness of the content of his world-view, the modern Western layman is rarely more 'open' or scientific in his outlook than is the traditional African villager.
>
> (Horton, 1971, p. 209)

Norris (1997) goes even further to suggest that there is a moral case for explaining the basis of our scientific beliefs and knowledge arguing that:

> To ask of other human beings that they accept and memorize what the science teacher says, without any concern for the meaning and justification of what is said is to treat those human beings with disrespect and is to show insufficient care for their welfare. It treats them with a disrespect, because students exist on a moral par with their teachers, and therefore have a right to expect from their teachers reasons for what the teachers wish them to believe. It shows insufficient care for the welfare of students, because possessing beliefs that one is unable to justify is poor currency when one needs beliefs that can reliably guide action.
>
> (1997, p. 252)

Finally, there is the democratic argument (Millar and Osborne, 1998) that individuals need a body of ideas-about-science or knowledge of how science works to comprehend and critically evaluate the issues and dilemmas posed by advances in science and technology in contemporary society. Research has demonstrated that the body of content knowledge offered by school science is rarely of use as most of the issues posed by contemporary science are raised by topics which are either new or rarely covered (Ryder, 2001). In contrast, research exploring the public interaction with science (Fuller, 1997; Irwin, 1995) would suggest that much of what non-scientists need to know in order to make informed judgements about science is knowledge of how science works rather than a knowledge of science itself – an argument supported empirically by the work of Osborne et al. (2003).

Common misconceptions about science

One helpful approach to this topic is to review what some of the commonly held ideas about science are and why they are considered to be wrong. One of the most familiar ideas is that scientists simply measure features of the material world. That is, they take their instruments, gather data and then look for patterns in their findings which they then generalize as summary statements about how the world works. This is the most common view of science held by students in schools (Driver et al., 1996) and is seen as a product of the way science is taught (Millar and Osborne, 1998).

How does this belief come to be so commonly held? Indeed, much of the focus of school laboratory work is on collecting data. Students may be asked to devise fair tests, collect sets of data and then look for relationships or patterns. This activity is so common because the stock-in-trade of school science is persuading students of the validity of well-established, consensually agreed explanation. With this point in mind, teachers use experimental work to serve a rhetorical function of providing the supporting evidence for their vision of the world (Millar, 1998). One consequence is that little attention is paid to competing explanatory theories or the reliability or validity of the data. After all, if your goal as a teacher of science is to persuade, then the important thing is that the material world behaves in the manner you have predicted. Indeed, teachers of science will go to extensive lengths to 'rig' or 'conjure' the material world to behave in the manner that they have predicted (Nott and Smith, 1995). Scientists, in contrast, manipulate the material world for a fundamentally different goal: their aim is to develop new knowledge. Observation and data collection, for them, are driven not by a need to confirm an existing theory but rather by a need to collect data to decide between competing explanations (see Chapter 6 in this volume).

The theory dependence of observation

As a picture of science, why is the common misconception that is acquired, at least in part by the study of school science, highly unsatisfactory? The first important objection is that observation is a theory-dependent act. In short, what that means is that you can only see things through the conceptual lens you have available. Look at the photograph in Figure 2.1. What do you see – a meaningless array of black and white splodges?

However, if you are told that what you are looking at is a picture of a Dalmatian dog drinking at a puddle, many individuals can now decode the picture and 'see' what is there. Some of you may yet still be having difficulty – you cannot see it because you have not formed an idea of what it is you are looking for, which makes sense of your perceptions of black splodges on white paper. Indeed, some people find it impossible to see the dog even after several attempts. Another example is shown in Figure 2.2. What do you see? A young woman with a feather in her hair with her head turned away or an old woman with a large nose and her chin dropped into her fur, looking down?

Most people can switch between the two without much difficulty. Most teachers of science know, at least intuitively, that the theory dependence of

Figure 2.1 A Dalmatian dog drinking from a puddle
Source: Ronald C. James, 'Dalmatian', *Life* magazine, 19 February 1965.

Figure 2.2 A picture of a young woman?
Source: W. E. Hill, 'My wife and my mother-in-law', *Puck*, 16, p. 11, November 1915.

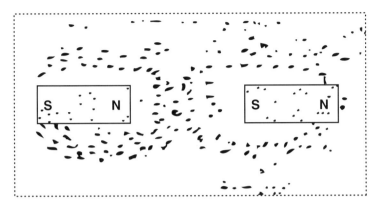

Figure 2.3 Common student representation of the pattern of iron filings around two attracting magnets
Source: Driver (1983).

observation is correct. Anybody who has ever used microscopes with young children recognizes that there is little chance of students observing what you would like them to see unless they are given a fairly detailed description of what they are looking for beforehand. The converse of this problem is, as pointed out by Driver (1983), when students do draw literally what they see which does not match the standard representation in science. For instance, students will commonly draw the pattern of iron filings around a magnet like that shown in Figure 2.3. Yet what we want them to draw is the standard representation show in Figure 2.4.

Logical positivism

This argument that observation is a theory-dependent act was first made most cogently by Hanson (1958). It spelt the death knell for a view of science

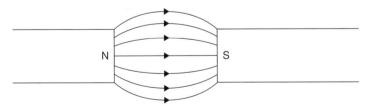

Figure 2.4 Common scientific representation of the field lines between two attracting magnets
Source: Driver (1983).

commonly called 'logical positivism'. The logical positivists were empiricists, in that they saw the laws of nature deducible from a set of empirical observable statements. From such observables, all scientific claims to knowledge would be logically derived. A good example would be Olber's claim about the Universe. Olber starts with the observable fact that the night sky is dark. He then argues that if the Universe were infinite, there would be a star at every point in the sky. If there was a star at every point in the sky, the sky would not be dark at night. As it is not, the Universe must be finite. In this way, Olber has logically deduced a statement about the world that he could be said to have demonstrably proved. Strict logical positivists would not entertain any theoretical entities for which there was no observational support. The problem with their position is twofold. First, it did not permit science to introduce theoretical entities which were too small to be seen such as atoms. Given the success of the atomic hypothesis in the work of eighteenth- and nineteenth-century scientists, this was increasingly untenable. Second, it rested on an assumption that what one individual sees is the same as another – that observation is independent of the observer and the set of theories that they carry with them. After Hanson showed that position to be false, this view of science collapsed more or less overnight.

The significance of theories in science

So if observation is not the bedrock of science, what is? The common answer to this question is that it is the explanatory theories that science offers about the material world. In the words of Rom Harré – 'theories are the crown of science, for in them our understanding of the world is expressed' (Harré, 1984, p. 168). Great leaps were, and are made in science not by deducing generalizations from multiple observations (though there is an important role for such acts, to be discussed later) but from imagining and creating models and analogues of the world that explain puzzling observations and, most importantly, enable testable predictions. Thus, Wegener's great achievement was to imagine that the continents had once been joined; one of Einstein's was to turn physics upside-down and imagine a world in which the speed of light never varied and work though its consequences; Pasteur's was to imagine that diseases were caused by tiny living microbial organisms which were too small to see; while Darwin imagined a world in which species were randomly advantaged by a process of mutation that gave them a competitive advantage. The alert reader might argue that not all of these theories were testable (Wegener's and Darwin's) – at least at the time they were proposed. However, in due course, they have enabled prediction. As has been argued elsewhere 'observation and experiment are not the bedrock upon which science is built; rather they are handmaidens to the rational activity of constituting knowledge claims' (Driver et al., 2000, p. 297) – handmaidens, that is, in that these activities provide the data necessary to test the theories. However, which data to look for and what significance they hold are determined by theoretical considerations and not by the data themselves. The standard Creationist critique that evolution is 'just a theory' shows a total lack of understanding of the importance that theoretical ideas play in science. Essentially, it reflects the common everyday use of the word 'theory' to mean a speculative guess. But scientific theories are much more than this, as will be shown later.

Scientific reasoning

One of the pervasive myths of our time is that there is such a thing as *the* scientific method (Bauer, 1992). This misconception assumes that scientists share a common approach to logically deducing the knowledge that they derive about the world. In its simplest form, this view sees science as a process of making predictions about the world. These predictions are then tested through the use of an experimental method which requires the salient variables to be identified. Then, all variables bar one (the independent variable) are kept constant and the experimenter measures the effect on the outcome or dependent variable – an idea which is consistently reinforced by the emphasis on 'fair testing'. The experiment is considered successful if the measured outcome confirms the prediction. This approach has its origins in the dominance of logical positivism as a description of the method of science in the first half of the twentieth century which saw the ideas of science as being logically deducible from observational statements.

This view of science is unfortunately a serious misrepresentation. First, it is important to recognize that there is no singular method of science. For instance, the methods of the theoretical physicist developing new models are very distinct from the entomologist working in the field, classifying new species. Both, however, are contributing to the scientific enterprise using the methods that are appropriate to their discipline. As Norris argues, 'Merely considering the mathematical tools that are available for data analysis immediately puts the study of method beyond what is learnable in a lifetime' (1997, p. 245). Likewise, the experimental organic chemist has a large range and repertoire of methods that have been acquired through years of practice.

This is not to argue that there is no underlying structure to the nature of scientific reasoning, however. Rather, the process of developing new knowledge begins with observations of the world and asking causal questions. For instance, Darwin asking why the finches on the Galapagos Islands were different but yet well adapted for the conditions on each island. Or Einstein asking why the Michelson–Morley experiment had failed to show that the measurements of the speed of light should differ depending upon whether you were approaching or running away from the light. In the case of school science, it might be wondering why the temperature of boiling water does not rise even

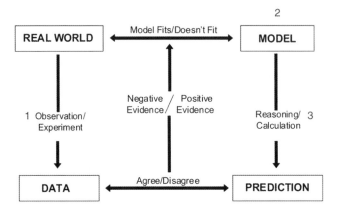

Figure 2.5 A model of scientific reasoning
Source: Giere et al. (2006, p. 29).

when you continue to heat it; why tiles feel colder than wooden floors; or how come two highly reactive gases – oxygen and hydrogen can react to produce the most pervasive and relatively unreactive liquid on the planet? Such a process represents step 1 of the model of scientific reasoning developed by Giere in his authoritative book on the topic, *Understanding Scientific Reasoning* (Giere, 2006) (Figure 2.5). It may be a single observation or many repeated observations but the mind of the scientist begins by interrogating nature and asking what the explanation might be.

Creativity and the role of models in science

Answering such questions is where the creative imagination of the scientist is brought to bear, for it requires the scientist to develop a model, representation or picture of the world – models which are often a radical way of thinking at the time. Thus Copernicus began by thinking, what if it is the Earth that moves around the Sun? How would that explain how we see – in particular the retrograde motion of the planets? Pasteur imagined that maybe there exist tiny living organisms in the air which spread mould to other living things. Einstein imagined a world in which the speed of light did not vary depending upon whether you were travelling towards the light beam or away from it, and Toricelli imagined that the only way to explain the empty space at the top of his tube was if it was a vacuum. Developing causal scientific explanations requires the scientist to draw on their existing conceptual knowledge and imagine a different form of the world. This process of conjecture is one of the key scientific processes and is both as creative and demanding as other forms of work because it requires the scientist to imagine the world differently and, in some cases, to invent entities which are too small to see such as atoms, molecules and microbes or too large to imagine such as galaxies and black holes. It is what makes science a creative endeavour, requiring the facility to imagine the world not as it appears but as it might be. For instance, this is very much the process that Crick and Watson were engaged in during their struggle to determine the structure of DNA. Wilkins and Franklin had produced the observational data in the form of photographs from X-ray crystallography. Moreover, Franklin and Wilkins had both acquired the expertise and knowledge to be able to produce such photographs which was no mean feat in itself. But it was Watson and Crick who dedicated their thinking to imagining what kind of structure could produce that kind of photograph and attempted to build a model, with one or two notable failures along the way. The question they were persistently asking was, what kind of structure would produce that kind of photograph and be able to replicate itself? In Figure 2.5, this process in science is represented by step 2. A much more elaborate description of this process can be found in Karl Popper's seminal book *Conjecture and Refutations* (Popper, 1963) where he makes the argument that making imaginative conjectures is a key element of science.

From the perspective of teaching science, there are two implications. First, that students need to be shown explicitly that this is a process that lies at the heart of science. Their models of the world need to be contrasted with the scientific model. So, for instance, the common misconception that plants get most of their 'food' from the earth needs to be contrasted with the scientific model that most of the mass in a tree has come from the air. School science often places a lot of emphasis on the process of collecting data rather than developing explanatory models (Gilbert and Boulter, 2000) and testing them. In so doing, it fails to show that developing innovative theories and models of the material world is the key intellectual achievement that lies at the core of science.

Forms of argument in science: 1 Retroduction

The initial development of such explanatory models often relies on a process of retroduction – what might be loosely termed as the provisional adoption of an explanatory hypothesis which seems to offer the best explanation of the observable facts. This form of argument is also known as abduction or inference to the best possible explanation. Such arguments begin with a puzzling observation, for instance, that the west coast of Africa seems to fit with the east coast of South America and the two seem to have similar rock strata and flora. The hypothesis is then generated that perhaps these two were once together and have drifted apart. If this was so, then it would explain the fit. The argument is somewhat circular and based on past events – hence it retrospectively explains phenomena in the material world. Nevertheless, it is an important starting point for science and is the form of argument developed by Darwin to explain the variation in the species on the Galapagos Islands and the form of argument used to establish the Big Bang theory for the origin of the Universe. A puzzling observation was made in 1964 by Penzias and Wilson that there was a form of microwave radiation coming from every direction in the Universe. What could explain this phenomenon? If the Universe expanded from a singularity at its beginning, there would indeed be lots of electromagnetic radiation produced which would have now become microwave radiation. As their observations showed that the microwave radiation does exist, the Big Bang theory was supported. The competing steady-state theory of the Universe was unable to explain such an observation which was essentially its death knell. In terms of Giere's model of the process of scientific reasoning (Figure 2.5), what is happening here is a comparison of the model with the observational data. Do the predictions (albeit retroductive) fit with the data here? If they do, then that establishes more confidence in the model.

Forms of argument in science: 2 Hypothetico-deductivism

The next important step in scientific reasoning is to use such conjectures to develop a hypothesis or prediction – step 3 in Figure 2.5. So, for instance, Pasteur is so confident in his theory that giving people a mild infection of a disease will develop resistance to the stronger forms of disease that he was willing to see his idea tested publicly (Geison, 1995). Toricelli predicts that if his hypothesis that the space at the top of his barometer is a vacuum and the mercury is being supported by the weight of air then, when he takes it up a mountain, the height of the column should be less as there will be less air pressing down. Sometimes there is a very long time between the theoretical prediction and its testing. For instance, Maxwell, in 1864, showed how light is simply a wave consisting of variations in the electric and magnetic fields that exist throughout space and that other forms of waves at different frequencies should be detectable. It was not until the work of Hertz in 1886 that such waves were shown to exist. Likewise, at the moment, theoretical models of the nucleus have predicted the existence of a fundamental particle called the Higgs boson. The new giant accelerator at CERN has essentially been built to test this hypothesis. Again, in terms of Giere's model (Figure 2.5), what is happening here is a comparison of the predictions with the data derived empirically. In all of these examples, the argument is stronger as they are genuine predictions. If these fail to match, what is modified or in some cases abandoned is the model itself. Einstein's prediction, based on his theory of General Relativity, that light from a star grazing the sun in an eclipse would bend by 19 seconds of a degree, which was confirmed empirically by Edgington in 1919, is one of the best-known examples of the use of the hypothetico-deductive method. What is important to note though is that the hypothesis is a product of the theory, not vice versa.

Falsificationism

The preceding section reveals another aspect of science elaborated by Popper (1963). This is that the crucial element that makes science distinctive from other forms of knowledge is the requirement that it generate theories which make testable predictions. After all, retroduction as a form of argument is used to some extent by historians and social scientists to explain a range of social events. However, science makes predictions based on theoretical hypotheses – a form of argument known as hypothetico-deductivism. If these predictions fail, then it calls into question whether the theory is correct. Popper's argument reveals an important idea that is commonly misrepresented in science. Having your prediction confirmed does not mean that science has shown it to be universally true. All that it means is that it has not failed under these conditions in these contexts. The more tests we can conduct of any given theory and its predictions, the stronger we believe it likely to be true. Indeed, Popper argued that falsificationism – the ability of science to show that a logical assertion was empirically false – was the critical determining feature of science as no amount of tests could ultimately confirm an idea is irrevocably true. Thus Popper argued that an idea was scientific if it was potentially falsifiable and that experiments should be seen not as tests of the validity of a hypothesis but whether it could be falsified. The problem with this view is that it is not how scientists, or for that matter most humans, work – that is we conduct experiments to test whether our theories are supported by the evidence and not whether they can be falsified. Also, adopted as a strict demarcating criterion of science, it would rule out a lot of biological science which does not use hypothetico-deduction.

Forms of argument in science: 3 Induction

The fact that theories have to be tested multiple times, if possible, leads science into its final form of argument which is induction. This is the form of argument that generalizes from multiple events or experiences, for example, all swans are white. For instance, when Thomson first advanced the idea that one of the constituents of the atom was an electron with a negative charge and $\frac{1}{1840}$ of the mass of a proton, it was initially a very tentative idea. However as 'we regularly set out to build, and often enough succeed in building – new kinds of device that use various well-understood causal properties of electrons' not only do such entities exist but their properties and nature are confirmed time and time again (Hacking, 1983). Likewise, the theoretical hypothesis that energy is conserved in all interactions is something that has been tested time and time again to the point where there is sufficient confidence to frame this property of the natural world as a 'Law'. Laws, in a scientific context, are simply inductive generalizations in which we have great confidence – such confidence that they have become taken-for-granted matters of fact. The extreme form of this view was articulated by Eddington when talking about the status of the second law of thermodynamics:

> If someone points out to you that your pet theory of the universe is in disagreement with Maxwell's equations, then so much the worse for Maxwell's equations. And if your theory contradicts the facts, well, sometimes these experimentalists make mistakes. But if your theory is found to be against the Second Law of Thermodynamics, I can give you no hope; there is nothing for it but to collapse in deepest humiliation.
>
> (Eddington, 1928, p. 81)

However, this does not mean that because a concept has attained the status of a law that it is universally true. To think so would be to misunderstand induction. For any inductive argument, no matter how strong, can be destroyed by new information. The argument, for instance, that all swans are white is destroyed by the existence of a single black swan. Likewise in school science, a child's inductive generalization that 'heavy things sink, and light things float' is contradicted by the fact that a grain of sand sinks. What, then, do such arguments mean about the nature of the claims that science makes about the world?

Realism and relativism

The knowledge that we generate about the world can never be absolutely certain. People who believe that science offers us literal truths about the world would be classified as 'naïve realists'. This is very much a common-sense view of the world strongly rooted in the idea that we can make statements about objects which are based on our sense experience and that we perceive the world pretty much as it is. The challenge to this view comes from the notion discussed earlier that observation is a theory-dependent process and dependent on organs of sense perception that can easily be deluded into what they are seeing. Moreover, many of the ontological entities that populate the phenomenological zoo of the material world are too small to be seen or too large to imagine. For instance, how can the quantum mechanical description of the world be an accurate representation when certain electromagnetic phenomena are explained using particles and others are explained using waves? Instead, the common position adopted by many scientists is that of critical realism. This is a position that recognizes that while there are limits to the sensory data we can gather and that our ideas are potentially fallible, there is nevertheless definitely a material world that exists external to ourselves. However, our knowledge of the world is filtered through the perceptual and cognitive mechanisms that we have available and that these have their limitations. Ziman, for instance, argues that the nature of scientific knowledge is akin to a map. The map is not the same as the reality but the degree of verisimilitude enables the user to make predictions and to find their way around. The most contemporary articulation of critical realism is provided by Bhaskar (1989).

Relativists, in contrast, hold that the theory dependence of observation makes our ideas about the world strongly dependent on the individual theories and ideas that we bring to a problem or examination of the world. In short, that there is no 'God's eye view of the world' which is accessible to us (Putnam, 1975). Relativists argue, instead, that there can be no absolute truths but rather that truth is established by drawing on a particular frame of reference, a language or a culture. Thus all human practices are socially embedded and can only be understood by observing them at work and by looking at how they seek to establish their claims to knowledge. In the case of science, the best-known study that has taken this perspective is the ethnography conducted by Latour and Woolgar (1986) of a laboratory engaged in conducting work in neuroendocrinology between 1975 and 1977. In this very detailed and thorough account, Latour and Woolgar looked at how scientists transform their initial tentative hypotheses to ideas which ultimately may become taken-for-granted facts. They argue that the scientific paper acts very much as a rhetorical device where data are selectively used to support a particular argument which will be acceptable to their peers and meet the social norms and criteria established by the scientific community. The result, they suggest, is that scientific activity is not 'about nature', but is a fierce fight to construct reality. Consequently:

> science is a form of fiction or discourse like any other, one effect of which is the 'truth effect', which (like all literary effects) arises from textual characteristics, such as the tense of verbs, the structure of enunciation, modalities and so on.
>
> (Latour and Woolgar, 1986, p. 184)

Further examples of such a stance can be found in the work of Collins and Pinch (1993), Traweek (1988) and Pickering (1984). Such views are undoubtedly radical and a challenge to many scientists. In the 1990s, there was a particularly fierce set of debates between scientists and the sociologists of science known as the 'science wars'. These reached a pinnacle with the publication of a hoax paper in a journal dedicated to the social studies of science (Sokal and Bricmont, 1998).

The sociological turn

But what were sociologists, with no knowledge of science, doing studying how scientific knowledge is produced? Surely, it needs somebody who understands the discipline deeply? The explanation lies in the writings of Thomas Kuhn and his seminal work *The Structure of Scientific Revolutions* (Kuhn, 1962). In this book, Kuhn argued that science consisted of periods of 'normal science' interrupted by periods of 'revolutionary science'. In periods of 'normal science' there was a communal adherence to the common values and norms shared by the community of what constituted acceptable ideas and thinking. This he called a 'paradigm'.

Scientists working within a given paradigm were essentially puzzle-solving, attempting to resolve outstanding enigmas that still existed but were not attempting to challenge or investigate the basic theoretical tenets of the work. Thus, what counted as scientific knowledge was produced by a community with agreed norms and social practices. As such, it was socially and culturally situated and not a privileged form of knowledge. Hence, such practices were as amenable to sociological examination and analysis as any other. In some senses, such arguments were very much the last nail in the coffin for the logical positivists whose basic tenet was that the knowledge claims of science were logically deducible from verifiable observational statements – both acts which they saw as being independent of culture, place or time and element of subjectivity.

The establishment of a body of scholarship known broadly as the sociology of scientific knowledge (SSK) as a legitimate way to study science in the early 1970s (Bloor, 1976), led to a critique of what now seem the idealized views that the scientific community held about itself. These are most strongly articulated by the work of Merton (1973) who portrayed them as communualism (a commitment to the free sharing of knowledge); universalism (a belief that scientific knowledge is independent of culture); disinterestedness (a personal detachment from the outcome of their work); objectivity (a belief that science is value-free); and scepticism (a commitment to critically questioning all claims to knowledge). These views are commonly summarized by the acronym CUDOS. However, the kind of detailed examination of the practices of science offered by the historians and sociologists of science have shown that these are values that the scientific community aspires to but rarely attains. For instance, Geison, in his account of the life and work of Louis Pasteur, based on access to his private diaries and notebooks, shows Pasteur's 'ingenious capacity for producing empirical evidence in support of positions he held a priori' (Geison, 1995, p. 16). Feminist philosophers are another group who have critiqued science to show that many aspects are culturally situated and that interpretations of such things as primate behaviour are the product of a masculine epistemology and values (Haraway, 1989; Harding, 1991). Likewise the notion of universalism is highly questionable given the body of research that is conducted for military or for private companies which is never published (Ziman, 2000).

The values of science

What the findings emerging from SSK and other studies have meant is that it is impossible to defend the argument that science is a value-free activity. First, science has its own internal values, the best-known of which is a commitment

Figure 2.6 Photograph of the night sky taken in the Southern hemisphere with the camera pointed at the Pole Star and with the shutter left open for 8 hours
Source: © Anglo-Australian Observatory/David Malin images.

to parsimony. Known as Occam's razor and first elaborated by a fourteenth-century friar – William of Occam. Occam's argument was that when confronted with two competing explanations of equal merit, we should pick the simplest. A good example is shown by the photograph in Figure 2.6.

The photograph was taken by mounting a camera on a tripod, pointing the camera at the South Pole Star (a fictitious entity as there is no star at this point) and leaving the shutter open for 8 hours. There are two possible explanations for the observation. Either all the stars in the Universe are rotating around the 'Pole Star' or the camera is fixed to an Earth that rotates once every 24 hours. Both are valid and on the evidence of the photograph alone it is impossible to choose between them. In this situation, the latter explanation is preferable because it is complete. The idea that all of those stars are moving in perfect circles around one star would demand another explanation making any theory more complex. Part of the reason for the acceptance of the Copernican explanation of the retrograde motion of the planets over the Ptolemaic theory was that it was much simpler and more elegant. Copernicus' theory showed that the motion was an apparent effect of the relative motion of the planets and stars. Ptolemy's explanation required the invention of an epicycle around which each star moved.

How though is science to defend itself against Latour's contention that it is not a privileged or distinctive form of discourse? The defence of rationality and objectivity of science comes from recognizing that science is a social practice and that the community of scientists has established social norms and values. However, while scientists may think what they like, the world is recalcitrant and will not always do what we would like. As Siegel has argued:

> There is no procedure that is constitutive of the scientific method or that insures that science is rational. What insures the rationality is the commitment to evidence—or, better, science is rational to the extent that it proceeds in accordance with such a commitment.
>
> (1989, p. 14)

It is Longino (1990) who takes this idea further in seeing the requirement for evidence as a standard of rationality which is independent of any research programme or culture. For her, it is a standard which is satisfied by the community engaging in intersubjective criticism through presentations to colleagues and peer review. While this process is amenable to distortion – for instance, with the ideas about environmentally acquired inheritance promoted by the Russian agronomist Trofim Lysenko – the critical spirit of the community acts to prevent the dissemination of theories which have been shown to be demonstrably false. Thus, science is 'objective to the degree that it permits *transformative* criticism' (Longino, 1990, p. 75). Such criticism is enabled by the existence of commonly agreed standards that make the members of the scientific community answerable to something besides themselves. A scientific community that supports plural and differing points of view is more likely to sustain objectivity and make their descriptions of reality more reliable. Reliable, that is, in the sense articulated by Ziman who argues that: 'The objectivity of a well established science is thus comparable to that of a well-made map drawn by a great company of surveyors who have worked over the same ground along many different routes' (1979, p. 108). Thus, while there may be many types of maps and representations of the same ground – all of which appear different, there is an underlying real entity that they have in common.

There is a more fundamental point to emerge from the account offered by Longino and others, for example, Pickering (1995). This is that scientific ideas are the product of a community who engage both in construction *and critique* – a critique which deploys the nature of reality as the ultimate arbiter. In that sense, scientists are engaged as much in holding ideas up for critical scrutiny as they are in imagining new ideas about the way the world might function. If we want young people to become critical consumers of scientific knowledge, then we must provide them with the opportunity not only to see how knowledge has been constructed (that is the evidence and reasons for our belief) but also an opportunity to engage in a scientific critique by using reasoning which is based on what they know about the material world. Such an approach would require greater use of opportunities to present their thinking and arguments to other students whose task would be to evaluate whether the conclusions are justified; to engage in a process of appraising two competing explanatory theories; and to identify why the wrong idea is wrong (as in the idea that day and night are caused by a moving Sun). As Ford argues, the teachers' role in such a context is 'not only to identify errors, but also to model the kind of thing that students are expected to do with their peers' and their own knowledge claims' (2008, p. 420). Ford suggests that one way to do this is to 'problematize' the standard content. So, for instance, the teacher could ask 'How do we know that matter is made of atoms?' or 'Why doesn't the Moon slow down like every other moving object here on Earth?'

Such an approach enables teachers to go beyond stating the bare facts – something which research would suggest is too often mind-numbing to young students. For instance, Van Praagh (2003) offers a good example in his account of teaching oxidation by asking a question – why does copper go black when it is heated? What could this be and why? This is what he writes:

> Smith says 'I think it is soot from the flame'. 'Good idea'. I write on the board 'Smith's theory – the black stuff is soot'. 'He may be right', I say. 'Any other ideas?' 'Yes, sir' says Robinson, 'I think it's an impurity driven out of the copper by heat.' So Robinson's theory goes on the board too. 'I know what it is', says Solly whose older brother is in the Fifth form. 'If you know, you will have to prove you are right – we'll add it to our theories.' Solly's theory: 'the black stuff is formed by the air acting on the copper'. 'How shall we decide who is right?, I ask. I get them to suggest three experiments to test the three theories.
>
> (2003, p. 44)

In this way, he has opened up the discursive space for students to engage in a process of testing their ideas against the material world and to use their findings to critique each other's theories. The argument of Ford (2008) and Duschl (2007) is that by engaging in such practice, students are more likely to develop an understanding of the nature of science and scientific reasoning, especially if the nature of the critique and its value are discussed by the teacher.

Research on students' and teachers' understanding of the nature of science and its development

In the second part of this work, we turn to discussing how the ideas presented in the first half are acquired, or not, by students and the effect they may have, or not, on teachers' practices. Lederman (1992, p. 332) has identified four lines of research into topics related to the teaching of the nature of science:

1. attempts to assess student conceptions of the nature of science (NOS);
2. curriculum innovations designed to 'improve' students' conceptions of the nature of the nature of science:
3. the assessment of, and attempts to improve, teachers' conceptions of the nature of science; and
4. identification of the relationship between teachers' conceptions, classroom practice, and students' conceptions.

In this last section of the chapter we will be looking predominantly at the first and the third of these areas.

Students' views, their sources and changes

Space does not permit a full treatment of the substantial body of research that has been conducted in this domain. Hence, what is offered here is a selection of the work of the most recognized researchers who have explored this area. Best known is perhaps Lederman who has written his own review of research in the field (Lederman, 2006) to which the reader wishing a more extensive treatment is referred. The dominant theme that has emerged from this work is that students view scientific knowledge as absolute and literal truths about the world and that the primary objective of science is to uncover or 'discover' new scientific facts (Driver et al., 1996; Lederman and O'Malley, 1990; Mead and Métraux, 1957). The falsity of the idea that scientific knowledge is absolute was the subject of the first half of this chapter. This latter idea – that scientists 'discover' new ideas – is correct in the sense that one of the goals of science is to develop our knowledge and understanding of the world. It is wrong, however, in the sense that knowledge is rarely 'discovered' at a finite point in time but emerges over a long period as a result of numerous experimental tests. For instance, new drugs are first detected using a process of looking for agents that are biologically active. These then have to be tested on a variety of living organisms and animals to model what their behaviour might be with humans. Finally, they have to be tested on humans using initially small-scale exploratory studies followed by larger-scale, double-blind, controlled studies. So the hypothesis that any new drug might be effective is never tested by the success of a single experiment but, instead, requires multiple tests where it is not falsified.

Lederman and O'Malley (1990) undertook a survey of changes to 55 US high school grade 9 to 12 (age 14–18) students' views of science after a year of science classes. The students were in three classes each taught by a different teacher. The instrument used to monitor the students' views consisted of items to which the students were invited to give open responses:

1. After scientists have developed a theory (for example, atomic the-
    ory), does the theory ever change? If you believe theories do change,
    explain why we bother to learn about theories. Defend your answer
    with examples.
2. What does an atom look like? How do scientists know an atom looks
    like what you have described or drawn?
3. Is there a difference between a scientific theory and a scientific law?
    Give an example to illustrate your answer.
4. Some astrophysicists believe that the universe is expanding while
    others believe that the universe is shrinking: still others believe that
    the universe is in a static state without any expansion or shrinkage.
    How are these different conclusions possible if all these scientists are
    looking at the same experiment and data?

Lederman and O'Malley coded the students' responses as either absolutist or
tentative, which roughly translates into the more orthodox terms of realist
or instrumentalist. An instrumentalist view is associated with the notion that
scientific ideas are tentative and can be arrived at through various methods
and are valued because they work rather than because they are true. For in-
strumentalists, the descriptions and explanations produced are not evaluated
with respect to their match to reality, but rather with respect to how useful
they are.

Over the year of the study, the students' responses to item 1 showed a shift
away from absolutist views towards more tentative views. Responses to item
2 showed the most marked shift towards tentative views. Responses to item
3 showed little change, while responses to item 4 showed mostly bafflement
on the part of students with the highest number of no responses and unclear
responses. It was a naturalistic study and so the three teachers had not been
asked to diverge from their normal teaching over the year. The authors conclude that these students' views on the nature of science developed out of the
science they were exposed to, and that the more science they learnt, the less
absolutist they became.

A more recent cross-sectional survey study undertaken by Kang et al. (2005)
explored Korean elementary, middle and high school students' NOS conceptions with 534 sixth graders, 551 eighth graders and 617 tenth graders. The
authors found that less than 20 per cent considered the purpose of science as
creating explanations. Instead, almost half the students considered scientific
theories as facts proven through experimentation and testing. Furthermore, a
smaller proportion of students considered scientific theories as well-educated
guesses. Only about 25 per cent of students considered scientific theories to
be the basis of scientific explanations and, even then, many of these students
were found to hold misconceptions of the notion of explanation when interviewed, which they viewed as descriptive rather than causal.

Similar findings emerge from a more extensive qualitative study conducted
by Driver et al. (1996). They undertook an interview-based study focusing on

whether students were capable of discriminating between theories and facts in science and how they related evidence and theories. Their study was undertaken with three different age groups (9, 12 and 16 years old). The authors created six probes that pairs of students had to discuss during an interview. In order to compare the results across ages, the probes presented used the same science content that was seen as being accessible to all age groups. This group of researchers concluded that students have difficulties determining the role of theories in science and how theories are evaluated against existing data. In particular, scientific theories were seen by many students as taken-for-granted facts that did not require any further supporting evidence – a view that was particularly dominant among the 9-year-old students. Furthermore, some students considered scientific theories as involving the correlation of variables. For example, when students tried to explain why a balloon with hot air inflates, they stated that the heat makes the air inside the balloon hotter, which makes the balloon blow up – essentially a tautology. Other students, especially the 16-year-olds, were more able to recognize that scientific theories are models that represent the phenomenon under discussion. Driver et al. (1996) found that, overall, older students demonstrated a more sophisticated understanding of scientific theories suggesting that students' understanding of the nature of scientific theories may improve with age and with science teaching that encourages or permits discussion and reflection on the nature of the subject.

The overwhelming conclusion is that school science has failed, and continues to fail to develop what might be termed a good 'vulgar' understanding of the nature of science. The extent to which this is a matter of concern is largely dependent on your perceptions of what the goals of the nature of science should be. Those who view the primary purpose of science education as an introduction to the explanatory accounts that science offers and what we know will not be troubled. Those who feel that any education in science should attempt to explain the route by which such ideas were derived and the degree of certainty and confidence we can place in them will view these findings with a degree of unease. To echo sentiments written over 80 years ago:

> If science teaching is to mean anything more than the acquisition of a few tags of knowledge and a certain skill in manipulation we must accord to science a place among the humanities. The teacher must try to give his pupils the conception of science as a process of development through human endeavour. He must avoid the dogmatic attitude shown in many elementary text books and help the pupils to gain some critical insight into the conclusions of science. The old dictum that science is exact measurement obviously requires modification and the teacher of science must endeavour to make his pupils realize the limitations and scope of physical measurements.
>
> (Turner, 1927, p. 191)

Science teachers' views about the nature of science and its effect on the teaching of science

There have been several attempts to survey teachers' views of the nature of science (Mellado, 1998). The majority of the methods devised have been aimed at pre-service teachers in the USA. Various strategies have then been adopted to help pre-service teachers develop their own understanding of the nature of science. Nott and Wellington have gone so far as to produce a questionnaire that enables respondents to determine their 'Nature of Science Profile' (Nott and Wellington, 1993) although this was developed mainly to provide a stimulus for discussion and is not a valid, psychometric instrument.

Koulaidis and Ogborn (1989) surveyed the views of 54 teachers of science and 40 student teachers associated with the Institute of Education, London, during 1984–85. They designed a questionnaire to monitor ideas on the nature of scientific method, the criteria of demarcation of science from non-science, ideas on patterns of scientific change and ideas on the status of scientific knowledge. The teachers and student teachers who took part in the study were presented with statements such as:

- As science changes or develops, new knowledge generally replaces ignorance or lack of knowledge.
- New scientific knowledge follows no pattern of growth, being purely the result of what scientists happen to have done.
- In general, the better of two competing theories is the one nearer the truth.
- In general, the better of two competing theories is the one which gives more useful results.

The teachers were invited to agree or disagree with the statements. Having analysed the teachers' responses, Koulaidis and Ogborn present a set of three broad tendencies that mark out the constellations of views which characterize most of the teachers and student teachers in their sample. These were 'inductivists', 'hypothetico-deductivists', and 'contextualists'. The last are individuals who have a broadly Kuhnian perspective which sees science as being a socially situated product. Contextualists were further divided into three groups: (1) contextual rationalists who were essentially realists with a pragmatic view about what science could achieve; (2) relativists; and (3) undecided contextualists. The picture that emerged was not one of homogeneity. Both relativism and hypothetico-deductivism got scant support. Nor was inductivism very popular, though as many as 16–18 per cent chose answers reflecting this view when questioned about the scientific method. On all three themes, when undecided contextualists were included, between 35 and 50 per cent chose some version of a contextualist position. And, if undecided contextualists are considered to be relativists, then two-thirds of the biology teachers expressed relativist views. Chemistry teachers were the most eclectic and mixed in their views while physics teachers showed the strongest tendency to be rationalists.

However, Koulaidis and Ogborn refer to these physicists as undecided rationalists due to their lack of consistency. In the Koulaidis and Ogborn study, student teachers were found to have somewhat different views on the nature of science from experienced teachers. This evidence suggests that not only does the subject content influence one's views, but it looks as though experience in the classroom may modify those views as well. These findings contrast with other surveys which have shown teachers and students to hold views that Koulaidis and Ogborn associate with empiricism and inductivism, for example, the Blanco and Niaz (1997) study carried out in Venezuela.

Another significant study was that conducted by Gallagher (1991), between 1984 and 1987, who undertook an ethnographic study of 25 secondary science teachers from five schools in two different districts in the USA. The aim of this study was to gain an understanding about the practice of science teaching in secondary schools and the forces that shape it. During more than two years, his team observed over 1,000 science classes in the five schools, participated in several hundred informal conversations with the teachers, and conducted numerous formal interviews with the teachers and their administrators. In their classes, the 25 teachers devoted virtually no time to discussion of matters related to the nature of science, such as how the knowledge included in the curriculum came to be or the processes by which scientists validate knowledge – the only exception being an initial treatment of 'the scientific method' and an emphasis on the 'objectivity of science'. Gallagher argues that such emphasis is used to endow a higher epistemic status on science compared to other subjects. His explanation for his findings was that teachers of science lack any education in the history, philosophy or sociology of science. Moreover, they have never been practising scientists themselves and their education has itself given very little emphasis to answering the question 'How do we know?' These arguments are supported by King's findings (King, 1991) that teachers' lack of education in the history and philosophy of science left them bereft of suitable ideas about how such topics could be taught about in the classroom. Clearly little had changed since the 1950s when Anderson (1950), in a study of 56 Minnesota high school teachers, ascribed ignorance of knowledge of the scientific method to teachers being too busy imparting the factual aspects of the curriculum to be interested and/or concerned about how science works.

What effect does this state of affairs have on the teaching of science? Lederman and Zeidler (1987) looked at the views on the nature of science and classroom actions of 18 American high school biology teachers, each with a minimum of five years service (average 15.8 years service). They also carried out classroom observations of the teachers at work as well as giving the teachers a 48-item questionnaire to complete. From their analysis of the data they concluded that the views the teachers expressed on the nature of science and scientific knowledge had little relationship, and therefore effect, on the actual classroom actions of the teachers. Similar findings also emerged from a detailed study conducted by Hodson (1993) of six teachers which sought to establish whether teachers' views about the nature of scientific inquiry were reflected in their choice and design of learning experiences. Hodson found that even those teachers who held clear and coherent views about science did not plan their laboratory-based activities using those views in any consistent manner. Rather, they concentrated on the immediate concerns of classroom management and on concept acquisition and development.

For beliefs to have any effect on actions, there must be choices of alternative actions. For most science teachers the choices are not formulated in terms of different approaches to the nature of science and scientific knowledge. Instead, the choices they face are managerial/technical. The influence of these imperatives of the classroom on teachers' actions was reported in a small-scale case study carried out by Tobin and McRobbie (1997). They looked in detail at the classroom practice of an experienced Australian chemistry teacher (called Mr Jacobs in the study) and his expressed beliefs about the nature of science. Although Mr Jacobs would talk in terms of science being an evolving discipline that was uncertain and changed over time, his classroom actions were not congruent with such a view. Instead, they were dominated by his own views on the nature of learning and the students' needs gathered from long experience. His main goal was to help the students to pass the examinations and tests with good marks. To this end, his teaching methods reflected science as being a catalogue of facts that the students had to remember and repeat in examinations. Where students had to solve chemical problems, Mr Jacobs provided them with algorithms to follow and the students were entirely happy with Mr Jacobs' methods. This practice added to the conservative inertia of what Tobin and McRobbie call the enacted curriculum. Duschl and Wright (1989), too, have found that issues of perceived students' needs, curriculum guide objectives and accountability all mitigated against consideration of the nature of science (see also Brickhouse, 1989, 1991).

Even if the nature of science is explicitly addressed by teachers, the extent to which explicit teaching of the nature of science can help to develop students' understanding is an open question. Zeidler and Lederman (1989) report a survey of 409 US students who studied with 18 high school biology teachers. The students completed a questionnaire at the beginning and end of a Fall (autumn) semester and were categorized as showing either a realist view of science or an instrumentalist view of science. Shifts in the students' responses between the beginning and the end of the semester were computed. Some students became more realist in their views while others became more instrumentalist. During that semester a researcher collected data on the classroom behaviour of the 18 teachers. Transcripts were made of classroom talk, observation schedules were used to record events, and copies of notes on blackboards were taken down. The teachers' classroom language was then matched against the shifts in the students' responses. The researchers satisfied themselves that there was a correlation between the shifts in scores shown by the students and the classroom discursive nature of the lessons in which they had participated. From the evidence they collected, Zeidler and Lederman conclude that, 'Teachers' ordinary language in the presentation of subject matter was found to have significant impact on students' conceptions of the nature of science.' This and other more recent studies (Khisfe, 2008; Khisfe and Abd-El-Khalick, 2002) both lend weight to the view that student understanding of the nature of the discipline will only develop if the concepts are explicitly explored in classrooms.

However, teaching about the nature of science explicitly would appear to be a necessary rather than a sufficient condition. For instance, Leach et al. (2003) found in a study in English high schools with seventy 16–17-year-old students, that a substantial minority of the students made no progress in their understanding. In their intervention, the teaching consisted of short, focused lessons that sought to emphasize the role of models in science. Hence one explanation the authors offer for their findings is that developing an understanding of the nature of science requires the use of a 'drip-feed' approach and that the topic permeates the curriculum. Likewise, Bartholomew et al. (2004) worked with a group of 11 teachers over a course of a year to support their efforts to teach a set of ideas about science emerging from an earlier Delphi study (Osborne et al., 2003). Their focus was simply on measuring the extent to which these ideas were engaged with and used by teachers in their teaching. They found the results were very mixed. From their work, they were able to identify five dimensions of practice which made some teachers more effective than others. These were:

- their understanding of the nature of science;
- their conception of their own role, that is, a facilitator of learning versus a dispenser of information;
- their use of discourse in the classroom, that is, the extent to which it was open and exploratory as opposed to the use of closed, initiation–response–feedback (IRE) discourse;
- their conception of the learning goals. The goals of teachers who were less successful were dominated by knowledge acquisition as opposed to those who held a wider range of goals for their lessons such as the development of critical thinking skills.
- the nature of the classroom activities. Those who were more successful developed activities that were seen by the students to be genuine learning experiences rather than exercises that were contrived and of questionable validity.

It is possible to see such findings as an implicit criticism of teachers – that if only they could change their views, or if they were better educated, or had a better understanding, none of these issues would be problematic. To do so would be a mistake. For instance, is it any wonder that science graduates come to their teacher education courses convinced of the certainty of science and of the pre-eminent position of science among other school subjects when that is the way science has been presented to them? The evidence from a range of studies seems to be that pre-service teachers' views, rather like children's views of science, can be classified as 'naïve', 'inconsistent' and 'resistant to change'. Lederman et al. conclude that: 'It does not appear that pre-service teachers have well-formed knowledge structures . . . the structures that do exist are largely the result of college coursework and are often fragmented and disjointed with little evidence of coherent themes' (1994, p. 18). What we do not know much about is how pre-service teachers develop understanding and awareness of ways to teach 'the nature of science'. It may be the case that they do not have an understanding of the link between what they teach, how they teach and the impact on their students' view of science and scientists. It may also be the case that they do not believe that they can make much difference to their students or even that they should be making much difference!

Final comments

In 1996, the UK Government proposed that there should be a National Curriculum for Initial Teacher Training (NCITT). In terms of the nature of science, the proposals stated: 'As part of all courses [of initial teacher training], trainees must demonstrate that they know and understand the nature of science' (Teacher Training Agency, 1998). This requirement rests on a premise that the nature of science is a concept that is well understood and commonly agreed. While there does seem to be an emergent consensus about the ideas that should be taught (Lederman, 1992; McComas and Olson, 1998; Osborne et al., 2003), implementing that in the practice of schools science still has far to go. Research has demonstrated that the supposition that if teachers 'know and understand the nature of science' then they will incorporate elements of the nature of science in their lessons is flawed. The major advance of the past decade has been a consensual agreement that the nature of science or 'how science works' should be an important element of the school science curriculum. Such policy documents rest on a final key assumption that teachers themselves have at least a working knowledge of key features of any contemporary picture of the nature of science; that they have the pedagogical content knowledge to teach the topic effectively; and then, that children will grasp its significance and salience. To say that this is questionable, particularly given the saturation of everyday culture with images of scientists that still perpetuate the image of the lone, Caucasian, male scientist working in isolation searching for the moment of 'discovery' in search of scientific truth would be in grave danger of understating the case.

Further reading

Harré, R. (1984) *The Philosophies of Science: An Introductory Survey,* 2nd edn. Oxford: Oxford University Press.

Hodson, D. (2008) *Towards Scientific Literacy: A Teachers Guide to the History, Philosophy and Sociology of Science.* Rotterdam: Sense Publishers.

Matthews, M. R. (1994) *Science Teaching: The Role of History and Philosophy of Science.* New York: Routledge.

3 Science for citizenship

Jonathan Osborne

Introduction

Bhopal, Chernobyl, Three Mile Island and *Exxon Valdez* are just some of the names associated with *environmental disasters* in the past 30 years or so. BSE (mad-cow disease), human-made climate change, ozone depletion, coral bleaching and species destruction are an additional set of topics which can be added to this litany. What do they all have in common? Put simply, they all represent a set of human-made manufactured risks that are commonly perceived as products of science and technology. In contrast, the post-war generation grew up within a cultural milieu that saw science as *a source of solutions*. Science, after all, had succeeded in placing a 'man on the moon'; the development of penicillin had saved millions of lives; and deadly diseases such as polio and smallpox were being eliminated. There was no challenge which science could not meet. Yet, over the past half-century, that image has been transformed. Transformed by the recognition that the human activities that science and technology have enabled can pose serious threats to our way of life. Instead of offering solutions, science and technology have become for many *a source of risk* (Beck, 1992). A perusal of the headlines of scientific stories in broadsheet newspapers in any given week demonstrates how such a perception is now deeply embedded in contemporary cultural contexts with topics such as 'Aircrew risk breast cancer', 'Climate change poses threat to water quality', 'Genetic crops pose threat to birds and bees' and 'Glass of wine halves chance of pregnancy'.

Thus, socio-scientific issues and their accompanying ethical, political and moral concerns from BSE to climate change increasingly dominate the media, public and family life. Although science is one of the major achievements of Western civilization and permeates our culture rather as mica pervades granite, ever since that fearsome mushroom cloud rose over the Nevada desert and Rachel Carson published her book *Silent Spring* (Carson, 1963), the pretence that science and scientists are separate from society and its applications has been unsustainable. What this means is that science is now viewed with much greater ambivalence than before by most societies. It no longer offers a technological miracle – a dazzling quick fix to human problems. Rather, the public attitude is much more circumspect and there is a recognition that with every benefit there is, as a corollary, a cost which is often environmental either in reducing biodiversity, permanently altering the landscape (dam construction), or reducing the resources available to future generations (oil exploitation) (Gregory and Miller, 1998; Irwin, 1995).

Yet, as the then UK chief scientific advisor, Sir David King, commented in 2007 (King, 2007), the five major challenges facing humanity – generating sufficient energy, providing an adequate supply of clean water, growing enough food, controlling and eliminating disease and, last but not least, dealing with climate change – are all problems to which science and technology must make a substantial contribution. Indeed, *The Independent's* (1999) comment that 'the real challenges for the future are scientific' seem to have a prescience that even the writer could not have foretold.

In such a context, what role, if anything, does science education have to contribute? For the political and moral dilemmas posed by modern science have raised concerns about the public understanding of science first expressed by scientists in the Bodmer Report (1985) which argued that there was a need to improve the general 'scientific literacy' of the adult population if the adult population were to engage in the public debate. C. P. Snow put it more bluntly in his now infamous lecture in Cambridge 50 years ago on the 'Two cultures' (Snow, 1959). Snow argued that not to know science was to be an 'outsider' – an alien to the culture as much as somebody who cannot recognize the cultural referents that are a product of the 'greats' of English literature. But does the science education that we practise really help to develop the kinds of competencies and knowledge – the scientific literacy – that our future citizens are likely to need? And should this be one of its purposes?

Such arguments about aims are important because aims matter. A teacher without an aim is like a ship without a rudder, unable to see the route or the strategies that will provide an education that is appropriate to their students' current and future needs. So, beginning with a discussion of aims, this chapter explores and summarizes the scholarly arguments and research evidence that have revolved around the purpose and function of science education. And, if science for citizenship or scientific literacy is to be an aim, this chapter then considers what implications for contemporary classroom practice might be.

Aims of science education

Why teach science, and in particular, why teach science to all students? Such a question is often asked by students, albeit in the more simplistic form of 'Please Sir/Miss, why are we studying this?' While the daily treadmill of teaching offers little opportunity to stand and stare and consider such questions, the answers are important in determining the kind of science that is offered to young people, and the emphasis that is given to different aspects of science.

Broadly speaking, there are four arguments for science education which can be found in the literature (Layton, 1973; Millar, 1996; Roberts, 2007; Thomas and Durant, 1987) These are called the utilitarian argument, the economic argument, the cultural argument and the democratic argument, and are reflected by particular curriculum emphases. In what follows, each of these is described and discussed, and their strengths and weaknesses examined.

The utilitarian argument

This is the view that learners might benefit, in a practical sense, from learning science. That is, scientific knowledge enables them to wire a plug or fix their car; that a scientific training develops a 'scientific attitude of mind', a rational mode of thought, a practical problem-solving ability that is unique to science and essential for improving the individual's ability to cope with everyday life. It is also claimed that science also trains powers of observation, providing an ability to see patterns in the plethora of data that confront us in everyday life. Such arguments may well resonate with the reader – they are after all the stock-in-trade responses that are part of the culture of science teaching. Sadly, however, they do not stand up to close examination.

First, there is little evidence that scientists are any more or less rational than the rest of humanity. As Millar (1996) argues, 'There is no evidence that physicists have fewer road accidents because they understand Newton's laws of motion, or that they insulate their houses better because they understand the laws of thermodynamics' (p. 11).

Second, the irony of living in a technologically advanced society is that we become *less* dependent on scientific knowledge, for the increasing sophistication of contemporary artefacts makes their functional failure only remediable by the expert, while simultaneously, their use and operation are simplified to a level that requires only minimal skill. Electrical appliances come with plugs pre-wired while washing machines, computers, video-cameras, etc. increasingly require little more than intuition for their sensible use. Even in contexts where you might think that scientific knowledge would be useful, such as the regulation of personal diet, research on students' choice of foods show that it bears no correlation to their knowledge of what constitutes a healthy diet (Merron and Lock, 1998).

Any idea that science trains powers of observation has long been undermined by the recognition that observation is a theory-dependent process (Hanson, 1958). Studies of perception reveal that observers tend to pay attention to objects or features with which they are familiar – that is observers are influenced by the ideas that *they bring to* their looking and see first what they expect to see. As Driver (1983) showed in her work, students often find it difficult to see check cells on a microscope slide, or the accepted pattern of iron filings surrounding a magnet because they lack a clear concept of what they are looking for (see, also, Chapter 2 in this volume). Further support is provided by research which shows that children's performance on observation-type tasks is significantly improved if prior instruction is offered about the kind of structures they expect to observe (Bremner, 1965; Hainsworth, 1956).

The inevitable conclusion to be drawn from such work is that a utilitarian argument for knowledge is open to challenge on a number of fronts.

If there is a convincing instrumental argument to be advanced, it is that a knowledge of basic human/animal physiology is essential to engage in meaningful conversations with doctors and surgeons. One limited example, however, is an insufficient foundation for the edifice of science education offered by schools. In short, the instrumental argument is one that science teachers would be ill-advised to use with their students, and ill-advised to use with headteachers and curriculum managers for science's claim to such a large slice of precious curriculum time.

The economic argument

This is the argument that an advanced technological society needs a constant supply of scientists to sustain its economic base and international competitiveness. From this perspective, science is seen as providing a pre-professional training and acts as a sieve for selecting the chosen few who will enter academic science or follow courses of vocational training. It is the substance of the argument which has been made in a range of reports across the years beginning with the Dainton Report (1968). Since then, such reports have reappeared with increasing frequency. Thus there has been the European report *Europe Needs More Scientists* (European Commission, 2004), the US Report, *Rising above the Gathering Storm* (National Academy of Sciences: Committee on Science Engineering and Public Policy, 2005), the UK report *The Race to the Top* (Lord Sainsbury of Turville, 2007), and the Australian report on opening up pathways into science, technology, engineering and mathematics (STEM) careers (Tytler et al., 2008). All of these reports portray the role of science education as a 'pipeline' (in some cases literally) which will sustain the future supply of scientists and engineers and which will maintain the economic competitiveness of their respective societies.

There are two basic problems with the economic rationale for compulsory science education. First, is the simple statistic that the proportion of school students who will go onto work in STEM professions is a minority. In 2008, the number of students emerging with STEM or STEM-related qualifications (for example, computer science, agricultural science) was approximately 250,000 (HESA, 2009). This forms 37 per cent of the total graduate student cohort but only a small percentage of the large number who take science courses to age 16 (approximately 750,000+ in the UK) or later. Therefore, to argue that the education of the future STEM professional should be the dominant or sole determinant of the aims of the science curriculum, and hence its content, is hard to justify, particularly when the majority of school students will not go into STEM careers. Undoubtedly, a case can be made that the whole populace will benefit from a sustained supply of professionals and that such a system ultimately benefits all. However, does the idea that the experience and educational needs of the majority should be sacrificed to meet the needs of the majority *really* make sense?

A much more fundamental objection to this argument is that it is framed totally in terms of an argument about supply. Absent from the discussion has been any critical examination of future demand. While all agree that it is virtually impossible to predict future demand, a cursory examination of the basic assumption embedded in many of the aforementioned reports, that the future society will be like our existing one, shows the weakness of the argument. Who, for instance, 30 years ago could possibly have predicted the rise of the Internet and how that would transform occupational employment diminishing the significance of manufacturing and enhancing the employment of those who worked in service and professional industries that dealt with ideas and financial instruments? For instance, the author of this chapter has been taught a long lineage of knowledge and skills which are now redundant, for example, mathematics using logarithmic tables and a slide rule, the workings of the triode valve, black and white photography using chemical solutions and more. Those who would advance the economic justification have a responsibility to engage in some kind of minimal future gazing and ask ourselves what kinds of trends we can perceive. Hill (2008), for instance, makes a cogent case that we are moving to a 'post-scientific society' where basic research will no longer be done by advanced societies. In part, this is because many aspects of it are increasingly mechanized; in part, because it is expensive in terms of facilities and staff; and in part, because there are many competitors particularly from emerging economies. For Hill,

> A post-scientific society will have several key characteristics, the most important of which is that innovation leading to wealth generation and productivity growth will be based principally not on world leadership in fundamental research in the natural sciences and engineering, but on world-leading mastery of the creative powers of, and the basic sciences of, individual human beings, their societies, and their cultures.
>
> (2008, p. 1)

Hill argues that in such a society, firms will hire fewer scientific professionals than in the past, and their role will be more to serve as translators and exploiters of new science than as original contributors to the body of scientific knowledge. Indeed, the number of people engaged in occupations that require specific expertise in science and engineering in the USA is only 4 per cent. In the UK, the most systematic and comprehensive analysis of what scientists themselves *do* was carried out by the Council of Science and Technology Institutes (1993). Their report listed 46 occupations where science was a main part of the job (such as a medical technician), or a critical part of their job (such as a nurse). Some 2.7 million people fell into these categories, a figure which represents only 12 per cent of the UK workforce. A further million people have their work enhanced or aided by a knowledge of science and technology. This represents at most, a further 16 per cent of the total UK workforce (Coles, 1998). Even if the demand has been growing since there is little evidence that there is a shortage of supply (Butz et al., 2003; Jagger, 2007; Lynn and Salzman, 2006; Teitelbaum, 2007). For instance, in the USA, the production of individuals with a PhD in the life sciences has increased by 50 per cent between 1993 and 2003 yet the number of tenure-track academic positions has remained virtually static; the unemployment rate for scientists and engineers tracks the national unemployment rate; and salaries for STEM professionals have not risen relative to the rest of the population (Teitelbaum, 2007). Similar concerns can be found in the report of a workshop funded by the National Science Foundation to examine the likely future skill demands for the working population (National Research Council, 2008). If these visions of the future hold any validity, then espousing the argument that school science has an instrumental value for a career in science is at best dubious and at worst morally questionable.

Coles' (1998) analysis of scientists and their work, their job specifications and other research, summarizes the important components of scientific knowledge and skills needed for employment as:

- general skills;
- knowledge of explanatory concepts;
- scientific skills:
  - application of explanatory concept,
  - concepts of evidence,
  - manipulation of equipment;
- habits of mind:
  - analytical thinking;
- knowledge of the context of scientific work.

Coles' data, collected from interviews with a range of 68 practising scientists, suggest that a knowledge of science is only *one* component among many that are needed for the world of work. Furthermore, his data show that the knowledge that scientists *do* need is quite specific to the context in which they are working. In contrast to the domain-specificity of the knowledge requirements, the scientists in this research stressed the importance of the domain-general skills of data analysis and interpretation; and general attributes such as the capacity to work in a team and an ability to communicate fluently, both in the written word and orally – aspects which are currently undervalued by contemporary practice in science education. Likewise, Gilbert (2005) has argued that the future society will be dominated by a conception of knowledge not as a noun or object – something which is offered up in the classrooms of the world for students to absorb – but knowledge as a process or verb – something which must be actively constructed and worked on. The skills required to engage in the knowledge society are those of the system-level thinker who is adept at taking elements from one field of knowledge, relating them to other fields and producing new ideas or new ways to do new things. A school curriculum which would support the development of such skills should develop an understanding of the major themes of science and how it works *as a system* rather than a miscellany of scientific facts (Cohen, 1952).

Hence, baldly stated, even our future scientists would be better prepared by a curriculum that reduced its factual emphasis and covered less but uncovered more of what it means to practise science. Coles' findings suggest that the skills developed by opportunities to conduct investigative practical work, such as that required in the UK – the ability to interpret, present and evaluate evidence, the ability to manipulate equipment and an awareness of the scientific approach to problems – are outcomes which are to be valued as much as any knowledge of the 'facts' of science.

The cultural argument

This is the argument that science is one of the great achievements of our culture – the shared heritage that forms the backdrop to the language and discourse that permeate our media, conversations and daily life (Cossons, 1993; Millar, 1996; Snow, 1959). In a contemporary context, where science and technology issues increasingly dominate the media (Pellechia, 1997), this is a strong argument, succinctly summarized by Cossons:

> The distinguishing feature of modern Western societies is science and technology. Science and technology are the most significant determinants in our culture. In order to decode our culture and enrich our participation – this includes protest and rejection – an appreciation/ understanding of science is desirable.
>
> (1993, p. 339)

One narrow articulation of the cultural value of science has been offered by Hirsch (Hirsch, 1987) who argued that there is a basic repertoire of facts and events that every American needs to know. However, just as nobody would claim that a knowledge of the chronology of the Kings and Queens of England provides any understanding of the cultural value of history, neither does a knowledge of a miscellany of scientific facts. What is perhaps missing from school science is a recognition that the crowning glory of science is the explanatory accounts it offers of the material world (Harré, 1984) – explanations which required enormous creative endeavour to imagine. For instance, a world where the Earth moved rather than the Sun (Copernicus); where diseases are spread by tiny living organisms (Pasteur); and where the speed of light is invariant with respect to any motion of the observer (Einstein). In every case, whether it be Darwin's theory of evolution, Mendeleev's development of the Periodic Table, or Wegener's theory of plate tectonics, such ideas were the fruition of a creative endeavour to see beyond the self-evident and to bring into being new imagined entities. The work of the best scientists is, therefore, just as creative as that of the best writers and artists. Yet it is as if science and science education suffer from some collective amnesia leaving the study of its own roots to the historians of science. Why might this be so? One explanation is that the project of science is closure. Once a question is answered, science and scientists move onto the next concern. All that is of value for the next enquiry is the knowledge that has been established, not how it was established. Yet, just as a society which forgets its roots loses its sense of identity and who it is, so does science lose some sense of its significance and sense of its own worth. Whatever history there is to be found in school science is commonly reduced to a few potted biographies and the march of science is commonly presented as a linear succession of successful discoveries. Nowhere are the blind alleys, the false trails or even occasionally plain fraud to be found (Brush, 1974; Matthews, 1994).

The implication of such arguments is that science education should be more of a course in the appreciation of science, developing an understanding not only of what it means to do science, but of what a hard-fought struggle and great achievement such knowledge represents. Therefore, understanding the culture of science requires some history of science, its ethics, scientific argument and scientific controversy – with more stress on the human dimension and less stress on science as a body of reified knowledge. In short, a reduction of the factual emphasis with more emphasis on the broad 'explanatory stories' that science offers and the development of a better understanding of a range of 'ideas-about-science' (Millar and Osborne, 1998).

The democratic argument

Proponents of this view point to the fact that many of the issues facing our society are of a socio-scientific nature. For instance, should we permit stem cell research? Should we allow electricity to be generated by nuclear power plants or, how can we limit the effects of human activity on climate change? The nature of contemporary society has changed from one where science is perceived as a source of solutions to one in which it is *also* seen as source of problems (Beck, 1992) or, as Giddens would argue, where our concerns have moved from external natural risks such as famine, droughts or earthquakes to manufactured risks – risks which have been generated by human activity. Moreover, as disciplinary knowledge becomes increasingly specialized and fragmented, we become evermore reliant on expertise. Social systems such as hospitals, railways, and air travel gain a complexity beyond the comprehension of any individual. Consider, for instance, the number of individuals and systems involved in ensuring the safe flight of one aircraft between London and Paris. In such a context, trust in expert systems and their regulatory bodies plays a large part in our faith that they will function effectively (Giddens, 1990).

If, then, the challenges of the future are likely to be the moral and political dilemmas posed by the expansion of scientific knowledge, a healthy democratic society requires the participation and involvement of all its citizens (or as many as possible), in the resolution of the choices that contemporary science will present. This is only likely if individuals have at least a basic understanding of the underlying science, and can engage both critically and reflectively in a participatory debate. Such an argument is elegantly captured in the *European White Paper on Education and Training* (European Commission, 1995):

> Democracy functions by majority decision on major issues which, because of their complexity, require an increasing amount of background knowledge. For example, environmental and ethical issues cannot be the subject of informed debate unless young people possess certain scientific awareness. At the moment, decisions in this area are all too often based on subjective and emotional criteria, the majority lacking the general knowledge to make an informed choice. Clearly this does not mean turning everyone into a scientific expert, but enabling them to fulfill an enlightened role in making choices which affect their environment and to understand in broad terms the social implications of debates between experts. There is similarly a need to make everyone capable of making considered decisions as consumers.
>
> (1995, p. 28)

This view sees the future citizen not as a producer of scientific knowledge – the notion underlying the economic argument for science education – but, rather, as a critical consumer of scientific knowledge (Millar, 2006). The latter is the idea that lies at the heart of a science education for the future citizen. Such an education, it is argued, requires a much greater emphasis on how science works (Fuller, 1997; McComas and Olson, 1998; Osborne et al., 2003).

Moreover, scientists, like other members of a democratic society, must be held to account. As a society, we provide large sums to fund and support their research. Should it be directed towards work that promises a material and tangible benefit, for example, enhanced food production, a vaccine for malaria, or should we support work which has little obvious benefit such as the construction of a new, orbiting space station or the Large Hadron Collider? Most contemporary scholarship would argue that the discussion of such issues would benefit if future citizens held a more critical attitude towards science (Fuller, 1997; Irwin, 1995) – essentially a stance, which while acknowledging its strengths, also recognized its limitations and ideological commitments. However, it is difficult to see how this can be done by a science education which offers no chance to develop an understanding of how scientists work, how they decide that any piece of research is 'good' science and which, in contrast to the controversy and uncertainty that surrounds much contemporary scientific research, offers a picture of science as a body of knowledge which is unequivocal, uncontested and unquestioned (Claxton, 1997).

In summary, no single one of these cases – the instrumental, the economic, the cultural or the democratic – establishes the case for science to be taught on the compulsory curriculum. Rather, the case for school science is based on all of these arguments and the emphasis that is placed on any one will vary with the nature of the course and the age group. Thus, the course, 'Science for Public Understanding' (Hunt and Millar, 2000) may well put a substantial emphasis on the democratic rationale while Advanced Placement physics in US high schools may justify itself more through the economic imperative. Attempting to justify the case for school science simply in terms of one of these arguments is always likely to fail as there are good counter-arguments – some of which have been considered. Nevertheless, having a basic mastery of their substance and form will help many a teacher to defend school science against the forlorn cry of 'Why are we learning this?'

Education for citizenship

Confronted with issues such as whether we should build more nuclear power stations, support stem cell research or fund the development of more energy-efficient cars, what kind of science education would help our future citizen? Gee (1996) argues that becoming 'literate' means becoming knowledgeable and familiar with the discourse of the discipline. That is the 'words, actions, values and beliefs of scientists', their common goals and activities and how they act, talk, and communicate. Such knowledge has to be acquired through exposure to the practices of scientists and explicitly taught so that children can become critically reflective. Rather like learning a language requires children to develop a knowledge of the form, grammar and vocabulary, so becoming scientifically literate would require a knowledge of science's broad themes, the reasons for belief, at least some of its content and, in particular, its uses and abuses.

Norris and Phillips (2003) take a different view, arguing that there are really two kinds of literacy – 'fundamental' and 'derived'. Fundamental scientific literacy is the knowledge which is required to make meaning from sentences of scientific English. This is more than the ability to recognize individual words – knowing the vocabulary, so to speak. Rather, the meaning of any given word can only be constructed from the context of its use – from examining the specific concatenation of words and inferring what they mean. Only with this form of literacy is it possible to achieve the 'derived' form of scientific literacy – that is the ability to comprehend, analyse and critique scientific text. This does not mean that one must be attained before the other. Norris and Phillips are at pains to point out that the two forms are deeply intertwined, but that the fundamental form of scientific literacy is a necessary requirement to engage in activities that require the use of the derived form. For many students, however, it is the use of the derived form – the ability to reflect critically on the dilemmas and choices posed by contemporary science which helps to give meaning to developing the fundamental form (see, also, Chapter 7).

Table 3.1 Estimated percentages of adults qualifying as civically scientifically literate by country/area

Country/Area	1998	2006
United States	12	25
European Union	5	22
United Kingdom	10	26
Germany	4	24
Denmark	8	22
Spain	3	9

Source: Millar (1998, 2006).

Attempts to measure 'scientific literacy' have usually focussed on the fundamental form and, even then, very much on a knowledge of the vocabulary and its processes (Miller, 1997). The results of such empirical studies question the achievements of science education, painting a depressing picture of the average person's knowledge of science. Since 1987, a number of well-funded surveys have been conducted in the UK (Durant et al., 1989; Research Councils UK, 2008), Europe (European Commission, 2005) and on an annual basis in the United States, since 2001 (National Science Board, 2008). These surveys have been conducted using a mix of closed questions using true–false quizzes containing items such as 'Is it true that:– 'lasers work by focussing sound waves?', 'all radioactivity is man-made?', 'antibiotics kill viruses as well as bacteria?' and other open questions. These surveys also asked respondents to tell the interviewer in their own words, what (for instance) is DNA? In addition, questions were included that assessed the public's understanding of the procedures of science.

Combining these data with that for their understanding of the processes of science, Miller (1998) and Millar (2006) have arrived at a view of the numbers who could be deemed to be civically scientifically literate, or at least partially so (Table 3.1). Defining a standardized score of 70 (with the mean set to 50 and a unitary standard deviation), as the level of knowledge necessary to read science and technology articles in the science section published in Tuesday's *New York Times* or the French magazine, *Science et Vie*, Miller estimates the percentage of adults who are scientifically literate as relatively low.

Given that in his 1998 paper, Millar used a lower score of 67 to define scientific literacy, these results point to a significant improvement in the understanding of science in the general populace which may be attributed to improved communication about science or even an improved science education. Clearly what is at question here is whether Millar's somewhat arbitrary definition of scientific literacy is too demanding. Many science topics are covered in tabloid newspapers in a brief, but nevertheless informative manner. In other areas of science and technology, such as the implications of nanotechnology, it could be argued that such general measures of literacy are of little predictive value in such a domain-specific area.

In the 2005 Eurobarometer survey (European Commission, 2005), the average number of correct answers to 13 knowledge type questions was 66 per cent with the highest being Sweden with 79 per cent and the lowest Turkey with 44 per cent. While the answers to some questions such as 'Do antibiotics kill viruses as well as bacteria?' were somewhat troubling, with only 46 per cent identifying this as false, the overall level of success is suggestive that the public knowledge of science is not quite as appalling as the picture portrayed by the Bodmer Report (1985). Moreover, there has been a positive improvement since the last survey in 2001. Nevertheless, these results do invite the question of whether the systematic exposure to formal science education within schools is generating a sufficiently scientifically literate populace?

However, it should be said that this body of survey research into the public's knowledge of specific aspects of science is subject to a number of criticisms. First, while such data portray the public as deficient and lacking in scientific knowledge, a range of studies carried out in a variety of contexts – with sheep farmers in Cumbria coping with the aftermath of Chernobyl (Irwin and Wynne, 1996); parents of Down's syndrome babies; individuals living near a chemical plant; and electricians at Sellafield (Layton et al., 1993), all demonstrate that the public can engage with scientific expertise in a manner which is both locally and contextually situated and acquire new scientific knowledge on a need-to-know basis. Rather, just as one's memory of a foreign language fades into the dim and distant past without use, so do the 'facts' of science unless there is a regular need to use such information. Hence, the results obtained by such surveys of the public knowledge of science are unexceptional and we must ask if a survey of the public understanding of English literature would obtain a similar set of disappointing data. Indeed, research would suggest that, at least for the US populace, this is so (National Science Board, 2008).

A succinct summary of the body of research on the public relationship with science undertaken by social scientists has been provided by Jenkins (1998) who argues that it shows that the interests of citizens in science are differentiated by the science, social group and gender. For most of us, interest in science is related to decision-making or action, and that for such purposes when necessary, we choose a level of knowledge adequate for the task in hand and learn what is essential. As Jenkins concludes, 'the "non-expert" citizen turns out to be rather complex in his or her dealings with science' and those interactions 'cannot be explained simply in terms of ignorance' (p. 14).

For science education, such findings have an important message suggesting that the over-emphasis on content, coupled with the negative attitudes it engenders (see Chapter 11) is an unproductive endeavour. Indeed, an examination of 30 recent public controversies about science conducted by Ryder, found that:

> looking across the understandings identified as significant for the individuals involved in the case studies, subject matter knowledge did not tend to be the central focus. Indeed in many of the studies relevant subject knowledge was unknown to science (e.g. the

epidemiology of the BSE agent). Overall, much of the science knowledge relevant to individuals in the case studies was *knowledge about
science,* i.e. knowledge about the development and use of scientific
knowledge rather than scientific knowledge itself.

(2001, p. 35; author's emphasis)

Thus, it could be argued that if the public's use of the disciplinary content
of science is so situationally specific, would it not be better to spend time
developing an understanding of what science is, how it is done, its broad areas
of study and the major ideas that it has contributed to our culture rather than
attempting to construct an understanding 'brick by brick' or 'fact by fact'?
After all, the research on the public knowledge of science cited previously
would appear to suggest that it is a structure without any permanence. Such
arguments have long been made by those who study the public and their
relationship with science (Fuller, 1997; Irwin, 1995). Fuller, for instance argues
that:

> most of what non-scientists need to know in order to make informed
> public judgements about science fall under the rubric of history, phi-
> losophy, and sociology of science, rather than the technical content
> of scientific subjects.

(1997, p. 9)

Further empirical evidence to support this case comes from a Delphi study
conducted by Osborne et al. (2003) with a group of 25 participants consisting
of equal numbers of leading scientists, science teachers, science communicators, historians, sociologists and philosophers, and science educators. This
study used a three-stage, open-ended questionnaire in which the responses
of the responses of the participants at each stage were analysed and summarized and fed back after round 1 and round 2 to see if the group could come
to any consensus. Despite the well-known disparate and occasionally antag-
onistic views of this community, they found eight features of the nature of
science that the group agreed should be part of the compulsory school science
curriculum (see, also, Chapter 2 in this volume). These were:

- Scientific Methods and Critical Testing
- The Role of Creativity in Science
- Historical Development of Scientific Knowledge
- Science and Questioning
- The Diversity of Scientific Thinking
- The Relationship between Science and Certainty
- The Role of Hypothesis and Prediction
- The Role of Competition and Collaboration.

Granted, one cannot have a knowledge of science without acquiring some
of its major conceptual ideas or understanding some of the methods science
uses to justify its claims. But as Gee (1996) argues, teaching for acquisition

alone leads to successful but 'colonized' students who have no knowledge about their own discipline, such as its history or its evidential base, leaving them bereft of many of the faculties necessary to engage critically with the assertions and opinions of scientists who claim, for instance, that eating genetically modified foods is absolutely safe. Too much emphasis on content then leads to 'too little analytic and reflective awareness and limits the capacity for certain sorts of critical reading and reflection' (Gee, 1996, p. 139). History teachers, in contrast, have made such a transition. They now see their subject as one in which content is subsidiary to developing the skills of historical analysis needed to make sense of contemporary life and resolve uncertainty (Donnelly, 1999). While arguments such as this are not new (Turner, 1927), they have been given increasing emphasis by the body of scholarship that has emerged in the past two decades from those engaged in studying the sociology of scientific knowledge and those working in the public engagement of science. It is arguments such as this which have led to a major element of the English National Curriculum now being devoted to the topic of 'How science works' whose central focus is on teaching a body of ideas *about* science (see, also, Chapter 2 in this volume).

Implications for science teaching

Teaching *about* science would require that more emphasis is given to developing the following attributes: an understanding of the methods and processes of science; an awareness of the context and interests of scientists, their social practices; and an ability to analyse, or at least consider, risks and benefits (Millar and Osborne, 1998; National Academy of Science, 1995). Merely teaching about the applications of science is insufficient for, as Ziman (1994) argues, such approaches simply take a quick stride from science to technology but usually fail to go on and consider the implications for society at large, thus perpetuating the notion that science offers a technical fix for all our problems. However, contemporary science raises issues whose solution requires careful consideration of ethical and moral values, for example, should we grow genetically-modified organisms; should we restrict car use; or should we conduct research on animals?

The ideology that dominates the teaching of science is one which sees the act of scientific enquiry as a value-free activity. However, such a view is not tenable. First, science has its own intrinsic values which are variously described as: mechanistic, materialistic, masculine, reductionist, idealized, objective, impersonal, rational, universal, communal, value-free, disinterested, parsimonious, authoritarian, socially sterile and positivistic (Putnam, 2004). Second, science does not take place in a social vacuum, being a practice which is both shaped by and which shapes society. Decisions about which line of enquiry to pursue and how it is pursued are influenced by the values of the individuals working in science just as much as any other social practice. As

Willard points out, 'values emanate from practice and become sanctified with time' and 'the more they recede into the background, the more taken for granted they become' (1985, p. 444). The attempt to sustain a hermetic seal between science, society and its applications simply increases the gulf between science-as-it-is-taught and science-in-the-real-world alienating many students, particularly girls (see Chapter 11 on attitudes) – a sentiment clearly expressed by a student in Osborne and Collins' (2001) study of student attitudes towards school science:

> But still, like, this morning we were talking about genetic engineering. She didn't want to know our options and I don't reckon that the curriculum lets them, lets us discuss it further. I mean science, okay you can accept the facts, but is it right, are we allowed to do this to human beings?
>
> (2001, p. 451)

The Science-Technology-Society (STS) movement has sought, in contrast, to situate learning about science in a social context, arguing that the presentation of science as an academic, value-free subject was seriously out of date. This led to a series of courses and materials such as *SISCON* (Solomon, 1983), *Chem-Com*: Chemistry in the Community (American Chemical Society, 1988), *SATIS* (The Association for Science Education, 1986) and the *Salters Science* courses produced by the University of York – all of which have sought to make the consideration of the applications and social implications of the course a core feature. During the past decade, two courses have evolved which have arguably gone a step further – *Science for Public Understanding* (Hunt and Millar, 2000), which has recently been renamed *Science and Society* indicating a return to its roots and *Twenty-First Century Science*. The latter was an attempt to design a course consistent with the principles to be found in the report *Beyond 2000: Science Education for the Future* (Millar and Osborne, 1998) and a full rationale for this course is elaborated in Millar (2006).

More guidance for developing the skills and competencies for citizenship is dependent on the brief lights shone by specific pieces of research in a range of areas, and the substantial body of work that has been undertaken in the history, philosophy and sociology of the subject in the past 30 years. From such work, several areas stand out for attention in school science education.

Argument in science

When scientific claims are made, theories are often challenged and progress is made through dispute and conflict (Kuhn, 1962; Taylor, 1996). Assessing alternatives, weighing evidence, interpreting texts, evaluating the potential viability of scientific claims are all essential components in evaluating scientific arguments (Latour and Woolgar, 1986). Science-in-the-making is also always characterized by a number of uncertainties: empirical uncertainty due to lack of evidence; pragmatic uncertainty due to a lack of resources to investigate the problem; and theoretical uncertainty due to a lack of a clear theory of what is causing the events of interest. Arguments between scientists extend into the public domain through journals, conferences and the wider media and it is only through such processes – checking claims and public criticism that 'quality control' in science is maintained (Longino, 1990). Increasingly such arguments now spill out beyond the boundaries of science into the public domain.

Yet as currently practised, science education uses evidence to persuade students that the *singular* account offered by the teacher is self-evident and 'true'. There is little attempt to develop an understanding of the logic and reasoning that is used to argue for, or against, a scientific hypothesis (Giere, 2006). This contrast, or gulf between science-as-practised and science-as-taught can only be resolved if students are occasionally given the opportunities to study more than one interpretation of a set of data and critically examine the arguments for both cases (Driver et al., 2000; Monk and Osborne, 1997). Research on individuals' abilities to argue from evidence to conclusions (Kuhn, 1991; Kuhn et al., 1997) suggests that the majority of individuals display a naïveté in their argumentation skills. Kuhn found that individuals display a range of errors in reasoning such as 'false inclusion' – essentially seeing correlations between two variables as being causal; the failure to use exclusion (controls) – a method essential to scientific reasoning as it allows the elimination of extraneous factors from consideration; the domination of affirmation over negation – that is looking for evidence to confirm an idea when scientific ideas survive because they are *not* disproved; and a tendency to dismiss factors as irrelevant, thus eliminating the potential for disconfirming evidence. Somewhat dishearteningly, Kuhn found that schooling made no difference after the end of junior high school, a finding which suggests that too little attention is paid to the practice of reasoning and argument in high schools.

The implication is that rather than presenting science as a succession of successful discoveries, young people should occasionally be offered the opportunity to study aspects of science-in-the-making so that they can begin to understand why scientists might disagree, and why so much uncertainty surrounds scientific work at the boundaries of our knowledge. One approach would be to undertake more detailed case studies of scientific discoveries such as those suggested by Matthews (1994), Solomon (1991, 1992) and Osborne (1998). Such case studies show that whenever a new explanation is offered for a phenomenon, there are always at least two competing theoretical interpretations offered. Resolution often takes many years – as it did with Galileo's arguments for the heliocentric theory of the solar system; Torricelli's assertion that there was a vacuum at the top of the barometer when there were good logical arguments that 'nature abhorred a vacuum'; or Wegener's almost lunatic (at the time) assertion that the continents had once been one and drifted apart. The other advantage of such case studies is that they introduce into science that aspect that often seems to be missing for so many students – people. Thus stories can be told about Joule on his honeymoon, Marie Curie and her lover

Langévin, Pasteur's deceit with his anthrax vaccine, Rosalind Franklin circulating scornful, black-edged cards announcing the death of DNA HELIX – all of which add an essential extra human dimension to the practice of science which has been systematically erased from standard texts.

Developing an understanding of evidence

Another necessary task is to develop a more substantive grounding in what constitutes evidence in science – what Gott and Duggan (1995) term 'concepts of evidence'. This approach requires that much more time be given to exercises that require the quality of data to be assessed – how accurate is it, how much error was there in its measurement, and how much can it be trusted? In science lessons, a regular feature should be exercises in transforming data from one form to another, from tables to graphs and vice versa so that students can develop fluency in a skill which is not only essential to evaluating scientific findings but has value far beyond the boundaries of science wherever bodies of data are used to support arguments.

It is also somewhat strange that much of science education, as practised, shows an obsessive concern with the methods of the physical sciences. Science is presented as a form of empirical enquiry based solely on a hypothetico-deductive model of investigation (see Chapter 2). In contrast, much research reported in the media is based on epidemiological or correlational studies (Bencze, 1996), with the use of controls, and blind or double-blind testing – concepts which are rarely even mentioned, yet alone modelled in the science classroom. Yet simple exercises tabulating hair colour against eye colour, or hours spent watching television against hours spent doing homework, are activities that open a window into one of the principal methods of science.

Contemporary science

Some illumination about where science educators might concentrate more of their efforts comes from examining the growing body of scholarship emerging from the study of science communication, particularly that in the popular press. After all, as Nelkin and Lindee argue, 'For most people the reality of science is what they read in the press. They understand science less through direct experience or past education than through the filter of journalistic language and imagery' (1995, p. 2). In the past decade, that has changed somewhat with, for instance, 50 per cent of Americans reporting in 2008 that television is their main information source, 23 per cent newspapers and 14 per cent the Internet (National Science Board, 2008).

One study which examined the trends in science coverage in three major US daily newspapers over the period 1966–90 found that the disciplinary divisions were medicine, health, nutrition and fitness (73 per cent), technology (5 per cent) and natural/physical sciences (22 per cent) (Pellechia, 1997). The implication, therefore, is that an understanding of the biological sciences and its methods is *the* important science to address if we wish to provide a knowledge that will be both valued and valuable. Yet school science is still dominated by the exact sciences of chemistry and physics and rarely explores the distinct differences that exist between these domains of science.

Providing an opportunity to read and discuss contemporary reports about science offers another means of extending students' ability to understand and interpret science (Jarman and McClune, 2007; Wellington, 1991). Researchers in the area of science communication (Evans et al., 1990; Hinkle and Elliot, 1989; Perlman, 1974) have argued that the following components are important factors in determining the importance and significance of any reported science story:

- The location and length of coverage as these give a measure of its importance.
- The source of the original research, as papers published at conferences have less prestige than, for instance, those published in *Nature*.
- The identification of the researcher(s) by name and their professional status, for example, Dr, Professor, as this enables some discrimination about the level of significance to give the report.
- The institutional affiliation of the researcher(s), for example, university, government, industry, as such information enables us to judge, at least in part, whether the interpretation of the findings might be coloured by allegiances, commitments and values of the researcher.
- Comments from the researcher(s) who conducted the study(ies) which indicates that the report is at least attempting to offer their own interpretation of the findings.
- Comments from other scientists. One characteristic of science is that it is a process of organized scepticism. The natural procedure of science is to examine all findings with a view to disbelief. Quotes, or comments in support, suggest that the findings have at least convinced some of the peer community of the value of the findings, whereas comments expressing disbelief warn that the findings are contested.
- Contextual factors. Media reports have a tendency to characterize scientific research in terms of 'breakthroughs', resulting in over-sensationalization of what might be quite tentative findings. Therefore, one important characteristic is information that informs the reader whether these findings accord with, or deviate from, previous findings.

Developing the ability to read science in a critical, 'educated' manner requires opportunities to explore some of these issues in the science classroom. Again, most of the background knowledge underpinning this set of evaluative criteria is not knowledge of science itself, but knowledge of how science is practised – science in its social context; knowledge that will only be developed by the occasional opportunity to read, discuss and explore contemporary science. Evidence that formal science education currently leaves students ill-prepared to make such judgements emerges from the work of Norris and Phillips (1994)

Table 3.2   Categories of salient information in media reports

Feature	Description
Social context	Information about the prestige and bias relate to who did the research. Who funded it and where it was conducted or published.
Method	Information about how the research was conducted, including such topics as research design and procedures.
Theory/agent	Information about why the reported effects might have occurred, including questions about the properties of the putative causal agent and/or possible underlying mechanisms.
Data/statistics	Information about precisely what was observed in the reported study or about statistical tests.
Relevance	Information about the importance or applicability of the findings.

Source: Zimmerman et al. (2001).

which showed that of a sample of 91 able, grade 12 Canadian science students, less than half could identify causal statements, fewer than a tenth recognized justifications and almost half confused statements of evidence and conclusions in reading media accounts of science.

Another study, undertaken by Zimmerman et al. (2001), exposed another weakness in the skills and knowledge that even individuals educated in science bring to evaluating media reports of science. Using a taxonomy of the salient features of information provided (Table 3.2), they asked students to rank which they considered most important in evaluating any journalistic report about science. In addition, they asked a group of five experts in the field of science communication to rank these features for their importance as well. What they found was a significant disparity between the views of experts and those of students. For instance, whereas all five of the experts suggested that information about 'related research' and the 'relevance of the research' was critical to the evaluation of any report, the comparable figures for students were only 32 per cent and 41 per cent respectively. Conversely 84 per cent of the students suggested that seeking information about the underlying theory was important and 86 per cent said seeking information about the data and statistics was important, whereas only one of the experts considered them important. Given that the students participating in this research were well-educated undergraduates and yet lacked the appropriate conceptual framework to evaluate this work, these findings are suggestive that their formal education is failing to develop a body of knowledge about science, and how to read it critically, which may be essential for citizenship.

Exploring ethics and values of science

Finally, science does not exist in a vacuum and its practice raises important moral and ethical issues for society that students might want to consider.

Many science teachers are reluctant to venture into such waters, perpetuating an illusion either that human problems are amenable to technical solutions where values and human needs can be weighed by experts using value-free methods, or that ethics and values are not part of science. While this is understandable given their own background and education, it places a hermetic seal between school science and the daily lives of young people. Such a division appears arbitrary and, for them, weakens the relevance of the subject. After all, many of the political and moral dilemmas confronting both society and young people are of a socio-scientific nature and research shows that students do want to discuss such issues (Solomon, 1992). Furthermore, as Kolstoe asks, 'How, for instance, it is possible to weigh some people's wish for a new power plant based on coal against other people's wish for clean air?' (2001, p. 298) without any consideration of values? The resolution of such dilemmas can only be achieved by recognizing that science is only one of several social domains that can contribute relevant information to the debate. For most people, interest in science and technology is a product of an interest in decision-making and action. And, if one of the roles of education is a preparation for citizenship, this cannot be undertaken without some consideration of values. In short, it is difficult to conceive of a science education which is a preparation for citizenship without some opportunities for a structured exploration of the application of science in a social context and the dilemmas that are produced (see, for example, Corrigan et al., 2007).

Research into systematic attempts to consider the ethical aspects of science and science-related issues has been conducted by Fullick and Ratcliffe (1996), Ratcliffe and Grace (2003) and Solomon et al. (1992). Such work has been a feature of curriculum initiatives such as SATIS (The Association for Science Education, 1986), the *Salter's Science Course* and the Canadian course *Logical Reasoning in Science and Technology* (Aikenhead, 1991). The approach is usually based on group discussions of socio-scientific issues, from the local and specific such as what type of materials it is best to use for window-frames, to the global such as what can be done to solve the world food problem. All research and findings on such activities reinforce the view that a clear structure must be provided, both for the conduct of the discussion (Baines et al., 2009; Johnson et al., 2002; Oulton, Day ct al., 2004; Oulton, Dillon et al., 2004) and for the identification of options and evaluating their relative merits (Ratcliffe and Grace, 2003). One pedagogical approach is the use of consequence mapping in which students map on a sheet of paper the primary and secondary consequences of choices such as storing spent nuclear fuel underground, producing energy from wind turbines or conducting research on animals. Such exercises provide opportunities to practise and develop an 'an armoury of essential skills: listening, arguing, making a case, and accepting the greater wisdom or force of an alternative view' (Ratcliffe and Grace, 2003, p. 61) which are the foundations of responsible citizenship in a participatory democracy (Advisory Group for Education for Citizenship, 1998). Research is now also emerging that would suggest that engaging in such activities does begin the process of enhancing

Table 3.3 Table showing the possible risks of men dying in the UK at the age of 40

Ways of dying	Rank	Risk (based on mortalities)
All natural causes at age 40	2	1 in 850
An accident in the home	7	1 in 43,500
An accident on the railway	10	1 in 500,000
An accident on the road	4	1 in 8000
Being hit by lightning	11	1 in 10,000,000
Radiation/nuclear industry	8	1 in 57,000
Homicide/murder	9	1 in 100,000
Influenza	3	1 in 5000
Leukaemia	5	1 in 12,500
Playing football	6	1 in 25,000
Smoking 10 cigarettes a day	1	1 in 200

the students' skills of argumentation while simultaneously providing interest and relevance (Nolen, 2003; Zohar and Nemet, 2002).

A very basic goal should be the opportunity to consider not just the strengths of science but also its limitations – that is, that there are limits to certainty and that many decisions involve an assessment of risk. Indeed, the public are generally bad at making good estimates of risk overestimating unfamiliar risks (flying in an aeroplane) and underestimating familiar risks (driving a car). Table 3.3 shows the risks of various ways of dying by age 40 in the UK (British Medical Association, 1990). When asked to rank these risks in the left-hand column most people commonly fail to identify the highest risk.

Exploring the concept of risk helps to show that while the desire for certainty might be understandable, in reality, it is a nebulous illusion. Science does not offer us a clear path to 'navigate the sea of uncertainty' (Adams, 1995, p. 199) that we sail in our daily lives. An understanding of the nature of risk, its evaluation and its determination, therefore, is a vital tool for interpreting scientific information – from assessing the reliability of the weather forecast to making decisions about the storage of nuclear waste. Moreover, the message that science-at-the-cutting-edge does not offer unequivocal resolution of the many risks that confront us is *the* fundamental message that any course in science must communicate if the public are to begin to understand the information that science provides. Any science education for citizenship would be remiss, therefore, if it did not explore some of these ideas of risk (see, also, Dillon and Gill, 2001).

Conclusion

This chapter has attempted to explore the arguments for science education, and, in particular, for a science education that is a preparation for citizenship rather than life as a professional scientist. Studies of science, as used in the media and everyday life, suggest that 'citizen's science' requires less emphasis on the 'facts' of science and a broader knowledge of how science works. While work in this field is limited, it rests on a premise that 'to know science' is a statement that one knows not only *what* a phenomenon is, but also *how* it relates to other events, *why* it is important and *how* this particular view of the world came to be. Any science education which offers only aspects of the conceptual achievements of science in isolation constructs an artificial divide between science, technology and the social context of its production, and is unlikely to provide an adequate education for the future citizen. Current practice is rather like introducing a young child to jigsaws by giving them bits of a one-thousand-piece puzzle and then assuming that they will persist and acquire the whole picture and an enthusiasm for jigsaws. An education for citizenship would, in contrast, offer the broader overview of the content of science (the 100-piece version) and a sense of both the achievements and limits of science. The goal is simply enabling – to help students acquire the confidence and a measure of intellectual independence that will assist them to participate as informed and responsible citizens when faced by the inevitable dilemmas that will be posed by science and technology in the years to come. Whether the issue is global (climate change) or local (building wind-farms), a healthy democratic society needs young people to engage with such issues. Helping students to do so is one of the responsibilities that school science cannot, and should not avoid.

Further reading

Corrigan, D., Dillon, J. and Gunstone, R. (eds) (2007) *The Re-emergence of Values in Science Education*. Rotterdam: Sense Publications.

Driver, R. (1983) *The Pupil as Scientist?* Milton Keynes: Open University Press.

Fuller, S. (1997) *Science*. Buckingham: Open University Press.

Irwin, A. (1995) *Citizen Science*. London: Routledge.

Jarman, R. and McClune, B. (2007) *Developing Scientific Literacy*. Maidenhead: Open University Press.

Layton, D. (1973) *Science for the People: The Origins of the School Science Curriculum in England*. London: Allen and Unwin.

Millar, R. and Osborne, J. F. (eds) (1998) *Beyond 2000: Science Education for the Future*. London: King's College London.

Ratcliffe, M. and Grace, M. (2003) *Science Education for Citizenship*. Buckingham: Open University Press.

Ryder, J. (2001) Identifying science understanding for functional scientific literacy, *Studies in Science Education*, 36: 1–44.

4 Thinking about learning

Learning in science

Jill Hohenstein and Alex Manning

Introduction

What counts as learning? Learning can be defined as a relatively permanent change in thought or in behaviour that results from experience. Such a definition captures changes that occur over a lifetime, such as the adoption of a particular political perspective as a result of living in a specific cultural situation over a long period of time, as well as relatively unconscious adaptations in posture following repeated experiences of sitting in front of a computer. This broad range of behaviours is obviously larger than what you, as a classroom teacher, will usually be concerned with. Therefore, in this chapter, we narrow the focus to present a brief overview of theories of learning and the status of current thinking about learning.

Before beginning our discussion of the theories concerning how people learn, we should draw your attention to a debate in the field about styles of learning. We do not have space to devote very much attention to this debate. However, given the importance learning styles have received in educational policy in the UK and elsewhere, it seems worthwhile to mention them. There are many models of learning styles. Probably the most popular model involves labelling learners as Visual, Auditory, or Kinaesthetic, and can be linked to tests such as the Learning Styles Inventory (LSI; Dunn and Dunn, 1992).

A recent review of research conducted in the 'field' of learning styles revealed that tests such as the LSI had very little validity in terms of effective classroom pedagogy (Coffield et al., 2004). And while at least one of the models they examined seemed to hold up to criteria such as internal consistency, test–retest reliability, construct validity and predictive validity, the main point the report makes could be summed up as follows, 'self development is more likely to result from increasing learners' knowledge of the relative advantages and weaknesses of different models, than from learners being assigned a particular learning style' (Coffield et al., 2004, p. 132). That is, labelling a learner with a certain type of style is unlikely to benefit the learner as much as helping learners to understand the usefulness of applying a particular strategy to the task at hand (see, also, Chapter 5 in this volume).

So, whereas there may be some valid use of tests of learning styles, we focus here on general theories and research into learning. We also point out ways that these theories can be particularly exemplified in science learning. A further note worth mentioning is that we do not take the perspective that the learning that occurs in science is any different to the learning that occurs in other subjects (or in non-academic arenas). The topic of science may present specific contexts that pose challenges, some of which may even be unique to science. However, the manner in which learners form understandings should not differ between subjects.

Theories of learning

Origins of contemporary theories of learning can be traced to philosophers in the past three centuries, and possibly earlier. These theories have shaped our approaches to teaching and the mechanisms by which we help learners to learn. Many theories of learning can be categorized as either behaviourist or cognitivist (some span both).

Behaviourism

Behaviourism is based on the view that we cannot see anything that occurs in the mind and, as such, the mind becomes irrelevant to understanding human action. As a result, behaviourism focuses on externally observable inputs and outputs to determine what governs learning. This theory is related to the philosophy of Hobbes ([1651] 1968), who suggested that humans operate by way of inputs and outputs, and thus constructs such as 'mind' and 'free will' are not useful explanations of the way people function and as such, people are simply material systems.

Extreme behaviourism claims that infants enter the world *tabula rasa*. Behaviourists believe infants learn about the world through various forms of association, including conditioning, both classical (Pavlov, 1927) and operant (Skinner, 1974). Classical conditioning is a form of training of behaviour using stimulus and response. For example, a dog has innate responses (salivation) to a stimulus (food), which gradually becomes associated (through repeated pairing) with a new stimulus (a bell). The learned behaviour is then salivating in response to the sound of a bell. Classical conditioning is associationist in nature because learning occurs through the forming of associations between stimuli.

Operant conditioning occurs through the shaping of behaviour through incentives, lack of incentives and punishments. A monkey may learn to press a lever to dispense food by at first giving it food when it approaches the part of the cage where the lever is positioned. Then, as time progresses, food is given only when the monkey touches the lever. Finally, the monkey must actually press the lever to receive food. When the monkey receives the food, it obtains positive reinforcement for its behaviour, which is thought to maintain behaviour over time. On the other hand, if a negative stimulus can be removed by a positive action (an unpleasant buzzer desists when the monkey presses a button), then the monkey learns to repeat the action (button pushing) through negative reinforcement. Finally, if the monkey were to receive negative feedback (such as a shock) following an action, this punishment should lead the monkey not to repeat that action, thereby avoiding the punishment.

These principles of conditioning are thought by many to be true of humans as well as non-human animals. In the science classroom associationist learning might be thought of as a pupil who responds well to teacher praise. The suggestion is that a pupil who receives praise from their teacher as a consequence of following correct experimental procedure, may learn that praise will be linked with following instructions. Similarly, receiving a good or bad mark on an assignment would be thought to evoke some learning of an association between the study habits and effort, in addition to the content of the work in the assignment, and the 'feedback' that comes in the form of marks. On the other hand, the evidence that such praise or feedback really works is relatively scarce.

Behaviourism in the form of conditioning as outlined above has, as a perspective, fallen out of favour. Nevertheless, more modern approaches that rely on associationism, such as connectionism (Rummelhart and McClelland, 1986; Elman et al., 1996) would suggest that we should view learning as a series of pairings of inputs and outputs that create associations that operate in much the same way as a computer program does. These inputs and outputs are connected via networks that link the concepts that a person has acquired. Of course, there are structural mechanisms in the brain that assist or constrain learning in various ways, however, it is primarily the associations that govern learning. Building on the analogy between the brain and computers, some researchers have designed computer programs that are able to learn a language (Seidenberg and Elman, 1999), though these programs admittedly have much further to go before they can replicate the powerful learning demonstrated by the human brain. Furthermore, though the Connectionist model of learning acknowledges some innate limitations of the brain, these computer models may be more precisely described as associationist in that they rely largely on environmental stimuli (the inputs) to structure learning.

One thing to bear in mind is that many (especially those coming from a constructivist background, see below) would suggest that pupils do not arrive to the science classroom as 'blank slates', as they have formed ideas from the world around them. Furthermore, secondary science teachers will work with pupils who have previously been taught science elsewhere. Therefore, if science teachers are to use associationist principles in their philosophies of teaching, they will need to take into account the types of learning experiences that pupils are likely to have had.

Cognitivism

Many contemporary approaches to learning place some value on the internal workings of 'the mind' in contrast to behaviourist theories. An early cognitivist theory of this kind proposes that learners progress through a series of stages, each affording a greater degree of intellectual ability. Piaget (1952) is perhaps the best known of the stage theorists. His ideas suggest that for the first two years of life, a primary objective that infants have is to explore the world around them through their developing sensorimotor skills. After that, children enter the pre-operational stage (ages 2 to 7), in which they tend to be egocentric in their thoughts, seeing the world from their own viewpoint, and not able to complete mental 'operations' that older children can do. From ages 7 to 12, in the concrete operations stage, children are able to operate mentally on the things around them. For example, they can begin to conserve volume, number and mass. A classic Piagetian task involves pouring equal amounts of liquid into two glasses of the same shape and size. After the child has agreed that the glasses contain the same amount of liquid, the liquid from one glass is then poured into a different sized glass (either taller and thinner or shorter and fatter). Children who can conserve volume will be able to say that there is still the same amount of liquid, supposedly because they can mentally reverse the operation of pouring the liquid from the first glass to the second of differing size. Finally, around the age of 12, children enter the formal operations (or adult) stage of cognitive development. This stage is characterized by the ability to think abstractly about many different concepts and to use logical reasoning. It is important to note that over the years the age at which children are able to accomplish the tasks associated with various stages has been called into question. For instance, it is now accepted that most 5-year-olds can pass various conservation tasks (Adey et al., 2002; Shayer and Adey, 1981; Donaldson, 1978).

Some research even goes so far as to suggest that some of the proposed qualitative developments suggested by Piaget are present from birth (see Quinn and Eimas, 1997). The latter view is associated with a perspective on learning known as enrichment, in which the ability to understand some principles such as objects have physical boundaries is present very early in development (for example, Spelke and Kinzler, 2007) and what changes is the building upon these initial understandings in a gradual, domain-specific way. This viewpoint can be compared with a stage model of development like Piaget's in which children pass through a series of qualitatively different levels of understanding that may be more general in nature. In fact, many in the field continue to demonstrate that development is stage-like in nature with only some subtle differences to Piaget's original proposals (for example, Case et al., 1996). We are not necessarily endorsing one point of view over another. However, for you as an educator, it is worth paying attention to the fact that research has not necessarily resolved the issue of whether children pass through stages of development.

Stage theory, particularly that of Piaget, has had a large impact on school curriculum development. In particular, Piaget's suggested stages can be compared with school curricula. For example, in the UK National Curriculum for Science, there is an intended progression through four Key Stages of schooling. Pupils aged 5 to 7, KS1, are to be taught 'about the senses that enable humans and other animals to be aware of the world around them' (Humans and other animals 2g). It is interesting to note that Piaget's ideas of children who are 'pre-operational' are used to introduce pupils to the ideas of senses and understanding surroundings. Such tasks should theoretically help children to progress to the next stage of development. In addition to the points mentioned above, there is difficulty in pinpointing a learner's stage using chronological age as there has been noted to be a range of ability at age 12 that maps onto a 'seven year' difference in stages (Shayer and Adey, 1981). However, stage theory remains a foundation of developmental and educational psychology today.

Piaget relied on principles that suggested that the maturation of children's developing brains over time allowed them to pass through these stages. Piaget and his followers proposed that the mechanism for advancing from one stage to the next would be a cognitive conflict – an encounter with a new construct or experience that would prompt the reorganization, or accommodation, of the mental framework leading to a new stage of mind able to assimilate the new concept. (Accommodation can be contrasted with assimilation, a mechanism of learning that involves adding information to previously existing concepts, without changing their structure.) In this way, Piaget recognized that children construct their own understandings. That is, it is the children who must make the effort to acquire new information and adjust understanding appropriately. Cognitive conflict is one of the theoretical principles underpinning the Cognitive Acceleration through Science Education (CASE) programme. Pupils are presented with experiences that challenge their expectations; objects that float in water despite being heavy or sink though they are small. Pupils then need to reconsider their ideas in the light of this experience (see Chapter 5 in this volume for further discussion of this topic).

Constructivism

A number of researchers in the field of education took the notion that children construct their own understanding and expanded upon it. This idea is now known as constructivism (Phillips, 1997). Constructivists maintain that learning depends on the way in which learners create new mental schemas based on previous knowledge (and/or stage of development) and that learning is directly correlated with motivation to learn. A principal proponent of 'Radical Constructivism', von Glaserfeld (1989) argued that the learner should take on responsibility for learning, as opposed to relying on the teacher to 'transmit' the necessary information or concepts. In other words, learners must make sense of material based on their active interpretations of ideas they encounter in many sources, including teachers' lessons, books, television and the Internet.

This view is sometimes interpreted as meaning that children need to 'discover' concepts for themselves in order to construct their own understanding (see Mayer, 2004). However, besides being a practical impossibility (if we did not rely on the work of others who came before us, we would not have enough time to 'discover' the world's aspects from scratch), research has demonstrated that discovery is not as effective as guided instruction in producing new learning (Fay and Mayer, 1994; Inhelder et al., 1974; Klahr and Nigam, 2004; Lee and Thompson, 1997). In fact, Pea and Kurland (1984) found that students in a pure discovery learning situation, involving hands-on experience, were no better at planning a program in LOGO, a computer environment, than were students receiving no experience at all with the computer environment. Such research indicates that perhaps a better interpretation of constructivism involves acknowledging the learner's agency in any learning context, rather than suggesting *all* responsibility lies with the learner. Instead, it may be useful for teachers to consider how learners conceive of scientific phenomena prior to engaging in a lesson on a given topic.

Children often develop conceptions about scientific phenomena, and require guided instruction to hone these ideas. These conceptions have been variously called by different names: misconceptions, alternative conceptions, folk science, intuitive ideas, alternative frameworks and everyday science. Driver et al. (1994) present a wide range of studies that explore children's ideas in science. For example, the view that we are able to see objects because light travels from our eyes to the object or that plants' mass comes from nutrients in the soil are two instances of children's naïve scientific ideas that can be reorganized through instruction. On the other hand, learners' alternative or everyday conceptions can be powerful and difficult to override (Novak, 2002). As teachers, you must work hard to help learners to overcome the predisposition to rely on previous ideas, at least when thinking 'scientifically'.

Leach and Scott (2000) proposed the idea of a 'learning demand' in order to help teachers find ways to help learners make sense of scientific material. These learning demands offer 'a description of the differences between everyday and scientific ways of thinking about the world, and the resultant challenges that learners will face in coming to internalize and understand scientific accounts of phenomena' (Leach and Scott, 2000, p. 45). As they describe it, learning demands can help teachers to identify where learners are likely to experience difficulties in understanding the scientific as opposed to the everyday way of thinking.

Sometimes constructivism can be taken to mean that because individuals construct their own understandings about the world, there can be no such thing as a right answer, or absolute fact – because each of us creates our own explanations. This interpretation has been criticized on the grounds that knowledge, particularly scientific knowledge, is based upon repeated empirical observations of phenomena leading to objective facts (Osborne, 1996). Of course learners need to make sense of these facts. However, learners should not be left to construct their own reality instead of being taught the widely accepted scientific explanations.

There is a related theory, social constructivism, that proposes that learners create their own understanding through interaction with their environment, often guided by more knowledgeable people around them. Some of the work most closely tied to social constructivism comes from Vygotsky (1978) and Bruner (1966) among others. It suggests that ideas are first encountered by learners in the social environment, mostly in the form of language. After some experience with these ideas, the ideas become incorporated into children's habitual knowledge and become 'second nature'. The role of knowledgeable others, such as teachers, becomes one of guiding learning experiences through questions and stimulating commentary. Such guidance has been termed 'scaffolding' (Wood et al., 1976). Alexander (2004) has developed this idea in his work, *Towards Dialogic Teaching: Rethinking Classroom Talk*. Lemke (1990) articulates some of the distinctions in the way science is talked about, particularly in a classroom, and the way everyday language is constructed. He suggests that one of the most important means of allowing students to make sense of scientific material is to make explicit the differences between everyday language and scientific language, in addition to highlighting the reasons that science has such a special language. Mercer and colleagues (Mercer, 1996, 2002; Mercer et al., 2004; Mercer and Littleton, 2007) have devised an intervention to train pupils to use language in such a way as to require respect for all in a group, encourage explanation of one's thoughts, and ensure that everyone in a group speaks. When learners receive training in this sort of 'exploratory talk', they perform better on tests in science. This type of focus on working with learners, emphasizing a social environment, has provided fruitful information about how to instil learners with the language of science through discussion (see also Chapter 7).

Vygotsky (1978) also contributed to ideas of learning through a concept called the Zone of Proximal Development (ZPD). The ZPD assesses an individual's potential level of understanding or skill in a dynamic way. The ZPD may be thought of as the area between what people can accomplish on their own, to that which they could achieve with the help of someone more experienced. For example, a pupil, once taught, is able to deal with forces acting parallel or perpendicular to a plane/surface. Yet, if the force is acting at an angle to the plane/surface the situation becomes more complex. The pupil then requires the help of a teacher to suggest the use of trigonometry to resolve the force into the parallel or perpendicular direction, with which the pupil is familiar. Use of the ZPD in teaching has clear implications. A teacher will be most effective in helping a learner to acquire new understandings when challenging the learner at the upper limits of their ZPD, rather than at too low a level (thereby not challenging the learner) or at too high a level (where the concepts will be inaccessible).

Sociocultural theory

A growing set of theories, known as sociocultural theory, has been built upon Vygotsky's ideas about development, emphasizing the importance of people's sociocultural experiences in influencing development (Rogoff, 2003). These theories suggest that knowledge of a person's cultural experiences can help determine how best to approach teaching and learning for that individual. For instance, people in a small village in Guatemala may learn a great deal about weaving, a practice regarded as very important in their society, through watching others work and being physically guided while learning themselves. On the other hand, a child in a science classroom in England may learn about the processes of schooling and, we hope, some principles of physics while attending to a teacher and watching an experiment. Each of these situations has separate expectations about how people will behave in approaching learning. Sociocultural theory argues that what these two learning experiences share is the 'intent participation' of the learner. That is, the learners become part of a community (either weavers or science classroom participants) by taking part in the practices of their surroundings. They carefully watch how others act, interact with them and emulate the behaviour of more experienced others in order to act appropriately. In each case, the more engaged the learners are with the material, the more they will advance their skills in the discipline. Engagement will depend on a number of factors, including relevance. The more relevant the material to be learned is to the learner's everyday experiences, the higher the chances of their being engaged.

Connecting learning experiences

The previous sections have covered a variety of different perspectives on the importance of several features of learning. Behaviourism tends to highlight the environment, particularly associations between different inputs and outputs that manifest in effective (or ineffective) learning. In contrast, cognitive theories tend to focus on the individual, with varying levels of emphasis on the social environment the individual interacts with. Sociocultural theories mainly consider the ways that the culture people find themselves in helps them to appropriate accepted forms of interaction.

Though each of these theories approaches learning from a somewhat different perspective, we would suggest that they all agree that a learner's previous experience needs to be taken into consideration in any teaching environment. Each theory may explain the need to consider prior learning experiences differently. For example, from a behaviourist perspective, knowing what a learner is already capable of will provide some insight into where to start a teaching plan, and knowing which reinforcement is effective for a particular learner will help an instructor to decide how best to 'train' new behaviours. In contrast, according to a constructivist theory, understanding something about a learner's alternative conceptions may help teachers attempt to persuade learners to adopt a scientific framework as more acceptable in understanding scientific phenomena. Finally, from a sociocultural perspective, the knowledge of a learner's previous experience can allow a teacher to ease the transition from one 'cultural perspective' to another, in this case, from the everyday to the scientific perspective. As such, the theories may use different reasoning to come to a similar conclusion: teaching and learning require making connections between understandings.

Some have suggested that one of the most important factors in learning is the formation of connections between different concepts and learning experiences (Vosniadou and Ortony, 1989). The idea that one should build new learning into existing knowledge structures makes sense from the perspective of any learning theory. As such, it becomes essential for educators to make explicit the different principles and concepts in different learning experiences and show how they are related.

Ausubel (1968) noted that connecting new knowledge with existing knowledge structures is at the heart of developing understanding in a specific topic, as is illustrated in the following quote:

> During the process of reformulating information or constructing knowledge, new associations are formed and old ones altered within the individual's knowledge networks or structure. These links connect the new ideas together and integrate them into that individual's existing cognitive representations of the world. Adding more and better links results in a more elaborated and richly integrated cognitive structure that facilitates memory and recall.
>
> (King, 1994, p. 339)

That is, the opportunities for enhancing both understanding and memory of material are increased when what is being learned is related to previously learned material.

Strategies for integrating new and old knowledge have been investigated in myriad studies. We cover but a few of the recognized strategies, including analogy, questioning, concept or mind maps and the promotion of self-regulated learning.

The use of analogy to directly relate old understandings with new ones is fairly common in the classroom. Learning through analogy involves comparing a familiar (or source) concept with a new (or target) concept, where the two are related in some form. Those analogies that compare two concepts that are similar in structural, rather than superficial, ways can be especially powerful learning tools (Gentner, 1983). To illustrate, noticing the superficial similarities in the colour of two animals such as a shrimp and a snake may be less helpful to learning about the functional attributes of these animals than noticing that a snake and a shrimp both shed their outer layers. Such a functional similarity is likely to provide more understanding about the structure of these two animals than will any superficial similarity.

Analogy has been studied as a natural occurrence in the work atmospheres of scientists (Dunbar, 1995). In addition, analogy has been shown to be effective in teaching students at varying levels (Bulgren et al., 2000; Gentner et al., 2003). The use of analogies can be particularly helpful in science classrooms given the amount of material that is covered involving concepts that people do not have access to without the proper tools (Gilbert, 2004; Harrison and Treagust, 2000). For instance, a model of the double helix is not DNA; however, it can provide a helpful tool for understanding the structure of DNA. One of the challenges in using analogies and models in teaching is to get learners to understand that a model is a representation and that different representations of a phenomenon may be more appropriate for discussing different types of relationships. Harrison and Treagust (2000) illustrate, using a case study of a grade 11 student, how the understanding of models can develop and how having a flexible understanding of models can afford the student a better understanding of (in this case) atoms.

The use of guiding questions and explanations is another strategy for connecting knowledge from one situation to another. Often, teachers are seen to control classroom talk by involving students in a round of questions that take the form of Initiate, Respond, Evaluate (IRE) (Cazden, 2001; Lemke, 1990; Mehan, 1979; Mortimer and Scott, 2003; Scott et al., 2006). Whereas this pattern of questioning can be seen as beneficial in some contexts, such as determining what students' previous knowledge consists of (Wells, 1999), some have suggested that the predominance of this form of questioning can restrict student engagement with the topic (for example, Lemke, 1990). The identification of this IRE pattern led many to explore the use of more open-ended and authentic questions in teaching (Nystrand et al., 2003; van Zee et al., 2001; Wells and Arauz, 2006). For instance, van Zee et al. (2001) examined the use of the 'reflective toss' in which teachers elicited student deep-level thinking by 'throwing' a question out to the class. Black and Harrison (2004) explore science specific questioning, with the intention of providing practical advice to science teachers, in applying the generic ideas presented in their preceding publications. They consider generic questions stem and apply them to specific science topics (see, also, Chapter 9).

In contrast to studying teachers' use of questions, some researchers have looked at how students can ask each other questions in order to increase understanding. In one such study, one group of students engaged in peer questioning in which classmates encouraged each other to apply concepts to a new situation, relate new materials to known materials, provide justifications for concepts and draw personal conclusions. In contrast, a second group were not encouraged nor supported to interrogate the subject matter learned. In analyses of test results, the first group scored more highly in understanding, applying and retaining information that they were learning than did the second group (King, 1994). Similar to the work reported earlier by Mercer and

colleagues, students' effective learning involved the use of providing justifications for statements, this time as a result of questioning each other.

A third strategy for making connections is the use of concept maps/webs
(Novak, 1990). Children can be asked to develop their own ideas and show
connections between them or be asked to connect ideas the teacher provides.
The intention is to reveal to the learner how seemingly separate ideas might
fit together or conversely to show the teacher how a learner currently links
concepts (Kinchin and Hay, 2000). Connections made with connective words
are more useful than mere lines. Under the topic, 'waves', one group of learners might link 'light' and 'sound' as 'both waves' while another group might
acknowledge they are indeed different types of waves, then make further connections to transverse and longitudinal.

The final strategy we note here is associated with promoting self-regulated
learning among students. Self-regulation refers to the idea that learners can
generate their own plans, assessments and transfer of understandings. Paris
and Paris (2001, pp. 97–8) identify ways that student autonomy can benefit
learning and be encouraged. Their review finds that:

1. Self-appraisal leads to a deeper understanding of learning.
2. Self-management of thinking, effort, and affect promotes flexible
   approaches to problem solving that are adaptive, persistent, self-
   controlled, strategic, and goal-oriented.
3. Self-regulation can be taught in diverse ways.
4. Self-regulation is woven into the narrative experiences and the identity strivings of each individual.

This concept of self-regulation can be related to the ideas of constructivism
discussed earlier. Promoting learners' autonomy or self-regulation in educational contexts should build on learners' own need to make sense of and
make relevant, material covered in science lessons.

Learning and motivation

Ultimately, learning is dependent upon a learner's response or attitude to new
material (Pintrich et al., 1993). This idea is rooted in the work by Posner et al.
(1982) that suggests that in order for conceptual change to occur, four conditions ought to be met: (1) the learner must experience dissatisfaction with
their previous understanding; (2) a new conception must be intelligible;
(3) the new conception must also be plausible; and (4) the new conception
must seem useful, or have explanatory power. With this in mind, it seems
logical that for dissatisfaction to occur with an understanding, learners must
have goals for improving their understandings. We now turn to examine a
few ideas about motivation in the classroom.

Motivation, or the affective drive to act in any given way, is related to the
affective appeal of an activity. How much people like a topic is related to how

much they will want to pursue learning in that area. Thus, many teachers would like, and feel the need, to make everything they do with their class inherently interesting (Nisan, 1992). The ROSE project, Relevance of Science Education, has carried out international comparisons of learners' perceptions of science, revealing interesting results as to which topics appeal to learners and differences between genders and countries.

> When asked what they wished to learn about, there are marked differences in the responses of boys and girls. For girls, the priorities lie with topics related to the self and, more particularly, to health, mind and well-being. The responses of the boys reflect strong interests in destructive technologies and events. Topics such as 'Famous scientists and their lives' and 'How crude oil is converted into other materials' are among the least popular with both boys and girls.

> There are major differences in the out-of-school experiences of boys and girls. Those of girls are associated with activities involving the natural world, such as planting seeds or crafts such as knitting or weaving. In the case of boys, activities that might be described as mechanical are to the fore, although the engagement of girls with the use of simple tools should not be overlooked.
> (Jenkins and Pell, 2006, pp. 6–7)

These gender differences are common to many of the 44 countries involved with the ROSE project. We might use these differences in interest to promote participation; we could also consider how we might develop the areas of low interest (see, also, Chapter 10 in this volume).

Differences between countries have also been revealed. Sjøberg and Schreiner (2005) discuss the link between the development of the country and student interest. Data suggest there is a strong inverse relationship, the higher the level of development, the lower the level of interest in learning about science and technology (2005, p. 13). All of these data derived from the ROSE project reflect different levels of motivation to learn about different kinds of science.

In addition to theories of learning, many theories of motivation can also be labelled behaviourist or cognitivist. Behaviourist theories tend to claim that providing positive or negative reinforcement in response to behaviours will provide incentive for future behaviours. For instance, giving someone praise after getting the answer to a question correct would be seen as motivation to answer other questions correctly. Such acting for receipt of (or absence of) reinforcement has been called extrinsic motivation. That is, people act so that they will receive a reward, not because they choose to do so. This approach for motivating students has been criticized because it is predicated on the continued presence of rewards. In fact, external rewards have even been seen to decrease interest in otherwise motivating tasks (Deci and Ryan, 1985).

On the other hand, cognitivist theories of motivation focus on intrinsic motivation, or the desire to learn for learning's sake. One such theory emphasizes the need to facilitate people's mastery-orientation as opposed to their performance-orientation (Dweck and Leggett, 1988). Mastery-orientation is a state in which people pay attention because they want to understand the material at hand, such as to follow through with a desire to understand why we see rainbows. Performance-orientation is more related to extrinsic motivation and is exemplified by the desire to achieve a particular score or grade, such as an A* in a given science exam that includes questions about why we see rainbows. The content could be the same in each type of motivation; it is the underlying reasons for acquiring the content that differs. Evidence suggests that mastery-orientated students tend to rise to challenges in difficult situations, attribute success to internal causes, and use effective strategies for solving problems, such as in-depth questioning (Alexander et al., 1998). In contrast, performance-orientation is complicated by the fact that most mastery-oriented learners also have some desire to perform well. However, being performance-oriented without being mastery-oriented appears to provide for less-efficient learning than does mastery-orientation alone. To illustrate, in a study of undergraduate students, Grant and Dweck (2003) asked participants to fill in surveys that provided indications of their goal orientation. When confronted with either experimentally manipulated or real coursework difficulties, students who were mastery-oriented tended to retain motivation and plan more than did students who were performance-oriented. However, when performance-oriented students performed well, they also maintained intrinsic motivation and help-seeking behaviours.

Two examples can be used to illustrate mastery-orientation's advantages over performance-orientation. First, performance goals are often not directly controllable. For instance, if two people have the goal of getting the highest score on an exam, unless they both achieve perfect scores, one of them will be disappointed. Second, when encountering failure, people who have adopted a mastery-orientation tend to continue to attempt to learn and see the experience as valuable whereas people with only performance-orientation are more likely to be anxious and avoid situations where they will possibly fail in the future (Midgley et al., 2001).

Conclusion

In this chapter we have discussed the key learning theories; behaviourism, cognitivism, constructivism, social cultural theory and how they might be considered in the context of science learning but importantly how these theories are not necessarily specific to science. It could be argued that science is different to other subjects in abstractness and often far removed from learners' experience. In discussing connected learning experiences, we hoped to explore ways you as the teacher might facilitate your pupils' learning, through use of analogies/models, questioning techniques, concept mapping and developing pupils as learners. In addition to this, we presented research posing the importance of motivation towards learning. It is after all essential that you not only understand how your pupils learn and ways to promote learning but also how to engage them in science.

URLs

The National Curriculum, http://curriculum.qca.org.uk/
The Relevance of Science Education, http://www.ils.uio.no/english/rose/

Further reading

Bransford, J. D., Brown, A. L. and Cocking, R. R. (eds) (2000) *How People Learn: Brain, Mind, Experience and School*. Washington DC: National Academy Press.
Driver, R., Squires, A., Rushworth, P. and Wood-Robinson, V. (1994) *Making Sense of Secondary Science: Research into Children's Ideas*. Oxford: Taylor and Francis.
Mercer, N. (1996) The quality of talk in children's collaborative activity in the classroom, *Learning and Instruction*, 6(4): 359–77.
Mortimer, E. F. and Scott, P. H. (2003) *Meaning Making in Secondary Science Classrooms*. Maidenhead: Open University Press.

5 Science teaching and Cognitive Acceleration

Philip Adey and Natasha Serret

In the CASE project we have demonstrated that science teaching can be used to raise students' general intelligence.

Introduction

Such a bold claim should raise a great many questions in the minds of a healthily sceptical scientist. In this chapter, we propose to address a couple of those questions, and to see what answers research can provide – and with what level of confidence.

CASE stands for Cognitive Acceleration through Science Education. The original project was set up in 1981 by Michael Shayer at Chelsea College (which soon thereafter merged with what was then King's College). The aim of the project was to explore in a systematic way methods of raising the cognitive, or 'thinking', ability of a wide range of students in normal secondary (high) schools. Although the project used the science curriculum as a context, the intentions went far beyond the delivery of more effective science teaching. Drawing on Piagetian and Vygotskian perspectives on cognitive development, CASE uses science as a 'vehicle' for raising students' general cognitive processing ability, that is, their general intelligence. In brief, the approach rests on three main principles (or 'pillars'): (1) *cognitive conflict*, or creating scenarios which challenge students' current thinking; (2) *social construction*, or encouraging students to build understanding through meaningful dialogue with peers and the teacher; and (3) *metacognition*, making students conscious of their own thinking and problem-solving processes. These principles are embodied in a two-year intervention programme called *Thinking Science* (Adey, Shayer and Yates, 2001), now in its third edition. It comprises 30 science activities that are taught to students aged 12–14 years and is supported with an intensive professional development programme that encourages teachers to revisit their personal philosophies about intelligence, learning and teaching and translate this process into classroom practice.

In this chapter, we will outline the main psychological principles underlying the CASE approach to stimulating thinking; we will show how understanding the nature of cognitive development relates directly to structuring the science curriculum, and then show how the psychological principles inform a programme of cognitive stimulation. We will describe what it is like to use CASE methods in the science classroom and show some effects that the CASE intervention can have on cognitive development and on achievement (in science and beyond). Issues of implementation, especially as they relate to professional development, will be discussed. Finally we will touch briefly on the issues of progression and differentiation.

The underlying principles

In this section we will consider the nature of 'intelligence' and then see how its main characteristics can be accounted for by various models of the mind.

What counts as 'intelligence'?

Let us first deal with the issue of 'IQ'. Alfred Binet (Binet 1909, well described by Perkins 1995) is often considered to be the 'father' of intelligence testing. He was originally commissioned by the Department for Education in Paris to try to quantify educational sub-normality, so that children below a certain level could be provided with special education. Notably, one of Binet's students was Jean Piaget – of whom more anon. The idea of intelligence testing was taken up in the United States by Thorndike and his colleagues (Thorndike et al., 1986) who developed a quantitative measure that yielded an Intelligence Quotient (IQ). For each individual, this indicates how their intellectual ability compared with others of the same age. This process of turning descriptions into measurements offered great reliability and predictive validity, but it lost much of the richness of description of intelligent behaviour (Shayer, 2008). An IQ score will give you a pretty good idea how an individual will fair in normal academic achievement, but it will not tell you much about why, or what you might do about it.

   We often ask teachers to think about what counts as intelligent behaviour in their students. What sort of thing does a student have to say, or write, or do, to make you say, 'that's smart'? (You might like to consider this yourself for a minute, before reading on.) As you might expect, we get a great many answers, but the most common are things such as:

- can apply existing knowledge to new situations;
- makes connections between different areas of knowledge;
- sees a pattern in data;
- asks searching questions.

   If you have ever looked at verbal, numerical, or pictorial intelligence tests (for example, Lohman et al., 2001; Raven, 1960; Wechsler, 1958). you will have noticed that many of the items demand just this type of thinking: making connections, seeing analogies or patterns, or abstracting some general pattern. This is no accident since from Binet's earliest attempts to define and measure intelligence, psychologists have considered connectivity to be one of the prime hallmarks of intelligence. Spearman (1927) described the 'education of relations and of correlates' as the two fundamental attributes of intelligence. Perceiving the relations and connections between aspects of the environment allows one to understand a new concept, solve a new problem, or formulate a new idea by transformation of the concepts, problem solving skills, or ideas already available. Cattell (1971) also considered these properties to underlie fluid intelligence. So it seems that psychologists who devise intelligence tests agree broadly with teachers about the nature of intelligence. It has something to do with making connections or connectivity.

So, connectivity is a feature of intelligence upon which there is little disagreement. Other supposed characteristics of intelligence are more controversial. For example, how *generally* is an individual able to apply her or his intelligence across a wide range of tasks? This relates to the vexed question of whether there is just one, or many types of intelligence. The answer is – there is one, and there are many. Howard Gardner (1993) and Gardner et al. (1996) have proposed that there are at least seven independent types of intelligence. They have called these numerical, spatial, verbal, kinaesthetic, musical, interpersonal, and intrapersonal, and more recently have proposed also environmental (or naturalist) and spiritual. The theory of multiple intelligences allows one to suppose that a child may be 'brilliant at maths but useless at English' and, by extension, that everyone has some sort of talent that can be developed. This is an idea that is very comforting to teachers and perhaps explains why the notion of multiple intelligences has become quite fashionable in some educational quarters. In a book devoted to 'what research says' to the science teacher we are bound to look critically at evidence, and the evidence for the existence of completely independent abilities in different intellectual areas is not good. Certainly, intelligence is not a monolithic unidimensional ability that allows us to fully define an individual with one IQ number, but all measures of different aspects of intellectual ability do correlate with one another (Anderson, 1992). By any sensible statistical analysis (Carroll, 1993), the most reasonable way to explain the vast amount of data which comes from multiple testing of individuals is in terms of (1) a general underlying intelligence ('g') plus (2) a number of specific abilities such as verbal, numerical, and spatial. Any intellectual behaviour is then a product of a general processing ability and a number of specific abilities.

A third, and in the context of this chapter most important, characteristic of intelligence is *plasticity*. To what extent can the general intelligence of an individual be modified? In a chapter entitled Cognitive Acceleration, it will not be surprising to hear that our answer is 'Quite a lot', and we will offer evidence to support that claim.

Here we will consider four approaches to intelligence that help to account for these key characteristics of connectivity, generality (plus special abilities) and plasticity:

- an *information processing* approach, treating the mind as a computer;
- the perspective which sees intelligence as a set of *stages of cognitive development* as described by Jean Piaget and his co-workers in Geneva;
- the idea of the social nature of intelligence developed by Vygotsky; and
- a neurophysiological approach which relates to 'brain-based education'.

We will see how these approaches are complementary, each contributing something to our understanding of the difficulties encountered by students with science concepts, and how we might help them overcome those difficulties. For a more detailed consideration of the nature and structure of intelligence, see Adey et al. (2007).

Information processing

Information processing (IP) theories (for example, Case, 1975; Johnstone and El-Banna, 1986; Anderson et al., 1997) start by considering the mind as being somewhat like a computer. There are inputs, processing, storage, and outputs.

Input: pay attention!

We have a sensory system of eyes, ears, and so on which convert physical stimuli such as light and sound intensity and wavelength, pressure and temperature into electrochemical signals running along neurones from the sense organs to the brain. Every waking minute of our lives, we and our students are subject to a vast input of such sensory experiences. Effective learning requires us, first of all, to attend especially to those stimuli which are relevant to the learning task in hand and shut out those which are not. Our minds need to filter out perhaps 95 per cent of the stimuli received, in order to avoid hopeless overload and confusion, but self-control over our attention is limited. Everybody, at some time, has found their mind wandering during even the most interesting lecture, piece of music, or play. Masters of modern media have learned the art of maintaining audience attention by rapid change of pace, story line, or viewpoint. They know that variety plays an important role in grabbing attention.

Of course, other factors are important also – degree of tiredness, hunger, temperature, humidity, carbon dioxide and concentration all play their part and perhaps most obviously, the intrinsic interest of some subjects. For example, sex is intrinsically interesting for good reasons of species survival.

Storage: long-term memory

Evidence for the existence of long-term memory is clear and shows that apparent failure of memory is not due to material being lost from the store but to temporary or longer-term failure of the central processing mechanism to recover information that is there. This is illustrated by the common phenomenon of an elderly person who may forget what happened yesterday but whose memory of their childhood becomes much clearer.

Following the remarkably prescient work of Hebb (1949), Ausubel (1968) described knowledge held in long-term memory in the form of networks of interconnected bits of information. The more sophisticated the elaboration of these networks, the better prepared is the whole mind to assimilate new information about a particular topic, since the working memory processor has a richer source of existing knowledge to which to relate new inputs. This explains why it is easier for us to understand and to learn new things in a field with which are already familiar, and why starting to learn in a completely new field is so difficult. Hence Ausubel's (1968) famous advice: 'Ascertain what a child already knows and teach them accordingly' (p. 1).

Processing: working memory

Suppose that, as a teacher, you pull out all of the stops in terms of keeping attention: you use a variety of paces, materials and changes of attack, using visual, verbal, and numerical material and make it all as relevant as you can to your students' interests. On occasion you can do all that is possible to gain and maintain attention and yet you are conscious that not a lot of learning is taking place. Perhaps the problem lies not so much in holding attention, as in the ability of your students to process the information you are providing.

IP theories propose a 'working memory' function of the mind (Anderson, 1992; Baddeley, 1990) as the central processing mechanism that takes in signals from sensory inputs and from long-term memory and makes meaning of them. The neuronal signals from sense organs themselves have no 'meaning', rather they are simply a chain of electro-chemical events. Working memory receives these signals and information from long-term memory, compares and combines them, and creates new syntheses or simply recognizes an external input as corresponding to a known configuration from long-term memory. Three important features of working memory are:

- stuff goes in and out of it very fast – maybe lingering no longer than 3 seconds;
- its capacity is limited;
- its capacity develops with age and stimulation.

Pascual-Leone (1976, 1984) has suggested that the number of bits of information that working memory can handle grows from just two at birth to a maximum of seven in mature intelligent adults. One way of testing working memory span (Towse et al., 1998) is to present a series of very simple sums (for example, $5 + 1 = \ldots$) and ask the person to remember the answer to each. After four, five, or six sums the person is asked to recite all the answers so far. Holding more than seven proves to be very difficult, even for intelligent adults. (If you just give someone a string of numbers to remember, they can recite the string to themselves, or find a pattern to help them *chunk* the number and so lower the working memory demand. Interspersing the sums, trivial in themselves, is intended to deny this possibility.)

This view of the growth of working memory provides a useful explanation of the development of intelligence, and ties in with our picture of intelligence as concerned with multi-variable thinking and the ability to hold a number of ideas in mind at once. The view meets our connectivity requirement for intelligence, since in order to see the connection between two things, both have to be held in mind at once. At an elementary level, when water is poured from a squat beaker into a tall beaker, an average 4-year-old will believe that the amount of water has changed (Piaget and Inhelder, 1974). This observation can be explained if one supposes that limitations in the child's working memory prevent him/her from considering *at the same time* the height of the water and the breadth of the water, and so constructing a compensation explanation for the amount of water remaining constant (see the classroom dialogue later). At a senior secondary science level, the ability to really understand the law of moments (as opposed to memorizing the algorithm and slotting in the numbers) requires that the student hold in mind two masses, two distances, and whether the system is in balance or not. That's five bits of independent information, and quite a demand on working memory.

Much of what we want our students to learn in science is complex, abstract and involves multiple elements (just think of photosynthesis as an example). A full understanding of such concepts and their implications and connections is a very demanding task on a child's ability to take in and make meaning of new information. It is hardly surprising that the complexity of what we are trying to teach often becomes filtered down by our students' understanding to over-simplifications which amount to misconceptions.

A final component of working memory which deserves attention is the 'executive system'. This is what is proposed to control attention and act as a gatekeeper for what information is processed by working memory and where it goes. The mechanism by which this executive system works is not well understood, and in some formulations it appears simply as a way of explaining away the unexplainable (for example, 'The executive *decides* what to pay attention to' – this invokes a little man in the machine which then invites the endlessly regressing question of how such 'decisions' are made). Understanding the executive is essentially understanding consciousness, a notoriously hard nut for psychologists and philosophers alike (Greenfield, 1995; Blackmore, 2003).

Output

If working memory succeeds in making meaning from its inputs, it may produce outputs to activate motor nerves for speech, writing or other action or for storage in long-term memory. This is sometimes a relatively simple matter of 'here is the formulation, let us pull out well-practised verbal routines and output them'. Such is the substance of normal, trivial, human discourse. But in teaching and learning we want to encourage our students to produce more thoughtful outputs that encompass something novel (to them). This is a far more complex and difficult process. It is illustrated by the frustration shown by a student who 'knows the answer but cannot put it into words'. And this explains why encouraging meaningful dialogue – providing students with opportunities to articulate and test their understanding in the classroom – will prove to be one of the most powerful stimuli to the development of intelligence.

Stages of cognitive development

We noted above that one of Alfred Binet's students was a young French-Swiss psychologist called Jean Piaget. Although Piaget learned about Binet's approach to measuring intelligence well, he was actually more interested in the philosophical question of what it means to 'know' something. What is the mechanism by which we acquire, store, and pass on knowledge? This is the study of epistemology. Specifically he was interested in the regular and systematic 'mistakes' that children of different ages seemed to make and what possible mechanisms of the mind might explain these 'mistakes' and their eventual correction. This led to a lifetime of observations of children (starting with his own), probing their responses to apparently simple phenomena such as objects dropping to the ground, water being poured from one vessel to another and (for older children) the factors that influence the rate of swing of a pendulum. Detailed analysis of children's responses allowed Piaget and his co-workers to develop a rich and detailed description of the development of intelligence from birth to late adolescence (for example, Piaget, 1950; Piaget and Inhelder, 1974, 1976). Piaget's Stage Theory of Cognitive Development (Inhelder and Piaget, 1958) describes cognitive development as a continuum of gradual intellectual change. This continuum is typically divided into four broad sequential stages, with detailed sub-stages within each:

0. *Sensorimotor intelligence*: This period is generally accepted to cover the first two years of a child's life where activity is governed by perception and oriented towards action. Natural reflexes, including early responses such as blinking at bright light, characterize the first few months after birth. This is followed by successive and incremental periods of 'circular reactions', repeated acts that are carried out initially for their own sake, then deliberately repeated to achieve goals such as pleasure and later forming the basis for early regular thinking patterns ('schemata').

1. *Preoperational thought*: While action remains central to all mental activity, at this stage action can be internalized and, with access to early language, a child can use and understand words that represent these internalized actions.

2. *Concrete operations*: A major development characterizing this stage is the ability to hold more than one idea, although these ideas need

to be introduced and handled physically, using concrete examples such as cubes for counting. In his classic experiments Piaget observed children employing reasoning such as seriation (putting things in order), classification and conservation of number, volume, and weight as objects or materials are moved or reshaped. He used his findings to describe the parameters within which concrete thinkers work for each schema. Broadly speaking, for an average child, concrete operations span the age ranges of primary education into early secondary education, that is, around 6 to 13 years of age.

3.   *Formal operations*: From about 11 years old, some children start to develop abstract reasoning that is logical and systematic, without the support of concrete objects. Formal thinkers are not bound by experiences that are solely personal or real. They can propose and formulate new ideas and test and manipulate these in their abstract form as well as in concrete reality. Mature formal thinkers can hypothesize, examine, analyse, deduce and evaluate. They can hold many variables in mind at once and operate upon them. They can use abstract ideas in conjunction with one another and see actual events as a subset of many possible events. A survey in the 1970s (Shayer and Adey, 1981) showed that only about 30 per cent of 16-year-olds in England and Wales had reached this stage of thinking, and more recent research (Shayer et al., 2007) suggests that that percentage has actually declined over the past 25 years.

This developmental sequence shows the connectivity idea very clearly. If you are going to see connections between science concepts (say, to see the relationship of respiration to photosynthesis), you need to be able to hold in your mind at once the important characteristics of each and also be able to compare them. This is multi-variable thinking. Many models that are central to scientific understanding, such as current flow or kinetic theory, are abstractions. You cannot handle them physically, but only come to understand them through a thorough familiarity with their characteristics and applications in the real world. The investigation of cause and effect, the design of experiments, requires the ability first of all to hold all possibilities in mind and then systematically to eliminate possible causes one by one. This conception of formal operations offers a powerful explanatory model for the difficulty encountered by students with some concepts in science.

A word of warning is in order: the Piagetian idea of the gradual development of intelligent behaviour through a series of stages is occasionally misinterpreted as implying that nothing can be done to encourage cognitive development, as if it were some inevitable unfolding process to which the teacher can do little but wait for the full flowering. This is a serious misconception both of Piaget's original work and of a modern neo-Piagetian perspective. The burden of this chapter is that the development of intelligence, cognitive development, is plastic and is amenable to influence by teachers and parents.

The social nature of intelligence

Lev Vygotsky was a Soviet psychologist born in the same year as Piaget, 1896, but who died of tuberculosis at the age of 34. Early in his life he studied cultural differences in the development of reasoning across the many people of the Soviet Union and he was impressed by the impact of the socio-cultural context on the particulars of the development of intelligence. He developed this idea into a principle of social construction of knowledge, pointing out that ideas often originate in the social space, as a result of constructive dialogue between people, and only then become internalized as the thoughts of individuals (Vygotsky, 1978, 1986). While there certainly are examples of the lone genius working out new principles entirely by their own internal dialogue (Einstein? Picasso? Wittgenstein?), these are rare and even then, their work depended on or grew out of the work of others. The vast majority of advances in the sciences and arts are made by a number of workers at the forefront of their field feeding off one another's ideas.

At the level of learning, this principle of social construction is illustrated by Vygotsky's well-known 'Zone of Proximal Development'. That is the difference between what learners can achieve unaided, and what they can do with a little help from peers, older students, teachers, or others asking probing questions, leading on from what they have achieved to what they can achieve. This process of moving a person on to a stage of greater understanding, without direct telling, is sometimes called 'scaffolding' (Wood et al., 1976).

Brain-based education

Cognitive neurophysiology is making enormous strides in developing our understanding of the structure and function of the brain. Aspects of the localization of brain functions have been known for many years from evidence of patients with brain lesions, but a range of new techniques has led to an explosion in knowledge of brain architecture (Greenfield, 1998; Johnson, 1997). Modern electron microscopy has allowed anatomists to look directly at neurones (nerve cells) in the cortex, while various scanning techniques such as Positron Emission Tomography (PET), Magnetic Resonance Imaging (MRI), and Event-Related Potentials (ERP) do allow for genuine experimentation, of the form, 'Let's see what areas of the brain are activated by . . .'. For our present purposes, a few results from such research are relevant.

1. Rats brought up in a stimulating environment, forced to solve problems to reach food, develop far more complex neural networks than initially matched rats brought up in laboratory cages and fed regularly (Greenhough et al., 1987). This is direct evidence that the brain develops physiologically in response to external stimulus.
2. The brain first starts to form in the human embryo about 12 days after conception. From then until birth, there is a massive growth

in the number of neurones in the brain (around 250,000 per minute before birth). After birth, growth in the number of neurones virtually ceases, but there are a series of phases of growth of connections between neurones and decay of (apparently) unused connections. These growth and decay cycles occur in different locations in the brain at different ages, but are not completed until some final organization in the forebrain in early adolescence. All of this development is as much under the influence of the environment as it is of any 'genetic unfolding'. Johnson (1997) provides a comprehensive account of brain development.

3. Scanning studies show both the localization of certain functions to particular parts of the brain, but also (a) the great difficulty of actually describing the precise nature of those functions, and (b) the brain's ability to adapt to damage. That is, functions associated with one brain area may be taken over by other areas (Goswami, 2006).

The neuronal level of considering the development of intelligence shows up the inadequacy of the 'brain-as-computer' idea floated earlier. Notwithstanding these developments in our understanding of the brain, we are still a long way short of being able to use these new understandings to prescribe educational procedures. The brain is part of a living organism, and the process by which it develops depends at least as much on its ability to select and reinforce useful neuronal pathways as on any pre-programming. This is a position strongly supported by the work of Edelman (1987), and predicted many years ago (and in surprising detail) by Hebb (1949). The idea that direct measurements of brain activity can be made under different learning conditions is likely to appeal to science teachers as apparently cutting through a lot of jargon and speculation associated with cognitive psychology. Unfortunately it is not that easy. There remains a major issue with interpreting brain scans and proposing and testing hypothetical models of the structure of mind. John Bruer (1999) has warned educators against expecting too much too soon from neurophysiology. It would be wise to treat any claims for educational procedures 'based on brain science' with considerable scepticism, and if in doubt to seek out reputable peer-reviewed academic publications to support claims made. Examples of topics which are often over-simplified to the point of uselessness are left-brain/right-brain contrasts, learning styles, and extreme forms of brain localization of functions (Goswami, 2006).

Using the theory

In the next section we will see how the theories outlined above are used for Cognitive Acceleration, but before we get to that we will show how Piagetian stage theory in particular has a direct use in analysing the science curriculum for cognitive demand, and so allowing work schemes to be designed on a rational, scientific, basis.

From the 1970s onwards, we developed a tool called a Curriculum Analysis Taxonomy (CAT) that allows anyone – with a bit of effort – to analyse curriculum material for its level of difficulty. The CAT is in the form of a table with stages of cognitive development as column headings, and aspects of scientific thinking in rows. The levels of thinking are given in terms of Piagetian substages of cognitive development:

1	preoperational
2A	early concrete operational
2A/2B	mid concrete
2B	late concrete
2B*	concrete generalization
3A	early formal operational
3B	mature formal operational

Figure 5.1 reproduces one of the pages of the CAT. Published originally in 1981, this secondary-level CAT is now available in Adey, Nagy, et al. (2003) and a primary one in Adey (2008).

We described, above, high level thinking as requiring an individual to be able to hold in working memory, at one time, four, five, or more bits of information and to be able to relate them to one another. This *multi-parallel processing* is what Piaget describes as formal operations. If you look at Science in the English National Curriculum, at the Level Descriptors in each Attainment Target, it is possible to use this particular notion of intelligence to assess the relative difficulty of different concepts. Here is a very small sample from the English science curriculum to illustrate the process of cognitive analysis. Notes on level of demand are inserted in square brackets.

> **AT2, Level 5**: Pupils describe processes and phenomena related to organisms, their behaviour and the environment, [*descriptive* work is generally concrete, say 2B for these fairly complex phenomena] drawing on abstract ideas [... but drawing on the abstract ideas for explanations lifts it to formal, at least 3A] and using appropriate terminology, for example, the main functions of plant and animal organs and how these functions are essential. They explain processes and phenomena, in more than one step or using a model, such as the main stages of the life cycles of humans and flowering plants [multi-factor models where the components interact in complex ways certainly require formal operational thinking, 3A+]. They apply and use knowledge and understanding in familiar contexts, such as different organisms being found in different habitats because of differences in environmental factors ['this goes with that' sort of thinking is mature concrete, 2B].

> **AT3, Level 6**: They (pupils) take account of a number of factors or use abstract ideas or models in their explanations of processes and

Curriculum Analysis Taxonomy 1: Different aspects of the development of the child's interaction with the world

Function	1 pre-operational	2A early concrete	2B late concrete	3A early formal	3B late formal
1.1 Interest and investigation style	Things are believed to be exactly as they appear to immediate perception. Perception dictates decisions. Faced with a mature person's idea of evidence, will deny it, explain it anthropomorphically, or be silent. Does not perceive contradictions.	Will register what happens, but for interest to be maintained after the first obvious observations needs a seriative or simple associative model. Unaided investigation style does not go as far as producing concrete models. (See 1.4, 2A and 2B.)	Will include seriation¹ and classification as tools of perception in finding out what happens, but needs to be provided with a concrete model by which to structure experimental results (classes must be given, and examples of the application shown). Finds interest in making and checking cause-and-effect predictions.	Finds interest in looking for why, and following consequences from a formal model. Confused by the request to investigate empirical relationships without an interpretative model. Can use a formal model, (see 1.4, 3A) but requires it to be provided. Can generate concrete models with interest. Sees the point of making hypotheses, and can plan simple controlled experiments, but needs help in deducing relationships from results and in organising the information so that irrelevant variables are excluded at each step.	Finds interest in generating and checking possible 'why' explanations. Will tolerate absence of an interpretative model while investigating empirical relationships. Takes it as obvious that in a system with several variables he must 'hold all other things equal' while varying one at a time, and can plan such investigations and interpret results. Will make quantitative checks involving proportionality relationships.
1.2 Reasons for events	Interprets phenomena egocentrically, in terms of own self.	See 1.1, 1.3 and 1.4 Cause-and-effect only partly structured – this goes with that; so uses associative reasoning. Simple one-factor causes, such as 'force', etc.	Bipolar concepts such as 'alkali destroys acid'. Can use ordering relationships to partially quantify associative relationships: 'as this goes up, that goes down', 'if you double this you double that', i.e. 'the reason' involves describing the relationship or categories, not providing a formal model. Cause-and-effect structured according to general concrete stage schemata as 'adding acid makes the pH lower'.	Looks for some causative necessity behind a relation established with concrete schemata.² Allows for the possibility of a cause that is not in 1:1 correspondence with observations. Can consider the possibility of multiple causes for one effect, or multiple effects of one cause. Can suspend judgement and allow results of controlled experiments to constrain choice among various cause-and-effect explanations. Can handle formal models as explanatory provided their structure is simple (see 1.4).	Because aware of multiple causes and effects, can think of reality in a multivariate way, so can make a general or abstract formulation of a relationship which covers all cases in an economical way. Can use deduction from the properties of a formal model – either from its mathematical or internal physical structure – to make explanatory predictions about reality.

Figure 5.1 A page from the Curriculum Analysis Taxonomy

Notes: ¹Seriation: putting objects in order according to a property such as length, mass, etc.

²Schema (pl. schemata): a general way of thinking, a 'reasoning pattern' which can be applied in many contexts.

Concrete schemata are those characteristic of concrete operational thinking.

Source: © P. Adey, M. Shayer, C. Yates 2003. *Thinking Science Professional Edition.*

phenomena, such as word equations. [Multi-factor thinking and abstract ideas are hallmarks of formal operations, at least 3A.] They apply and use knowledge and understanding in unfamiliar contexts, such as relating changes of state to energy transfers in a range of contexts such as the formation of igneous rocks. [This looks like 3B mature formal thinking, applying abstract ideas in novel contexts, very demanding.] They describe some evidence for some accepted scientific ideas, such as the patterns in the reactions of acids with metals and the reactions of a variety of substances with oxygen. [Now this essentially descriptive level is more accessible, no more than concrete generalization, 2B*.]

AT4, Level 6: They take account of a number of factors in their explanations of processes and phenomena, for example, in the relative brightness of stars and planets. They also use abstract ideas or models, for example, sustainable energy sources and the refraction of light. They apply and use knowledge and understanding in unfamiliar contexts. They describe some evidence for some accepted scientific ideas, such as the transfer of energy by light, sound or electricity, and the refraction and dispersion of light.

[The wording is of course parallel to that for AT3 at the same level, and the cognitive analysis will be similar, but the phenomena in the last sentence quoted are less directly observable than those in the chemistry example and therefore perhaps a stage more difficult.]

There are a number of implications of this type of analysis. One of the most striking is the general correspondence of National Curriculum levels with the level of thinking required. The curriculum was written by teachers and others with a great deal of practical experience of teaching the subject, and revisions were made in the light of feedback from teachers concerning, among other things, the relative difficulty that their students found with concepts at different levels in the curriculum. So the actual experience of teachers trying to get across ideas gives a very good intuitive feel for the cognitive demand of those ideas. What the Piagetian (or information processing) analysis does is to provide a theoretical explanation for teachers' intuitive logic, and demonstrates the value of research in helping to make sense of experience and providing a predictive tool.

So, what do we do about it? Identify a problem as cognitively demanding, decide it is beyond the capability of your Year 8Z group, and retire to the prep room for a cup of coffee and wait for them to mature gently to a higher stage of thinking? Not very practical, as you might have to wait a long time. In fact, without the stimulation of your teaching, you might have to wait forever. The whole point is that although cognitive development occurs in part in response to natural maturational processes, it also depends importantly on response to cognitive stimulation. In the next section we will enlarge on this process.

Stimulating high level thinking

What conclusions can we draw from our brief review of psychological and neurophysiological approaches to understanding cognition? An important message that emerges is the intimate interaction of human evolution, individual heredity, and environment. The course that an individual's cognitive development actually takes will be determined by a continual interaction between evolutionary predispositions, specific genetic make-up, and environmental influences. The importance ascribed to environment in the development of intelligence places a serious responsibility on us as teachers (and as parents) as we shape the learning environment to influence the cognitive development of children in our charge.

More specifically, what lessons can be learned from the models of the mind outlined above about how we might most effectively stimulate the development of general intelligence, so that our students can process and make meaning of our teaching more effectively? Cognitive Acceleration draws from these general principles its own three main pedagogical principles, briefly mentioned in the Introduction: cognitive conflict, social construction, and metacognition. Here we will elaborate on these a little more fully, and then show how they work out in classroom practice.

Cognitive conflict

Piaget described cognitive development as a process of the mind reaching a succession of stages of equilibrium, when the experiences of the outside world could be processed by the current state of the mental machinery. Further development occurs when events in the outside world cannot be explained by current processing ability, and a new level of thinking must be sought to handle the challenge. It is activities which students find a bit difficult which are most likely to promote cognitive development. Vygotsky (1978, p. 82) says, 'the only good learning is that which is in advance of development'. In other words, the busy-work we all occasionally engage in with our pupils, when we give them work well within their capability, may keep them quiet and give an inspector a picture of a busy and peaceful class, but it doesn't do much for cognitive development. To encourage cognitive growth, we need to provide a modicum of cognitive conflict – experiences which push students to the limit of their current processing capability, and just a little beyond.

Social construction

In a science classroom where cognitive acceleration is promoted, students can experience cognitive conflict when they witness an unexpected or surprising event or when they encounter alternative ideas that seem to contradict their current understanding. The natural instinct for students (or in fact anyone) is to want to talk about it and the social interactions that accompany cognitive conflict become a rich opportunity for deep learning and general intellectual development. True, such social construction can be harder to manage for the class teacher than simple transmission but what might sometimes appear to be classroom chaos is in fact just what is needed for students to develop understanding. Much the same conclusion was reached in our account above of the output phase in the Information Processing model.

Also, as indicated above, Vygotsky (1978, 1986) stressed the significance of social interaction and culture in the development of cognition in humans and this feature is reflected in his ideas on semiotic mediation and the zone of proximal development. According to Vygotskian theory, cognitive development involves biological processes (maturation) and social processes where humans construct meaning through their interactions with one another. In society, this development is mediated between peers through the manipulation of psychological and cultural tools. Vygotsky illustrates how the transforming effect that technical tools have on the structure and processes of manual labour is similar to the impact that psychological tools can have on mental operations. Sign-based tools such as counting and mnemonics are seen as psychological devices for mastering and mediating mental activity. But, for Vygotsky, the 'tool of tools' (Wells, 1999, p. 7) was language.

In classrooms where thinking is promoted, opportunities for social construction are fully exploited. Students work through problems collaboratively in small groups. Teacher and student questions such as, 'Can you explain why...?', 'How did you decide...?' are seen as vehicles for prompting students to think aloud and explain their reasoning. In this way talking is a crucial and valued part of the thinking process.

Metacognition

If students are to take control of their own learning and development (which they must do, since we cannot be there driving them along every minute of the day), then they have to become conscious of themselves as thinkers and learners. Metacognition means *thinking about your own thinking*. Although inducing metacognition in students is not at all easy, it is well worth persisting with. Probes of the type 'OK, you've got the right answer, now explain how you got it' often produce the standard answer of, 'We dunno, we just did it.' Going beyond such responses is important. Holding up for inspection the type of thinking a student has been using makes it more likely that that type of thinking can be used again. Making thinking explicit is a prerequisite for making it generally available. The importance of metacognition is based on:

- Piaget's idea of *reflective abstraction*, which he considers to be an essential characteristic for formal thinking; and
- Vygotsky's idea of *language as a mediator of learning* (putting thoughts into words so that they can be shared and inspected).

Michael Shayer (Adey and Shayer, 1994) describes the process as *going above*: looking back and down on a completed bit of thinking so that its features can be recognized and it can be used again. Perkins and Saloman (1989) have shown the importance of metacognition in the development of general cognitive skills which can be transferred from one context to another, and Brown et al. (1983) and Larkin (2001) have provided more details of the nature of metacognition.

In translating psychological perspectives on cognitive development into a clearly defined set of pedagogical principles, the CASE literature describes these three features as the central 'pillars' of teaching for cognitive acceleration that now guide and characterize all cognitive acceleration programmes, extended from the original KS3 science to KS3 maths, technology, and a wide variety of primary CA materials. This pedagogical framework is also extended to six pillars (Adey and Shayer, 2002). The three additional pillars include *concrete preparation*, the first 5 minutes or so of a CASE lesson when some of the words which are going to be used are introduced, and the nature of the problem discussed. This phase sets the students up in preparation for the surprising or difficult-to-explain event, which causes conflict. Another is *bridging*, linking the type of thinking developed in the CASE lesson with other opportunities in the science curriculum or beyond where that type of thinking will be useful. The sixth pillar is the set of *schemata* (singular *schema*) or general ways of thinking such as seriation, classification, proportionality, and probability which underpin all scientific thinking. These schemata form the content matter of the 30 *Thinking Science* (Adey, Shayer and Yates, 2001) activities comprising the published curriculum materials of CASE. Students in Years 7 and 8 (aged 12–14) are mostly just entering the doorway to formal operational thinking, and the activities are structured by the schemata which Inhelder and Piaget (1958) describe as characteristic of formal operations. They all require multi-variable thinking, and all can be identified as underlying aspects of the National Curriculum in science that appear from about level 5 and 6 onwards.

An example

We can illustrate these principles with one CASE activity, called 'Treatments and Effects'. The schemata addressed are causality and correlation. Students are offered this picture (Figure 5.2).

It is emphasized that all other conditions are kept the same across the two samples of carrots, and the question is: 'Does *Growcaro* make carrots grow larger?'

This is an activity one can do with Year 5 children, with Year 8, with Year 11, and with science teachers, obviously expecting increasingly sophisticated ways of dealing with the raw data and interpreting the results. An immediate response might be 'Yes, because there are more big ones with the *Growcaro*.' To which the challenges (which will create some conflict in younger students) are 'How many more?'; and then 'Is this enough to be convincing?', 'What can you tell by comparing the number of large and small carrots in each row?'

With Growcaro

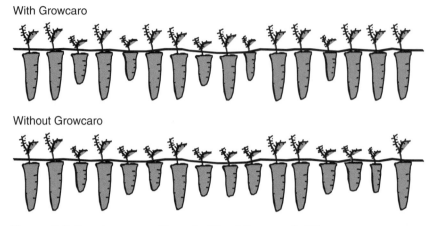

Without Growcaro

Figure 5.2 Carrots grown with and without *Growcaro* fertilizer

(4 data points). From this (explicit or implicit) table (Table 5.1), at a concrete level, students can use an additive strategy, 'There are 6 more large ones than small ones with *Growcaro*, but 2 more small ones than large ones without.'

Table 5.1   Comparison of carrots with and without *Growcaro* fertilizer

	Small	*Large*
With *Growcaro*	5	11
Without *Growcaro*	9	7

At an early formal level, students start to use ratios, '11/16 are large with *Growcaro* only 7/16 without.' These ratios might be simplified or converted into percentages. Going up another cognitive step, teachers often question the sample size. Although science teachers often know that you should have large samples, they sometimes find it quite difficult to explain why. Finally, one could get into something like a chi-squared statistic to test for statistical significance. And to all of that may be added discussion of side issues such as the economics (how much does *Growcaro* cost?), green considerations (is *Growcaro* organic?), or taste (yes but do the big carrots taste good?).

So this simple activity, like all CA activities, has the potential to cause cognitive conflict in students of a wide range of cognitive ability, but, of course, this process has to be well managed by the teacher. The following extract of whole class discussion comes from a class engaging with one of the activities from the primary *Let's Think Through Science!* (Adey, Nagy, et al., 2003). As mentioned earlier, primary students are generally working within Piaget's concrete stage of thinking and find working with multiple variables challenging. In the example of talk below, some 7–8 year-old students still struggle to handle *breadth* and *height* of water as a fixed volume is poured from one container into another. It also illustrates how the class teacher manages cognitive conflict and uses student talk to develop thinking.

At this point in the lesson, groups of students have all agreed that they have 100ml of water and have been asked to pour this into a new, different, unmarked container and decide how much water they have. Unable to conserve volume, one group decide to re-measure their amount of water using a ruler and measuring the height of the water in the container.

>   *T*: How much have you decided that you think is inside the container?
>   *P*: 20 ml.
>   *T*: 20 ml, why do you think 20 ml? Where did you get that answer from?
>   *P*: You know how the ruler has got like mm, well that's like ml so we just put the ruler here and checked.

Rather than dismiss this alternative suggestion and teach the correct idea, the teacher promotes this cognitive conflict. She does a demonstration in front of the class and pours the water from a short, wide container into a tall, thin container. Each time she measures by using the ruler technique suggested by the first group.

>   *T*: If I use the ruler and I measure how much is in here . . . and I measure it and I get about 10 ml. And then if I try now, see if I can pour carefully into this container, try not to spill it and then I use the same ruler to measure how much water is in this container I've got about 150 ml. What do you think about that? Is there anyone who would like to explain to me, what do you think about that?

Some children (experiencing cognitive conflict) start to respond to this spontaneously and mutter among themselves:

>   *P*: It looks like there is more because this is thinner. It looks smaller because that's bigger. (Points to the two different containers)
>   *T*: What did he say, Isabel? Can you repeat that so that everyone can hear?
> *Isabel*: It looks like there is more.
>   *T*: Right, it looks like there is more in that one because it is taller. Who agrees . . . This group, do you still think that the ruler might be a way the measuring it? That group, are you still happy that your way is a way of measuring it? I did say that we would listen to Reece. Reece, what do you want to say?
> *Reece*: Do you see what they have done, yeah? They got 20 because there is only a little bit in there, yeah, but the size of the space, it will spread out then, you can't just do it like that because that won't be how high the water has risen. If the other, yeah, will show you how deep it is because if you put it by the thing, it will show you how high the water has risen but if it is in a large space, like a big space, it won't, it will fill up smaller than it would in the littler space like that container.

Although all CA activities are designed to trigger conflict, the professional challenge for teachers lies in how to realize the cognitive potential of classroom talk, these Vygotskian 'social spaces' where ideas are generated and developed. At every step, a class can be asked to talk about the problem in their groups and – as partly exemplified above – to justify their claims, to challenge others' and generally to engage in high level social construction. Following on from this, they are asked to explain their thinking, and how it developed through the lesson, what mistakes they made, what made them change their minds, and generally to be metacognitive about the experience.

Does Cognitive Acceleration work?

The effects of CASE on students has been widely reported (Adey and Shayer, 1993, 1994; Shayer, 1999) and here we will provide just the briefest summary. In the original experiment from 1984–87, teachers in ten schools tried the materials with some classes, and identified other matched classes as control groups, just following their normal science curriculum. Students in CASE classes (a) made significantly greater gains in cognitive development over the two-year period (Years 7 and 8, or 8 and 9) of the CASE intervention; (b) one year after the intervention (end of Year 9 or 10) scored significantly higher on tests of science achievement; and (c) three or two years after the intervention, when they took their GCSEs, scored significantly higher grades in science, maths, and in English than their colleagues from control classes who had not experienced CASE activities. We consider this long-term effect, combined with the transfer of effects from a science context across the curriculum to English, as evidence that the CASE intervention has had a fundamental effect on the students' general ability to process information – their general intelligence. Here at last are the grounds on which the statement which opens this chapter are founded.

After those initial results were published in 1991, there was an immediate demand for schools to participate in CASE, and we started to run a two-year professional development programme at King's for science departments and for CASE trainers across the country. Now that there was strong evidence for the efficacy of CASE in raising levels of cognitive development and academic achievement, we could no longer run simple treatment versus control experiments (how do you explain to the parents of control children that they cannot have something of proven effectiveness?). Subsequent evaluations were based on comparing the value-added from initial Year 7 mean ability levels to eventual KS3 and GCSE grades for CASE and non-CASE schools. In other words, we were able to compare the overall academic achievement of schools matched for initial intake abilities. We consistently found that CASE schools out-performed non-CASE schools, again in English as well as in science and maths. We believe that the evidence that CASE does raise KS3 and GCSE grades is quite convincing.

Since the successful impact of the CASE intervention programme, the CA pedagogical framework has been applied to a wider range of curriculum subjects that include maths (Adhami et al., 1998) and the arts (Gouge and Yates, 2008) as well as to different age phases (Adey, Shayer and Yates, 2001; Adey, Nagy, et al., 2003; Adey, 2008).

Issues of implementation

Teaching for cognitive stimulation leads to some significant benefits, but implementing the approach in school is not all plain sailing. The upside is the improvement shown by students in deep-level processing which comes about from improved ability to hold in mind (working memory) many variables at once. Such multi-variable processing allows an individual to evaluate evidence against an initial belief or hypothesis, holding both the preconception and the evidence in mind at once. The genuine development of more sophisticated concepts in science requires such multivariable thinking. In general, higher-level thinking allows students to derive far more benefit, in terms of efficient learning, from any good instruction.

But these benefits are purchased at a cost. Twenty-five years on since the inception of a cognitive acceleration programme, many schools are becoming reacquainted with the principles of CASE. The challenges facing this new generation of teachers, as they attempt to infuse thinking into their twenty-first-century science classrooms, are similar.

Cognitive Acceleration takes time

Interventions designed for cognitive stimulation may occupy 20 per cent of the time allocated to the science curriculum and given the perception that the curriculum is already overcrowded, it seems reasonable to ask where this time is going to come from. In practice, the situation is nothing like as bad as it seems. For one thing, many of the process objectives as described in the 'How Science Works' section of the curriculum are addressed directly by the thinking intervention (see, also, Chapter 2). For another, after one year of work on improving thinking, students are able to understand the regular content-oriented instruction so much better that they make far better use of the time available to them. In some respects, current curriculum developments across the UK and beyond are creating space for thinking. For example, the new *Curriculum for Excellence* in Scotland has attempted to streamline the content in order to promote assessment for learning. All of the subject areas outlined in the new Welsh curriculum guidance are underpinned by a skills framework with one strand devoted to thinking and discussion. In England, the Key Stage 3 curriculum has been slimmed down, giving teachers greater autonomy and flexibility and encouraging use of a wider and more relevant range of learning contexts. Time spent in Year 7 and 8 focusing on the development of children's intellectual ability, however, pays off – with great capital growth and interest – in subsequent years.

Cognitive Acceleration necessitates change

An important consideration is the shift in pedagogy and attitudes towards learning and intelligence that are required for effective cognitive stimulation. To accept the principle that intelligence is not fixed has huge implications for the ways in which learning and teaching are approached, organized and facilitated. Group work needs to be recognized as a structure which allows learners to reach their zone of proximal development (Daniels, 2001; Newman et al., 1989) and not be seen simply as a convenient way of managing large numbers of students. This requires cultivating a classroom environment and establishing ground rules in which ideas such as changing your mind, learning from others and making mistakes are valued, as highlighted in the SPRinG (Social Pedagogic Research into Grouping) project (Blatchford et al., 2003) and in the programme 'Thinking Together' developed by Dawes et al. (2000).

Cognitive Acceleration might challenge perceptions of teacher and student roles in classroom discussion, such as the traditional dynamic between the teacher who leads the talk and the student who reciprocates. Recent projects have attempted to address this by going beyond the general distinctions be-tween 'open' and 'closed' discussions. Mortimer and Scott (2003) offer a way of looking, a 'communicative approach', at a sequence of teacher–student in-teractions but warn of misleading dichotomies between authoritative (using talk to get across a scientifically accepted viewpoint) and dialogic (using talk to elicit range of ideas) and interactive (students and teacher talk together) and non-interactive (teacher does all the talking). They suggest instead that these are dimensions and that decisions over the degree of interaction and dialogue needed should be considered in terms of the learning demand of the activity. For example, a teacher might decide that a more authoritative, non-interactive approach works best where the science is more commonsensical and easier for students to grasp. Or, a teacher might decided to spend more time engaging in a dialogic, interactive discussion with students to explore those aspects of science that are more counter-intuitive (see, also, Chapter 7).

Cognitive Acceleration lessons require the use of more than one kind of talk and the challenge for the teacher and the students lies in finding the best kind of talk to meet the specific purpose of different phases during a lesson. Some re-searchers have developed frameworks that identify specific types of classroom talk and the purposes that they satisfy. For example, Mercer's (1996a, 1996b) 'social modes of thinking' build progressively from disputational talk (where there are mainly short exchanges and individualized decision-making), to cu-mulative talk (where a shared understanding is built through repetition and elaboration but is not evaluated) to exploratory talk (where constructed mean-ing and reasoning are publicly evident in the statements, justifications and al-ternative hypotheses offered by members of that group). In Alexander's (2004) oral repertoire, *scaffolded dialogue* is used to describe a kind of talk where common understanding is achieved through structured and cumulative questioning and is thus collective, reciprocal, supportive, cumulative and purposeful.

Cognitive Acceleration requires professional and collegial support

For many, if not all, teachers the shift from content delivery to teaching for intellectual stimulation is radical and it will not easily be achieved alone, or by relying solely on print or ICT resources. Certainly the effect will not be achieved by a one-off INSET day. The model we developed for introducing CASE to a school includes seven INSET days and a number of coaching visits to the school, over a two-year period. While this may be the Rolls-Royce of professional development (PD), the in-depth study we have done of the factors which make professional development effective (in the sense that it actually brings about change in students' learning) shows that at least the following elements are essential:

1. *Time*: Teachers often need plenty of time to meet some of the underlying theory, to become familiar with the activities, and above all to practise the new skills.
2. *Coaching*: Change in teaching practice rarely comes about from INSET days in nice in-service centres. Support is needed in the classroom, as a teacher tries the new approach with the direct support of a critical friend.
3. *Collegiality*: One of the most consistent findings from research into effective PD is that a lone teacher finds it very difficult to make significant changes to their practice. By far the best way to approach this change in skills is by participation of a whole science department together, mutually supporting one another and calling in some outside assistance as necessary (Fullan and Stiegelbauer, 1991; Joyce and Showers, 1988).
4. *Senior management*: Introducing any significant teaching innovation, especially if it does not have the explicit stamp of approval of the QCA or Ofsted, requires a headteacher with faith and vision to see beyond the current buzz of official ideas to the longer-term benefit of their students, and to see through the intensive process of change.
5. *Quality of PD*: Nothing is more ironic than the Professor's monologue extolling the values of student activity and dialogue. PD designed to introduce ideas of cognitive conflict, social construction, and metacognition needs to induce in teachers, yes, cognitive conflict, social construction, and metacognition.
6. *Quality of the innovation*: The best-delivered and structured PD in the world will have no effect on student learning is what if being promoted is rubbish. There must be some evidence, preferably beyond

the anecdotal ('Our kids seemed to love it') that the innovation can have a positive impact on learning.

This model of effective professional development is described in full in Adey et al. (2004), and Chapter 13 of the present volume is devoted to the issue of professional development.

Progression and differentiation

Ensuring progression and differentiation within the teaching and learning of science are considered to be key indicators of good practice. To conclude this chapter, we will deal briefly with how the psychological models introduced earlier, and the notion of stimulating general intelligence, have an impact on our ideas of progression and differentiation in the science curriculum. What do progression and differentiation actually mean and what do they look like, particularly in a science classroom that promotes thinking?

Progression

What it means to make progress in science, as with any subject, is a complex and multi-faceted process (Monk, 2001) and, in the previous edition of *Good Practice in Science Teaching*, progression is described in several ways, as:

- a shift from a naïve conception to a more scientifically acceptable concept;
- the child's ability to process increasingly more complex ideas;
- the sequential difficulty within a topic;
- the order in which a child's learning takes place.

(Harrison et al., 2000)

The kinds of everyday explanations that we develop to make sense of the world around us have been described as 'spontaneous concepts' (Vygotsky, 1986) and as 'alternative frameworks' (Driver, 1983, 1995). They are personal, resistant to change and can be very different to the sometimes counter-intuitive but scientifically accepted explanations, the 'non-spontaneous concepts' that are introduced in science lessons. Students often experience serious cognitive conflict when their ideas clash with those presented by science. Enabling students to progress, to make that shift, is part of a teaching dilemma that Vygotsky described as the 'learning paradox'. He warns us that simply telling the students what they need to know is not the solution. This he says, 'accomplishes nothing but empty verbalism, a parrot-like repetition of words by the child, simulating knowledge of the corresponding concepts but actually covering up a vacuum' (Vygotsky, 1986, p. 150).

The Science Process and Concept Exploration research reports (SPACE, 1990–92) documented a range of children's 'alternative' ideas on concepts such as Light, Earth and Space, Sound, Processes of Life and Electricity, and the Nuffield primary teaching guides that emerged out of this work provide teachers with constructivist strategies that help students to make meaningful conceptual shifts (see Chapter 4 of this volume). Classroom approaches that target Vygotsky's 'learning paradox' were also developed in the Children's Learning in Science Project (CLIS) (1987), a programme designed by Rosalind Driver and her colleagues Hilary Asoko, John Leach, Philip Scott, and others at the University of Leeds.

A central feature of CLIS is that children are given a full opportunity to describe their explanations for common phenomena, to share them in groups and with the whole class, for example, through posters. They are invited to design critical tests of their ideas, to put them to the test of evidence. Frequently, the experiments have surprising (to the children) results, causing them to readjust their explanations and ideas. It is interesting that in developing an approach that enables students to make progress in their conceptual understanding, this programme employs all of the features we have described above as necessary for cognitive stimulation: the *cognitive conflict* of the surprising results, *reflection* on 'what we thought then, what we think now, and why we have changed' and *social construction* justifying, arguing, relating evidence to explanations, and so on.

A high-stakes testing culture and content-focused learning agenda can leave teachers feeling that they do little else than race through a curriculum and make learning a very unrewarding and de-motivating experience (Harlen and Deakin-Crick, 2002). The Piagetian framework underpinning Cognitive Acceleration provides for each lesson to be driven by a particular type and level of reasoning which concentrates teaching and learning on conceptual complexity. The sequence of activities in the CASE programme offers a more difficult (yet more rewarding and eventually more efficient) progression up levels of cognitive development than does a content-focused work scheme. CASE activities have well-defined lines of progression within each reasoning pattern. For example, activity 10 (relating thickness of branches to how high up a tree they are), activity 11 (exploring a balance beam) and activity 12 (relating the length of a wire to the current that flows through it) show clear progression in terms of reasoning based on inverse proportionality, beginning with the simple notion that 'as one variable goes up the other goes down' to the quantified relationship between current and length.

On this view, progress can take place along two dimensions. A student can progress in terms of accumulating more and more knowledge at a given conceptual level (for example, learning more and more concrete information about dinosaurs). But s/he can also make progress up the conceptual scale understanding increasingly complex relationships (for example, forms of classification of dinosaurs, the relationships of form to function or of survival to the environment). Both types of progression are necessary.

Differentiation

At the heart of Dickinson and Wright's (1993) handbook of classroom strategies for differentiation is the idea of 'intervening to make a difference'. To differentiate means to recognize that learners differ not only in their conceptual understanding, but also in their prior experiences, their motivation and the ways in which they learn best and to respond to these differences when teaching. There are several approaches to differentiation. These include differentiation by Organization, by Task, by Outcome, or by Support.

Streaming or setting students according to ability offers schools many advantages and disadvantages (Boaler and Wiliam, 2001). It can mislead a teacher or school into thinking that differentiation can be addressed solely through *organization*, allowing the teacher to work with a class of roughly similar ability and to tailor their teaching to meet the particular needs of that group of students. While this approach may narrow the range of abilities within one class, it does not eliminate all the subtle differences between students or take into account the possibility that different students might respond to different topics or learning contexts differently. Furthermore, seemingly objective processes, such as testing, employed to decide which set a student belongs to, often reveal only a partial picture of achievement and subjective decisions can be influenced by latent attitudes towards ethnicity, social class and gender. The danger is that, once locked into this system, some students become de-motivated or are denied access to the kinds of learning opportunities that would have enabled them to flourish so that the prospect of moving up (or down) a set is limited. This picture is far removed from the idea of 'intervening to make a difference'.

In Cognitive Acceleration, differentiation is addressed through a combination of *outcome* and *support*. The ideal context is where students work through cognitive challenges in small groups of moderately mixed ability, so that everyone can work in their zone of proximal development (Vygotsky, 1986) and tap into their dormant potential that is activated through collaboration. In the CASE programme, different activities are not provided to specific groups of students (differentiation by *task*). However, effective CA means more than setting an 'open-ended' task (differentiation by *outcome*) and collecting in the various responses. The Piagetian stage-wise account that informs CASE offers a rich description of where individuals might encounter cognitive conflict, and how to assess current levels of cognitive development. This, coupled with an appreciation of the differences in students' alternative frameworks and personalities, enables a teacher to map out the different learning trajectories within an activity and select the most effective strategies to *support* students in their individual development.

Conclusion

In the Introduction to this chapter, we offered psychological accounts based on cognitive development, mind-models, and cognitive neuroscience. We were at pains to show that these did not represent finite constraints on what young people can achieve and we hope we have shown how aspirations that teaching should both cognitively challenge and develop young people can be realized by science teachers, working within a broad context of the science curriculum. From the specific example of CASE, we have seen that time taken out of delivering content to focus on challenging students' thinking does pay off, quite quickly, in terms of academic achievement. It certainly requires something of a paradigm-shift in the mind-set of many teachers, from an emphasis on 'covering' content to focusing on the quality of dialogue that takes place between teacher and student and between student and student – recognizing puzzlement, uncertainty, admission of confusion as far more hopeful pathways to ultimate academic achievement than a neatly filled book of notes.

Further reading

Adey, P. (ed.) (2008) *The Let's Think Handbook: A Guide to Cognitive Acceleration in the Primary School.* London: GL Assessment.

Adey, P. S. and Shayer, M. (1994) *Really Raising Standards: Cognitive Intervention and Academic Achievement.* London: Routledge.

Alexander, R. J. (2004) *Towards Dialogic Teaching.* Cambridge: Dialogos.

Goswami, U. (2006) Neuroscience and education: from research to practice? *Nature Reviews Neuroscience,* 7: 406–13.

Inhelder, B. and Piaget, J. (1958) *The Growth of Logical Thinking.* London: Routledge & Kegan Paul.

6 Practical work

Robin Millar

Introduction

Practical work is a prominent and distinctive feature of science education and it is not hard to see why. The aim of science is to increase our understanding of the natural world, what it is made of, and how it works. A fundamental commitment of science is that claims and explanations should be supported by observational data. The aim of science education is to expand students' knowledge of the natural world, and help them develop an understanding of the ideas and models that scientists use to explain its behaviour. Science teaching naturally involves 'showing' learners certain things, or putting them into situations where they can see things for themselves. Simply 'telling' them is unlikely to feel appropriate, or to work.

In countries with a long tradition of laboratory-based science teaching at school level, practical work is seen by many teachers as an essential aspect of their everyday practice. It is often claimed that it leads to better learning – that we are more likely to understand and remember things we have done than things we have merely been told. It is also considered by many teachers, and by others with an interest in science education (see, for example, House of Lords Science and Technology Committee, 2006; SCORE, 2008), to be the key to catching and holding learners' interest in science and encouraging them to pursue the subject further.

Some science educators, however, have sounded a more questioning note. Hodson argues that:

> Despite its often massive share of curriculum time, laboratory work often provides little of real educational value. As practiced in many countries, it is ill-conceived, confused and unproductive. For many children, what goes on in the laboratory contributes little to their learning of science or to their learning *about* science and its methods.
>
> (1991, p. 176)

Osborne similarly argues that practical work 'only has a strictly limited role to play in learning science and that much of it is of little educational value' (1998, p. 156). Others have voiced similar doubts (for example, Bates, 1978; Hofstein and Lunetta, 1982). The claim that practical work strongly influences students' motivation to study science has also been challenged (Abrahams and Millar, 2008).

So which of these contrasting images of practical work in school science is the more accurate? What does research have to say about the role of practical work in science teaching and, in particular, about its effectiveness as a teaching and learning strategy? These questions are the focus of this chapter.

Defining terms

It may be useful to begin by clarifying what is meant by 'practical work'. In this chapter, 'practical work' will be used to mean *any science teaching and learning activity in which the students, working individually or in small groups, observe and/or manipulate the objects or materials they are studying*. This is slightly tighter than the 'classic definition' proposed by Lunetta et al. (2007, p. 394) which also includes activities based on secondary sources of data. This conceptualization, however, opens the door to a very wide range of activities, such as exercises where students are asked to analyse and interpret given data, perhaps in a table or graph. These would not normally be seen as 'practical work'.

It could be argued that teacher demonstrations meet the definition above, as they provide opportunities for students to observe natural events and may also involve some students in the class in manipulating objects or materials. In this chapter, however, teacher demonstrations will be treated as a separate category. 'Practical work' will refer to activities undertaken by students, not carried out by teachers.

The term 'practical work' seems a better label for the kinds of lesson activities discussed in this chapter than alternatives such as 'laboratory work' (or 'labwork'/'lab'). Observation and manipulation of objects and materials *might* take place in a school laboratory, but could also occur in an out-of-school setting, such as the student's home or in the field. The learning processes involved in collecting and interpreting data are the same, wherever the activity takes place. The term 'experiment' (which students often use), or 'experimental work', carries a more specific meaning – of an activity which involves an intervention (Hacking, 1983) to produce the phenomenon to be observed or to test a hypothesis. Although some practical work in school science is like this, some is not.

Another term often used in discussions of practical work is 'investigation'. In this chapter, an 'investigation' means a practical activity in which students are not given a complete set of instructions to follow (a 'recipe'), but have some freedom to choose the procedures to follow, and to decide how to record, analyse and report the data collected. They may also (though this will not be taken as a defining characteristic) have some freedom to choose the question to be addressed and/or the final conclusion to be drawn. Like 'experiments', 'investigations' form a sub-set of 'practical work'.

The variety of practical work

Practical work in school science has a range of aims. Many authors have proposed ways of classifying these. Hodson (1990, p. 34) suggests that the main reasons given by teachers for using practical work in science teaching are:

- to motivate pupils, by stimulating interest and enjoyment;
- to teach laboratory skills;
- to enhance the learning of scientific knowledge;
- to give insight into scientific method, and develop expertise in using it;
- to develop certain 'scientific attitudes' such as open-mindedness, objectivity and willingness to suspend judgement.

Hofstein and Lunetta (2004, p. 38) offer a similar list of aims but with some differences of emphasis. They suggest that the principal aims of practical work are to enhance students':

- understanding of science concepts;
- interest and motivation;
- scientific practical skills and problem-solving abilities;
- scientific habits of mind;
- understanding of the nature of science.

Hofstein and Lunetta note that the last two points are relatively recent additions to lists of this sort. A later article by Lunetta et al. (2007) includes a similar list (2007, p. 402), but with the addition of 'argumentation from data' to the third aim above. Lazarowitz and Tamir (1994) include the more specific aim of challenging students' misconceptions. In the central section of this chapter, reviewing the research evidence about the effectiveness of practical work, I will use a classification of the aims of practical work based on those discussed above to structure the discussion.

Rather than classifying aims, some researchers have tried to classify types of practical activities. Woolnough and Alsop (1985) suggest that practical tasks undertaken by students can be classified as:

- exercises (to develop practical skills and techniques);
- experiences (to give students a 'feel' for phenomena);
- investigations (to put students in the role of a 'problem-solving scientist').

To these they then add a fourth category – activities intended to support the learning of scientific ideas, concepts and theories – arguing that these are more effective if presented as teacher demonstrations rather than as practical tasks undertaken by students.

More detailed schemes for describing practical activities, in order to high-light similarities and differences, have also been proposed. Lunetta and Tamir (1981) developed a classification scheme to compare practical tasks in two US high school physics courses. Another was developed by the European *Labwork in Science Education* project (Millar et al., 2002) and used to explore the character of science practical work in upper secondary (senior high) school and university courses in six European countries (Tiberghien et al., 2001). An analysis of a sample of 165 laboratory instruction sheets found few activities that required students to test a prediction, or choose between two explanations. In general, the focus was on observable features of the situation studied rather than explanatory ideas. Many chemistry activities taught a standard procedure, and many physics ones focused on processing numerical data. A modified version of this classification scheme was used by Kapenda et al. (2002) to study practical work in lower secondary (junior high) schools in Namibia. They found that teachers' objectives inferred from lesson observation were often wider than those indicated in their written lesson plans or teaching materials. Much of the value of this sort of research lies in the classification scheme itself, which may be a useful tool for other researchers and for teachers wanting to analyse and review their practice more systematically.

Teachers' views of practical work

Several research studies have explored teachers' declared views on practical work. A study by Kerr (1963) asked a sample of secondary (high) school teachers in England to rank in importance the ten aims of practical work, shown in Table 6.1. Kerr included teacher demonstrations within his definition of practical work. Over 700 teachers in 151 schools responded. Kerr concluded that there was 'a significant measure of agreement among teachers as to the educational values arising from practical work' (1963, p. 95) though this was less

Table 6.1 Kerr's aims of practical work (as used by Beatty and Woolnough, 1982a)

1. To encourage accurate observation and description.
2. To promote a logical reasoning method of thought.
3. To develop specific manipulative skills.
4. To practise seeing problems and seeking ways of solving them.
5. To prepare students for practical examinations.
6. To elucidate the theoretical work as an aid to comprehension.
7. To verify facts and principles already taught.
8. For finding facts and arriving at new principles.
9. To arouse and maintain interest.
10. To make phenomena more real.

marked at upper secondary level. A similar approach was taken by Thompson (1975) (with upper secondary school teachers) and by Beatty and Woolnough (1982a, 1982b), but using an extended list of 20 aims. More recently the same 20-item list of aims was used by Swain et al. (1999, 2000) to compare the views of teachers in Egypt, Korea and the UK, and to explore changes over time in the views of UK teachers. They report inter-country differences that might stem from differences in curriculum emphasis or dominant epistemological perspective, but also considerable stability in UK teachers' views. Aims 1, 2, 9 and 10 (Table 6.1) were ranked highly in all studies of UK teachers.

Some questions might, however, be asked about the methods and instruments used in these studies. It is difficult to state aims of practical work clearly and concisely, and specific choices of words may significantly affect responses. Conclusions drawn from the responses may lack validity – a respondent's interpretation of the statements of aims may differ from that intended by the researchers. The repeatability of a person's ranking of 10 or 20 statements, particularly in the middle of the rank order, is also questionable. Perhaps most significantly, Kerr (1963, pp. 43–6) and Thompson (1975, p. 36) report discrepancies between teachers' rankings and their actual practice. Beatty and Woolnough (1982a, p. 30) similarly acknowledge that their data may not reflect what is taking place in classrooms and laboratories. Wilkinson and Ward (1997) also report marked differences between Australian teachers' stated aims for practical work and the aims perceived by their students. Teachers' ranking of aims may tell us more about the rhetoric of practical work, at the time the study was carried out, than about the practice.

A rather different research approach was used by Donnelly (1998) in a study of teachers' views of teaching their subject. Drawing on data from 40 interviews with science teachers in five schools in England, Donnelly suggests that science teachers typically categorize lessons, or parts of lessons, as 'practical' or 'theory', and that the overwhelming majority see practical work as a constitutive element of 'being a science teacher'. That is, they see it as something which is simply part of what you do as a science teacher, rather than a strategy consciously chosen from a range of options to achieve a specific learning outcome. The fact that many lessons take place in laboratories is likely to be a factor in sustaining this perception. Donnelly reports that only one teacher in his sample expressed qualified scepticism about the value of practical work. He emphasizes that his account is intended to be descriptive, not judgmental. Donnelly's interpretation is in line with the observation of Duschl and Gitomer (1997) that science teachers tend to see their practice in terms of 'tasks and activities rather than conceptual structures and scientific reasoning' (p. 65). Teaching is then a matter of staging a sequence of activities, rather than of producing intended cognitive or behavioural changes. If this is so, it has significant implications for efforts to improve the effectiveness of practical work – suggesting that a necessary first step is to help teachers to see each practical activity as a means to an end, and not as an end in itself.

The effectiveness of practical work in teaching and learning science

For many people a central question about practical work in science education is: is practical work effective? Does it lead to better learning? To structure the discussion of this question, I will use a classification of the aims of practical work based on those of Hodson (1990) and Hofstein and Lunetta (2004) discussed above. I will consider in turn the research evidence concerning the use and effectiveness of practical work:

- to enhance the learning of scientific knowledge;
- to teach laboratory skills;
- to give insight into scientific method, and develop expertise in using it;
- in stimulating students' interest and increasing motivation to study science;
- in developing understanding of the nature of science.

This omits one of the aims of practical work included in some lists: to develop scientific 'habits of mind', or 'scientific attitudes', such as open-mindedness and objectivity. There is, to my knowledge, no research on the effectiveness of practical work in helping to achieve learning outcomes of this sort; indeed it is difficult to see how they could be evaluated. This aim is perhaps better seen as an aspiration than as a measurable outcome.

Practical work to enhance the learning of scientific knowledge

Many studies, mainly from the United States, have explored whether science courses with a practical emphasis lead to better student learning than more textbook-oriented alternatives. A series of studies of three activity-based science programmes from the 1970s (*Science – A Process Approach (SAPA)*, *Elementary Science Study (ESS)* and *Science Curriculum Improvement Study (SCIS)*) reported conflicting outcomes, some showing learning gains from the new programmes and others reporting no significant difference. To attempt to resolve this uncertainty, Bredderman (1983) undertook a meta-analysis of 57 studies of these three programmes, considering nine different outcome measures including students' scientific knowledge. He concluded that:

> The overall effects of the activity-based programs on all outcome areas combined were clearly positive, although not dramatically so. Thirty-two per cent of all 400 comparisons favoured the activity-based program and were reported as statistically significant at the 5% level or above. Only six per cent favoured the non-activity-based program group.
>
> (1983, p. 504)

The smallest mean effect size,[1] however, was for measures of science knowledge (0.16), with the largest for measures of science process (0.52). Bredderman also notes that fewer than 25 per cent of these studies used random assignment to the treatment and control groups. This significantly weakens the evidence of positive effects, as better outcomes are to be expected in the classes of teachers who have voluntarily adopted a new approach compared with teachers who have not. A similar meta-analysis by Shymansky et al. (1983) of over 100 experimental studies of 27 activity-based science programmes for US elementary, junior high and high schools reached a somewhat different conclusion from Bredderman, reporting that students following activity-based programmes made the greatest gains on measures of scientific knowledge and science process skills. Atash and Dawson (1986), however, in a synthesis of 10 studies of activity-based programmes found a small positive effect (0.09) on a composite measure of all learning outcomes but a negative effect (−0.45) on measures of scientific knowledge (that is, the average score of those following activity-based programmes was lower than that of the control group).

To try to account for this variation in reported findings, Stohr-Hunt (1996) explored the relation between time spent by students 'experiencing hands-on science' (p. 101) and science achievement. For the latter, she used scores on a 25-item multiple-choice test of science knowledge and reasoning ability used in the US National Education Longitudinal Study of 1988. A random sample of 1,052 schools, followed by random sampling of students within these, produced a sample of over 24,000 eighth-grade (age 14) students. Data on time spent on hands-on science activities came from a teacher questionnaire. Stohr-Hunt reported that students who experienced hands-on activities once a week or more scored significantly higher on the achievement measure than those who experienced such activities once a month or less.

Studies of the effect of whole programmes are inevitably rather 'broad brush'. A science programme is a complex intervention, with many facets. The quality of the hands-on activities used, rather than simply their quantity, may have a major influence on learning outcomes. We may learn more about the effectiveness of practical work for teaching scientific knowledge from studies on the teaching of a specific science topic. Watson et al. (1995) carried out one such study, using naturally occurring differences in the exposure of 14–15-year-old students in England and Spain to practical work in the teaching and learning of combustion. The topic is taught in both countries with quite similar learning objectives. In England, it is usually taught with high practical content, whereas in Spain the amount of practical work is low. A sample of 150 students attending mixed-ability co-educational comprehensive schools in each country completed a written diagnostic test of their understanding, developed for this study. Testing did not immediately follow teaching, but took place at a time when both samples would have studied some elementary chemistry including combustion. The researchers also interviewed the students' teachers to get fuller information on how combustion had been taught. There were marked differences between the samples in their responses, for example, in the terms they used and the examples they gave. And there was, as might be expected, considerable variation in student understanding within each sample. The researchers concluded that English students' greater exposure to practical work 'had only a marginal effect on their understanding of combustion' (1995, p. 487).

In a study with somewhat greater control over the content and sequence of instruction, Yager et al. (1969) compared the learning outcomes of three different ways of teaching the *Biological Sciences Curriculum Study (BSCS)* course: discussion only; discussion-demonstration; and discussion-laboratory. Sixty students (age 14) in one school were allocated randomly into groups following each of these approaches. Yager et al. found no statistically significant difference between these groups on measures of biology knowledge, attitude towards biology, understanding of science and scientists, or critical thinking ability. Only on ability to manipulate laboratory materials and equipment was there any measurable difference in favour of the group that had undertaken laboratory practical work.

There are few studies like the two discussed above, which compare the outcomes of teaching a science topic with and without practical work. There are, however, many studies comparing the outcomes of teaching a topic using small-group practical work and teacher demonstration. Garrett and Roberts (1982) discuss and review studies carried out up to the early 1980s. They comment on the variation, and lack of clarity, out in the use of key terms across these studies, for example, about the size of 'small' groups, and about the role of students during a demonstration. They also draw attention to weaknesses in sampling and in the outcome measures used in many studies, and variations in study design from simple experimental-control group comparisons, to those in which students experience the same interventions (or teaching approaches) in a different order. Referring to 'small groups' and 'demonstrations' as different 'tactics', they reach the conclusion that these research studies 'have provided no clear cut indication of the superiority of one tactic over the other and the overall evidence would seem to suggest that there [is] no difference between them at least in any generalisable way' (1982, p. 139).

More recent studies have reached similar conclusions. Atkinson (1981) compared the outcomes of teaching a unit on the Gas Laws using practical work or teacher demonstration to secondary school students (age 16) in Australia. Students who had done practical work retained a memory of some 'episodes' associated with these, but did not link these strongly to explanations. On tests of scientific knowledge and transfer of skills there was no significant difference between the groups. Thijs and Bosch (1995) compared teacher demonstrations and student practical work for developing students' understanding of forces on objects at rest. The subjects were 160 students (age 15) in six classes of above average ability, taught by five teachers in two schools in the Netherlands. Three classes were taught using teacher demonstrations, and three undertook the same tasks as small-group practicals. The teaching sequence in all classes was based on the 'anchor-bridges method' suggested by Clement et al. (1989), thus ensuring some similarity in the content and sequence of instruction. It is, however, unclear how students were allocated to each 'treatment' and hence how well the groups were matched. Learning outcomes were measured by written probes of concept understanding, analysis of students' written class work, and observers' notes during lessons. Thijs and Bosch reached the conclusion that 'overall cognitive effects of small-group practicals and teacher demonstrations do not differ' (1995, p. 320). They did, however, note a gender effect: girls performed less well than boys in the sample who did small-group practicals.

Another experimental study, of the outcomes of a unit on electrolysis for Jamaican 10th grade students (age 14–16 years), compared an experimental group (66 students) taught using a combination of lecture, teacher demonstration, class discussion and small-group practical work with a control group (72 students) who did not undertake any small-group practical work (Thompson and Soyibo, 2002). Although the primary focus of the study was on the effect on students' attitudes to chemistry, the study also looked at students' scientific knowledge. Thompson and Soyibo found a statistically significant difference in the mean attitude scores of the two groups after the unit, in favour of the experimental group. The evidence of impact on conceptual understanding, however, was less clear – complicated by statistically significant differences between the two samples on the pre-test, with one scoring significantly higher on multiple-choice items and the other significantly higher on structured open-response items. Although there were statistically significant differences attributable to treatment in mean scores on both types of item, in favour of the experimental group, there was no correlation between these and attitude gains. Thompson and Soyibo concluded that, 'further studies, involving larger samples, are needed' (2002, p. 34) (see, also, Chapter 11).

The absence of clear and compelling evidence of the learning benefits of small-group practical work over teacher demonstration or non-practical teaching is perhaps surprising in view of the strong endorsement of the importance and value of practical work by many science teachers and other important stakeholder groups. It has prompted researchers to seek explanations in the nature of the practical tasks used and they way they are presented. This research is explored further in the next section.

Learning through practical work

Many researchers have attributed the apparent lack of effectiveness of practical work to an over-reliance on 'recipe following' or 'cookbook' practical tasks. These, it is argued, result in activities which may be 'hands on' but are rarely 'minds on'. When doing such tasks, students often lose sight of the purpose of the activity and carry out the steps rather mechanically without much reflection or real engagement.

Gunstone (1991) highlights the value of Predict–Observe–Explain tasks for making practical tasks more 'minds-on'. These are tasks in which the student is asked to predict what will happen in a certain situation (and perhaps also to give their reasons), and only then to do it. If what they observe differs from what they predicted, they are then asked to explain their observations (White and Gunstone, 1992, Chapter 3). Gunstone (1991) uses an example from the teaching of electric circuit theory to discuss how practical experience can contribute to learners' construction of theoretical ideas. He notes that observation is always influenced by the ideas we bring to it, which can affect what we choose to observe, what we actually observe, which observations we regard as relevant and which we deem irrelevant, and how we interpret them. Gunstone argues that, to be more effective in promoting learning, practical work must be embedded in a carefully planned sequence of learning activities which emphasizes links between observations and ideas and allows students some control in making these links.

⟨Some science educators have suggested that a specific role for practical work is in challenging students' misconceptions. Lazarowitz and Tamir (1994, pp. 99–101) review several studies of practical work designed to do this. Chinn and Brewer (1993), however, sound a note of caution. They analysed the ways in which scientists and science students might in principle respond to unexpected or apparently anomalous data, which are not in line with their expectations. They identify seven different responses, only one of which is to accept the data and revise your explanation or theory. In a subsequent empirical study, Chinn and Brewer (1998) tested their taxonomy by presenting a sample of over 120 undergraduates with data (in the form of a short text) that contradicted a theory they currently held, and recording their responses. The majority of responses fitted one of the categories of their taxonomy, with only a minority being prompted to revise their theory. Gauld (1989) used a similar taxonomy of possible responses to unexpected observations to classify the responses of 14 students (age 14) in a class in New Zealand to their observations during practical work on electric circuits. Again it was very clear that observations did not automatically cause students to change their incorrect beliefs. Similar findings were reported by Shepardson and Moje (1999), from another study of the same science topic. Again this used in-depth case studies of a small number of students (4 from each of two US grade 4 (age 10) classes in different schools).

Several science educators (for example, Driver, 1975; Gunstone, 1991; Hodson, 1993b; Millar, 1998a) have suggested that the apparent lack of effectiveness of much practical work is due to a fundamental flaw in its design. Many practical activities are implicitly based on the view that explanatory ideas will 'emerge' from careful study of a phenomenon, perhaps shaped by the guidance that a teacher or a worksheet provides. From this perspective, practical enquiry is a kind of 'reading of the book of nature'. But explanatory ideas do not simply 'emerge' in this way, however carefully you observe or measure. Rather, they are conjectures, proposed to account for the available evidence, in a process that involves imagination as well as logical deduction and inference. It is easy for someone who already knows an accepted scientific explanation to underestimate the difficulty learners have in 'seeing it'. Ideas which have become second nature to a teacher are often not apparent to a learner – and do not become 'obvious' from the data in the way the teacher may expect. By taking more account of this 'imaginative' step from evidence to explanation, we may be able to devise more effective practical activities and more effective ways of staging them, which take proper account *both* of the first-hand data from the practical activity *and* of the teacher's subject knowledge. As Driver notes, 'If students' understandings are to be changed towards those of accepted science, then intervention and negotiation with an authority, usually a teacher, is essential' (1995, p. 399).

Two case studies from the research literature illustrate these issues well. Scott and Leach (1998) discuss a lesson where a teacher is developing the idea that reducing the amount of air in a vessel reduces the air pressure. The teacher sets up a demonstration with two partially-inflated balloons inside a bell-jar. The air is then gradually removed from the bell-jar by a vacuum pump. The students observe the balloons gradually inflating and are interested in this unusual way of blowing up a balloon. The teacher asks them for an explanation. Several suggest explanations based on the idea that the vacuum created by the pump is 'sucking out' the skin of the balloons. The teacher, in contrast to these explanations, wants them to think in terms of the air pressure being reduced in the space around the balloons, so that the pressure of the air inside the balloons is now able to push the skin outwards. So he picks out specific aspects of the demonstration, for example, that the balloons are tightly sealed, and so the quantity of air inside them is fixed. And he reinforces some, though not all, parts of students' explanations, praising one boy who has mentioned that the air pressure in the bell-jar has been reduced, and then repeating slowly and deliberately 'so if we make less air in the jar there's less air pressure in the jar . . . '. The teacher is engaged in the style of science teaching that Ogborn et al. (1996) call 'see it my way' – helping students to see the world through 'new spectacles'.

Another case study described by Roth et al. (1997) and McRobbie et al. (1997) also illustrates the ineffectiveness of practical experience on its own and the importance of interaction with an authority. They discuss six weeks of observation of a Canadian grade 12 class (age 17), in which a physics teacher is trying to develop students' understanding of force and motion. Students' interpretations of their data varied, and often differed from what the teacher had anticipated (and hoped for). Their own ideas influenced what they observed and recorded. The teacher thought his instructions were clear and self-evident, but the students did not share his theoretical perspective on motion which made sense of the practical activities, and the result was confusion for many. Significantly the students who learned most were those who had the confidence to ask the teacher many questions, and were thus enabled to make better use of the information provided.

The two examples above illustrate the importance of discussion around a practical activity, to help students 'make sense' of their observations. In a study

Figure 6.1 The fundamental purpose of practical work: to link two domains of knowledge
Source: Tiberghien (2000).

of three practical inquiry-based lessons in each of two classes of 12–13-year-old students in the UK, however, Watson et al. (2004) found that the quantity and quality of discussion of the inquiry were low. The practical tasks were seen by students as routine procedures, to provide the material for a written account. In a more recent study in the UK, Abrahams and Millar (2008) observed 25 practical lessons in eight schools and interviewed the teacher and a sample of students (aged 12–16) about aspects of the lesson. Some of the practical activities observed required little engagement with explanatory ideas; others were critically dependent on making links between the domains of observables and of ideas (Figure 6.1). Abrahams and Millar noted no observable difference in the way tasks of the two kinds were presented in lessons, either in the oral or written instructions provided, or in the discussion around or during the task. In almost every lesson, all of the teacher talk was about how to carry out the practical task, not about the ideas that made sense of it. A first step towards improving the effectiveness of practical work may therefore be raising teachers' awareness of the wide variation in demand between practical tasks and helping them to recognize those that are of high demand, so that they build in specific ways of supporting students' thinking and reasoning in such tasks.

Using information and communication technologies (ICT) to enhance learning

One approach for enhancing the effectiveness of practical work is increasingly supported by research evidence. This is the use of interactive computer-based simulations in which students experiment with virtual manipulatives rather than physical manipulatives. Several recent studies have concluded that the use of such simulations, before or alongside practical work with real objects and materials, leads to better student learning.

The fundamental reason for using information and communication technologies (ICT) to support practical work is to address an issue highlighted by Johnstone and Wham (1982) – that practical activities have a high level of 'noise' which can distract students from their central purpose. In a typical practical activity, students have to deal simultaneously with the ideas and concepts that give the activity meaning, the practical manipulation of apparatus and materials, perhaps involving some quite fine motor skills, the planning and sequencing of actions to carry out procedures and record outcomes, and the social interactions involved in group work. ICT offers a way of reducing this noise and helping students to focus on the central question the activity is addressing.

Zacharia and Anderson (2003) investigated the use of simulations presented before laboratory activities designed to develop students' conceptual under-standing of mechanics, waves and optics, and introductory thermal physics. The subjects were 13 postgraduates (in-service and trainee teachers) without physics qualifications. Students were randomly assigned to the simulation or non-simulation condition for different sub-topics within the overall teach-ing intervention. Diagnostic written tests were used to assess understanding. Results indicated that exposure to simulations improved students' ability to offer acceptable predictions and explanations, and led to significant concep-tual change in the areas tested. Finkelstein et al. (2005) used a larger sample of undergraduate students (n = 231) at a large research university in the USA to study the effectiveness of an interactive computer simulation for teach-ing basic electric circuit theory. The experimental group (n = 99) used the computer simulation, while the control group (n = 132) used real laboratory equipment. Assignment to these groups appears to have been on convenience grounds, rather than random. The researchers reported that students who used the simulation achieved higher scores, both on an assessment of conceptual knowledge and on a task involving assembling a real circuit and explaining how it worked. In a study with much younger learners, Klahr et al. (2007) var-ied several conditions, including the use of physical or virtual manipulatives, in a task involving the design and testing of toy cars. The participants were 56 school students (20 girls, 36 boys) with a mean age of 13.1 years from two middle schools in the USA. In this case, the researchers found no significant difference in learning outcomes between the conditions they tested – but note that virtual manipulatives have pragmatic advantages in terms of class man-agement and organization, and possibly cost, and might therefore be preferred for enabling active student involvement and engagement in learning.

In another study of learning of electric circuit theory, Zacharia (2007) used a sample of undergraduate students following a pre-service course for elemen-tary school teachers in Cyprus. Students were assigned randomly to an experi-mental group (n = 45) or a control group (n = 43). The control group used real experimentation throughout, while the experimental group used virtual ex-perimentation for part of their programme. The experimental group achieved higher gains on conceptual tests taken before, during, and after the interven-tion. A similarly designed study of 68 students from the same pre-service teach-ing programme explored learning of heat and temperature (Zacharia and Con-stantinou, 2008). The experimental group used virtual manipulatives (VM) and the control group physical manipulatives (PM). Unlike previous stud-ies, the curriculum and the instructional approach were explicitly controlled. The groups made similar conceptual gains on written tests. In a subsequent investigation, involving 62 students of similar background (Zacharia et al., 2008), the experimental group used PM followed by VM, and the control group PM only. Here the experimental group made larger conceptual gains than the control group. In another similarly designed study of 66 10–11-year-old students in Finland, Jaakkola and Nurmi (2008) found that a combination of simulation and laboratory experimentation on electric circuits led to better learning outcomes than either approach used on its own.

This is a relatively new area for research, but there is growing evidence that the use of activities involving virtual manipulatives in conjunction with activities involving physical manipulatives leads to measurable learning gains. Studies reported are, however, of a relatively limited number of science topics, and the use of virtual manipulatives may not be applicable to all the science topics we might wish to teach (see, also, Chapter 8).

Practical work to teach laboratory skills

In contrast to the preceding section, this one is brief. There is consistent evidence from research studies that students are better at using practical science equipment and carrying out standard procedures if they have been taught by practical methods that have given them opportunities to do these things for themselves. It comes from studies such as that by Yager et al. (1969) (discussed above) and the studies included in the meta-analyses by Bredderman (1983) and by Shymansky et al. (1983) (also discussed above). It is scarcely a surprising finding. Indeed, we would be surprised were it not the case. Some of the findings of the Assessment of Performance Unit (APU) in England (discussed more fully later), however, suggest that the students' competence in using some very common measuring instruments is lower than we might expect, given the prominence of practical work in English schools. For several of the instruments tested, less than half of a large sample of 15-year-olds could take a reading to the expected precision and accuracy. The major problems were associated with interpolation between marked values on a scale, and were greatest when this involved decimals (Gamble et al., 1985, pp. 18–19). It should, however, be acknowledged that these students' competence was being assessed out of context, in making measurements for no obvious purpose beyond the assessment itself. It is quite likely that the quality of measurements made purposefully, in a well-understood context, would be rather better.

Practical work to give insight into scientific method, and develop expertise in using it

In many countries, the school science curriculum aims, in addition to broadening students' scientific knowledge, to provide an insight into the scientific approach to enquiry. This approach often leads to the inclusion (or advocacy of the inclusion) in the teaching programme of some open-ended investigations, in which students are given, or propose, a question or problem that can be explored empirically, and then have to decide what data to collect, how to present and analyse these, and what conclusions to draw. It is sometimes suggested or implied that students can develop their scientific knowledge and understanding of the natural world through investigative work. This, however, seems implausible, given the lack of research evidence that structured and directed practical activities are effective in achieving this outcome. A commoner, and more defensible, view of investigations is to see them as tools for developing students' understanding of the scientific approach to enquiry and providing practice in using it.

A great deal of research has been carried out on the development of students' understanding of scientific enquiry, and their ability to undertake scientific investigations and to reason appropriately from data. Some research has been undertaken by cognitive scientists, with a central interest in how human ability in reasoning and problem-solving develops with age and educational experience. Another body of research, mainly by science educators, centres on issues and questions that arise from practice or from policy innovations such as the introduction of Attainment Target Sc1 in the English National Curriculum (DES/WO, 1989). As Klahr et al. (2001) note, however, there is relatively little interaction between these two research programmes.

Research by cognitive scientists

The interest of cognitive scientists in scientific reasoning stems largely from the fact that Piaget's theories see certain kinds of reasoning, such as control of variables, as characteristic of the stage of formal operations (see, also, Chapters 4 and 5 in this volume). Two major reviews by Zimmerman (2000, 2007) provide an excellent overview of research on the development of the reasoning skills involved in design of investigations and evaluation of evidence. Some studies have sought to document the performance of a chosen group, others to evaluate interventions that aim to improve students' performance.

Some studies of investigation design have deliberately chosen to minimize the role of prior knowledge and focus on content-independent strategies. Siegler and Liebert (1975) used a problem that required US Grade 5 and 8 students (age 11 and 14) to find the correct combination of four on/off switches to make an electric train run. A systematic approach involved testing all 16 possible combinations, but few succeeded in doing this. After instruction on how to identify and represent the possible solutions, performance improved markedly, particularly in the older group. One important finding from this and other similar studies was that students who kept a written record of their attempts were significantly more successful than those who relied on memory.

In another study of experimental design, Kuhn and Angelev (1976) looked at the outcomes of a 15-week intervention with US fourth and fifth graders (age 10–11) which set them practical tasks involving formal operational thinking: exploring how mass and length affect the time of swing of a pendulum, exploring which combinations of given colourless liquids produce a yellow colour when mixed, and a non-practical task to find which ingredients affect the quality of bread. A sample of 82 subjects was divided into six subgroups, of which four were given variants of the intervention, differing, for example, in intensity (number of lessons/week), or in the presence/absence of teacher demonstration of correct solutions; the other two were controls. The researchers reported improvement as measured by immediate and delayed post-tests, linked to intensity of the intervention, but not enhanced by more direct teaching. The sample, however, was small and, as Kuhn and Angelev noted, these findings need to be checked across a wider range of task contexts.

Indeed, later studies have reached the opposite conclusion about the effects of direct instruction. Chen and Klahr, for example, from a study of 7–10-year-olds (n = 87) reported that 'when provided with explicit training within domains, combined with probe questions, children were able to learn and transfer the basic strategy for designing unconfounded experiments. Providing probes without direct instruction, however, did not improve children's ability' (1999, p. 1098). Another study, of 112 US Grade 3 and 4 students (age 9–10), corroborated this finding (Klahr and Nigam, 2004). Children taught the control of variables strategy (CVS) made greater pre-test to post-test improvement than those who were simply exposed to a series of tasks that required the use of the CVS. The need for short direct teaching interventions to teach the CVS is, however, still contested by other researchers such as Kuhn and Dean, who argue that there is evidence of learning when young children simply 'engage in repeated encounters with situations that require these skills' (2005, p. 866). As control of variables is the aspect of scientific enquiry on which much the largest body of research exists, it is worth noting that this research effort has not yet produced consensus about how the central ideas can be taught most effectively. It is an indication, if one is needed, of how difficult it is to produce clear and compelling evidence of the effectiveness of educational interventions.

Turning then to studies of students' ability to evaluate evidence. Many of these use non-practical probes, in order to have control of the data that students are being asked to reason about. Even so, the findings are directly relevant to the use of practical work in teaching and learning, as this inevitably involves the interpretation and evaluation of empirical data. A much-cited study by Kuhn et al. (1988) explored through interviews how subjects interpret given pieces of evidence, some supporting and some challenging their prior beliefs about a causal link. In one probe, a sample of US Grade 6 and 9 students (age 12 and 15) and adults were first asked which food, of each of a set of given pairs, they thought would make a difference to whether or not a person caught a cold. They were then presented with a series of pieces of evidence about the diet of individuals and groups, told whether or not they caught colds, and asked to say what conclusions they would draw and to identify any implications for their 'theory'. From a set of such probes, Kuhn et al. suggested that many subjects, including some adults, tend to see evidence and theory as a single representation of 'how things are'. The ability to differentiate evidence and theory increased with age. Some subjects ignored or distorted discrepant information, echoing the findings of Chinn and Brewer (1993) discussed earlier.

The claim that many children do not distinguish evidence and theory (or explanation) has, however, been challenged. Koslowski (1996) makes the important point that ideas about possible explanatory mechanisms are important in evaluating evidence. If we cannot imagine any mechanism linking two variables, we are unlikely to see covariation (the value of one variable increasing or decreasing steadily as the other increases) as evidence of a causal connection. Conversely, if we can see a possible causal mechanism, we may well continue to believe there is a causal link despite evidence of non-covariation. Through a series of studies, Koslowski showed how the presence or absence of a plausible mechanism influences subjects' interpretations of covariation and non-covariation data.

Millar (1998b) argues that Koslowski's work explores 'logical reasoning' rather than 'scientific reasoning', because it asks subjects about the implications for their theory of given *conclusions*, whereas scientific reasoning is about the relationship between theory and *data*. A key element of scientific reasoning is knowing how to deal with uncertainty (error) in measurements. To explore this issue, Kanari and Millar (2004) observed 60 students (aged 9, 11 and 14) in schools in England undertaking a practical investigation of the effect of each of two named independent variables on a dependent variable. Two situations were used, in both of which the dependent variable covaries with one of the independent variables but not with the other. One investigation was about the time of swing of a simple pendulum (the effect of length and mass), the other about the force needed to pull a small box across a level surface (the effect of weight and area of bottom surface). Half of the sample (randomly selected) did each investigation, and were subsequently interviewed about the actions of children observed on a video-recording carrying out the other investigation. The study was designed to test the hypothesis that recognizing and dealing with measurement error is a major challenge for students, and that this will result in fewer reaching the correct conclusion about the effect of the variable that does not covary with the outcome than of the variable that does. This hypothesis was strongly supported by the data. Almost all students, at all ages, drew the correct conclusion about the effect of the covarying variable. But only 50 per cent drew the conclusion that the non-covarying variable had no effect (the same proportion as would have arisen from guessing). This finding suggests that students need more opportunities to reflect on, and learn how to deal with, the inevitable uncertainty (error) in all measurements, and more practice in using data to discriminate between instances of covariation and non-covariation.

In another study of young subjects (US Grades 2 and 4; age 8 and 10), Masnick and Klahr (2004) found that many children could recognize sources of error in an investigation, and could assess its importance in different situations, but have yet to integrate their ideas about error into a more coherent whole. Only a few, for example, referred to errors in justifying conclusions from experiments. Masnick and Klahr noted improvement between their two age points, but concluded that researchers have much more to learn about students' understanding of measurement error.

Finally, some studies have explored experimental design and evidence evaluation together. One is the study by Kanari and Millar (2004) discussed above. Another, by Klahr and Dunbar (1988), set subjects the task of discovering the purpose of the RPT button on a programmable robotic toy (called Bigtrak). From their observations, they propose a general model of Scientific Discovery as Dual Search (SDDS), in which subjects' actions are seen as involving a mental search of the 'spaces' of possible hypotheses and possible experiments. In a subsequent study of 22 US Grade 3–6 students (age 9–12), Dunbar and Klahr (1989) found that children did not always check that their hypothesis is consistent with previous data, had difficulty abandoning a current hypothesis (perhaps through limited ability to search the space of possible hypotheses) and often designed experiments to 'prove' the current hypothesis rather than to test it. Although the name Klahr and Dunbar give to their model includes the term 'scientific discovery', it is striking that their study used a technological task which has some rather significant differences from many scientific tasks. The student sample was also very small. So, general conclusions about 'scientific reasoning' are not strongly supported. The SDDS model, however, may in itself be a useful product of research, offering a general framework for interpreting students' actions in scientific investigation tasks that involve generating and testing hypotheses, or possible explanations for a phenomenon.

Research by science educators

Research by science educators on students' performance of science investigations has tended to focus on issues arising directly from classroom practice and curriculum policy. In England, the work of the Assessment of Performance Unit (APU) between 1974 and 1990 has had a major influence on the curriculum and on subsequent research. The APU was set up to assess and monitor the performance of students aged 11, 13 and 15 in England and Wales in several subjects including science. For science, the APU assessment framework had six categories:

1. use of graphical and symbolic representation;
2. use of apparatus and measuring instruments;
3. observation;
4. interpretation and application of (a) presented information and (b) science concepts;
5. planning of investigations;
6. performance of investigations.

The last of these categories was seen as incorporating all of the others, and hence as a culmination of science learning. This in turn lent weight to the view that school science should include investigative practical work and that students' ability to carry out investigations could and should be assessed. Over a period of 15 years, the APU collected data from around 16,000 students in 600 schools. The findings are summarized by Black (1990) and presented more fully in a series of 11 major research reports, 11 short reports for teachers, and four large review reports (for references, see Black, 1990). Further analysis of APU data by the Evaluation and Monitoring Unit (EMU) of the Schools Examination and Assessment Council (SEAC) led to two short reports dealing directly with students' performance of practical science investigations (Archenhold et al., 1991; Strang et al., 1991). Given the sheer volume of data reported, it is only possible here to provide a very selective overview of the APU findings on performance of investigations. Around 60 per cent of 11-year-olds, for example, were found to be able to put a problem into a form that could be investigated scientifically, but the proportion able to carry out subsequent stages of the investigation, such as identifying variables to be changed and controlled, taking steps to increase validity of the data collected, and using results to draw a conclusion fell steadily to around 20 per cent. Around half of all 11-year-olds were able to control variables in some situations, and the proportion that controlled variables increased with age. At all ages, tasks involving comparison of cases were found to be easier than those with a continuous independent variable whose values have to be set by the investigator. Pupils in general did less well in investigations set in everyday contexts than those set in clearly 'scientific' contexts – suggesting that many did not see a need to 'act scientifically' in everyday settings.

While the APU reports provide a rich and often fascinating picture of students' performance of practical investigations, they do not lead to a general model to account for observed variations in performance and characterize the main stages of progression. The evidence points, rather, to the conclusion that performance on investigation tasks is strongly content-dependent (Donnelly, 1987; Strang et al., 1991) – that it is influenced more by what a student knows about the domain of the investigation than by their investigative, or science reasoning, 'skills'.

Despite this evidence of the strong content-dependence of student performance, there was a surge of interest in England in the late 1980s in the 'process approach' – the view that science education should focus on developing students' ability to carry out certain content-independent 'science process skills', such as observing, classifying, hypothesizing, designing experiments, and so on. These skills, it was argued, were transferable to situations beyond school science and were more durable than content knowledge (Screen, 1986). Criticisms of the process approach in principle (for example, Millar and Driver, 1987; Millar, 1989; Gott and Duggan, 1995) are supported by a study by Lock (1990) who administered four practical tasks to a sample of 36 students of secondary school age. Their performance of elements of these tasks involving observation, planning, interpretation, and reporting was assessed. The analysis looked at the correlation between a student's performance on the same 'skill' in two different tasks. For several, including observation and reporting, this correlation was low. Given that factors such as general educational attainment, or attainment in science, would be expected to account for much of the observed variation in performance on all of these tasks, this again suggests that performance on tasks involving 'skills' such as observing, hypothesizing, designing experiments, and so on, is strongly content-dependent, indeed that these 'skills' are not well-defined constructs in a psychometric sense.

The English National Curriculum, introduced in 1989, was more strongly influenced by the work of the APU than by the 'process approach'. It included one Attainment Target, carrying a 50 per cent weighting in assessment terms at the primary (elementary) stage and 25 per cent at secondary (high school), on 'Exploration of science', requiring that 'Pupils should develop the intellectual and practical skills that allow them to . . . develop a fuller understanding of . . . the procedures of scientific exploration and investigation' (DES/WO, 1989, p. 3). This target set out, in line with the other attainment targets, descriptions in content-independent terms of a set of 10 hierarchical levels of performance – a requirement which strongly influenced the drafting committee's decision to eschew a 'process approach'. Instead, progression was described principally in terms of the ability to plan and conduct investigations of increasing complexity of the effect of one or more independent variables on a dependent variable. This focus might be seen as influenced by the APU's choice of tasks, which can in turn be traced back to the role of control of variables in Piaget's theories. It was criticized by some as presenting an unduly narrow view of scientific enquiry, which underemphasized the role of theoretical ideas and frameworks in deciding what to investigate, which variables to consider in doing so, and how to interpret and evaluate the outcomes (Donnelly et al., 1996). It also led to a perceived need for more research to map out in greater detail the nature and extent of progression in variables handling ability.

In a publication prior to the introduction of the National Curriculum, Gott et al. (1988) distinguished categoric and continuous independent variables. Foulds and Gott (1988) then proposed a hierarchy of investigations, from those involving a single categoric independent variable (IV), to those involving a single continuous IV, to those involving more than one IV – while acknowledging the evidence from their own work and that of others (including the APU) that task content strongly influences student performance of all types of investigation. In a project commissioned by the National Curriculum Council (the then regulator of curriculum in England), Gott and his co-workers explored a more elaborated version of this hierarchical model, which sub-divided the top category into tasks involving two categoric IVs, and tasks involving two continuous IVs. They then analysed the responses of a large sample of students (n = 2,208; age 11–13) to 23 investigative tasks spread across the four levels of their hierarchy. The findings are presented in a research report (Foulds et al., 1992), and summarized in a subsequent book (Gott and Duggan, 1995, Chapter 4). Again, a major finding was that task content strongly influences performance, but Gott and Duggan also concluded that a model based on the type and number of independent variables can help to account for observed performance of variables-type investigations and provides a means of characterizing student progression. Like other studies, they reported improvement with age, in this case principally in interpreting data collected. Again, tasks in scientific contexts were done better than those in everyday settings. Finally, they reported that student 'motivation appears to be high, although the evidence to support this statement is of an anecdotal nature' (1995, p. 64). This finding may, of course, be partly due to the relative novelty of such tasks at that time.

Perhaps a more significant finding from this work is that teaching of what Gott and Duggan term 'concepts of evidence' led to improved performance. The idea that the quality of a student's performance of a science investigation task is a consequence of their knowledge of specific facts and ideas about data collection and interpretation, and about experimental design (procedural knowledge), rather than their planning or investigating 'skills', was explored further in the *Procedural and Conceptual Knowledge in Science (PACKS)* project (Millar et al., 1994). The PACKS model of the investigative process (1994, p. 222) identifies the student's understanding of the purpose of the task, and their understanding of measurement, as two important elements of procedural knowledge. The first may account for the finding from several studies that investigations in a scientific context are done better than ones in everyday settings. Millar et al. (1996) reported significant numbers of students reinterpreting tasks set within a scientific 'frame' and carrying them out within a 'modelling' or 'engineering' frame – aiming to produce a desired effect or phenomenon, or to maximize or optimize a desired effect, respectively. To explore students' understanding of measurement, Lubben and Millar (1996) used written probes involving interpretation and evaluation of given data. They suggest that only a minority of students by age 16 are fully comfortable with the use of repeated measurements to assess the reliability of a measurement, and the use of the range of a set of repeat measurements when judging whether an observed difference should be treated as a 'real effect'.

Building on similar ideas about procedural knowledge, Roberts and Gott (2004) propose the use of a written test of procedural understanding in science to improve assessment of practical capability. In a subsequent study (Roberts and Gott, 2006), they report that scores on this test do not correlate strongly with measures based on students' written reports on an extended project, raising the question of which approach, or combination of approaches, provides the best measure of students' understanding. This finding is similar to that of Baxter and Shavelson (1994) who evaluated several surrogates for direct one-to-one observation in assessing student performance on inquiry tasks. Only students' written reports correlated adequately with observation. Others, such as performance on computer-simulated investigations, and written tests consisting of short-answer or multiple-choice questions, correlated only weakly.

One stimulus to explore other methods of assessment of practical capability is the high cost of practical assessment based on extended tasks, alongside the recognition that performance is very strongly content-dependent, meaning that several tasks are needed for a reliable assessment of any individual student. In England, another source of discontent has been evidence of the narrowness of practice stimulated by national curriculum Attainment Target 1 and its assessment. Watson et al. (1999a) note how the idea of a 'fair test' has come to dominate teachers' language and practice – and that this is often understood by students in ways that go well beyond its intended meaning as 'an investigation in which variables are controlled'. They found that primary and secondary pupils in England, of very different ages, were carrying out investigations with similar levels of demand in ways that displayed similar levels of performance (Watson et al., 1999b). In addition, the variety of investigations used was very restricted. They report that 30 per cent of all investigations carried out by pupils in the 9–13 age range were in the same four contexts, and that most pupils by age 13 had twice investigated solubility or rate of dissolution (usually of sugar in water). The *ASE-King's Science Investigations in Schools* (*AKSIS*) project sought to broaden and improve practice. It took the view, in line with several of the studies and projects discussed above, that 'too much reliance is placed on learning skills and processes by doing, rather than being taught them explicitly' (Watson et al., 2006, p. 196). To address this, the project developed a set of resources to support explicit teaching of ideas about investigation design (Goldsworthy et al., 2000). Goldsworthy reports improvement in the quality of pupils' investigative work in the classes of teachers who had participated in in-service courses based around these resources (cited in Watson et al., 2006, p. 199).

The effectiveness of practical work in stimulating students' interest and increasing motivation to study science

It is often claimed that practical work stimulates students' interest in science and increases motivation to continue studying science beyond the point where it is a compulsory subject. Research studies from many countries report that students enjoy practical work in science. Lunetta et al. (2007, pp. 389–400) list several studies reporting positive student views of practical work. For example, Ben-Zvi et al. (1977) reported that Israeli students regarded practical work as more interesting than teacher demonstrations, lectures or watching video recordings. Dawson and Bennett (1981) asked lower secondary (junior high) school students in Australia to rate their liking for 17 teaching methods. Methods involving student activity (doing practical tasks, making models) were rated highly.

An online survey in the UK of students' views of the science curriculum, which was unusual in that the survey instrument was developed by a panel of school students, collected responses from almost 1,500 students aged 11–18 (Cerini et al., 2003). One item asked respondents to identify the three methods of teaching and learning (from a given list of 11) they found 'most enjoyable', and the three they found 'most useful and effective in helping you understand your school science'. 'Doing a science experiment in class' was chosen as one of the three most enjoyable by 71 per cent, putting it third after 'going on a science trip or excursion' (85 per cent) and 'looking at videos' (75 per cent). As 'doing a science investigation' was also one of the options listed, and was in the top three choices of 50 per cent of the sample, this might suggest that practical work as a whole is ranked higher than third for 'enjoyment'. However, 'doing a science experiment' and 'doing a science investigation' were markedly less highly rated as 'useful and effective' for understanding, appearing in the top three choices of 38 per cent and 32 per cent of students respectively. One weakness of this study is in the use of the terms 'experiment' and 'investigation' which may not have been understood by respondents in the way the researchers intended. Also, the study used an opportunity sample, and the online delivery is quite likely to have introduced bias. For this reason, we might have more confidence in the reported difference between 'enjoyable' and 'useful and effective' ratings than in the absolute values of either (see, also, Chapter 11).

Gardner and Gauld (1990) speculate that students may find practical work enjoyable because it offers a change from other kinds of activity. Donnelly (1998), in a study discussed above, suggests that the labels students typically use to describe types of science lesson activity are 'practical', 'writing' (by them), and 'talking' (by the teacher). Bennett suggests that students' declared liking for practical work may stem from the fact that it provides 'welcome relief from listening to teachers and from writing, a task which many pupils report as being something they particularly dislike about science lessons' (2003, p. 86). Several student comments reported by Abrahams (2009) tend to corroborate this hypothesis. These were recorded in field-notes made during observations of 25 unselected science practical lessons in English secondary schools. Abrahams noted that most student comments about practical work were comparative, and that it was often said to be enjoyable compared to writing, rather than *per se*. These students also reported doing less practical work in biology than the other sciences, yet more said that they were planning to continue with biology after age 16 – casting doubt on the claim that practical work is a factor that strongly motivates subject choice.

While most studies report positive student views of practical work, Head, from a sample of students' writing in science, reported that 'a significant minority . . . expressed a dislike for practical work' (1982, p. 637). He suggested that a fuller understanding requires more precise information, for example, on the types of practical work that students find motivating. Kempa and Dias (1990) suggest that students generally enjoy practical tasks where the purpose is clear, which provide an appropriate level of challenge, and which allow them some control over what they do. But they also suggest that students may have individual preferences about instructional modes, which may result in differing views about the learning value of practical work and a range of affective responses to it. Murphy (1991) summarizes evidence from the APU data and from other studies of gender differences in performance on practical tasks. She notes in particular that there may be striking differences between boys' and girls' perceptions of the same practical task and hence in their responses to it, and argues for classroom strategies that 'take account of boys' and girls' present preferred styles of working and interests as well as providing opportunities for them to reflect critically on them' (1991, p. 121) (see, also, Chapter 11).

The effectiveness of practical work in developing understanding of the nature of science

It is nowadays quite widely accepted that science education should seek to develop students' understanding of the scientific enterprise itself – of the nature of scientific knowledge, the methods used to generate and test knowledge claims, and so on. This is usually termed 'understanding of the nature of science'. Lederman and Abd-el-Khalick argue that students are unlikely to come to an understanding of key components of the nature of science

> solely through learning about the content of science or its processes...a concerted effort on the part of science educators and teachers to explicitly guide learners in their attempts to develop proper understandings of the nature of the scientific enterprise is essential.
>
> (1998, p. 83)

While this might be so if the aim is a reflective understanding of the epistemology of science, it seems likely that fundamental ideas about science, such as the central role of data from observation and measurement in developing scientific knowledge, are learned, perhaps tacitly rather than as explicit declarative knowledge, through the experience of doing practical work.

There is little research evidence on the effectiveness of practical work that has been explicitly designed to develop students' understandings of the nature of science. In one study in the USA, Carey et al. (1989) evaluated a teaching unit in which 12-year-old students tried to discriminate between two explanations for the role of yeast in making dough rise: that yeast is alive and breathes out a gas, and that there is a chemical reaction between yeast and other ingredients in which a gas is evolved. Twenty-seven students were interviewed before and after participating in the unit to probe their understanding of the nature and purpose of scientific enquiry. The researchers concluded that children of this age have epistemological views that are different from those of scientifically literate adults, with many holding what they term 'a "copy theory" of knowledge: knowledge is a faithful copy of the world that is imparted to the knower when the knower encounters the world' (1989, p. 526). From this viewpoint, scientists can only be wrong 'through ignorance, that is, by not having looked at that aspect of nature' (1989, p. 526). For these children 'knowledge directly reflects reality, so the problem of examining the fit between the two does not arise' (1989, p. 526). Post-intervention interviews suggested that many students were able to move beyond this kind of under-standing, and to see experiments as tests of ideas. The study did not explore whether this understanding was durable, or transferrable to other contexts.

While the evidence of this single study is that practical work, carefully designed and staged, can change students' ideas about the nature of science, we should also be aware of an underlying tension between teaching about the nature of science, and teaching core scientific knowledge. The principal objective of much practical work is to develop students' understanding of well-established scientific knowledge. Its purpose is to communicate ideas, rather than to provide a warrant for accepting them. Reflecting on this issue, Layton concluded that:

> It is difficult to see how both objectives, an understanding of the mature concepts and theories of science and an understanding of the processes by which scientific knowledge grows, can be achieved simultaneously...The problem of reconciling these objectives in school science teaching has been considerably underestimated.
>
> (1973, pp. 176–7)

This 'problem' is well illustrated by the evidence of teachers' practices and views reported by Nott and Smith (1995). They looked at teachers' responses to practical tasks where the students do not observe the intended phenomenon or do not draw the intended conclusion from their observations. Teachers had a repertoire of ways of 'talking their way through' such situations. Many were also willing to use practices such as tampering with practical set-ups, without the students' knowledge, to ensure that students made the intended observa-tions (Nott and Wellington, 1996). This finding suggests that these teachers, whatever they might say in other contexts, implicitly recognized a significant difference in purpose between the teaching and research laboratories. In gen-eral, the teaching of well-established scientific knowledge is likely to involve practices that carry implicit messages about warrants for belief that are rather different from those we might put forward when talking explicitly about the epistemology of science (see, also, Chapter 2 in this volume).

Research on practical work – the way forward

The central question explored in this chapter is: what does research have to say about the effectiveness of practical work as a teaching and learning strategy? So what, in a nutshell, might we say in answer to this question?

Any sensible discussion must surely start from the recognition that science is, in a fundamental sense, 'a practical subject'. Its subject matter is the natural world; the core of the scientific approach is its commitment to privileging observational data in developing and evaluating knowledge claims. Research evidence, however, clearly shows – in line with what a thoughtful analysis would anyhow suggest – that explanatory ideas do not 'emerge' from data. Indeed, they are often not at all obvious even when you have the data. The evidence from research is that much practical work makes little difference to students' understanding of scientific ideas. Many studies have found no significant difference in understanding between students taught a range of topics with and without hands-on practical work. Some other studies, however, suggest that the reasons may lie in the way practical work is used. Studies of carefully designed practical tasks which 'scaffold' students' efforts to understand show evidence of better learning, as do studies of virtual experimentation in association with physical experimentation. Both increase the minds-on element of the learning activity. More research on the design of practical activities, in particular the design features that encourage more thoughtful student engagement and are likely to lead to better understanding, are surely needed. This is particularly important for practical activities intended to develop understanding of concepts, explanations, models and theories.

In evaluating the effectiveness of practical work, we also need to consider carefully the 'unit' we evaluate. We cannot expect a single practical activity, even one with a very clear learning objective, to result in long-term change in students' understanding. Practical activities should be seen, and evaluated, within a teaching sequence that includes activities of diverse kinds, designed as a whole to promote learning of certain ideas or skills. In the research studies reported on the learning outcomes of topics taught with and without practical work, little information is provided on the nature of the practical activities or on how they were supported by other lesson activities before and after. More studies are needed of the role of practical work within carefully planned teaching sequences, on topics where we believe that practical work makes a significant contribution to understanding. Hart et al. (2000) also make an important distinction between the 'purpose' of a practical activity from the perspective of the learner, and its 'aim' in the teacher's eyes. They argue that students frequently do not really know what, in learning terms, they are doing the practical activity for. Recognizing and addressing this issue is surely central to improving its effectiveness.

What general conclusions might be drawn from research on practical work intended to develop students' understanding of scientific enquiry? One very clear finding of research is that performance of investigative practical tasks is strongly context-dependent. Another is that evidence of improvement in performance with age is less clear-cut than might be hoped or expected. On balance, the research evidence, from several studies of different kinds, suggests that improvement is more likely to come from carefully planned explicit teaching of some key ideas and understandings about measurement, investigation design, and data analysis, than from practice alone. It also seems clear, however, that the science education community has not yet developed a clear, or agreed, analysis of the knowledge and understandings that underpin the kinds of practical performances we would like to see students display when undertaking a science investigation. As a result, there is no clear rationale for choosing the investigative tasks we put to students, or for describing clearly the observable features of the progression in performance we would like to see. Without a clearer definition of the learning outcomes we desire from this sort of activity, it is difficult to see how more research in this area can make significant progress. The need is for better theoretical frameworks to guide research, rather than for more empirical data.

Finally, one research finding that seems clear from several studies (discussed above), and from informal experience, is that students in general like practical work in science. While this is not in itself a justification for its use, it is a significant incentive to work on ways of making practical work more effective in promoting learning – and in the process perhaps changing short-term student engagement into a longer-term interest and enjoyment in science.

Note

1. 'Effect size' is calculated by dividing the difference between the mean scores of the experimental and control group by the standard error of the scores of the control group. For an educational intervention, an effect size of > 0.4 is quite large.

Further reading

Hodson, D. (1993) Re-thinking old ways: towards a more critical approach to practical work in school science, *Studies in Science Education,* 22: 85–142.

Lunetta, V. N., Hofstein, A., and Clough, M. P. (2007) Teaching and learning in the school science laboratory: an analysis of research, theory, and practice. In S. K. Abell and N. G. Lederman (eds) *Handbook of Research on Science Education.* Mahwah, NJ: Lawrence Erlbaum, pp. 393–431.

Woolnough, B. E. (ed.) (1991) *Practical Science.* Milton Keynes: Open University Press.

Woolnough, B. E. and Alsop, T. (1985) *Practical Work in Science.* Cambridge: Cambridge University Press.

7 The role of language in the learning and teaching of science

Maria Evagorou and Jonathan Osborne

> *Learning to become a legitimate participant in a community involves learning how to talk.*
>
> (Wenger, 1998, p. 105)

> *Science exists because scientists are writers are speakers. We know this, if only intuitively, from the very moment we embark upon a career in biology, physics or geology. As a shared form of knowledge, scientific understanding is inseparable from the written and spoken word. There are no boundaries, no walls between the doing of science and the communication of it; communicating is the doing of science. If data falls in the forest and no one hears it . . . Research that never sees the dark of print remains either hidden or virtual or nonexistent. Publication and public speaking are how scientific work gains a presence, a shared reality in the world.*
>
> (Montgomery, 2003, p. 1)

Introduction

Language is central in everyday life since it is one of the tools for understanding the world around us, communicating with peers, expressing our ideas and developing our knowledge. Even though language is not the only tool for understanding or apprehending the world, 'becoming an educated person necessarily involves learning some special ways of using language' (Mercer and Littleton, 2007, p. 2). Within classrooms, language is the principal means of communication, the tool used to reflect upon our thoughts, and share our experiences with others (Mercer et al., 2004), and is thus both a technology for transmitting information (Rivard, 2004) and a means for interpreting our experiences (Sutton, 1998).

But why are language and literacy so important for science? First, as Keys (1999, p. 115) states, 'Language does not merely describe or reflect pre-existing conceptual structures; language actively creates those structures.' In theorizing about the natural world and developing explanations for the phenomena we observe, we are forced to refer to objects we can see, or to imagined entities such as atoms, germs and electric current, or to concepts such as velocity, power or force. Language is the tool by which such reference is achieved. More specifically, in science, language is the means by which we envisage new ideas, comparing the structure of an atom to the solar system, the flow of an electric current to the flow of water in a pipe, or the packing of atoms to the way oranges are stacked at the greengrocers. In this manner, our ideas are made tangible and communicable. Scientific knowledge is thus dependent inextricably on language and language is also central to our ability to think. As Billig (1996, p. 141) argues: 'Humans do not converse because they have inner thoughts to express, but they have thoughts because they are able to converse.'

Language is also central to the activity of doing science. For, once we have ideas or hypotheses, they must be tested and data collected. Such data must be coded and represented using a range of representational forms that can vary from tables and charts to computer visualizations so that the meaning is comprehensible to others. Drawing on all of these representational forms, the scientist attempts to communicate their specific meaning and their claims to have uncovered new knowledge. It is impossible to envisage an activity we could call science without such tools. Likewise, in learning science, language is also central to communicating the ideas of science. For, surprising as it may seem, research shows that science classrooms are places where the activities of talking, writing and reading – all language activities, are those which predominate (Newton et al., 1999).

Such points, it might be argued, are not unique to science. Scientists, however, use language in special ways. Not only is there a specialist scientific vocabulary consisting of words which are recognizably unfamiliar but there are familiar words such as 'energy', 'power' and 'force' which must acquire new meanings. Moreover, the charts, symbols, diagrams and mathematics that science deploys to convey ideas, are essential to communicating meaning and students must learn to both recognize and understand their use. The challenge for the teacher then is to introduce and explain this new vocabulary; the challenge for the student is to construct new meanings from such a language. Not surprisingly then, the most prominent theories of learning consider learning and teaching as mediated by the use of language (see, also, Chapter 4 in this volume). From an information transmission perspective, communicating an idea requires it to be encoded by the speaker into words and decoded by the listener. The common difficulties with this process are captured by the cartoon in Figure 7.1. The constructivist view of learning sees the process of decoding as one which depends upon the existing prior knowledge which the listener can bring to that process. Constructing meaning from a text is not simply a process of word recognition. Rather, the words must be interpreted and their meaning weighed and argued over. The implication of this perspective is that the teacher is not just a teacher of a new language – the language of science, but that they must also help by acting as an interpreter – somebody who can explain how to derive the correct meaning from the discourse and texts that populate the science classroom.

Figure 7.1 Elliptical orbit explanation

What then does it mean to be literate in science? A seminal contribution is offered by Norris and Philips (2003) who argue that there are two forms of scientific literacy: a fundamental sense and a derived sense. The fundamental sense is one which sees the process of reading and writing as a constitutive element of science itself and where reading is a process of comprehending, analysing and interpreting texts. Norris and Phillips argue that reading and writing are not functional tools necessary to accomplish the scientist's goal (a view that many teachers of science commonly hold). If they were, and if the processes of reading and writing were to be removed, then there should still be some residual activity that is recognizable as science. Thus, reading and writing are constitutive of science itself in that they are 'essential elements of the whole' (Norris and Phillips, 2003, p. 226). By this they mean, for instance, that the trace on the oscilloscope has no meaning unless it is both labelled and its meaning interpreted, either orally or in writing. In what sense can the young child measuring the temperature of boiling water be said to be 'doing science' unless she records the measurement and shares her value with others? The scientist is reliant on a whole battery of semiotic tools to construct meaning, such as graphs, charts, diagrams, symbols, mathematics and language itself. Indeed, science has its own reserved language where familiar words are used for unfamiliar concepts, for example, the 'colour' of a quark, the 'resistance' of a wire or the 'field' produced by a magnet.

The ability to undertake to comprehend science requires a body of appropriate background knowledge and a set of interpretive strategies that help to decode texts that can often be difficult and complex. In contrast to literacy in its fundamental sense, literacy in its derived sense refers to the ability to critically evaluate and analyse scientific texts. This task can only be undertaken by people who are literate in a fundamental sense. This stance should not be taken to imply that individuals should only engage in activities intended to develop their fundamental literacy in science. Clearly the two are interrelated. For instance, when discussing the merits of nuclear versus wind power, the teacher has an opportunity to develop students' skills to think critically by examining both the arguments for and against as well as developing their fundamental literacy by exploring their understanding of the concepts of energy transfer, nuclear fission and electrical power.

Nevertheless, because reading and writing are activities that are constitutive of science, and because the language of science is complex and foreign to many students, we see teaching science as fundamentally a process of teaching a language – one in which the teacher has both to help students to interpret and construct meaning from scientific text and one in which they must provide opportunities to develop their fluency and capabilities with that language. In the classroom, three main forms of language are used as tools for understanding, communicating, and developing knowledge: talk, writing and reading. In this chapter, therefore, we explore specifically the role of each of these language forms in the learning and teaching of science, and provide examples of language activities that can be used to enhance student learning.

Why language is central to the teaching of science

All professions rapidly establish a reserved language for communication. This form of coded shorthand is essential to enhancing the functional purpose of language – to communicate complex concepts in an effective and comprehensible manner. The study of how language achieves this purpose is known as functional linguistics. In the case of science, it has evolved a highly complex means of communicating ideas within the scientific community and, as Halliday and Martin (1993, p. 202), two leading exponents of functional linguistics, argue:

> Technical language has evolved in order to classify, decompose and explain. The major scientific genres – report, explanation and experiment – have evolved to structure texts which document a scientist's world view. The functionality of these genres and the technicality they contain cannot be avoided; it has to be dealt with. To deal with it, teachers need an understanding of the structure of the genres and the grammar of technicality.

A corollary of this view is that the teacher of science is fundamentally a *teacher of a language and that* their task is to educate their students how to construct meaning from the texts of science by reading, writing and talking science. While a primary focus might be to develop an understanding of the major concepts and explanatory theories that science has to offer, such understanding will only be developed by the student constructing new meanings and concepts (Driver et al., 1994) by engaging in language acts – either written or oral. In such a manner, the discourse of the scientific community is appropriated by the individual.

More fundamentally, language is essential to science as our ideas and concepts about the world are constructed in a hierarchy. From our everyday interaction with the macroscopic world we construct representations of objects which are tangible and accessible to sensori-motor experiences, for example, the Moon, the eye, a chair, a spring. These we can represent with diagrams, pictures and are aware that others will have, most likely, have had experiences with such objects (Harré, 1986; Osborne, 1996). Reference to such objects is then a means of fixing the meaning of descriptive terms in the commonality of our shared experiences. However, many of the entities that we wish to discuss in science, for example, a cell, an electric current or a reaction rate, are unobservable entities which are only accessible to our senses through instrumentation. All such entities depend on *a representation* which must draw on our knowledge of commonly observable entities. So a cell is pictured as a kind of brick, electric current is talked of in terms of a flow of current, and particles are visualized as hard balls. To talk about these and construct representations of them we are dependent on the use of metaphor and simile. And 'In this way, through metaphor, new vocabulary can be created within the existing structure of language, so securing the intelligibility of the term in the context of use' (Harré, 1986, p. 77). Teachers commonly engage in a language game of 'seeing it my way' (Ogborn et al., 1996) using analogies and metaphors to construct student understanding. As such, metaphor is not simply a useful adjunct for scientific thinking but an essential component of theory itself enabling the construction of mental models. Such models can then be manipulated to make predictions which lead to the discovery of hidden causes, or the postulation of new theoretical entities. For instance, Harvey's observation that the volume of blood emerging from the heart on each contraction could only be explained if it was seen to be analogical to a pump and not an organ producing blood.

Indeed, the vast majority of scientific theories are descriptions and hypotheses about imagined entities, for example, the electrons, cells, and molecules which populate the world and the processes by which they interact. In constructing a picture of such objects with students, language is not a peripheral adjunct but a core means by which students' understanding and visualizations are realized. Support for such a view comes from research into the use of analogies to engender conceptual change (Treagust et al., 1996). These researchers examined the use of an analogy by students in explaining refraction and found that almost two-thirds of the students (from a sample of 29) in the class where a teacher used an analogy were able to generate a plausible explanation compared to less than a tenth of the class that made no use of such an analogy. As the authors concluded, 'The analogy provided students with language they could comfortably utilise to transform an abstract idea into an articulate explanation' (1996, p. 222). Analogy is, therefore not merely desirable but an essential tool to develop student understanding.

Difficulties with language in science

A common misapprehension is to think that constructing meaning from language is a simple process. Much of education is deeply rooted in the belief that the transmission of information is a straightforward act where success is the norm and failure is the exception and the notion that learning occurs through some kind of conduit between the teacher, and the taught is a metaphor which dominates much of our thinking (Reddy, 1979). Reddy suggests that the reality is more often the converse, that is, most acts of communication are failures and success is the exception. Why is this? We speak of needing to 'get it across' or conveying a message. In this sense, ideas are objects that can be put into words and which language captures. These are then sent over a conduit or channel of communication to another person by way of words. The other person then extracts the ideas from the words. Such a metaphor entails the view that ideas can be extracted and can exist independently of people.

Everyday thinking of this nature, however, fails to acknowledge that reading and making meaning are constructive acts. Constructing meaning is not simply a process of decoding words as words only make sense in the context of their use (Wittgenstein, 1961). For instance, the word 'weight' in the sentence 'he felt the full weight of the law bear down on him' does not have the same meaning as that in the sentence 'weight is a force which is measured in Newtons'. The basic problem here is that words have multiple meanings and their meanings can only be decoded from the context. As Phillips (2002) argues, in such a context, constructing meaning involves the integration of both the information provided by the text or the teacher – *and* the reader's knowledge. Through this process, something over and above the words is created. A student who has never met the use of a word within a specific context or meaning will be unable to construct the meaning the teacher intends. Given that there is evidence that the average science course between age 14 to 16 introduces 6–8 new words a lesson (Merzyn, 1987), an essential task for the teacher of science is to show how the word is used in appropriate contexts and to explain the meaning it carries.

Evidence that students have difficulty decoding the meanings of words in their context comes from a considerable body of research that has been conducted looking at students' ability to construct the correct meaning from sentences containing specific words known to be 'troublesome'. Work by Cassels and Johnstone (1985) led them to believe that many pupils and older students misunderstood the language of science but this was *not* caused primarily by

Table 7.1 Difficult words in science

abundant	adjacent	contrast
incident	composition	contrast
complex	component	converse
spontaneous	emit	exert
relevant	linear	negligible
valid	random	sequence

Source: Cassels and Johnstone (1985, p. 14).

problems with *technical* language. The main problem lay in the vocabulary and usage of normal English in a science context. Hence, they decided to probe pupils' understandings by using multiple-choice tests which examined their grasp of words in different contexts (Cassels and Johnstone, 1985). With these tests they were able to survey a huge sample of students across 200 different secondary schools. Typically, students would be presented with multiple-choice questions of the form: 'Which sentence uses the word <u>excite</u> correctly?':

   a. Just the thought of the party began to excite him.
   b. Dogs should not be allowed to excite on pavements.
   c. The freshly made tea was left to excite to improve its flavour.
   d. The girl began to excite a page from her book.

Cassels and Johnstone (1985) described pupils' understanding of very few words as 'disastrous'. Understanding of a larger number of words was deemed to be 'satisfactory', for example: appropriate, estimate, isolate, modified, standard, contribute, detect, disperse, essential, and exclude. However, *very few* words were well understood in all of the different types of multiple choice tests used. Table 7.1 shows words for which understanding was found to be 'weak' or 'very weak'. As the authors point out, in 'a surprising number of cases pupils take the *opposite* meaning to that intended: negligible = 'a lot'; initial = 'final'; random = 'well ordered' (Cassels and Johnstone, 1985, p. 14).

Subsequent studies have repeated this work in one form on another. For instance, Pickersgill and Lock (1991) conducted a similar study from which a list of 20 words emerged and concluded that 'for many students these words are inaccessible'. Similarly to Cassels and Johnstone's (1985) study, they too found that pupils often take the opposite meaning to the true one, that is, the antonym.

Another study which adopted a different approach used 50 non-technical and 25 technical terms with a sample of 306 students with an average age of 17. This study compared the percentage who claimed to know a word's meaning with the percentage that actually did (Farrell and Ventura, 1998). Unsurprisingly, the latter percentage was 'notably smaller' than the former. For instance, 91 per cent claimed to know the use of the word 'relative' but only 44 per cent actually chose the correct use; 99 per cent claimed to know the use of the word 'power' but only 54 per cent did, and so on.

Teachers of science can easily use words ambiguously themselves. For instance, the word 'electricity' although apparently technical could be, and is, used to refer to 'electric charge', 'electric power', 'electrical voltage' or 'electrical current'. Its precise meaning can only be determined by examining the context of its use, as in the sentence, 'The demand for electricity was low' where it is referring to electrical power, as opposed to the sentence 'The electricity nearly killed him', where it is referring to electrical current (Wellington and Osborne, 2001). Clearly, students will find it difficult to construct the intended meaning from such sentences unless the exact referent is specified.

Logical connectives

Logical connectives, for example, words such as 'however', 'therefore', and 'because', are essential to the process of constructing an argument as they establish the relationships between claims, warrants and data. They also help to contrast and compare similar and different phenomena. Gardner (1975) found 75 connectives that posed difficulty to the 15-year-old pupils in his research in that they made the text more difficult to comprehend or understand. The common response by authors and publishers of science texts has been to excise them in an attempt to improve readability (Wellington and Osborne, 2001). Yet, as Halliday and Martin (1993) point out, logical connectives are not an adjunct to scientific text – they are fundamental elements used to explain and justify the claims that science makes about the world. As they point out – 'science is unthinkable without the technical language science has developed to construct its alternative world view' (1993, p. 202). The appropriate response for anybody attempting to provide an education that develops students' ability to read and comprehend scientific text is not to excise such words but to realize that time must be spent assisting students to construct meaning from text and to develop their skills in their use.

Science as a multi-semiotic language

As we have already pointed out, the language of science is more than words. Rather, meaning in science is constructed through a judicious use of charts, graphs, symbols, mathematics, diagrams and words. Because of the way it uses different forms of representation to construct meaning, science is said to be a multi-semiotic (Lemke, 1998) or multimodal (Kress et al., 2001). As Lemke (1998) argues:

> Science does not speak of the world in the language of words alone, and in many cases it simply cannot do so. The natural language of science is a synergistic integration of words, diagrams, pictures, graphs,

maps, equations, tables, charts, and other forms of visual mathematical expression.

The essential problem for science is that natural language is very limited in its ability to describe continuous variation, shape and the interrelationships of structure, form and function. Indeed, as Lemke argues, often it *cannot* do so. For instance, consider the common standard diagram of the heart. Imagine for an instance, if you will, how difficult it would be to describe this organ to another without the use of diagrammatic representation. Likewise, many other phenomena and their patterns of interaction are best described in the language of mathematics which becomes a bridge between verbal language and the abstractions scientists seek to express. So complex are some of the concepts and ideas that science wishes to capture and communicate that its language becomes dependent on a synergy of semiotic signs – that is, symbols to represent elements, quantities and units; graphs and charts to summarize frequencies and patterns in the data; tables to summarize numerical data; and mathematics to express relationships between physical variables. That these are all interdependent can be seen from a cursory examination of any contemporary scientific paper. Temporarily excising one of these components makes the process of constructing its meaning significantly harder, if not impossible. Thus, the task confronting the student is not one of learning the language of science but one of learning a set of plural *languages* used by science. As Lemke elegantly describes it, the use of so many 'languages' makes communication in science appear to be as if: 'we said the first words of each sentence in Chinese, then the next few in Swahili, and then the last few in Hindi, and in the next sentence we started in Swahili, . . . and so on.'

Moreover, the language of science is cumulative. This simply means that each conversation in any given scientific domain builds on ones that have gone before – science thus progresses in a fundamental way that many other disciplines do not. The consequence is that the discourse of science increasingly deviates from the language of everyday life and other forms of communication. Compare, for instance, the writings of any nineteenth-century introduction to gravity with any contemporary text on gravitational theory with its matrix mathematics, tensor calculus and more. The two are virtually incommensurable. For the learner, this is an additional barrier to entry extending the period of apprenticeship or, alternatively, restricting the field of study to an even narrower domain so that they know more and more about less and less.

Learning science is learning a new language

The effect of all these linguistic practices, however, is to erect a 'monolithic castle of impenetrable speech' (Montgomery, 1996, p. 7) which intimidates the outsider or the young person who is new to science. Why, our students ask, does science insist on using this strange and unfamiliar form of speech? The consequence is that for too many young people science remains distant, elevated and strange. The pedagogic point, however, is that such distance will *not* be reduced by an education which fails to explore such modes of writing, to discuss their rationale and their justification.

The simple message of this analysis is twofold. First, that learning science is akin to learning a new language and, second, that teachers of science are teachers of that language. The latter point, in particular, is key. For teachers who recognize it will do two things. One, they will attempt to scaffold students' access to that language through the use of activities that require students to talk, read and write science. They will demonstrate and model how that language is used, what are good uses of the language, what are poor or weak attempts and why, following Lemke's (1998) dictum, that: 'the one single change in science education that could do more than any other to improve student's ability to use the language of science is to give them more actual practice using it.' In short, they will see their task as being one in which they help students, not only to learn the concepts in science, but as much, if not more, a process of helping students to construct meaning from the texts of science.

What does research have to say about ways in which students' use of language can be supported? Much of the work has been explored more extensively in the book *Language and Literacy in Science Education* (Wellington and Osborne, 2001) which focuses on reading, writing and talking science – all of which are now discussed briefly.

Talking science

Bakhtin (1981) argues that the essence of gaining competence in a field is through appropriating its language. It is, for instance, impossible to imagine learning a foreign language without engaging in exercises that require the use of talk. Yet, when it comes to appropriating the language of science, opportunities for students to talk science within classrooms are minimal, occupying less than 5 per cent of classroom time compared to up to 40 per cent of the time that students spend listening in lessons (Gallas, 1995; Newton et al., 1999). Summarizing the importance of talk, Jones (1988, p. 27) states that:

> Pupil talk in a lesson has many functions. It increases the understanding of concepts, enables pupils to learn how to communicate clearly with others, makes them active learners, gives them a diversity of view points and a critical tolerance of others.

Empirical evidence to support this claim comes from studies that have examined the use of group discussion in the teaching and learning of science

(Howe et al., 1989; Howe et al., 2000; Howe et al., 1992; Mercer et al., 2004; Zohar, 2004). However, talk in the science classroom is commonly dominated by teacher talk, or overshadowed by writing and reading (Jones, 1988).

Scott and Mortimer (2003) have developed a framework which identifies four forms of talk in science classrooms: interactive authoritative, interactive dialogic, non-interactive authoritative and non-interactive dialogic. Classrooms are dominated by the authoritative forms of dialogue which supports a view of teaching as a form of transmission – one where the knowledgeable person imparts the information to the learner. In particular, this form of dialogue is dominated by a pattern where the teacher initiates (I) the dialogue by asking the question, the student responds (R), normally with a short phrase-like answer which is not a complete sentence, and the teacher then gives an evaluative (E) response (Cazden, 1988; Lemke, 1990). This form of dialogue is commonly known as IRE or IRF where the 'F' stands for feedback. In some ways it is puzzling: it is not typical of normal discourse as we do not talk to each other by asking a series of questions; moreover, the person who knows the answer does not normally ask a question of someone who, in all probability, may well not know the answer. So what is its function? Wells (1999) and Mortimer and Scott (2003) argue that its primary function is that of making knowledge public so that others can perceive patterns, relationships, appropriate vocabulary and that the questioning invites all to participate in the construction of knowledge which is common to all. Studies in the UK (see, for example, Wegerif and Mercer, 1997) have shown that most of the talk time in science lessons consists of such teacher talk.

There are, however, many criticisms of this form of interaction. First, research shows that the majority of the questions are closed and make low-level cognitive demands on students (Lemke, 1990). Few questions are open-ended and invite extended reasoning by students, so it minimizes their opportunity to actually talk science. At its worst, the process can descend into a parody where students engage in a game of guessing what is in the teacher's mind (Wellington, 1981). Second, the interaction often permits a large number of students to hide their lack of engagement with the subject at hand. Third, it is a very hard interaction for a teacher and students to sustain, requiring students to listen hard and the teacher to respond in a thoughtful and supportive manner. Its predominance can only be explained in terms of the mental models of learning that permeate the classroom which see the teacher's function as one of putting knowledge out there in the classroom space for their students to absorb (Strauss and Shilony, 1994). Mary Budd Rowe found that teachers commonly waited less than a second for an answer to their questions (see, also, Chapter 9 in this volume). The consequence was that student answers were often restricted to brief phrases or one-word answers. Training teachers to increase the 'wait-time' before obtaining a response to an average of 3 seconds led to a significant improvement in the quality of student contributions and answers (Rowe, 1974). But perhaps the most telling critique is that of Bakhtin (1981, p. 343) who argues:

> Authoritative discourse permits no play with the context framing
> it, no play with its borders, no gradual and flexible transitions, no
> spontaneously creative stylizing variants on it. It enters our verbal
> consciousness as a compact and indivisible mass; one must either
> totally affirm it, or totally reject it.

The latter phenomenon is particularly apparent in students' response to science as can be seen from the following excerpt (Osborne and Collins, 2001, p. 452):

> *Cheryl*: ... so when they teach you science, you know that this is it, okay? There is nothing, you can't prove it wrong.
> *Leena*: In what way does that make it different to other subjects though?
> *Shakira*: I mean, you just have to accept the facts, don't you?

Dialogic interaction, in contrast, is the normal kind of daily discourse we experience. Its use provides a means for the students to work collaboratively in developing their knowledge. As Alexander (2004, p. 34) states, discussion is 'the exchange of ideas with a view of sharing information and solving problems' and dialogue is about 'achieving common understanding through structured and cumulative questioning'. As he argues, 'Discussion and dialogue are the rarest yet the most cognitively potent elements in the basic repertoire of classroom talk' (2005, p. 30). Mercer and Littleton (2007, p. 25), who have investigated collaborative classroom talk, argue that it is 'more than children working together ... participants are engaged in a coordinated, continuing attempt to solve a problem or in some other way construct common knowledge'. And indeed, their research on the use of small group discussions in the teaching of science in primary schools has shown that it develops both students' knowledge and student reasoning (Mercer et al., 2004).

Findings from previous studies in the UK have also shown that well-structured oral and collaborative activities 'maintain children's time on task more consistently than do solitary written and text-based task' (Alexander, 2004, p. 14) and when engaged in dialogic teaching, the learners develop interactive skills such as listening, responding, asking questions, presenting and evaluating ideas (Alexander, 2004). Other studies (Azmitia and Montgomery, 1993) show that the quality of the children's dialogue is a significant predictor of their problem-solving abilities, a finding that suggests that improving the quality of the dialogic interaction can also improve students' learning. In higher education, too, there is good evidence that disrupting the traditional lecture format with small group discussions of the lecture material leads to enhanced understanding (Smith et al., 2009). Given the body of evidence for its value, however, why is it such a minimal feature of science classrooms?

First, the technique is unfamiliar and challenging and its use unsettles teachers' sense of competence and confidence, particularly when the use of small-group discussion can result in student behaviour which is uncoopera-tive, off-task and unproductive. As van Lier (1996, p. 91) points out:

> Many beginning teachers embark on group work with great enthu-siasm, only to find that the class degenerates into an unmanageable chaos. They have probably selected an interesting and challenging activity which will take a group of students (perhaps four of five in a group) ten minutes or longer to do, implying a division of labour, a great deal of synchronization of talk and action, and a joint final product. They do not realize that, unless students have been carefully prepared, they are not likely to be able to carry out such concerted work independently.

Hence, such activities, just like any other, need to have clear goals, a well-defined structure, clear time limits and time spent establishing the agreed rules of interaction (Osborne et al., 2004). In the primary classroom, such an approach to promoting dialogic talk has been developed by Wegerif et al. (1998). The particular form of talk which they view as being of cognitive benefit was what they termed *exploratory talk*. This process requires a set of agreed rules which require that all relevant information is shared; the group seeks to reach agreement; the group takes responsibility for decision-making; reasons are expected; challenges are accepted; alternatives are discussed before a decision is taken; and all in the group are encouraged to speak. Learning such rules is, however, not something which happens instantaneously and only comes with repeated practice. Gallas offers an interesting exploration of how she introduced talk activities (and a thoughtful rationale for them) in her book *Talking Your Way into Science* (Gallas, 1995).

Supporting talk in the classroom requires a knowledge of some of the stan-dard structures that support small group interaction such as pairs, envoys and jigsawing (Johnson et al., 2002). A resource which has been shown to be effec-tive (Keogh and Naylor, 1999) at supporting talk in science classrooms is the concept cartoon (Naylor and Keogh, 2000). This strategy involves presenting a common phenomenon as a cartoon, for example, water boiling, a boy skiing or three street lamps which are accompanied by three to four people around them making statements about what they think will happen and why. The car-toons provide an easily accessible stimulus for initiating discussion. However, research would suggest that the cartoon selected for use needs to be appro-priate to the level of students' background knowledge (Aufschnaiter et al., 2008).

Another potential way to support talk in the science classroom which re-searchers have explored involves the use of *discussion-based* tools which have emerged from a programme of research on computer-supported collaborative learning (Andriessen et al., 2003). Discussion-based tools are tools that can fa-cilitate communication, either on-line using asynchronous communication or face-to-face using synchronous communication, with other learners. Discussion-based tools are based on the recognition that the construction of knowledge is not an individual process but rather a collective process including ideas and arguments that come together (Scardamalia and Bereiter, 1999). Furthermore, according to Lampert et al. (1996), discussion-based tools allow students more time before formulating a contribution, something that usually does not happen within classrooms and, in that way, contribute to the discussion in a more coherent way. These tools can also reduce social and emotional obstacles that students may have about expressing their opinion in public where they might struggle to represent their ideas appropriately and, in that way, enable more students to take part in the discussions (Scardamalia and Bereiter, 1999). Examples of such environments are the Knowledge Forum/CSILE and the ExplanationConstructor (Reiser, 2002; Sandoval and Reiser, 2004). Research with these environments has demonstrated that technology-enhanced learning environments can be used to successfully scaffold dialogic argumentation (Scardamalia et al., 1994).

Finally, it is worth noting the work of Rivard (2004) who investigated the effect of using different types of language activities (talk only, writing only, combination) with students of different abilities. Low ability students were found to benefit mostly from talk activities, while high ability students from writing activities – though using a combination of both led to better retention of scientific ideas by low achievers. Thus, he concluded that a combination of writing and talking activities can benefit both the low and the high ability students.

Reading in science

In a major study of reading across the curriculum, Lunzer and Gardner (1979) found that pupils in the first year of secondary school spent only 9 per cent of their science lesson time reading. This had increased to only 10 per cent in the fourth year of secondary education. Of this small amount, a large proportion (up to 75 per cent in some cases) was reading from the blackboard or from an exercise book. Over 90 per cent of all pupils' reading occurred in 'bursts' lasting less than 30 seconds. A later study by Newton et al. (1999) found that the time devoted to reading had been reduced to less than 3 per cent. While the common perception is that science is a practical, hands-on subject, it is important to remember that reading is an important scientific activity. 'Minds-on' is as much a part of real science as 'hands-on' and working scientists read journals for several hours a week. Written texts are not just peripheral but central to science and students need help to be able to comprehend and read scientific text in whatever form it is presented to them – be it a textbook, a newspaper report or a video. For instance, Norris and Phillips (2003) found, in a study involving 91 grade 12 science students that fewer than half of the students were able to interpret causal statements as such; less than one in ten recognized justifications for action as justifications; and just as many students (almost half) took statements of evidence to be conclusions as took statements of evidence to be evidence. On the positive side, 'nearly 90% recognised observations and descriptions of method as such, and just over half recognised conclusions as such' (1994, p. 961). If students at the end of their formal science education are unable to correctly construct meaning from standard scientific texts, how much more difficult must it be for younger students? Once again, the message of this research is that students need to be helped to read and interpret the meaning of scientific texts.

To assist students to read scientific texts, however, it is important that teachers of science recognize the major distinction between reading fiction and non-fiction texts. In the former, reading is *receptive* and there is little or no requirement to reread any given section. This is the kind of reading undertaken when reading a novel. Reading science texts, in contrast, is characterized by *reflective* reading (Davies and Greene, 1984) where the reader is forced to pause, reread and reflect to construct an understanding of the meaning of the text. Science texts, which have a high density of unfamiliar lexical terms, are difficult to construct meaning from and decode. Teachers who use strategies that develop the skills that enhance reflective reading will enhance the chances that their students will ultimately comprehend the text. With this objective in mind, Lunzer and Gardner (1979), and then Davies and Greene (1984), developed a whole set of strategies called 'Directed Activities Related to Texts' (DARTS) which supported this approach to reading in science. Their approach is based on either the deconstruction of text (Analysis DARTS) or the synthesis of text (Reconstruction DARTS). Table 7.2 summarizes the range of different strategies that can help students read texts.

The essential rationale for the use of DARTs is that they help students either to deconstruct the text (and hence to comprehend its meaning) or to construct scientific text (and hence to comprehend its meaning). In essence, both activities can be seen as two sides of the same coin. Teachers of science stand very much in the position of knowledge intermediaries between science and the neophyte student – a role that requires representing the language of science in a form that is comprehensible. The inevitable consequence, however, is a difficult tension between attempting to tone down the technical language of science to make it more accessible and educating students into the language of science. Adopting the former approach invariably leads to a loss of detail and subtlety and 'their deletion means, without exception, loss of knowledge' (Montgomery, 1996, p. 10). The converse is to raise the entry cost to learning science – to make science seem distant and inaccessible. This is a particular concern where learners are English language learners – that is, English is not their first language (Brown, 2006; Moje et al., 2001). However, if education in academic science is the goal – and commonly it is – research would suggest that DARTs are an essential part of helping students to construct meaning from science texts as these kinds of activities will help students to comprehend the texts of science.

Table 7.2 A brief summary of directed activities related to text (DARTS)

Reconstruction DARTS	Analysis DARTS
1 Completing text, diagram or table (a) *Text completion* Pupils predict and complete deleted words, phrases, or sentences (cf. Cloze procedure). (b) *Diagram completion* Pupils predict and complete deleted labels and/or parts of diagrams using text and diagrams as sources of information. (c) *Table completion* Pupils use the text to complete a table using rows and columns provided by the teacher. **2 Unscrambling and labelling disordered and segmented text** (a) Pupils predict logical order or time sequence of scramble segments of text, e.g. a set of instructions, and rearrange. (b) Pupils classify segments according to categories given by teacher. **3 Predicting** Pupils predict and write next part(s) of text, e.g. an event or an instruction, with segments presented a section at a time.	**1 Marking and labelling** (a) *Underlining/marking* Pupils search for specified targets in text, e.g. words or sentences, and mark them in some way (b) *Labelling* Pupils label parts of the text, using labels provided for them. (c) *Segmenting* Pupils break the text down into segments, or units of information, and label these segments. **2 Recording and constructing** (a) Pupils construct diagrams showing content and flow of text using, for example: a flow diagram, a network, a branching tree, or a continuum. (b) *Table construction* Pupils construct and complete tables from information given in text, making up their own headings (rows and columns) (c) *Question answering and setting* (i) Teachers set questions; pupils study text to answer them (ii) Pupils make up their own questions after studying text (either for the teacher to answer, or other pupils). (d) *Key points/summary* Pupils list the key points made by the text and/or summarize it.

Writing in science

The genres of scientific language

A challenge for the science learner comes from the genres of scientific language commonly deployed by the discipline. For students, the most familiar in their everyday lives is narrative – a genre which is characterized by features such as human actors, plots and a sense of agency. In contrast, in science, the most familiar form is the experimental report where the personal is excised and pupils are encouraged to write in the passive voice. So rather than writing 'we took the Bunsen burner and heated the copper sulphate', the standard genre of science requires the wording 'the copper sulphate was heated'. Reports of this type or explanations in science remove the human agents, the scene, the motives and any sense of temporality and many students find the excision of the personal odd, difficult and alienating. Narrative accounts, in contrast, are often subjective accounts of experience. Science writing, however, seeks to distance itself from human values and portray the knowledge it offers as something which is a reflection of a real world which is independent of any observer. Why is this done? The reason is that there is a good functional reason behind the choice of the passive voice (Martin, 1998). For instance, in the example above, for the scientist, the point of interest is the material world (in this case the copper sulphate) and what was done to it (heating) *not* who heated it. Choosing to write in this form places the emphasis on what is of primary interest.

Another feature of science and all professional languages is the use of complex nouns or adjectives (Halliday, 1998). Many of these have their roots in Latin, for example, 'centrifugal', which is a combination of the Latin for centre (*centrum*) and the words 'to flee' (*fugo*). Hence the word 'centrifugal' literally means the force which flees the centre. Further examples are words such as 'photosynthesis', 'kinetic', and 'metatarsal'. With such words, insights into their meaning can be helped by examining their etymology and how it is constructed from its components to synthesize a new word – a process which helps to make the word appear less alien and its meaning more recognizable. The point at issue is not whether the use of such words is justified, or whether alternative modes of communication might be more effective, rather it is that that is *how science is written*.

Similar to reading, writing is one of the activities rarely seen in the science classrooms (apart from copying) and, in those cases in which the students engage in writing, writing is more often associated with note-taking, copying from the board, or filling-in-the-gaps activities. Nevertheless, writing is an essential part of science since it requires students to select the appropriate terms and then to relate those terms in a meaningful manner (Prain and Hand, 1996). By its very nature, the act of writing is a reflective process forcing the writer to consider the meaning of the words they choose.

There are three main arguments supporting the use of writing activities in the science classroom: writing to learn, writing to reason and writing to communicate. First, through writing, students are given opportunities to formulate their own ideas about concepts, and to combine them into 'an increasingly more complex network of theoretical propositions' (Rivard, 2004, p. 421) and reflect on their understanding of the concepts. Writing during science lessons is an important means of refining and coordinating new ideas with existing knowledge, and constructing and evaluating new ideas (Keys, 1994; Rivard and Straw, 2000) and this is what Keys (1999) and Yore et al. (2003) label as *Writing to Learn*. An example of a *Writing to Learn* activity is presented in a study by

Keys (1999), drawn from a summer school during which the students visited a zoo and were asked to record their observations about an animal, and then write a report on the behaviour of that animal to be given to the zoo-keeper. Students' reports suggest that some of them were able to use their observations and make connections with existing knowledge, and in so doing developing their knowledge about animals.

The second argument for the use of writing in the science classroom is the use of *Writing to Reason*. From this perspective, writing is important as it allows students to comprehend, interpret, analyse and criticize evidence – and, in that way, engage in critical analysis, synthesis, and evaluation. In this manner, writing in science can be viewed as providing opportunities to learn how to construct evidence-based explanations and, as Wellington and Osborne point out, 'to use the ideas and language of science' (2001, p. 83) for themselves. Hence, writing (for example, a report) can be used as an activity that will engage students in reasoning about the experiment, constructing a case using their data for their conclusions, and developing their understanding of the underlying mechanism of the phenomenon they are exploring.

The third argument for using writing in science learning is that it is through publications and discussions that some claims are accepted and transformed into what is called scientific knowledge (Sutton, 1998). *Writing to Communicate* the findings of empirical inquiry is, therefore, very much a central feature of the scientific process. Only by asking students to engage in such a process can they begin to understand an important element of science and that writing is used to communicate the outcomes of scientific work to a broad audience (Hand, 2008). However, research shows that the vast majority of writing done by students in the classroom is for the teacher as examiner (Davies and Greene, 1984). Not surprisingly, this leads to performance learning where the activity is extrinsically motivated by the students' valid perception that it is the teacher's judgement of the outcome which matters more than the intrinsic merits of the process. Changing the audience, where the student is asked to write for other students, or to write in a different genre and presenting their results, for instance, as an article for a newspaper or a poster at a conference is a simple means of transforming the basis of student motivation and their interest in the work (Wellington and Osborne, 2001).

Supporting writing is possibly more complex than reading as there are several different genres of writing in science and these have their own epistemic rationale. Martin (1998) argues that the major genres of science are:

1. The report, which has four forms:
    (a) Reports that classify.
    (b) Reports that decompose explaining the whole in terms of its constituent parts.
    (c) Reports that describe functions and processes.
    (d) Reports that list properties.
2. Explanations.

3. Experimental accounts, which consist of:
    (a) Procedural texts explaining how to do experiments.
    (b) Recounts of experiments that have been conducted.
4. Exposition, which presents arguments in favour of a position.

Writing in these forms has to be supported by a structure which helps students to organize their writing into the required form and style of writing. Such a structure is commonly called a 'frame' (Wray and Lewis, 1997), and it guides the writer to the key features of the genre as well as being a planning tool used to organize the writing. An example of a frame for writing up experiments is presented in Box 7.1.

Box 7.1 A frame for writing up experiments

Aims

- What is the purpose
- Why are we doing this?
- What are we hoping to show?
- Do we have a hypothesis in advance?

Method

- What is the recipe for doing this experiment?
- What are the instructions?
- What special precautions did we take to ensure that the experiment worked well?

Results

- How should we display the results – table, bar chart, line graph?
- These words may help you in your writing:
    This shows that
    Another piece of evidence is
    A further point is
    I would also argue that
    You can see that
    This means
    Therefore

Conclusions

- What do my results show?

Source: Wellington and Osborne (2001, p. 72)

As shown in the frame in Box 7.1, a set of prompt questions guide the students on what to include in their reports, and also to reflect on their results and conclusions. Wray and Lewis (1997) and Wellington and Osborne (2001) offer a range of writing frames to help support students in writing reports, explanations, arguments and experimental reports, and Hand (2008) discusses the Science Writing Heuristic (SWH), a frame that promotes *Writing to Learn* strategies.

The role of argumentation in supporting language activities

Argumentation – the making of reasoned claims which are supported by data or evidence – is a specific form of discourse that can help students view science as an epistemological and social process in which knowledge claims are generated, adapted, reorganized, and, at times, abandoned (Lawson, 2003; Lederman, 1992). This is an important aspect of science as the research evidence shows that school science commonly leaves students with the impression that the goal of science is to establish absolute and certain facts (Driver et al., 1996). An education in science should, therefore, attempt to show not only *what we know* but *how we know* and that ideas have to be argued for. Such an understanding of the scientific enterprise is necessary because it helps students develop appreciation of the power and limitation of scientific knowledge claims (Millar and Osborne, 1998) – knowledge which is necessary in order to understand, evaluate and use the products of science and technology.

Argumentation is a major feature of the resolution of scientific controversies (Fuller, 1997; Taylor, 1996) and 'a social and linguistic process, where co-operating individuals try to adjust their intentions and interpretations by verbally presenting a rationale of their actions' (Patronis et al., 1999, pp. 747–8). It is also part of the practice of science for evaluating, refining and establishing new theories (Duschl, 1990; Holton and Brush, 1996). Therefore, it is considered to be a core element of the scientific enterprise. Indeed, the history of science shows that so many ideas – be it the Periodic table of the elements, the idea that matter is made of three fundamental particles, or that diseases are carried by microbial organism – were not easily accepted and had to be argued for. For example, Galileo struggled to establish the validity of Copernicus' heliocentric theory; Torricelli's arguments that the space at the top of his barometer was just that – empty space; and Pasteur's case that mould was spread by microbial organisms in the air.

Given that the rhetorical task of the teacher of science is to persuade students of the validity of the scientific worldview, it might then seem logical to avoid exploring misconceptions or erroneous scientific ideas. Yet without this opportunity, students are not given opportunities to reason for themselves, examine their own misconceptions and, most importantly, discuss scientific ideas. As Hatano and Inagaki (1991, pp. 26–7) state:

Discussion on a certain issue is likely to make students recognize that their comprehension is not adequate. In the course of discussion, students may be surprised to find out that there exist a number of ideas, plausible though different from their own...The presence of others expressing different ideas is especially advantageous, because it is hard to recognize as plausible those ideas which we merely read or otherwise get exposed to passively...Through these processes, students often begin to feel a healthy dissatisfaction with the adequacy of their comprehension.

Those researching the comprehension of texts have found that refutational texts – that is, texts which explain why the wrong idea is wrong as well as explaining why the right idea is right are more effective than standard texts at developing students' understanding of the accepted scientific idea (Guzetti et al., 1997; Hynd and Alvermann, 1986). Indeed, Guzetti et al. (1997, p. 71) found that students preferred such texts as 'they thought they could learn better from knowing the errors in their thinking or errors they might construct in their future thinking'.

Argumentation activities are, therefore, a powerful means of fulfilling Lemke's dictum that the one single means of improving students knowledge of science would be to give them more opportunity to use the language of science (Lemke, 1990). For instance, there are good arguments that would justify the idea that day and night is caused by a moving Sun and not a spinning Earth. After all, it is the Sun which appears to move, and, if the Earth was spinning once a day, the speed at the Equator would be in excess of 1,000 mph – greater than the speed of sound. Exploring why these arguments are erroneous, forces students to appreciate and construct their own understanding that motion is a relative phenomenon and that gravity on Earth is a very strong force. A second value of argumentation – from a cognitive aspect – is that it requires students to coordinate evidence with a claim and, in that way, develop their ability both to construct links and to evaluate the accuracy or validity of claims (Driver et al., 2000; Kuhn, 1993).

An example of a project that uses argumentation as a focus for discussion of scientific ideas is the *How far the light goes* project (Bell and Linn, 2000; Bell, 2004). Specifically, in this project, students explore evidence related to the furthest extent of light's propagation from sources of illumination. The evidence includes multimedia evidence such as movies, simulations and web pages and explanations and arguments about how the evidence relates to the debate topics. The students are presented with two theories about light propagation, Newton's and Kepler's theory, and evidence to support each theory, and are asked to engage in a debate about the validity of the theories. Other activities include presenting opposing claims to the students using concept cartoons and asking them to discuss and justify their argument, and if applicable conduct an investigation to find evidence to support their argument. The *IDEAS* pack (Osborne et al., 2004) also presents a number of activities and resources for the teachers that can be used in the science classroom to support argumentation.

Conclusion

Three major points emerge from the research reviewed here. First, that language is central to both science and science education. Second, that the teacher of science is a teacher of the many languages of science. Most of the teacher of science's time is spent using words, diagrams and other visual representations to assist students construct an understanding of the scientific ideas embodied in those languages. Third, that in learning science, it is essential to scaffold students' ability to decode and understand that language by the use of structured activities for reading science, writing science, talking science and arguing about science. As Lemke (1990) has illustrated, the discourse of science represents a specialized system of language that rests heavily upon themes and concepts that are not immediately apparent to the novice science learner. The language of science and scientific practices are, therefore, unfamiliar to students. In the science classroom they encounter new ways of using the language (talking, reading, writing). Thus, even for native speakers the language of science is often problematic, because their everyday modes of language use may not match the formal forms of language they find in school science (Bernstein, 1961). It is Sutton (1998) who makes the point that language is both an interpretive system (that is used for making sense of new experience) and a labelling system (for describing, reporting and informing). School science, he points out, predominantly uses language as a labelling system. This chapter has reviewed the now considerable body of research which has focused on how students can be helped to read, write and talk science – that is to *interpret and construct meaning*. Yet, the idea that language is an interpretive mechanism and its implications for teaching science still have not permeated our common ideas about the teaching of science. Rather, the social norms embedded in the teaching community are dominated by the paradigmatic view which sees teaching as a process of transmission (Strauss and Shilony, 1994). Transcending that view remains an ongoing challenge for research and practice.

Further reading

Alexander, R. (2005) *Towards Dialogic Teaching*. York: Dialogos.

Lemke, J. (1990) *Talking Science: Language, Learning and Values*. Norwood, NJ: Ablex Publishing.

Lemke, J. (1998) *Teaching All the Languages of Science: Words, Symbols, Images and Actions*, available at: http://academic.brooklyn.cuny.edu/education/jlemke/papers/barcelon.htm.

Mercer, N. and Littleton, K. (2007) *Dialogue and the Development of Children's Thinking.* London: Routledge.

Ogborn, J., Kress, G., Martins, I. and McGillicuddy, K. (1996) *Explaining Science in the Classroom.* Buckingham: Open University Press.

Wellington, J. and Osborne, J. F. (2001) *Language and Literacy in Science Education.* Buckingham: Open University Press.

8 Technology-mediated learning

Mary Webb

Introduction

Year 7 are studying cells. They have all learned how to use a standard micro-scope and have made preparations of their cheek cells and of onion epider-mis. Using a micro-projector, the class, with their teacher, have examined and compared various different plant and animal cells on the big screen in the classroom. Now several of the students are talking to their classmates in their virtual laboratory. Their avatars are comparing images of their slides of plant material and discussing their findings about the invention of the microscope. As some of their classmates are in Holland, they are interested in compar-ing their evidence about early microscopes and whether they were invented in Holland or England. Now the teacher asks the students to return to the real world and they report their findings and what they have learned to their classmates. They log off their computers and pack them in their bags.

For their homework, they explore a virtual microworld of cells where their avatars climb through plant and animal tissues and marvel at the cells' archi-tecture and the texture of the various structures using haptic (virtual touch) gloves. Their avatars consult their virtual assistant for help in orienting them-selves in a leaf and making sense of the different shaped cells that they have found. Their avatars prepare their joint report on similarities and differences between cells using a shared word processor through a large virtual screen that they summon whenever they want to add to it.

When Ritel and Josh have finished their homework, they decide to examine a nucleus where, by choosing to explore at higher magnification, they are able to take a molecular tour. Ritel already knows something about DNA from previous 'geeking out' on the web, where he read about recent research on several university websites and chatted online with a postgraduate researcher, so he explains to Josh why DNA is important. At that point, Ritel's mum walks past the computer, which is in the living room, and noticing the double helix on the screen, asks what he is doing. Ritel quickly switches from his ear-phones to a desk top microphone and the three of them look at the DNA molecule and discuss its importance. As Ritel's mum is a scientist, they ask her to explain how the DNA works.

All of the technologies in this scenario are available now, although the vir-tual environments are only just beginning to become widely accessible online. The virtual assistants are being developed and are currently still somewhat limited. Current desktop computers are easily capable of presenting the graphical features and supporting voice interaction. Haptic devices to enable us to appreciate textures have been developed, although they are not yet widely available. Recent technological innovations including web 2.0 and the semantic web, wireless networking and portable computing can enable new ways of learning in which the students interact more with each other using technology both within the classroom and beyond. The technologies can mediate interactions both between people and between people and their physical and virtual worlds. Therefore, we have the technology to support inquiry-based and collaborative learning approaches that extend beyond the classroom. Most scientific knowledge is available on the web, and access to 'experts' other than the teacher is possible for any student. Therefore, your role as a teacher and your students' role could be transformed – but is it and what does research tell us about the progress that we are making with technology-mediated learning?

Since the early days of computers, expectations that technology would enable or even transform science learning have been high. Science research has been transformed by computer technology, including the establishment of the new field of bioinformatics which has used computer technology, for example, to map DNA and protein sequences, thus opening up a range of new opportunities including many in medical science. The potential for supporting and enhancing learning through capturing and analysing data automatically, exploring simulations of scientific phenomena, modelling scientific processes, and being able to access and communicate global scientific information and expertise is high.

In some science classrooms, where teachers have explored new ideas and innovations with their students, science learning has been supported and enabled by a range of technologies for many years (Cox and Webb, 2004; Kozma, 2003). However, in spite of changes in science curricula for the twenty-first century that emphasize understanding of the nature of science, discussion of current scientific issues (Millar, 2006) and a strong focus on practical work and collaborative learning (see Chapter 1), the use of ICT in science education has generally been patchy and limited. In most science classrooms where technologies are deployed at all, they are generally used to support existing traditional pedagogical approaches, for example, teachers presenting ideas and simulations to the whole class in ways designed to interest their students, such as using multimedia displays and animations. Thus there is a gap between the vision of twenty-first-century science learning proposed by Millar and Osborne (1998) that could also be enabled by use of technology and the reality of learning in most science classrooms.

There is no basis for complacency in science education: evidence discussed in Chapter 11 suggests that many students are interested in school science but to a lesser degree than other subjects, and students continue to complain that school science consists of too much repetition, copying and note-taking with no time to discuss scientific ideas or their implications.

What is in this chapter?

In this chapter, research into science learning mediated by a range of new technologies is examined and discussed. The research is approached though a critical review of evidence of ways in which technologies have supported learning and teaching through traditional pedagogical approaches. In addition, evidence is explored of how the use of a range of innovative technologies can enable new pedagogical approaches in, and enhance the learning of, science.

As indicated by the title, this chapter emphasizes learning. This emphasis is obviously crucial for the success of any innovation in education. However, it has not always been evident in technology-driven initiatives in recent years where the stress may have been on the technology and not the learning. Technology can mediate learning by providing tools for learners to access and interact with knowledge; for teachers to interact with learners; and for learners to interact with their peers and learners to interact with other experts in the wider community beyond the school.

In order to understand the evidence of the effects of technology-mediated learning, a range of research approaches used is examined first. Establishing cause and effect between pedagogical approaches and learning in the context of rapid technological change is difficult and the chapter begins by exploring the nature of the evidence. The issues associated with researching these effects are then discussed and key questions that researchers and teachers need to ask about technology mediated learning are identified. In subsequent sections, research evidence for each of the major ways in which technologies may support science learning is explored.

The nature of the evidence relating to technology-mediated learning of science

Research into the use of technology in education has expanded and diversified as technologies have developed, and these rapid changes in technology make such research difficult, complex and challenging (see Marshall and Cox, 2008). Many studies into technology used in education, especially those funded by stakeholders, such as the government, have aimed to find answers to questions such as:

- How does a particular technological innovation influence learning and teaching?
- Is using new technologies more effective than other approaches to learning (for example, Cox et al., 1993; Harrison et al., 2004)?

These technology-focused evaluations present three main difficulties. First, it is necessary to compare approaches with and without new technologies or at least with different levels of use of technologies. This can have the effect of oversimplifying by regarding new technologies or 'ICT' as a single entity, whereas there are actually a wide range of technologies that may be deployed in a variety of ways to enable learning. Furthermore creating or identifying the kind of controlled conditions where such comparisons can be made is extremely difficult. This is because in addition to the usual problems associated with controlled conditions in classrooms, various technologies are becoming ubiquitous and students cannot be prevented from using them for the purposes of such research. Therefore, many studies that provide evidence of how specific technologies can enable learning have been conducted outside classroom settings or in experimental classrooms. Results of such experiments may not be directly relevant to classroom settings.

Second, assessments of the effects are generally made through existing measures of attainment whereas technologies provide new opportunities for learning and new ways of working so that traditional assessment methods may no longer be appropriate. Third, it is now well known that the pedagogical approaches used with the technologies are crucial for their success (Cox and Webb, 2004). However an extensive review and meta-analysis of international research into effective pedagogy in science education (Hipkins et al., 2002) revealed the difficulty of identifying effective pedagogy and separating it from other effects such as curriculum and assessment.

The consequences of these difficulties are that reliable findings that demonstrate the effects of ICT use on learning are rare. Where findings are reliable, they might only apply in the particular circumstances of the study rather than being generalizable. A literature review that set out to assess research evidence of the impact of the use of ICT on students' understanding of science (Hogarth et al., 2006) illustrates some effects of these problems. As a 'systematic review' it only included those studies that had a control and pre-post test design and used reliable methods. Therefore, a large number of other studies were excluded from the review as they did not meet these criteria. The researchers found reliable evidence that some uses of simulations improved understanding of science beyond that achieved by other means but found no other clear evidence of impacts of ICT on students' understanding of science.

Therefore, despite many years of innovation and research on the impacts of ICT on science learning, reliable evidence is limited. The implications of the nature of the research evidence for teachers making decisions about using technologies for science learning are:

1. The evidence base is relatively weak so it provides pointers rather than clear guidelines.
2. Rapid technological change means that evidence relating to particular technologies is out of date almost as soon as it is published. Therefore, in examining the findings it is important to focus on the new pedagogical approaches and learning opportunities that are afforded by the technologies and how they affect learning outcomes.
3. There are many opportunities for teachers themselves to explore new pedagogical approaches using technology and to research the outcomes.

Some large-scale evaluations have shown statistically significant correlations between the general level of technology use and attainment in science as measured by traditional methods (see the review by Cox et al., 2004). These correlational studies (for example, Harrison et al., 2002) cannot reveal causal mechanisms. However, they do support the hypothesis that some uses of technology may enhance learning which raises such questions as:

- Which technologies can support and enable science learning?
- What evidence is there of how using these technologies enhances the learning experience or enables better learning than can be achieved through more traditional approaches?
- What pedagogical approaches are needed to enable these opportunities?
- What are the roles of teachers, students and the technologies?

Studies that may help to answer these questions can be classified into six main groups (Cox and Webb, 2004):

1. Literature reviews and meta-analyses of technology use for learning.
2. Studies of effective teaching and teachers' views that make little reference to ICT use but are important because recent research on the contribution of ICT to attainment shows that ICT is effective only when combined with good teaching.
3. Short-term interventions associated with software design, in which a specific aspect of ICT use is evaluated.
4. Studies associated with the introduction of an additional general ICT resource such as the use of laptop computers, interactive whiteboards or the internet in science lessons. Many of these studies are looking for a wide range of effects.
5. Studies focused on specific aspects of pedagogy in science, involving development work with ICT over two to three years.
6. Longitudinal studies involving development work, usually over at least five years. These studies can be sufficiently detailed to address the changing nature of teaching and learning associated with the introduction of technology but are limited in scope. They may involve only one school or classroom (for example, Linn and Hsi, 2000).

Using simulations, models and animations for science learning

Much of science learning is concerned with understanding processes that cannot be easily observed. They may be too small, for example, biochemical processes, too slow, for example, plant growth or on too large a scale, for example, global warming. Therefore being able to observe, interact with and experiment on simulations of these processes opens up many opportunities for learning science. A wide range of simulation software has been developed and, in addition to software available to purchase, there are many free simulations on the web. Typically, such software incorporates an underlying model that is hidden in the program code and the students can change the values of the variables in the model. They then run the model as a simulation and view the output, usually as a graph, although some software provides animations as output.

As mentioned earlier, there is some strong evidence that uses of simulations can improve understanding of science beyond that achieved by other means (Hogarth et al., 2006). The evidence for why and how some simulations enable science learning will be examined in detail. To do this it is necessary to consider not just the technologies themselves but also the learning environment and pedagogy because evidence from many studies suggests that the identification of the learning needs by the teacher, and the choice of simulation software and how it is integrated into the learning environment, are all crucially important to the learning outcomes (Webb, 2005).

Supporting conceptual challenges in science learning through exploring simulations

Evidence from experimental studies suggests that achievement can be improved by integrating simulations into topics that students find conceptually difficult (Webb, 2005). Focusing on specific areas of difficulty and addressing these with carefully designed tasks, either with ICT-based simulations or without ICT, may lead to productive learning (Webb, 2005). Studies have suggested that using simulation software may enable cognitive change in a range of topics including the particulate nature of matter (Snir et al., 2003), mechanics (Tao and Gunstone, 1999), understanding of image formation by lenses (Tao, 2004), genetics (Soderberg and Price, 2003) and trajectory motion (Jimoyiannis and Komis, 2001). In this section some of these studies are reviewed as examples to examine the ways in which using simulations may enable learning.

Computer simulations of experiments can easily be integrated as short episodes without changing curricula. For example, Huppert et al. (2002) found that using a computer simulation program, 'The Growth Curve of Microorganisms' within a biology course for 10th-grade students (aged 15–16) in Israel did have a significant positive effect on their achievement. In this experimental study involving 181 students, the two groups of students received the same teaching and laboratory practical work but the experimental group also used computer simulations to perform experiments. The two groups spent the same time on this topic. In the classroom, students were taught the characteristics of the micro-organisms, their structure, the life processes, and their uses in daily life in industry and medicine. They studied population growth characteristics: that is the generation time; lag phase and the exponential phase of the micro-organisms' growth. In the laboratory work, students examined yeast cells under a light microscope as representatives of unicellular organisms. They studied their reproduction, learned how to count cells on a haemocytometer, how to dilute a yeast cell culture and how to calculate the number of cells in a sample. Students in the experimental group used their simulated laboratory to investigate the effects of various factors such as the initial number of organisms in a population, the temperature range and the nutrient concentration on the growth curve. The students were assessed by specific tests of biological knowledge; the population growth of micro-organisms and science process skills. Their stages of cognitive development, were also assessed using a test that assessed the Piagetian formal reasoning skills of conservation, proportions, control of variables, probability, combinations and correlation. The results enabled students to be classified as concrete reasoners, transitional reasoners, or formal reasoners.

The findings indicated that the concrete and transitional reasoning students in the experimental group achieved significantly higher academic achievement than their counterparts in the control group. Huppert et al. attributed these differences to the use of the simulations which allowed the students to carry out investigations more quickly than with standard practical experiments and focus on analysing the results and hypothesizing. The structure of the course helped to create a collaborative learning atmosphere, with students comparing results and exchanging ideas. In this study, all students in the experimental group achieved higher marks than their counterparts in the control group but the results for students in the formal operations stage were not significant. Therefore, students from the middle and lower sections of the ability range benefited more from being able to carry out simulated investigations. Conducting this series of experiments in a real laboratory would be difficult and time-consuming and this example illustrates how the integration of a simulation can provide additional learning affordances for students at particular developmental levels.

In an Australian study, Tao and Gunstone (1999) investigated the use of simulations specifically developed to confront students' alternative conceptions in mechanics. The simulations were integrated into 10 weeks of physics instruction for one class in high school and provided the students with many opportunities for the co-construction of knowledge while they worked in pairs at computers. These case studies of 14 students showed that during the process, students complemented and built on each other's ideas and incrementally reached shared understandings. Their interactions led to conceptual change for some of the students as measured by pre- and post-tests. However, some of the students did not change their conceptions and some changed but reverted back when tested again a few weeks later. Tao and Gunstone suggested that the more stable conceptual change occurred when the students' co-construction of knowledge was accompanied by personal construction.

Soderberg and Price's (2003) case study focused on a lesson where students, using a computer simulation, learned that evolution can be measured as the rate of change of allele frequencies in a population. The teacher used the lesson to help students to examine metacognitively their understanding of concepts in population genetics and evolution and recognize common misconceptions.

The lesson helped the students shift from thinking about genetics on an individual level to a population level. This study and others (for example, Hennessy et al., 2007; Linn and Hsi, 2000) suggest that it is the teacher's role in planning activities with simulations that enable suitable interaction as well as in facilitating those interactions that is crucial for effective learning. This finding accords with other research on teachers' pedagogical practices where the way in which the teacher regulates the learning has been characterized in terms of two levels of management: first, in lesson planning and second, in interacting during the lesson. This model sees the teacher's role as one that requires them to do the following:

1. Set up situations which favour the interactive regulation of learning processes.
2. Interactively regulate these situations (Perrenoud, 1998).

Experimental studies are beginning to identify types of support or scaffolding that may be helpful to optimize learning with simulations (Reid et al., 2003; Zhang et al., 2004) and they also highlight the complexity of the learning situation in which not all support has a positive effect on learning. For example, Zhang et al. (2004) designed three types of support for discovery learning with simulations: (a) interpretative support that helps learners to access their prior knowledge and understand the context; (b) experimental support that scaffolds learners in designing experiments, predicting and interpreting results; and (c) reflective support that increases learners' self-awareness of the learning processes. Their experiments suggested that all three types of support are needed, but students with higher levels of reasoning ability need less experimental support. The research in these studies had limitations: it was not undertaken in classroom settings, the tasks were fairly straightforward, and it took no account of social interactions in knowledge-building activities.

Research into how teachers can best support students' learning with technology through social interaction in group work is discussed in more detail later. However, in the current discussion of the nature of effective support and intervention in discovery learning or problem-solving with simulations, a recent review of research into the role of the teacher in promoting learning in small groups (Webb, 2009) is pertinent. The findings suggested that whether teacher intervention was more or less explicit and whether it was content-related or process-related mattered less than whether teachers identified students' thinking and strategies and then based their interventions on these assessments. In their efforts to create software tools and other resources for scaffolding students' learning, designers may be neglecting important theoretical features of scaffolding such as ongoing diagnosis, calibrated support, and fading, that is, gradual withdrawal of support (Puntambekar and Hubscher, 2005).

Most of the evidence presented in this section is based on research conducted with students aged 11–18 and little use is made of simulations in primary schools where real practical investigations, perhaps supported by data-logging and spreadsheets are felt by teachers to be more useful (Murphy, 2003). However results of one study in a Finnish science classroom, comprising 22 children aged between 6 and 7 years, did suggest that multimedia simulations can support children's social interaction and explanation construction in inquiry-based science learning (Kumpalainen et al., 2003).

Supporting conceptual challenges in science learning through building models

In the previous section we examined the evidence for learning through exploring simulations by predicting outcomes, changing values and running the simulations to see the effects. Such simulations have built-in models but in most simulation software these models are fixed and cannot be changed by the users. Modelling software, however, enables users to change and build their own models.

Some types of modelling can facilitate students' conceptual understanding of specific aspects of science. The use of molecular modelling software, for example, has enabled students to achieve higher grades on tests designed to assess conceptual understanding of chemical change (Ardac and Akaygun, 2004; Dori and Barak, 2001; Dori et al., 2003). For instance, Dori and Barak (2001) used a combination of physical and virtual modelling to support the development of conceptual understanding. They conducted an experimental study with 276 students from nine high schools in Israel using a new teaching method in which students built physical and virtual three-dimensional molecular models. The students in the experimental group gained a better understanding of the concepts illustrated by the model and were more capable in several important ways:

- defining and implementing new concepts;
- mentally traversing across four levels of understanding in chemistry: symbol, macroscopic, microscopic and process;
- applying transformation from two-dimensional representations of molecules, provided by either a symbolic or a structural formula, to three-dimensional representations, to a drawing of a model, and of applying reverse transformations.

Furthermore, the researchers found that the enquiry-based learning tasks encouraged understanding of organic compounds and provided students with tools for explaining their answers. In this research, the molecular modelling software provided building blocks that are equivalent to physical modelling kits that have been used in chemistry teaching for many years. As such, it is an example of how computer-based representations can support the development of understanding of different representations of phenomena. Examples of modelling in science that may develop improved conceptual understanding of dynamic processes also include mathematical modelling of climate change, predator–prey relationships and models in mechanics.

Understanding modelling through constructing models

Understanding the use of models and modelling in science is important for developing scientific understanding because models are used to explain and communicate findings in science and to plan scientific research as well as to help students to understand scientific ideas (Brodie et al., 1994). Duit and Treagust (2003) reviewed research into students' understanding of models, however, and reported that students 'find the diverse models that are used to explain science challenging and confusing' (p. 678). Generally, students are presented with models constructed by others and they may find difficulties in understanding their purpose, value and limitations. However, using modelling software, students can build their own models by identifying relevant factors and variables and hypothesizing relationships. Thus, even though students' models may be limited or simplistic, being able to engage in the modelling process may help them to understand the nature of models and modelling.

Some studies have begun to examine in detail students' reasoning while collaborating with a modelling environment, for example, while modelling plant growth students were able to reason at several different levels of abstraction (Ergazaki et al., 2005). Other studies, for example, examining modelling of one-dimensional collisions between moving objects based on programming in ToonTalk, a simple programming language for children to create games and animations, revealed the importance of providing a modelling environment with an appropriate level of complexity that enables students to focus on the scientific problem rather than the challenge of learning the software (Simpson et al., 2005). This study also showed the crucial importance of the teacher/researcher's role, and the ways in which the collaboration between students helped in generating a classroom discourse that supported scientific enquiry.

Supporting students in visualizing processes

Many areas of science involve visualizing structures and processes that cannot easily be observed. For example, expert geologists, when viewing a landscape, can visualize the processes that led to its formation. Developments in computing power and modelling techniques using visual representations as outputs have become increasingly important in medical research as well as for understanding current global issues such as climate change (Brady, 2009).

The relationship between spatial ability, gender and success in science and mathematics has been investigated over the past 20 years. Spatial ability includes the ability to visualize the concepts of area, volume, distance, translation, rotation, and reflection and to combine measurement concepts with projective skills. Generally, males develop spatial ability earlier than females and students with high spatial ability scores perform better in some areas of science (see Sorby, 2009, for a brief review). For example, in a meta-analysis of spatial studies, Linn and Petersen (1985) found that males outperformed females on mental rotation tasks and they attributed this difference to their preferred strategies: males were more likely to use a 'holistic strategy' that relied on visualizing the whole object whereas females were more likely to use an analytic strategy based on a systematic, stepwise approach.

Visualization skills can be developed through training (Piburn et al., 2005; Sorby, 2009). For example, Piburn et al. (2005), who used software designed for visualizing geological processes, found that detailed instruction in visualization techniques using the software enabled college students to go on to use the software to develop better understanding of geological processes.

Not surprisingly, then, one of the claims for computer–based representations, simulations or animations is that they can support students in visualizing phenomena. In reviewing the evidence for the value of animation alone (that is, without interaction), for enabling students to learn, Tversky et al. (2002) found that many animations fail to improve learning beyond that achieved by static representations. They attributed this to their finding that animations were often too fast or too complex. They suggested that designers need to focus on presenting only the information essential to the processes to be conveyed and eliminating extraneous but sometimes appealing information. Furthermore, schematizing the process rather than representing it realistically tends to make it easier to follow (Tversky et al., 2002).

The conclusion to be drawn from this work is that the visualization skills desirable for learning science can be developed and that animations and simulations can support students in visualizing phenomena but animations are not always helpful.

Using automated methods for collecting and handling data

In scientific research, much of the tedious work of data collection and analysis is now computerized. In educational contexts, hardware and software for automatic data collection are now easy to use and can support students in the design of data collection, logging data in the laboratory or field and analysis of data. Research suggests that benefits of using computers for data logging include time saving (Barton, 1997), an improved ability to interpret data (Linn and Hsi, 2000) (as discussed in the next section), and more focused student–student interactions and interactions with the computer that could support *deep learning* (Russell et al., 2004). Evidence suggests that the use of computers for data-logging enables students to focus on higher level skills. For example, in a study of lesson evaluations of 61 teachers, Rogers and Finlayson (2004) found that teachers perceived gains in the accuracy of data obtained electronically from experiments and the speed of graphical representation as being important for improving students' learning as the technology enabled them to focus more on analysis and interpretation of data. Where students were working in groups using data-loggers to record experimental results, this freed up the teachers to circulate and stimulate discussion and thinking about the findings. Furthermore, discussion between students and the teacher did not interrupt the recording process which proceeded automatically under software control, for example, one teacher commented:

> Whilst circulating, I was able to draw individual groups' attention to the emerging graph and to pose questions about what might be happening, thereby guiding them to ideas later expressed during the debriefing session.
>
> (2004, p. 295)

Interpreting data and graphs

Whereas most of the findings related to data-logging mentioned above were based on students' and teachers' perceptions, a number of studies in the United States have measured specific skills involved in interpreting graphs in order to investigate the value of microcomputer-based laboratories (MBL) which are basically sets of sensors and data-logging devices connected to computers to enable real-time data collection, graphing and analysis. A review of this research by Linn and Hsi concluded students are much better at interpreting the findings of their experiments when they use real-time data collection than when they use conventional techniques for graphing their data, and this greater understanding is carried over to topics where they have not collected the data themselves (Linn and Hsi, 2000).

Interpreting multivariate data is considered to be a complex problem requiring high-level skills and therefore beyond the reach of many students. However, classroom observations suggest that the use of software can enable a wider range of students than previously envisaged to interpret such data (Ridgway et al., 2008). The software can provide on-screen sliders to manipulate and compare variables easily across multiple views of the data so that students can easily observe the effects on the graphs of changing values of different variables.

Extending learning opportunities through fieldwork using technology

The benefits of extending learning outside of the classroom into the field and the built environment include first-hand opportunities to engage with scientific concepts within a wider range of contexts. Many of these experiences involve data collection that can now be done by mobile computers that enable automated data collection and analysis in any location. However, as King and

Glackin discuss in Chapter 12 in this volume, learning outside of the classroom presents additional challenges for teachers beyond those of classroom-based work. Teachers need to ensure that experiences outside the classroom generate learning that is complementary to classroom-based work by managing opportunities before, during and after the event.

In addition to mobile computers and data-logging devices, other technologies that could support and enable learning through fieldwork include webcams, remote access telescopes, remote monitors of air quality and temperature, wireless internet access, social networking technology, Geographical Positioning Systems (GPS), 3D-mapping data and associated software including 'photo-stitching' software. Photo-stitching enables photographs to be joined into panoramas including 360° views. This technique, combined with web and wireless technology, would allow people to discuss and compare structures at remote locations while viewing real-time images. Combining this range of technologies provides for possibilities of students working collaboratively at the same or different locations, recording various types of data and observations and comparing their findings with other data globally while moving between many different environments.

All the technologies mentioned in the section have undergone particularly rapid development in recent years and this progress has been accompanied by many small-scale research and development studies to explore their possibilities for supporting fieldwork and enabling learning. Scanlon et al., in a review of some case studies of mobile technology (Scanlon et al., 2005), suggest that the unique affordances associated with handheld computers include permanence, accessibility and immediacy as well as portability. Thus students can access the tools and data they need, wherever and whenever they need it.

In summary, the technologies outlined here appear to support the blurring of boundaries between the classroom and outside spaces as well as enabling more collaborative approaches. Much of the fieldwork could be replaced by the use of remote access devices through the web, as discussed in the next section, or through the use of virtual worlds. Challenges for teachers remain in ensuring that the opportunities of the outside spaces, remote access, virtual worlds and other technological tools are chosen and deployed to enable appropriate learning.

Research projects facilitated by online communication

It has long been recognized that research projects enable students to gain insight into how real science investigations may be conducted. However, they are difficult for teachers to manage because students and teachers need access to a wide range of information. Web-based resources and online communication can enable teachers to run such projects in collaboration with researchers and science centres. For example, Hollow (2000) reported case studies from schools in Australia and elsewhere of student research projects in optical and radio astronomy using remote access telescopes. The benefits of these types of experience were evident to teachers and students but are difficult or even impossible to quantify or describe in terms of students' attainment or achievement in any measurable way.

Internet-based resources have also facilitated individual science teachers in running simple research projects. For example, Wilson (2001) described how his class of students used a website to find out information about woodlice prior to carrying out practical investigations for GCSE science. The website gave them a greater choice of investigation and therefore supported their planning, and enabled them to relate to other work in their analysis.

An experimental study in Israel investigated ways of developing scientific inquiry skills in 15-year-olds using a software environment called MINT in which students from different schools received metacognitive guidance during the process of performing inquiry tasks in microbiology (Zion et al., 2005). The researchers found that both asynchronous communication and metacognitive instruction enhanced development of scientific inquiry skills over face-to-face discussion, but when these two methods were combined, inquiry skills become even better (Zion et al., 2005). They attributed at least part of the benefit of asynchronous communication to the process of writing ideas and being able to review them later during metacognitive activities.

Learning through researching on the web

Better internet access and a proliferation of web-based science resources have supported a massive increase in the use of the web for learning science through researching ideas and information. Using web-based material has enabled more student participation and generated more interest particularly in some of the drier science topics, according to observations made by Ruthven et al. (2004). In case studies in the UK, science teachers emphasized a need for carefully structured tasks to avoid unproductive web-surfing (Hennessy et al., 2005; Rogers and Finlayson, 2004; Ruthven et al., 2004). Teachers concluded that they needed to plan lessons carefully and filter information beforehand in order to ensure that students were dealing with useful, accessible and relevant information (Hennessy et al., 2005). They made use of electronic worksheets with salient hyperlinks, intranets with bounded databases and time-limited tasks to achieve focused work. Studies in the United States also found that students can use on-line resources for investigative work in science when extensive support and scaffolding are provided by the teacher (Hoffman et al., 2003; Linn et al., 2004). One approach to this form of learning is 'WebQuest': an inquiry-oriented lesson format developed originally by Bernie Dodge at San Diego State University. A wide range of WebQuests have now been developed and can be used and adapted by teachers (see http://webquest.org/). Another approach called the Web-based Integrated Science Environment (WISE) (see http://wise.berkeley.edu) incorporates a more specifically collaborative approach to pedagogy (Linn et al., 2004) as will be discussed later.

Student presentations and productions

When students are asked to research a topic using web-based and other resources, they are usually asked to create a product that makes their findings available to an audience of peers or others. PowerPoint presentations are probably the most common products and can become monotonous or repetitive for students, but some teachers encourage production of animations, podcasts and videos (for example, see Branigan, 2005). Students and teachers often report on the motivational effects and learning benefits of such activities but specific learning gains have not yet been demonstrated and are hard to measure.

Learning through playing computer games

The learning benefits of games and simulations in educational contexts have been researched for many years. Some educational simulations have game-like elements and the evidence for learning gains from simulations designed for education has been discussed in previous sections. Claims have also been made over many years for the beneficial effects on learning of games played for entertainment, but there is little evidence of such effects that transfer to other contexts (Buckingham et al., 2008). Nevertheless, the rapid developments in computer gaming including online 'multi-user' collaborative gaming, and their popularity with young people, suggest that teachers should develop an awareness of possible learning effects and new opportunities. While educational games and simulation programs have generally been based firmly on research on young people's understanding in science and can engage students in school settings, they do not incorporate many of the structural characteristics such as graphics, realistic setting, use of humour and character development that make video games enjoyable to play and encourage many young people to engage in computer gaming in their leisure time (Wood et al., 2004).

Although there have been various games with scientific content over the years, the majority of the recent successful major games have been set in historical or fantasy settings rather than scientific contexts. That may change with the release of *Spore*, designed by the creator of the best-selling video games, *The Sims* and *SimCity*. *Spore* allows you to 'evolve' a species from single-cell level to a civilization engaged in intergalactic warfare. While *Spore* is intended purely for entertainment and may not model scientific processes accurately, it might encourage young people to think about evolution. A video game developed by the Federation of American Scientists to teach scientific facts about immunology (*Immune Attack*) (see http://fas.org/immuneattack/) is being trialled by schools, and preliminary findings suggest that playing the game is developing an understanding of immunology as well as greater interest in science. Both *Immune Attack* and *Spore* are single user games but *Spore* integrates with web 2.0 technologies enabling collaboration and sharing of user-generated content as well as links to browser technology that could also enable people to share their searching experiences (Cocker, 2008).

Exploring science in virtual reality

Recently, new developments in gaming and related technology outlined above have begun to provide new learning opportunities, especially those involving virtual reality. Current developments include games linking seamlessly to virtual worlds and the use of haptic technology. Role-play and identification with virtual avatars (customizable 3D representations of a person) are central to learning in immersive worlds (Francis, 2006). Developments in virtual reality environments are proceeding rapidly as increasing computer power and software developments enable more realistic 3D representations of both the environment and the avatar. Hence, developers are striving to achieve a more immersive experience. For example, research based on self-reporting suggests that being able to customize their avatars increases users' sense of presence in the game and their motivation to continue playing (Bailey et al., 2009). Current facilities in Second Life that could enable learning are the ability to conduct virtual genetic experiments, interact with molecular models, explore inside a giant cell or a human body organ and project weather data onto 3D terrain models and to interact with other learners in these settings.

When the learner is immersed in a virtual reality environment, their learning will depend on various interacting factors including: their ability to move between real and virtual states (Sakonidis, 1994; Kim and Shin, 2001), their feeling of presence in the game (Heeter, 2003) and the correspondence between the real and the virtual world (Sakonidis, 1994). Therefore, understanding how virtual reality environments may affect students' learning is extremely complex and is, as yet, little understood.

Technology-mediated collaborative learning

Many of the studies discussed in this chapter involved collaboration between students and the benefits of such collaboration were generally noted by the teachers and students involved in the studies as well as the researchers. Quantifying the effects of collaboration and characterizing effective collaboration, however, are still major research challenges. Since the early years of research into computers in education in the 1980s, the benefits of collaborative learning supported by computers have been proposed and investigated. Based on a review of research into collaborative learning with computers, Crook (1998) has argued, however, that there are significant pedagogical challenges in enabling collaborative learning. Hence, while computers can support collaborative learning, suitable software design, appropriate deployment of computers in the classroom and other aspects of teachers' pedagogical approaches are crucial for effective collaboration.

Evidence for significant positive effects of collaboration on achievement comes from a meta-analysis by Johnson et al. (2000) based on 158 studies of 'cooperative learning'. It is important to note that when Johnson et al. use the term 'cooperative learning', they mean students working together to accomplish shared learning goals, a definition that is more usually applied to the term collaborative learning. Their analysis revealed a range of different pedagogical approaches to 'cooperative learning' but they reported that there is almost no research on the relative impact of these different approaches. The key finding of their meta-analysis was that all of the methods of collaborative learning have substantial effect sizes and all have been found to produce significantly higher achievement than did competitive or individualistic learning.

Identifying the optimum arrangements for effective collaborative learning in science is a continuing research challenge but some evidence suggests that the cognitive conflict that is also important in the Cognitive Acceleration through Science Education pedagogy (see Chapter 5) may be an important factor. For example, Bennett et al. (2004), in a review of studies of small group work in science, found evidence of significant improvement of students' understanding where group discussions were based on a combination of internal conflict (that is, where a diversity of views and/or understanding are represented within a group) and external conflict (where an external stimulus presents a group with conflicting views).

In the Technology-Enhanced Secondary Science Instruction (TESSI) project, collaboration between pupils was a key element for clarifying understanding and supporting deeper learning (Pedretti et al., 1998). The self-pacing aspect of the TESSI course required pupils to monitor their own learning, and contributed to their time-management and organizational skills, fostering a kind of self-regulation and direction extending beyond the immediate use of technology. In these studies, the use of technology was associated with a decrease in direction and exposition by the teacher, a corresponding increase in pupil self-regulation, and more collaboration between pupils. However, a small minority of pupils reported that they preferred to learn in a more teacher-centred environment, with detailed directions and firm deadlines.

The Computer Supported Collaborative Learning (CSCL) movement that started in North America has taken an inter-disciplinary approach to researching and developing the technological tools needed to enable collaborative learning and the theoretical perspectives that can inform research in this area (see Stahl et al., 2006). It is widely recognized that early designs for virtual learning environments (VLEs) including Blackboard and WebCT were based on an 'instructionist' approach to pedagogy and their tools were not well suited to collaborative learning. The aim of the CSCL community is to develop tools that support emerging understanding of collaborative learning processes (Stahl et al., 2006). Tools developed by the CSCL community include: computer-mediated communication (CMC) that incorporates 'interaction rules' that can be continuously reinforced and hence scaffold the interaction (Dillenbourg, 1999); interactive brainstorming environments; collaborative writing tools as well as tools designed to support interaction in domain specific environments, for example, a computer-based 3D model of a research laboratory (see Krange and Ludvigsen, 2008).

Much of the earlier research into CMC was conducted in higher education where using CMC in distance and 'blended learning', that is, various combinations of face-to-face and online learning are now widespread. This research has shown that early naïve assumptions that simply providing CMC tools will enable communication and collaboration were incorrect (Zhao and Rop, 2001): instead careful design of courses and scaffolding of interactions, at least in the early stages of a course, are required (Pena-Shaff and Nicholls, 2004). Furthermore, encouraging students to argue constructively online presents a considerable challenge (Nussbaum et al., 2004). Even in face-to-face settings enabling students to develop their abilities to argue from evidence to conclusions is an important and demanding aim for twenty-first-century science education that presents significant pedagogical challenges as discussed by Evagorou and Osborne in Chapter 7.

Research into CMC in schools has been less extensive than in higher education but studies starting from classroom-based learning are beginning to explore the opportunities provided by CSCL. An experimental study by Shell et al. (2005) showed how CSCL tools can be integrated into classroom learning and surveys of teachers' and students' perceptions suggested that the CSCL approach promoted knowledge-building strategies such as asking questions and collaboration.

One approach to using CSCL tools that also incorporates the use of web-based resources was developed by Marcia Linn and colleagues and is based on a design approach referred to as a 'Knowledge Integration Environment' (KIE) (Linn, 2000). This approach aims to scaffold learning of new knowledge through the application of four main tenets: (1) making science accessible for all students; (2) making thinking visible so students understand the process of knowledge integration; (3) helping students to listen to and understand each other's ideas and arguments; and (4) promoting lifelong science learning (Linn, 2000, p. 784). These four tenets are based on the 'pragmatic pedagogical principles' identified by Linn and Hsi (2000) that are discussed later in terms of new roles for teachers. Two factors that are crucial to enabling collaborative learning through the KIE approach are the selection of suitable web-based materials that students find personally relevant and scaffolding students in constructing and editing their arguments. For example, Bell and Linn (2000) used software called SenseMaker in which students, working in pairs, constructed graphical representations jointly of their arguments about light propagation. This software enabled them to represent evidence from the web by a dot in the SenseMaker argument with a link to its internet location. Students could make their thinking visible by describing and grouping the evidence using 'frames'. Students began with frames for the two sides of the debate: 'light goes forever until absorbed' and 'light dies out'. They could add new frames within existing frames or outside the existing frames. A software component called Mildred enabled students to ask for hints about the activities, evidence and claims to support their explanations. In this study, analysis of students' developing conceptual understanding through pre- and post-tests suggested that they were moving towards the accepted scientific understanding and their explanations were becoming more specific and detailed.

Another approach to CSCL used an online discourse system to support scientific argumentation within the classroom in the context of an inquiry based on thermal equilibrium for eighth-grade students (Clark and Sampson, 2007). The students built principles to describe the data they had collected in the laboratory. These principles were used to seed the online discussion and the software sorted the students into discussion groups based on the principles they had built so that each discussion group incorporated multiple perspectives. Students then followed a set of guidelines to critique one another's principles. Clark and Sampson's analysis suggested that this approach of 'personally seeded discussions' produced more in-depth arguments than those found in other studies of science discourse in classrooms. This resonates with Bennett et al.'s (2004) findings, mentioned earlier, that students' understanding is improved where group discussions incorporate internal conflict within a group. Moreover, Clark and Sampson (2007) argued that this use of software to import argumentation into the classroom may be easier than the extensive professional development that has been required to enable teachers to support argumentation in science lessons.

Incorporating CMC into pedagogical approaches can offer several new learning affordances through asynchronous discussions including: giving learners time to consider their responses; extending discussions beyond the timeframe of a lesson; enabling more students to share their ideas; and preserving discussions for later review. In order to take advantage of these new learning opportunities provided by CMC and social networking technologies, users also need different social and emotional skills in addition to those used in face-to-face communication (Jones and Issroff, 2005). These include the ability not only to share knowledge but also to share emotions by means of CMC and to develop knowledge in collaboration with others (Eshet-Alkalai, 2004). Yet, how learning and collaborating through social networking both in formal and informal educational settings are influencing students' learning strategies and practices is not yet clearly known.

Learning and skill development at home and leisure

Since Marc Prensky claimed that young people are 'digital natives', growing up in an environment where computers and communication technologies are ubiquitous, and being able to 'think and process information fundamentally differently from their predecessors' (Prenksy, 2001, p. 1), researchers and others have been examining and discussing this claim. It is obviously important to understand how young people are changing but the 'digital natives' paradigm may actually be unhelpful by diverting our attention from the *diversity* of young people's experiences with technology. For example, in a large three-year ethnographic study in the United States, that examined the participation of young people aged 8 to 20 in the new media, Ito et al. (2008) found that young people were engaged in a diverse range of experiences: many were interacting socially online and a smaller number were exploring interests and finding information that went beyond what they had access to at school or in their local community. In the past few years, evidence has been accumulating of how young people use technologies for leisure and educational purposes outside of school, for example, studies have shown the following significant developments.

- Use of the internet has changed ways in which young people communicate and interact socially (Abbott, 2005; Kent and Facer, 2004; Ofcom, 2006) as well as their access to knowledge (Green and Hannon, 2007).
- Use of technologies outside of the classroom is extensive and includes mobile phones (Ito, 2003), games (Facer, 2003), person-to-person sharing of music (Ebare, 2004), chat and instant messaging (Becta, 2007) as well as surfing, downloading material, construction of personal web pages and social networking in virtual worlds. Many young people are actively involved in this 'participatory culture' (Jenkins et al., 2006).
- Social virtual worlds such as Second Life (www.secondlife.com) are drawing people together for various self and group-determined purposes including educational ones (Schome-community, 2007).
- Some young people 'geek out' and become deeply interested, knowledgeable or skilled in a topic (Ito et al., 2008). They link into specialized knowledge groups of all ages from around the world to develop themselves and may gain reputation among expert peers.

It is clear that the world of young people is changing dramatically. Literacy now encompasses media literacy (Sefton-Green, 2007) and 'multi-literacies' (Street, 2006). Yet in spite of all this research, variations in use of technology among young people are little understood as research has focused on those highly motivated technology users with access to networks of knowledge (Green and Hannon, 2007) leaving unanswered questions about less motivated young people and low users of technology (CIBER, 2008). Moreover, there is little evidence to suggest that schools are building on students' growing digital literacy.

Teachers' pedagogical approaches with technology

The evidence discussed in previous sections suggests that the benefits of technology use for learning are achieved through interactions between students and technology and by peer interaction while using technologies. The technologies can act as mediators between learners and teachers in the physical or virtual worlds. This learning is further enabled when tasks are designed to be done collaboratively and scaffolded by the teacher either directly or by carefully designed worksheets. However, despite all these opportunities, research into science teachers' use of technologies in the UK suggests that teacher demonstration persists as the most common mode of use of technologies (Cox and Webb, 2004; Rogers and Finlayson, 2003, 2004).

Studies of science teachers who were engaged in developing the use of ICT for learning (John and Baggott La Velle, 2004; Rogers and Finlayson, 2004; Ruthven et al., 2004), found that the teachers perceived the ability for students to explore simulations and to see animations of processes that are difficult to visualize as particularly valuable for science learning. Although teachers believed that group-work using simulations would be beneficial for their students' learning, they were used mainly for class demonstrations. Teachers cited logistical constraints such as difficulties in booking a computer room or a limited supply of computers as reasons for these decisions (Rogers and Finlayson, 2004). Even teachers who were experienced in using ICT in science teaching and had access to technologies found difficulty in reconciling curriculum pressures with their beliefs in the value of students learning through experimentation (Ruthven, 2005). While these resource and curriculum constraints are undoubtedly significant factors, the pedagogical challenges and changing roles of teachers and students, as discussed in the next section, may be other important factors affecting teachers' use of technology.

New roles for the teacher and students?

There have been only very few projects that have gone beyond the constraints of traditional curricula and explored how good access to a range of new technologies can enable new approaches to learning, new curricula and new roles for the teacher and students. Reporting on one such project, that investigated pedagogical issues for science education within technology-enabled classrooms without typical curricula constraints, Linn and Hsi (2000, p. 337) produced a set of 'pragmatic pedagogical principles':

- Encourage students to build on their scientific ideas as they develop more and more powerful and useful pragmatic scientific principles.
- Encourage students to investigate personally relevant problems and revisit their scientific ideas regularly.
- Scaffold science activities so students participate in the enquiry process.

- Model the scientific process of considering alternative explanations and diagnosing mistakes.
- Scaffold students' feedback to explain their ideas.
- Provide multiple visual representations from varied media.
- Encourage students to listen and learn from each other.
- Design social activities to promote productive and respectful interactions.
- Scaffold groups to design criteria and standards.
- Employ multiple social activity structures.
- Engage students in reflecting on their scientific ideas and on their own progress in understanding science.
- Engage students as critics of diverse scientific information.
- Engage students in varied sustained scientific project experiences.
- Establish an enquiry process which can be generalized and is suitable for diverse scientific projects.

Most of these principles are not focused on the technology but on enabling students to interact with each other and with the teacher. As the technology took over basic organizational and management tasks, the teacher's role became more focused on enabling learning through interactions.

Linn and Hsi (2000) found that each student drew on different 'pivotal cases' to organize their thinking. Pivotal cases are examples that promote knowledge restructuring by helping students to link their thinking about science to observations from their everyday lives. For each class, the teacher needed to research students' understanding, analyse their thinking and identify pivotal cases that would build on students' ideas and inspire them to reflect on and restructure their views. The teachers then had to use these pivotal cases at appropriate times in discussion with the students. For example, students often find thermal equilibrium a difficult concept owing to their personal experiences. Therefore a student who believes that metals have the capacity to impart cold would be asked to consider 'How do metals feel in a hot or cold car?' For some students, thinking through the answer to such a question may clarify their thinking about why objects feel colder or warmer even if they are at the same temperature, but simulations that allowed them to compare the temperature and feel of objects have also been developed (Linn 2000).

Knowledge of pivotal cases and when to deploy them is an example of the 'pedagogical content knowledge' (PCK) that is one of the types of knowledge that all teachers need to deploy in their 'pedagogical reasoning' processes when planning lessons and interacting with students (Shulman, 1987).

Implications for teachers' pedagogy and practices in the future

As outlined in this chapter, the current evidence for benefits for technology-mediated learning and opportunities provided by current technological

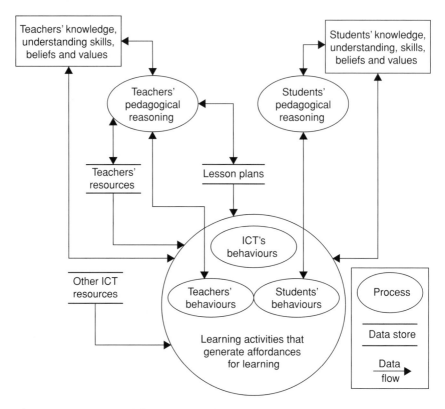

Figure 8.1 Framework for pedagogical practices relating to ICT use
Source: Adapted from Webb and Cox (2004, p. 239).

developments presents considerable challenges for teachers. The set of 'pragmatic pedagogical principles' listed in the previous section provides a useful checklist for teachers who are engaging with new technologies. Figure 8.1 presents an overview of how the behaviour of teachers, students and technologies combine to create affordances for learning within activities that may be classroom-based or outside the classroom and may or may not involve online elements. In this diagram, Gibson's original concept of affordance being a property of the environment and the possible actions of the learner is used (Gibson, 1979). Each of the processes in Figure 8.1 incorporates various subprocesses that use various sets of data. For example teachers' knowledge bases, according to Shulman (1987), include the following categories of knowledge:

- content knowledge;
- general pedagogical knowledge (knowledge related to general teaching issues, for example, teaching approaches, classroom management);

- curriculum knowledge (knowledge about the 'tools of the trade': schemes of work, resources, etc.);
- PCK;
- knowledge of learners and their characteristics;
- knowledge of educational contexts: groups, classes, school and wider community;
- knowledge of educational ends, purpose and values and their philosophical and historical grounds.

In order to design learning experiences that take advantage of technology-mediated learning, teachers need not only this extensive set of knowledge types but also knowledge of how the wide range of technologies available may support the content to be taught and which pedagogical approaches are appropriate. This knowledge has been described as technological pedagogical content knowledge (TPCK) (Koehler and Mishra, 2005) and is represented as an intersection between technological knowledge, pedagogical knowledge and content knowledge. Thus, Figure 8.1 gives some indication of the complexity of the processes with which teachers must engage and the range of knowledge and skills they may need.

Teaching has always involved a range of knowledge, skills and processes. However, a number of changes are being brought about by technologies and new opportunities for learning that increase challenges for teachers. Changes include:

- Students learning more outside school from web-based material and from other experts through the web.
- Expectations that teachers will use the technologies available to them to improve their teaching and their students' learning.

Opportunities enabled by technologies are many and varied, as has been discussed in this chapter. The complexity of the decision-making processes as outlined in Figure 8.1, and the extensive and continually changing nature of TPCK make the challenge of teaching in the twenty-first century quite daunting. Indeed, arguably, for a teacher operating on their own using twentieth-century pedagogy, there may be no future. The future lies in teachers working together to design learning experiences and enable learners to understand and manage their own learning. Thus learners may be enabled to undertake all or parts of a pedagogical reasoning process themselves to plan and manage their own learning as shown in Figure 8.1. Establishing how this may be achieved is another research challenge but the assessment for learning and associated pedagogy discussed in Chapter 9 suggests some possibilities. Opportunities also exist for 'software agents' that can participate in pedagogical reasoning as they build knowledge of learners' interests and learning experiences (Callaghan et al., 2004). This sharing of roles could change the nature of teaching and learning and present opportunities for more useful and more enjoyable learning.

Conclusion

In this chapter, research into the ways in which technologies can support learning and can mediate interactions between students and between students and teachers and between scientific ideas and students has been discussed. As technologies develop, they will be appropriated in various ways into activities in which learners and teachers interact with each other and new affordances for learning will emerge. Researchers will continue to investigate learning in these technology-rich environments and their studies will need to be informed from research into other areas of learning and education particularly including pedagogy, collaboration and argumentation. For the teacher, the research findings discussed in this chapter present a number of challenges including: the range of types of technology that can support learning; the ubiquitous nature of new technologies; the expectation from young people that they will use new technologies; the relative ease with which young people embrace new technologies and the large volume of TPCK that needs to be developed.

We can, however, identify some ways forward. Teachers working together can develop TPCK, and as well as working with colleagues locally, there are now many opportunities to benefit from and share with other teachers and scientists on the web. Linn and Hsi's (2000) pragmatic pedagogic principles provide a useful checklist for science learning activities whether or not you are using new technologies. At least some students will be developing skills with new technologies that they can share with you and other students.

In the longer term, software may become better at supporting and scaffolding learning but for the foreseeable future teachers have the major role to play in responding to new affordances provided by technologies, designing learning situations and regulating them interactively.

Further reading

Cox, M. J. and Webb, M. E. (2004) *ICT and Pedagogy: A Review of the Research Literature*. Coventry and London: British Educational Communications and Technology Agency/Department for Education and Skills.

Linn, M. C. and Hsi, S. (2000) *Computers, Teachers, Peers: Science Learning Partners*. London: Erlbaum.

Scanlon, E., Jones, A. and Waycott, J. (2005) Mobile technologies: prospects for their use in learning in informal science settings, *Journal of Interactive Media in Education* 25. Available at: http://hal.archives-ouvertes.fr/docs/00/19/03/16/PDF/Eileen-Scanlon-2005.pdf.

Webb, M. E. (2005) Affordances of ICT in science learning; implications for an integrated pedagogy, *International Journal of Science Education*, 27(6): 705–35.

9   Formative assessment in science

Paul Black and Christine Harrison

Introduction

This chapter describes ideas and advice that bear upon an important and yet challenging aspect of the teacher's role in promoting students' learning. Formative assessment is a key component of good practice; the first section justifies this assertion by explaining the principles which should form the basis for your thinking about the ways in which teachers help students to learn. This is followed by a brief account both of the research evidence which supports the claim that this aspect of teaching and learning is important, and then by other evidence which shows that it is poorly developed in normal practice.

The third section contains the main messages of the chapter, for it presents descriptions and analyses of examples of everyday activity in science teaching in order to explain and exemplify the range of practice of formative assessment. This is followed by a shorter section on the challenges that arise when teachers try to implement changes of the type suggested here. A closing section summarizes the main messages and relates some of these to current national policies in the UK.

Basic principles

Two phrases, 'formative assessment' and 'assessment for learning' are used to describe the activities discussed here. The main idea can be defined as follows:

> Assessment for learning is any assessment for which the first priority in its design and practice is to serve the purpose of promoting pupils' learning. It thus differs from assessment designed primarily to serve the purposes of accountability, or of ranking, or of certifying competence.
>
> An assessment activity can help learning if it provides information to be used as feedback, by teachers, and by their pupils in assessing themselves and each other, to modify the teaching and learning activities in which they are engaged. Such assessment becomes 'formative assessment' when the evidence is actually used to adapt the teaching work to meet learning needs.
>
> (Black et al., 2002 inside front cover)

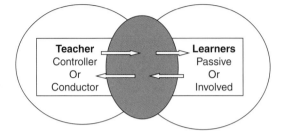

Figure 9.1 A model of formative interaction

The key point here is that the information is used to modify the activities. Thus, where a test is used only to record a mark or grade, and so to serve as a summary of a learner's achievement, it is summative, not formative: the test as such might be either formative or summative, it is the purpose for which the evidence is used, however, that matters.

A basic model is represented in Figure 9.1 (from Black and Wiliam, 2009). This is a model of a typical classroom episode, which starts when the teacher begins by presenting a task or question to the class (the arrows from left to right): pupils may then respond (the arrows from right to left), and in the light of that response the teacher has to decide what to do next. The responses of learners are frequently unpredictable, so it follows that genuinely formative interaction is contingent, that is, what happens will depend on how learners respond. The teacher's response may be to judge the response as a right or wrong answer, or the teacher may avoid this and try instead to draw other pupils into the discussion. If others join in, then there will be many such interactions in which the classroom (the shaded area) becomes a forum for general discussion. The process represented might either be an oral one, in which a two-way step might only last a few seconds, or a written interaction for which the time-scale might be much longer.

In terms of Figure 9.1, the teacher's task can be seen as involving:

1. deciding about the selection and presentation of the task, then,
2. interpreting the learner response, and then,
3. deciding what best to do next.

These three stages will be discussed in detail in the next section. However, there are some general principles about learning which should guide all of this activity. The first of these is that new ideas cannot simply be taken on board by a learner exactly as they are presented. Learners will always try to relate new ideas to those with which they are already familiar: hence the break between the arrows from left to right in Figure 9.1, which represents the fact that what is received will be an interpretation of what was intended, not a literal copy. For example, a teacher says to a 6-year-old drawing a picture of a daffodil: 'What is this flower called?' The child answers: 'I think it's called Betty' (Fisher,

2005). The child has identified the task in terms of her understanding of the term 'called'; her standard for a satisfactory answer is that of everyday talk, not that of a learning discourse in which the distinction between proper and generic names is essential. A teacher may think the answer is thoughtless – the break in the response arrows represents this possibility – and so be tempted to just ask other children the same question until someone give the 'right', that is, the expected, answer. However, a formative response would take the child's thinking seriously and require the teachers to formulate a way to open up discussion on various meanings of the phrase 'is called'. Thus, learning work will be most effective if teachers are attuned to the starting points in the learners' thinking, so that their contributions open up and guide interactions which will help learners to challenge and re-construct that thinking.

This first principle relates closely to the second, which is that the learner must be actively involved in such re-construction: learning cannot be done *to* the learner, it has to be done *by* the learner – re-building her or his own ideas. Hence dialogue, and not mere presentation by the teacher, is essential.

A third principle is implied in the above argument: learning is not a wholly individual activity, it is also social – learning through discussion is an essential feature. As Alexander (2004, p. 9) puts it:

> Children, we now know, need to talk, and to experience a rich diet of spoken language, in order to think and to learn. Reading, writing and number may be acknowledged curriculum 'basics', but talk is arguably the true foundation of learning.

Skilfully conducted, such dialogues can yield good results, but on their own they will not be sufficient. The learners may do well, but they will be dependent on the teacher's skill in steering the discussion in order to foster the maturing of their learning. What is also needed is that learners have a grasp of the target for their learning, one that is sufficiently remote that it challenges their efforts, but sufficiently close that they can guide their own work in the right direction. Maturity in learning requires such metacognition, that is, a realization that one has to be clear about where one is going, an appraisal of where one stands in relation to that target, and then some idea of how to progress in the right direction. So another aspect that is discussed further below is self-assessment, and the related activity of peer-assessment.

There is another aspect of feedback that is not covered by these principles. The idea can be illustrated by findings from research into the effects of giving feedback on written work, which shows that to give marks on a piece of work not only can be unhelpful *per se*, but can also lead students to ignore the comments altogether. For example, in research undertaken by Butler (1988), 12 classes were given identical teaching during which they were required to produce written work. Four of the classes were given back the work with no more than a mark, another four were given comments on their work with no mark, and the last four were given both marks and comments. The same test was given to all before and after the work. While those given only comments showed a 30 per cent gain in their scores, those with either marks or marks and comments showed no such gain. The giving of marks not only produced no gain in itself, it also wiped out the potential value for improving learning that might have been achieved through responding to the advice in the comments. Indeed, as another aspect of Butler's work showed, there can be deeper harm in that a focus on marks can produce what she and other researchers have called 'ego' or 'performance' orientation. This is an attitude in which both high and low attainers focus on comparing themselves with their peers, and which leads them to be reluctant to take risks and to react badly to new challenges, because of the potential to encounter failures which might damage their self-esteem. The opposite attitude can be described as task orientation, in which learners believe that they can improve by their own effort, are willing to take on new challenges, and to learn from failure. The evidence is that a diet of frequent marks can produce enhanced ego/performance orientation. In contrast, if feedback consisting solely of comments is provided, task-involvement is developed. Moreover, those with a task-involved mind-set go on to become more competent learners (Dweck, 2000).

The general principle involved here applies also to oral dialogue: any judgemental feedback, that is, which judges a contribution, showing, directly or obliquely, merely that it is right or wrong, may well have a negative effect, whereas responses which indicate how to improve performance can have a positive effect on learning.

Evidence from research on formative assessment

Evidence of success

From the literature published since 1986 it is possible to select at least 20 studies which describe how the effects of formative assessment have been tested by quantitative measures which compare students' test achievement with those of students taught by conventional methods (Black and Wiliam, 1998a, 1998b). All of these studies show that innovations which strengthen the practice of formative assessment produce significant learning gains. These studies range over all ages (from 5-year-olds to university undergraduates), across several school subjects, and over several countries. The experimental outcomes are reported in terms of effect size, which is the ratio of the net mean learning gain to the standard deviation of the pupils' scores. Typical effect sizes are between 0.4 and 0.7: an effect size of 0.4 would mean that the average pupil involved in an innovation would record the same achievement as a pupil in the top 35 per cent of those not involved and would correspond to a gain of between one and two grades at GCSE. An independent analysis of these same experiments showed that the learning gains were greater in those studies which implemented more of the several formative practices and where the feedback given was more detailed and helpful (Nyquist, 2003).

A key feature in almost all of these studies was the concept of 'feedback'. In a review of over 3,000 research reports of the effects of feedback on performance, Kluger and DeNisi (1996) selected 131 studies which met the most stringent requirements for research evidence of improvement of learning. Overall, the results, involving over 12,000 participants, showed a mean effect size of 0.4. However, the results of the different studies covered a wide range of sizes, and for around two in every five, the effects were negative. Positive effect sizes were only found where the feedback included advice on how to improve the work: these effect sizes varied in magnitude according to the quality and appropriateness of that advice.

That the type of feedback makes a critical difference was illustrated by an experiment in which 64 students of ages 7 to 8 were divided into two comparable groups (Day and Cordon, 1993). The difference between the two was that when students were stuck and asked for help, those in the first half were given only as much help as they needed to make progress – a 'scaffolded' response, while those in the other half were given a complete solution and then given a new problem to work on. Those in the first group learned more, and retained their learning longer, than those in the second. The students who were provided with a scaffolded response were helped to make their own progress. This approach provided an opportunity to learn rather than simply a route to reach the correct answer. This opportunity was taken away from the other students when they were given the complete solution as this led them to mimic the process rather than work out the steps in the solution.

While that last study was concerned with oral feedback in class, comparable results are found for feedback on written work. Elawar and Corno (1985) gave 18 sixth grade teachers in three schools in Venezuela seven hours of training on how to give constructive written feedback on the mathematics homework produced by their students (specific comments on errors, suggestions about how to improve and at least one positive remark). Another group of teachers graded homework as normal (that is, just scores) and a third group gave constructive feedback to half their classes and just scores to the other half. The students receiving the constructive feedback learned twice as fast as the control group students (which means that they learned in one week what the others would have taken two weeks to learn). Moreover, in classes receiving the constructive feedback, the achievement gap between male and female students was reduced, and attitudes towards mathematics were more positive.

A different feature of formative assessment is illustrated by the research of White and Frederiksen (1998), which was carried out with three science teachers in four Year 8 classes in two US schools. All the teachers had students engaged for 14 weeks in a succession of the same two 7-week projects, concerned with forces and motion, with their work based on a model of enquiry that was explained to the students. All were given the same basic skills test, and all had their work marked on the projects, and they also took a test of their understanding of the physics concepts. For a part of each week, half of each teacher's classes spent some time discussing their likes and dislikes of

Table 9.1 Mean project scores of the experiment and control groups

	Lower ability half	Upper ability half
Likes and dislikes	1.9	3.3
Reflective assessment	3.1	3.8

Note: The students were given a prior test of basic skills so results could be reported separately for the 'Lower half' and the 'Upper half' of each group.

the teaching, while the other half spent the same time on self-assessment and then peer assessments of their work. The results for the scores on a project undertaken by these two groups are shown in Table 9.1. The reflection by the students in their peer assessments and self-assessments produced a clear improvement, but what is also striking is that the gap between the previously weaker and the stronger students was more than halved. A similar pattern was found for the test of the physics concepts.

On the basis of the review of Black and Wiliam (1998a), the assessment group at King's College London has carried out several programmes of professional development with selected groups of schools designed to explore how teachers might turn ideas, which are suggested by the research literature, into methods that can work in daily classroom life. Two studies which both describe how new methods were developed, and show how these were of positive benefit, emerged from research involving six schools in Medway and Oxfordshire (Black et al., 2003; Wiliam et al., 2004) and the implementation of formative work in nine schools in Scotland (Hallam et al., 2004). There have also been many more local plans for sustained implementation of formative practice, at both primary and secondary levels.

Where such innovations have been evaluated, several features always stand out, namely:

- It is essential to enhance feedback between those taught and the teacher, thereby calling for *significant changes in classroom practice.*
- For assessment to function formatively, its findings have to be used to adjust teaching and learning, so indicating a need *to make teaching programmes more flexible and responsive.*
- Formative assessment, like all other ways to secure effective learning, requires that *pupils be actively involved.*
- Attention should be given to the ways in which *assessment can affect the motivation and self-esteem of pupils,* and to the benefits of *engaging pupils in self- and peer assessment.*

These points will be discussed later in this chapter.

The quality of practice

There is a wealth of research evidence that the everyday practice of assessment in classrooms is beset with problems and shortcomings. The Office for Standards in Education (Ofsted) reports have frequently and consistently drawn attention to the weakness of assessment practices in many schools, for example, in 1998:

> Assessment remains the weakest aspect of teaching in most subjects. Despite improvement, it remains poor overall in almost one school in eight in Key Stage 3 . . . Although the quality of formative assessment has improved perceptibly, it continues to be a weakness in many schools.
>
> (Ofsted, 1998, pp. 88, 91–2)

and more recently:

> Assessment remains, overall, the weakest aspect of teaching. Where assessment is ineffective, teachers do not routinely check pupils' understanding as the lesson progresses.

> In almost all institutions, there are systems for the assessment of young people's levels of literacy and numeracy. However, the resulting information is not used efficiently to inform teaching and learning.
>
> (Ofsted, 2007, pp. 30, 55)

While some of these weaknesses are to do with the impact of summative assessments, there is ample evidence of the weak quality of feedback in helping learning. In research which reviewed the effects of the national literacy and numeracy strategies, Smith et al. (2004) found that in questioning, only 10 per cent of the questions were open questions, and that for 70 per cent of the time contributions by pupils were no more than three words long and took less than 5 seconds. A similar review of the teaching of English in US classrooms showed that teacher–pupil discussions took up only 1.7 minutes in every 60 minutes (Applebee et al., 2003), while Alexander's (2004) booklet shows that studies of the quality of dialogue in primary schools in England over many years have produced similar results. Yet if pupils are not involved in discussing their learning, the teacher can have little evidence of their learning needs.

Other problems are found in the quality of the feedback on written work. For primary teachers particularly, there is a tendency to emphasize quantity and presentation of work and to neglect its quality in relation to learning. The collection of marks to fill up records is given greater priority than the analysis of pupils' work to discern learning needs and it is common for teachers to use approaches in which pupils are compared with one another, the prime purpose of which appears to them to be competition rather than personal improvement.

Competition can have a negative effect on learning. An extensive analysis of numerous research studies of pupils' learning through group work (Johnson et al., 2000) has shown that groups in which learners collaborate yield substantial learning gains over individual study, but that groups where students are competing with one another rather than collaborating produce almost no learning advantage over individual learning. Thus, while group work is very common in classrooms, it is its quality, and not its mere existence, which determines the help it will give to pupils' learning.

Of course, not all of these descriptions apply to all classrooms, and indeed there will be many schools and classrooms to which they do not apply at all. Nevertheless, researchers in several countries, including the UK, who have collected evidence by observation, interviews and questionnaires from many schools, have all drawn these general conclusions.

Implications for practice

This section discusses five main aspects of a teacher's work. The first three relate to classroom teaching, discussing, in turn, lesson preparation, responding to students' comments, and classroom dialogue. These are followed by sections about the formative use of written work, and about the development of peer and self-assessment – notably through group work.

Lesson preparation

If a teacher wishes to develop their classroom assessment practice, it is essential that they plan for opportunities in their lessons for formative interaction to take place. This means planning for learning opportunities in which students are challenged by the activities they do and by the questions that are asked of them, and through which both the teacher and learners start to explore students' beliefs and understanding about the topic studied. This is the starting point for deciding the next steps in learning and formative action ensues when there is a response to the findings of the initial exploration of current understanding. In other words, formative assessment activities work in pairs or two parts – exploration and action – and so need to be planned for in this way.

First, teachers need to think about the types of learning that they want their students to engage in and choose appropriate tasks. Perhaps the topic they are tackling involves the students learning and using some new vocabulary. For example, in learning about malaria, students need to use such terms as vector, parasite, and lifecycle. Teachers then need to think about what might be the best way for their learners to engage with and use these terms so that the teacher can observe how their learning develops. If students are asked to read about malaria in a textbook and answer questions in their exercise books, then the learning will only be apparent to the teacher when the books are marked: the immediate formative opportunity is lost. Moreover, the students will not know how well they are using the terms until their marked books are returned – some time after the occasion when they were actively thinking about malaria. The delivery of ideas by books, teacher exposition or video, and the checking of the ideas by written questions has limited formative value. If students can discuss new ideas on occasions when the teacher can, by listening, appraise what is understood and what is causing difficulty, then the feedback can be immediate and can become part of the discussion.

Perrenoud (1998) describes the interplay between learners and their teachers as 'regulation of learning'. In this, he describes some classrooms, as 'traditional', where learning is highly regulated and prescribed and the scope of the activities is tightly defined with the outcomes of the learning being largely content-driven. Here, there is little to help the students own their own learning and the main information given to the teacher is of deficits, that is, of what they cannot do within the limited opportunities afforded them. By contrast, in classrooms which may be called 'discursive' or 'negotiated', the tasks are more open-ended, giving students more scope to manage their own thinking, so making it the possible for the teacher to give more meaningful feedback to enhance this thinking (Marshall and Wiliam, 2006). In this type of classroom, 'regulation does not include setting up activities suggested to, or imposed on, the students but their adjustment once they have been initiated' (Perrenoud, 1998, p. 88).

It is clear from the work we have done with teachers, in a variety of subject areas and in different phases of education, that talk has a key role to play in learning. This means that planning for formative opportunities requires the teacher to plan for focused talk in the lesson. It is also important that teachers create learning scenarios where they can listen in to the talk, so that they can use the information that they pick up about learning, to make pedagogic decisions about next steps. One has to accept that progress in learning is often erratic and unpredictable: so the only effective strategy is to allow for this by looking for ways of helping learners make sense of the varied ideas that they may bring to the table, or that they develop as they struggle to transform these ideas.

Taking up the topic of malaria mentioned above, the following example shows how a teacher might create formative opportunities to check on and guide the learning. The teacher might begin by introducing the topic and stating that, by the end of the lesson, the class is expected to be able to explain two different lifecycles that are involved with malaria and to evaluate various ways of preventing its spread. The teacher provides the class with a series of cards, each bearing both one question relating to malaria and the answer to that question. The cards are coloured, with each question on a different coloured card (Figure 9.2).

The students walk around the class, each finding another student with a different coloured card: then the first student will ask the other the question, listen to the answer, and then discuss that answer in relation to the answer on the card. The answer may be right, or it might be wrong – this does not matter at this stage. The students then swap cards and each finds another student with

What are the symptoms of malaria? General tiredness and periods of high fever	What is the parasite called that causes malaria? A single-celled organism called *Plasmodium*
Why do you often find mosquitoes near ponds and lakes? The female lays her eggs in the watery surface and the larva develop in water	Which animal is the host for the malaria parasite *Plasmodium*? Humans
What is a vector? An organism that carries a parasite from one animal to another	Which animal is the vector for the malarial parasite? *Anopheles* mosquito
What is a parasite? An organism that lives in or on another organism (the host) so that it can feed or reproduce. Often causes damage to its host	Which animals get ill through malaria? Humans
Where does the malaria parasite reproduce? Inside human blood cells	What damage does the malaria parasite cause to its host? Destroys the red blood cells as the parasite reproduces and bursts through the membrane
How do mosquitoes pick up the malaria parasite? When the female mosquito pierces human skin with her mouthparts and sucks up blood	Why do female mosquitoes feed on human blood while males feed on plant sap? The females need the protein in blood to produce their eggs

Figure 9.2 Question cards used in the malaria lesson

a different coloured card and the questioning and answering are repeated. This continues until all 12 cards have been worked on by each student. The learning idea behind this activity is that processing involves relating new information to what we already know and changing what we know in the light of that new information.

During this activity, the teacher can listen to the question and answer sessions and begin to pick up which of the questions the students are finding difficult and which easy, which ideas they already have and which ideas they are able to add to their existing understanding. If the teacher is not clear about their current understanding after this first activity, they could perhaps ask them to work in groups, providing each group with all 12 cards and ask them to sequence the questions and answers in order to explain about the lifecycle of *Plasmodium* and the lifecycle of mosquitoes.

Again, this second activity allows both teacher and learners to gain an understanding of areas about which they are confident and areas they are less sure about. The formative step might then come from a series of questions from the teacher, chosen in the light of the difficulties that students expressed during one or other of the first two activities. For example, if there was some confusion between the two lifecycles, then a good starting question might be 'what is similar and what is different about *Plasmodium* and mosquito?' Many answers can arise from this question and the discussion that can ensue will enable the learners to sort out their understanding: thus learning is taking place alongside the assessment of the answers by the teacher.

The next part of such a lesson will depend both on the learning intention for the lesson and on how students responded to the first part. If the teacher feels they have sorted out most of their ideas about parasites, hosts and vectors, students might look at a diagram of the lifecycle of mosquito and talk through the stages with a partner. If the teacher thinks some confusion still exists, they might ask students to link up in one colour the lifecycle of *Plasmodium* and then in a different colour to link up the lifecycle of the mosquito and to discuss in their groups how the two lifecycles interact. Whichever choice is made will provide the starting point for the final activity, which will be to look at how the lifecycles of the two organisms can be broken, and here again there will be several choices that the teacher can make to engage the students in this last phase of the learning.

This approach involves planning not merely to 'cover' the topic, but also to develop understanding. It is based on the belief that learning is both an activity of the individual student and also an essentially communal activity: we learn most of what we know from and with each other through collaborative endeavour (see also Chapters 4 and 7 in this volume). The tasks and the questions 'open up' the learning so that, through them, the teacher can provide a framework within which new understanding can be fostered and can begin to scaffold new understanding for the students.

The content and pace of work are determined by the learning that is taking place. Sometimes students will need to spend longer than anticipated on sorting out their ideas, while at other times, the students pick up the ideas more quickly than the teacher anticipated, then the teacher should move on to the next part of learning. Flexibility is crucial and rigidly planned timelines will be unhelpful. It can be unsettling for teachers, at first, as school routines often follow ordered patterns, while formative assessment has to respond to and build on the peaks and troughs of learning. The task of the teacher is to identify and respond appropriately to these high and low points in learning, while the task of the students is to actively engage in their learning and so to come to realize that they can learn from their discussions – including their mistakes and the mistakes of others. Having a voice, learners may engage in deciding what is worthy of enquiry and effort. Finding they have a role to play beyond complying with given norms and repeating prepared information fosters improved learning behaviours in students, which have benefit both for that activity and for their future learning.

Formative assessment in practical work

Practical work plays an important part in science lessons, with observations or data collection providing the impetus for discussion and theorizing (see, also, Chapter 6). Within practical sessions, students can develop both their scientific understanding and their investigative skills. To do this successfully, the teacher needs to shape the practical session so that the learners understand the focus and purpose of what they are doing. Learners also need to be encouraged to relate the findings, ideas and process skills within one practical session with those in other sessions so that they begin to build up a good knowledge about science and how science works (see, also, Chapter 2 in this volume). What is vital here is that learners do more than simply complete a practical activity but use practical sessions to promote thinking, ask questions and theorize. An assessment for learning approach fits well with practical work since it calls on the learner to be actively responsible in their learning and to work collaboratively. Such an approach also highlights the importance of classroom talk (see, also, Chapter 7 in this volume).

Class practicals provide good opportunity for collaboration, but sometimes limit the number and amount of interchange of ideas between students. Teacher demonstrations can provide more opportunity for the teacher to focus the learners' attention on particular aspects of a practical and encourage more interchange between groups within the classroom. Through discussion, students can shape their thinking, while, at the same time, providing information for the teacher on areas that might benefit from revisiting or extending in that lesson or in future lessons. For this to function in a formative manner, the teacher needs to prepare opportunities for discussion with questions that elicit both understanding and misunderstanding. The following example, observed by one of the authors, demonstrates one way that such practice can be established.

A class of 15-year-olds had been studying diffusion and osmosis for two weeks and had done several experiments, including watching potassium permanganate solution diffuse into different sized cubes of agar, measuring how much larger or smaller pieces of potato became when placed in different solutions and also observing what happened when onion epidermal cells were placed in salt water and then transferred to water. For the demonstration, the teacher took a 30cm length of Visking tubing and tied a knot in one end to make a tube. She then pipetted a starch suspension into the tube and tied a knot at the top and told the class that she now had a 'Visking tube sausage filled with starch'. She then held the 'sausage' by the top-knot over a potassium iodide solution and asked the class. 'What do you think is going to happen when I drop the "sausage" into the iodine solution? Talk to your partner.'

The students began chatting about what might happen. The teacher listened in to the conversation of some pairs but refused to be drawn into the conversations. If they asked her a direct question, she raised her eyebrows and nodded, before saying 'let's think some more about that one.' After four minutes, the teacher wrote the word 'Ideas' on the board and turned to the class, who gradually brought their conversations to an end. She then selected six different pairs to comment on their ideas and she wrote up the main points they raised; two of these pairs were students she had listened to during the paired talk and one pair who had asked her a question previously. On the board were the following points:

- Iodine will turn black.
- Sausage gets bigger/fuller.
- Starch turns black.
- Iodine moves through the sausage wall.

She then asked the rest of the class if anyone had anything to add. One girl asked, 'Is it the iodine that turns black or the starch or both?' The teacher replied, 'Mmm, what do we think about that one? Iodine? Starch? Or both?' Although some hands were raised, the teacher signalled for hands to go down and continued, 'Okay. So now think about the idea *you* had and what *you think you will see* when I drop the "sausage" into the iodine solution. Also think what will happen if these other ideas are right. Could you get a particular result and it be explained by different ideas? Just think on your own for a minute.' There was then a pause before the teacher slowly lowered the 'sausage' into the boiling tube of potassium iodide solution. As the liquid inside the 'sausage' started to turn blue, conversation broke out among the students. After two minutes, the teacher said loudly, 'So, what do we think happened and why? Talk in your pairs and then check yourselves with another pair.' The teacher moved behind where the students were sitting, listening in to what they were discussing and this time she intervened in some conversations, asking students to explain what they had seen or said.

She then asked the students to use mini whiteboards to write their conclusion for the experiment. When they had completed the task, one of the pair raised their hand. When almost all the hands were raised, she asked the class to raise their whiteboards so that everyone could see one another's conclusions. 'What is similar and what is different about your conclusions?' she asked. This question led to a class discussion where the ideas were again checked, terminology agreed and a decision reached that the experiment had demonstrated diffusion rather than osmosis, after a lengthy discussion about why you could possibly argue that the process observed was a type of osmosis.

This classroom scenario illustrates the formative nature of this approach to teaching and learning. The practical demonstration provided an impetus for discussion and the teacher was able to listen into the paired talk on several occasions as well as observe how some students presented their ideas to the whole class. It was a voyage of discovery by both teacher and students: the teacher was able to judge how various learners reacted to what they saw and what they heard, while the students were given opportunity to express and articulate their ideas and have them challenged and shaped by their peers as well as being checked by their teacher. This approach provided the environment where learners felt comfortable in trying out their ideas while, at the same time, being assured that the teacher would support them in taking these ideas forward through the collaborative approach that she fostered. Early on in the lesson paired talk was used to anticipate what would happen in the experiment. The learning was consolidated and challenged by listening to a selection of ideas from six pairs of students and developed into a whole class discussion. During most of this time, the teacher did not intervene in the conversations but acted as a facilitator encouraging the learners to say more, while she listened in carefully to the detail of their conversations. Following this phase, pairs of students were asked to revisit their initial ideas and to write down their explanations and compare these with those of their pairs in the class. This time the teacher changed tack and did intervene in some of the conversations of particular pairs of students, before collecting ideas and agreeing a conclusion with the whole class.

The teacher was therefore able to explore, not just whether someone in the class could explain the phenomena they saw in the experiment, but how a wide range of students predicted and then explained their observations. In this way, the teacher collected important information about understanding of the topic and also the strengths and weaknesses in skills of explaining observations and articulating ideas of many of the students in the class. This process provided her with information to guide her in the pace and detail that she used within the lesson, as well as allowing her to plan the next steps in learning more appropriately.

Responding to students 'answers' or comments

Talk is vital in enabling students to develop their ideas and thinking and so make progress, because through active discussion ideas may be shaped and restructured. This is only possible, however, if classroom discussion develops beyond a series of rapid-fire closed questions to an environment where the activities are so presented and steered that they offer real opportunities for thinking and reflection.

If students are to receive feedback from the classroom dialogue, then the teacher's role is to help sustain and develop the talk and particularly to stop it being closed down. This is not an easy skill for teachers to develop since their understanding of the topic tempts them to correct students, or to respond positively only to correct answers, avoiding comment on the incorrect. The skill needed involves mediating and extending the talk by thought-provoking questions whatever the quality of the 'answers' (Harrison and Howard, 2009).

So, imagine the classroom where the students are asked to gather round and observe a beaker filled to the brim with water. The teacher asks the class to discuss with their neighbour what might happen if they tried to add more water. The teacher then asks whether the results would be the same if they added some salt and holds a beaker of salt above the water to prompt their thinking. The skill of the teacher is then to take ideas from the students without closing down the talk. It is tempting to take one of the words they offer, such as dissolve, and use it to explain to the class what is happening. However, taking such steps would provide minimal feedback to the many ideas the individual students might well be thinking about and discussing. Instead, these varied ideas need to be 'aired', so that individual students can compare their ideas with those of their peers.

In order to promote such activity, the skilful teacher uses questions and comments to help students reveal their own thinking and to challenge the thinking of others. The following are examples of such ' probes':

Questions of clarification:
What do you mean by that? Say a bit more. Can you give us an example?

Questions that probe assumptions:
Why would someone say that? What do you think happened?

Questions that probe reason and evidence:
What are your reasons for saying that? Are you saying . . . Which means . . . ?

Questions that probe implications and consequences:
What might happen if you did this . . . not that . . . ?
What other reasons might there be for that happening?

Questions about viewpoints or perspectives:
What would be another way of saying that? How do Sian's ideas differ from Gashan's?

Questions about the question:
What other questions might be useful? Explain how that question is going to help us.

(Harrison and Howard, 2009)

These types of questions and comments prevent learners hiding behind the keywords that they have recognized in a topic and so help to move from a recitation of facts to a deeper discussion of understanding. While learners may recognize when they do not understand the ideas arising within a discussion, it takes courage to think aloud and reveal publicly that they cannot engage with the shared meaning that is evolving through the talk; more often, those in most need of help may withdraw from the dialogue, or listen in, hoping to re-engage later with the sense-making (Harrison, 2006). If, however, such learners can find the confidence to offer their imperfect understanding, then others can respond in ways that might help all to re-examine the sense they are making of the shared meaning. It is only through entering the dialogue about shared ideas that the learner can begin to see other aspects of the ideas and so make judgements about where they are in their own sense-making. Non-engagement not only deprives the group of the learner's position, it prevents the learner from revealing their own sense-making to themselves.

The following examples demonstrate how formative interactions assisted students to become aware of and attempt to close some gaps in their science understanding. They also show how teachers noticed students' strengths and weaknesses and used them to foster student learning. The first exchange is between a teacher and a 13-year-old student that happened when the student was peer-assessing another student's work.

> *Teacher*: I am interested in why you have underlined these words in the conclusion.
> *David*: They're key ones. The ones it's about.
> *Teacher*: So are you crediting the words or the ideas?
> *David*: Both. He's got the words but not really explained what happened and why.
> *Teacher*: Mmm. So say again what you think he's done.
> *David*: Used the correct words but it's not an explanation. He's just described it. What happened. He's nearly there. He just needs to make it more of an explanation.
> *Teacher*: And your conclusion?
> *David*: (laughing)
> Yeh. Mine's like that too 'cept I didn't use all of them (the keywords) like Charlie did.

The second example took place in a Year 12 class, where the teacher helped a student draw out her ideas and realize where her misunderstandings were.

> *Teacher*: So what do you mean here by 'powerhouse of the cell?'
> *Marsha*: The mitochondria.
> *Teacher*: The mitochondria ...
> *Marsha*: Are the powerhouses. They power up the cell. Make it work.
> *Teacher*: So how does this link with what goes on inside cells?
> *Marsha*: I dunno. It's powering up. Bit like a machine I suppose. Switching things on.
> *Teacher*: So what needs to be switched on? What is going on inside cells? Inside the mitochondria?
> *Marsha*: Is it like to do with respiration?
> *Teacher*: Say a bit more about your thinking.
> *Marsha*: Well, cells respire and that releases energy so that's why ... why they are called powerhouses. It's where the respiration must be happening. Where sugars and glucose and things are being broken down to let the energy out ... Yes. That's it – respiration.

Classroom dialogue

There are numerous studies of classroom dialogue: the one by Dillon (1994) stands out by being practically oriented to the needs of teachers. We focus more closely here on the ways in which talk takes place at a number of different levels in science classrooms. Students might share ideas in pairs or collaborate to work out an answer in a larger group. There are also occasions in classrooms where ideas developed in smaller groups can be shared and challenged more widely. The teacher's role here is to orchestrate such discussion so that all learners can engage, whether contributing their group's idea, or raising their own, or simply actively listening to the ideas being offered.

Demanding questions require time for the learner to think about the question being asked, to think what the question means and then to formulate a suitable reply. For some questions this can be achieved by increasing the wait time (the time between a teacher asking a question and if no answer arises, answering it themselves). Rowe (1974) found that the wait time in primary science classes was very low, less than 1 second. Studies in secondary schools have shown that by increasing the wait time by 3–5 seconds there was a dramatic effect on the involvement of their students in classroom discussion. Our research (Black et al., 2003) showed that increased wait time led to:

- longer answers being given than previously;
- more students electing to answer;
- fewer students refusing to answer;
- students commenting on or adding to the answers of other students;
- more alternative explanations or examples being offered.

Improving classroom talk also involves teachers working on how they could encourage their learners to take further, before the whole class, the tentative ideas they expressed in the comfort of a small group. To help them with this process, teachers often envisage the talk as somewhat like a jigsaw. Within groups, individual students find and present pieces of the picture. Some pieces will be identified as important for the whole picture, while others will be discarded or set aside temporarily. Sometimes jigsaw pieces can be joined to others or reshaped to fit with others, such that the part of the whole picture that any group in the class possesses is likely to be clearer than the single pieces held by any individual within the group. In the next stage of whole class discussion, these group ideas can be held up and examined alongside those of other groups.

Class discussion, here, has a different role to play than that of the group dialogue. Discussion, etymologically, is derived from the Latin meaning 'smash to pieces' (Isaacs, 1999) and it is through the whole class discussion that ideas are judged and reshaped, having emerged and been moulded through group dialogue. In fact, in our work with secondary teachers (Black et al., 2003), the teachers saw the class discussion as a sieving process, where some ideas were refined enough to get through and others faltered and stuck and made little progress. The way that the teacher handles class discussion has a great deal to do with how effective this can be, to serve for learning while also being a sharing experience. So, choosing which group speaks first is important and decisions about how much of the group dialogue needs to be revealed before a second group is allowed to add, contrast or compare their ideas needs to be considered. The skilful teacher helps draw together the themes and ideas that emerge from the group dialogues while at the same time holding up these experiences for scrutiny, challenge and consolidation through the whole class discussion.

The class discussion that follows shows how the teacher encourages classroom talk while steering the ideas towards the learning with which he wants the class to engage. He started the lesson by showing the class two plants, one of which was clearly growing more vigorously than the other.

> *Teacher*: Why do you think these plants have grown differently?

Class erupts into loud discussion in pairs. Teacher goes over to sidebench and checks apparatus. After four minutes, teacher goes back to front and stops the class discussion.

> *Teacher*: Okay. Ideas? (About half the class put up their hands. Teacher waits for three seconds. A few more hands go up.) Monica – your group? Pair?
> *Monica*: That one's grown bigger because it was on the window. (Pointing.)
> *Teacher*: On the window? Mmm. What do you think Jamie?
> *Jamie*: We thought that.
> *Teacher*: You thought...?
> *Jamie*: That the big 'un had eaten up more light.
> *Teacher*: I think I know what Monica and Jamie are getting at, but can anyone put the ideas together? Window – Light – Plants?

Again about half the class put up their hands. The teacher chooses a child who has not put up their hand.

> *Richard*: Err yes. We thought, me and Dean, that it had grown bigger because it was getting more food.

Some pupils stretch their hand up higher. Teacher points to Susan and nods.

> *Susan*: No, it grows where there's a lot of light and that's near the window.
> *Teacher*: Mmmm. Richard and Dean think the plants are getting more food. Susan ... and Stacey as well? Yes. Susan thinks it's because this plant is getting more light. What do others think? Tariq?
> *Tariq*: It's the light 'cos its photosynthesis. Plants feed by photosynthesis.

Teacher writes photosynthesis on the board.

> (Black et al., 2003, pp. 38–9)

The sequence of interventions by the teacher in this example is noteworthy. First, he poses the question. Then there is a pause for thinking (while the students discuss in pairs or small groups) before he selects a student to answer. On hearing the first answer, the teacher can immediately 'bounce' the question back to others. This form of response prevents the teacher reacting to the first answer and so possibly cutting off the class talk. The second student might give the same or a different answer to the first student and may or may not respond to what was said in the first answer. Whatever happens, the point is that the classroom talk has started to move away from the teacher judging and towards giving a voice to the ideas of several students. The ultimate aim of many of these teachers is to achieve several 'bounces' before they express their reaction to the ideas. This pushes the talk in the direction of the learners, which in itself is beneficial to learning, and also gives the teacher essential 'thinking time', where he can plan what intervention is needed to help drive the learning forward. Yet the teacher here is far from passive – the frequent summaries and the request to 'put the ideas together' steers the discussion towards developing an understanding of the topic. It is worth noting also in this example that the students' contributions are in the form of whole sentences, and contain the terms 'think' and 'because': both of these are signs that the class is involved both in thinking and in formulating their thoughts.

Feedback on written work

For feedback on written work, as for feedback in oral discussion, a task is set up, the pupil responds, and the teacher should then respond. The task of framing that feedback so that it develops the pupil's learning is very similar, although for written work the teacher has more time to think about a response.

As was made clear above (under *Basic Principles*), to associate feedback with marks is counter-productive, in that it leads students to regard the work as a terminal test, so that the process is complete when a mark has been assigned. By contrast, if the focus is on feedback that helps learners to improve, they may profitably do more work, so that the exercise is seen as a step in the learning.

To cease to give marks on homework may be a shock to some, and cannot be done if it conflicts with school policy: this may, however, be negotiated. In some schools, teachers have continued to assign marks in their own records, but not write them on the students' work; in others, the arguments against frequent assignment of marks have led the whole school to abandon the giving of marks on homework. Students may be disconcerted if such a change is made without prior explanation. Experience had shown that students are content once such explanation is given:

> At no time during the first fifteen months of comment-only marking did any of the students ask me why they no longer received grades...Only once, when the class was being observed by a member of the King's team did a student actually comment on the lack of grades. When asked by our visitor how she knew how well she was doing in science, the student clearly stated that the comments in her exercise book and those given verbally, provide her with the information she needs. She was not prompted to say this!!!!
> (Derek, Century Island School, cited in Black et al., 2003, p. 45)

Parents likewise have been reassured if there is prior explanation of the rationale, for they, too, can understand better how improvement is to be achieved.

A change to comment-only marking makes new demands on the treatment of homework. Evidence of old habits of 'marking' has shown that many teachers give bland comments, often commenting on neatness, spelling and general tidiness rather than on the quality of understanding that the work reveals. Consider the following examples of comments by teachers on written homework:

1. Use paragraphs.
2. Sunita, you have completed a lot of work and it is very neatly done. However, your answers could be more sensitive.

These tell the pupil that the work is inadequate, but assume that she understands what is required. The pupil who received the first comment said, on interview, 'If I'd known how to use paragraphs, I would have done!'

3. Steven, the start you have made is very pleasing and the detail in your answers is improving. Read your responses again and see if you think they are complete, i.e. is all of the relevant information there?

This comment is more specific in explaining the criteria for improvement, but still assumes that the pupil will understand what is needed, that is, will Steven understand what counts as 'relevant information'?

4. This is generally fine but you are mixing up the terms particle, element and compound. Look at the glossary we made and use it to check through this piece again.
5. Sam, you seem to know what resistance is and you explain how it affected the brightness of the bulb. Can you suggest other things that could have affected the brightness of the bulb?

Here the requirement to improve is made more explicit, it is clear what an improved version should include. The reference to the 'glossary' helps the learner to find the resource needed, but the task for Sam is more demanding – he has to find out or think it out for himself.

Of course, particular comments cannot be judged outside the context in which they are made: a comment that might be helpful for one pupil may need to be put differently for another. Thus differentiation according to the needs of the individual is essential. However, the general principles are that praise in a comment should make clear what is good about the work, and comments on weaknesses should guide the pupil to improve by giving guidance about how to do so. Moreover, there is little point in writing such a large number of comments on a weak piece of work that the struggling learner is overwhelmed; the art is to choose a small enough number so that work can focus on the most important shortcomings.

Work with students has shown that they do not like their work covered with teachers' writing, and many particularly dislike red ink. A device used by one teacher was to only write comments on a reserved space at the front of the pupil's book, with a reference for each to the page and code label to which it applied. The comments were on a left-hand column, so that opposite them on the right the pupil could give the response, or a reference to the page where any revision might be found. These two columns thereby became a record of the learning dialogue. Such pages can be used for review at the end of a module, and might well inform a summative judgement more helpfully than a mere list of marks.

At first, a new attempt at the formulation of helpful comments may well take more time than did earlier 'marking'. Some have found that this extra time shortened as they became more familiar with the new approach. Many teachers found that productive comments written every 2–3 weeks were more useful than a mark on every piece of work. Indeed, it became clear that it was difficult to write comments on some tasks as they only needed checking to ensure that the pupil had transferred the information from their textbooks or class notes into the homework book: for these, self-checking or peer assessment could suffice (Black et al., 2003).

This last finding illustrates a more important finding of teachers trying to develop their art of formulating comments: just as for starting a classroom discussion, the nature of the task set to the pupil is crucial in its potential to evoke thoughtful writing. Here are three examples of tasks that might meet this requirement:

> What would happen if a villain sprayed the countryside with a chemical that destroyed chlorophyll?

> Why are some alternative energy sources more suited to Medway than to Derbyshire?

> If you wanted to slow down the reaction between magnesium and acid but get a steady supply of hydrogen gas, what would you do and why would you do this?

> (Black and Harrison, 2004, p. 12)

Self- and peer assessment and group work

The basic principles of learning set out above make clear that students have to develop the capacity to steer and reflect on their own learning, a principle which is central to the concept of metacognition. If learners have a clear understanding of the target of their own learning, then they can judge the level of their achievement by that target, and for this, self-assessment is essential. One important way to develop this skill is through peer assessment, in which students become resources for one another in learning.

For example, if students find it hard to understand what a target actually means, the teacher might present them with, say, three examples of relevant work by others, chosen to show a range of achievements. Students might be asked to work in small groups, first to put the three in rank order, and then to discuss how they came to decide that any one is better than another. When the judgements of various groups are exchanged, with their justifications, in a general class discussion, the discussion can lead to identification of the criteria for quality in the type of task considered. This approach could be helpful, for example, in starting work on open-ended investigations, whether as practical projects or as written work calling for library research.

A similar process can be used to involve students in assessing their own work alongside that of their peers. Thus, for a given piece of written work, a group may look at the responses of each of their members, decide how to place them in rank order, and then discuss their justifications for these decisions. In this process, they see how their own work compares with that of their fellow-students, and, in part through hearing the perceptions of their peers, begin to be objective about the strengths and weaknesses of their own work. A similar process can be used when the work assessed is the answer papers produced in a summative test. In such a case, the teacher would not write any marks or comments on the examination scripts which are returned to the students; it may even be helpful to expect pupil groups, in the course of studying and ranking the responses, to compose a marking scheme, for this will help them develop that understanding of the criteria of quality which will give meaning to any 'target' which has been expressed in necessarily abstract terms.

The value of such peer-group work depends on the quality of the collaborative discussion in groups. It cannot be assumed that the group will work in productive ways. One large-scale study of group work in classrooms (Baines et al., 2008) has described the various difficulties: some group members may not be engaged, some may, perhaps for self-protection, attempt to block the group's progress, some groups may wander off the point which they are there to address, and disputes, with reluctance to collaborate, may be further obstacles to progress. These difficulties can be overcome, but only if groups are given careful training and guidelines. For example, in developing such training in the work of Year 5 students in science, Mercer et al. (2004) formulated the following rules for the for their interaction:

- All students must contribute: no one member should say too much or too little.
- Every contribution should be treated with respect, all should listen thoughtfully.
- Each group must achieve consensus, which may call for efforts to resolve differences.
- Every suggestion/assertion has to be justified – arguments must be based on reasons.

In some cases, individual members of a group would be given responsibility for one of these rules; for example, one might be assigned to report the group's conclusions to the whole class, so that he or she would want to know what conclusions to report, while another might be given the role of challenging any assertion or refutation if a reason had not been given. As a result of this training, it was found that the use of terms that indicate reasoned argument, notably 'because', 'think', 'should', 'would' was three times more frequent after the training than before it. It was also found that these groups produced significantly higher scores on end of Key Stage test questions than students who not been trained in this way.

A common practice for a lesson is to set a task, and to give students time to discuss it in groups, and then receive reports from groups so that summaries and contrasts between the findings can provide comprehensive feedback, which will be the basis for taking the learning further. One advantage of this approach is that it gives opportunities and time for everyone to engage with the task. Another is that it provides the teacher with time to reflect on the various contributions as they are expressed. Unfortunately, several observations of such work show that it can fall far short of these ideals (Mercer et al., 2004; Baines et al., 2008). One common finding is that students sit in groups but do not work together collaboratively: thus, careful attention to the quality of the group discussions is essential. Another is that teachers find it difficult to respond if the group reports are either very diverse, or very unexpected. The challenge is for teachers to provide a model for the way students should respond to one another in their own discussions: that is, to use good listening skills, treat each other's answers with respect, and show that the goal is to explore and question the reasons for the points made rather than to pursue the correct answer.

A final aspect is the advantage of exploiting self-assessment more directly. One way to do this is to ask students to appraise their own work by indicating their degree of confidence in its quality, which can be done by 'traffic-light' labelling, with green for confidence, yellow for uncertainty, and red if the student is confused and insecure. The same icon-approach can be used in the course of a lesson as students respond to indicate their understanding of the teacher's presentations. Such visually simple labels will give the teacher, and peers working in groups, a quick indication of where, and with whom, the main problems have arisen. Where there are many reds, a fresh approach to the topic may be needed; where there is a mixture of yellow and greens, those showing green on a particular question may be asked to help those showing yellow or red. Of course, when a pupil has to explain their 'correct' explanation to others, they may realize that they do not understand it as clearly as they thought – but that, too, is part of their learning. Such reality checks are important in themselves, for being cautiously critical about one's own confidence is an essential habit.

Making it happen

The changes in classroom practice that are needed are central rather than marginal, and have to be incorporated by each teacher into his or her practice. That is to say, reform in this dimension will inevitably

take a long time, and need continuing support from both practitioners and researchers.

(Black and Wiliam, 1998a, p. 62)

Change in practice entails much more than introducing teachers to new ideas
and strategies. Assessment for learning requires changes in the ways teachers
work with learners, which some may find risky, and which may be challenging
at times. The process is like a voyage of discovery, a journey into new territo-
ries of teaching and learning (Harrison and Howard, 2009) and requires that
teachers be willing to look at their practice and to strive to make learning more
effective in their classrooms. For many teachers, the type of professional development required is unfamiliar, for the intention is not to show teachers what
to do, or how to fit in with what they already do, but rather to think about
the current learning behaviours of their classes and consider what pedagogic
decisions they need to create and nurture richer opportunities for learning
(see, also Chapter 13 in this volume).

In this process, teachers find that they also change in the way they react to and describe events on their professional voyage of discovery. One of
the striking features of our work with teachers has been the way in which,
in the early stages of professional learning, many spoke about the new approach as 'scary', because they were concerned that they were going to lose
control of their classes. Towards the end of the project, they described this
same process not as a loss of control, but as one of sharing responsibility
for the learning with the class – exactly the same process, but viewed from
two very different perspectives. In one perspective, the teachers and students
are in a delivery–recipient relationship, in the other they are partners in
pursuit of a shared goal. This duality was captured by one of the teachers
thus:

> What formative assessment has done for me is made me focus less
> on myself but more on the children. I have had the confidence to
> empower the students to take it forward.
>
> (Robert, Two Bishops School, cited in Black et al., 2002, p. 22)

Another of the teachers recognized the change that he made in the locus of
control:

> There was a definite transition at some point, focusing on what I was
> putting into the process and what the students were contributing.
> It became obvious that one way to make a significant sustainable
> change was to get the students to do more of the thinking. I then
> began to search for ways to make the learning process more transpar-
> ent to the students. Indeed I now spend my time looking for ways to
> get students to take responsibility for their learning at the same time
> making the learning more collaborative.
>
> (Tom, Riverside School, cited in Black et al., 2002, p. 20)

There are no instant recipes for success – teachers need to take decisions about the approach they take with their formative practice. What is called for is a continuous iterative process, starting on a modest scale, for example, with the learning of a particular class. The voyage as a whole will take a considerable time to complete, and, in fact, is never really finished, because as the teaching changes, the learners also begin to change which requires further adjustment to the developing pedagogy. What matters is that the approach is tailored to particular groups of learners to structure and so facilitate those activities that enable their learning. Judgement of success depends on weighing up the contribution to learning of the discussion in the classroom, how confident and enthusiastic students are to 'have a go' at learning and how well peers support and challenge one another when engaged in collaborative learning.

The task of change is too demanding for individual teachers to attempt on their own. The support of colleagues with whom they can regularly interact is essential. Indeed, given the challenging nature of the changes required, the benefits of collaborative reflection at teacher development are a powerful, even essential, aid to successful change. Glazer and Hannafin (2006) regard professional learning as a social exercise where 'reciprocal interaction' in a supportive 'community of practice' enables teachers to take responsibility for their own learning. In a professional development programme to promote classroom assessment in mathematics, Flexer et al. (1995) reported that teachers sometimes felt overwhelmed by the change process. However, when they received generally positive feedback from their own students and recognized that their classes had better conceptual understanding and problem-solving capabilities, the teachers become more convinced of the benefit of such changes. Their response was to attempt further change in assessment and instruction practices.

Teachers need to create opportunities in their classrooms for formative practice to emerge but, at the same time, to openly examine their practice with colleagues to explore what it reveals; this is not an easy balance to manage, as change in practice is often uncomfortable and possibly threatening to individuals. Leat and Higgins (2002) suggest that such development in pedagogy helps teachers take control of their professional lives, giving teachers permission to experiment with their practice in a structured way. Such development requires regular and sustained opportunity for professional dialogue, to promote teacher reflection and learning, so that new practices can be evolved, moulded and honed from existing classroom practice. Evaluation is a vital part of any plan. This process should be on-going, in terms of mutual observation and of sharing of ideas and resources to support professional learning (see, also, Chapter 13 in this volume).

So, moving teachers forward in a sustainable fashion requires more than the support of individual colleagues, requiring programmes that encourage professional communities of practice that involve both teachers and senior leaders in schools. Thus, such practices need support and encouragement from middle and senior management in schools, and ultimately from government, made effective through extensive professional development programmes.

Developing a shared understanding of how assessment for learning works in the classroom and how formative practice functions alongside other demands on teachers' time is essential for any change to be achieved and sustained in the long term. Teachers who have achieved success and confidence in their formative practice emphasize how essential patience and perseverance are, and how beneficial it is to be encouraged and enabled to pursue teacher development and professional learning through collaborative action research.

Conclusion

The discussions presented in this chapter should make clear that the practice of formative assessment lies at the heart of teaching and learning. This very feature means that it relates in a complex variety of ways to most other aspects of learning and teaching. For example, Figure 9.1 raises the issue of a comprehensive theory of pedagogy as a whole (as explored in Chapters 4 and 5 of Alexander, 2008), for example, the selection and presentation of questions and other tasks for pupils lie at the heart of the problem of ensuring that the aims of the learning are best served by the ways in which pupils are engaged and challenged. How discussion in science classrooms might assist (such as that described by Aufschnaiter et al., 2007), is relevant here, and such work might well be extended to exploration from a formative perspective. There is also a particular need for further research into the way that formative practices are best implemented within the different aims and cultures of different school subjects. It is clear, for example, that there are some sharp differences between formative practices in English and in mathematics (Hodgen and Marshall, 2005) but also that each of these teacher communities can learn from one another. This issue may be of increasing importance for science teachers, for the need to shift the priorities in science teaching, from the emphasis on training future scientists, to an emphasis on the science understanding needed by all citizens, has implications for the ways in which science teachers might need to interact with their students (see, also, Chapter 3 in this volume). For example, a discussion of the social or ethical implications of scientific discoveries requires an open approach, for in such topics there are no 'right answers'; the need in such cases is to help learners appreciate different points of view and to sharpen their skills in argument. Such discussions are more like those to which teachers of, say, English are accustomed.

A different issue that awaits exploration by further research is the ways in which implementation of formative practices affects different types of students. Some, but not all, of the research studies suggest that low attainers derive particular benefit from the changes, as shown in the White and Frederiksen study (1998), while hardly any studies report gender differences, or even report null findings. It could also be anticipated that pupils from cultural backgrounds in which it is unusual, even unacceptable, for the young to question or engage with argument with adult teachers, might find their beliefs about learning and about the role of the learner being challenged. All of these issues have practical import for the teachers and there is need for further research to guide them.

Teachers have responsibilities for both formative and summative assessment: recent work at King's College London has helped explore the problem that teachers of English and mathematics have in achieving helpful synergy between these two (Black et al., 2010): this issue should also be researched in science teaching. The several problems that teachers encounter at this formative–summative interface are summarized in the following paragraphs, which also illustrate how they are exacerbated by the pressures that have followed from the development of national policies that focus on testing for of accountability. The history of their development has been described in Chapter 3, entitled 'Principle, pragmatism and compliance', of Alexander's (2008) book. Essentially, national policies can be unhelpful here in two ways.

One way is to drive teachers to 'teach to the test', emphasizing use of rote learning to enhance response to tests which do not explore or reward pupils' ability to explain their understanding in any depth (Fairbrother, 2008). However, there is ample evidence to show that pupils who are taught with emphasis on understanding do in fact perform better, even in narrowly focused tests, than those taught to the test (Nuthall and Alton-Lee, 1995; Newmann et al., 2001), a finding that was borne out in the King's research on the effect on test performance of developing formative assessments in science and mathematics in some schools in England (Wiliam et al., 2004).

A second way in which national policies may be unhelpful has arisen because, while there has been widespread recognition of the potential of formative assessment to enhance students' attainments, there has also been misunderstanding of the evidence (Black, 2007). One error is to assume that assessment for learning is served by frequent summative testing: the evidence quoted here does not support this interpretation. A summative test may serve a formative function only if the evidence it reveals is followed up with the students to help deal with the faults shown by that evidence: if this is not done, then the frequent highlighting of students' test marks may in fact be as harmful as giving marks on homework.

A more subtle misunderstanding is possible in the way that target-setting is used. Again, where emphasis is placed on giving each student a level, this may lead to ego-orientation, seeing oneself as, say, a 'Level 4 learner' and, therefore, as a person who is not as smart as one's Level 5 or 6 peers. In any case, a National Curriculum Level is a very broad entity covering a range of topics and skills, so as such it carries little guidance about how to improve. By contrast, a target that is so clearly specified, in relation to recent achievement, that the student concerned can see how it can be attained, can provide both guidance and motivation. The difficulty is that the benefits of this approach are often quoted in support of the less helpful practice of using frequent testing to regularly check, for all pupils, and to report to them, their progress against the Levels of the National Curriculum which lack the specificity or clarity the student requires. None of the above is to argue, however, against the necessity and useful functions of summative assessment, a topic which is the subject of Chapter 10 in this volume.

What the experience of professional development programmes, such as our own, does make clear is that improving this aspect of the teacher's work can be a very challenging task, albeit one where the commitment and bravery required can bring significant rewards. The keys to success are clarity of purpose and a school-based approach which fosters, and so draws benefit from, a collegial approach to improving practice.

Further reading

Black, P., Harrison, C., Lee, C., Marshall, B., and Wiliam, D. (2003) *Assessment for Learning: Putting it into Practice.* London: Open University Press.

Dillon, J. T. (1994) *Using Discussion in Classrooms.* London: Open University Press.

Dweck, C. S. (2000) *Self-theories: Their Role in Motivation, Personality and Development.* Philadelphia, PA: Psychology Press.

Glazer, E. and Hannafin, M. J. (2006) The Collaborative Apprenticeship model: situated professional development within school settings, *Teaching and Teacher Education,* 22(2): 179–93.

Mercer, N., Dawes, L., Wegerif, R. and Sams, C. (2004) Reasoning as a scientist: ways of helping children to use language to learn science, *British Educational Research Journal,* 30(3): 359–77.

10 Summative assessment

Gold or glitter?

Julian Swain

> *But in this world nothing can be said to be certain, except death, taxes and assessment.*
>
> With apologies to Benjamin Franklin

Introduction

The scope of summative assessment

Assessing students is one of the oldest practices in education and the term 'summative assessment' is often regarded as the end of any assessment for students – having a supposed finality. In this chapter, using evidence from summative assessments and research, an argument will be developed that shows that summative assessment is an area worthy of more attention by teachers, of more research and further development and also of potential use to them in shaping their actions and decisions, for the benefit of both present and future students.

Students are complex and multifaceted beings. Like jewels, they are sometimes represented best as a whole rather than seen from a single side. The data on any student, like any jewel, can be put to many uses, for example, as part of different collections, which, in this case, may be classrooms, schools, local authorities or nations. Each student represents part of a nation's investment in the future and both collectively and individually, they give an indication of its quality and intellectual wealth. It is this variety of perspectives, from the individual to the whole, and its multiplicity of uses that can, and should be, looked at in order to provide new insights into the performance of educational systems. Summative assessment is the means of performing this task.

The summative assessment framework and the generation of summative data

Many of us tend to think of summative assessment as the end-of-topic test, national tests, or the terminal examination in Year 11, where the information issued is a statement of achievement for the student at that time. A hundred years ago, tests were limited to the classroom, now they have been 'globalized' and national and international tests are conducted in almost all countries of the world, comparing schools with schools and countries with countries. Hence the framework for looking at summative assessment is now more complex (Table 10.1).

There are external summative assessments which are often politically driven and ignore the technical issues and consequences. Here the results are used for certification or accountability. There are also internal summative assessments conducted by schools for their own use, such as setting or reviewing progress at the end of a topic or year. Others in schools are used for components of external assessments and national reporting. A third summative assessment strand centres on a specific child, usually with a view to identifying specific learning or social needs. Each of these types of assessment can use a range of methods to determine a 'result' and this can then lead to questions about their validity, reliability and consequential use.

This chapter mainly looks at recent types of external summative assessments and associated research by examining and discussing data from:

- schools, local authorities (LAs) and national tests;
- UK national examinations at ages 16 (GCSE) and 18 (GCE);
- the national programme of the Assessment of Performance Unit (APU) in the UK;
- the international studies such as TIMSS and PISA.

With the exception of GCSE and GCE certification, where the assessment outcome is primarily for the students' use, most of the other systems use a bottom-up approach, where the individual student in the classroom provides the data for local, national and international comparisons, giving the impression that the individual student is less important than the system of testing in which they find themselves. While this is comparison is inescapable, the research on summative data and its applications, summarized here, has its greatest value when its implications for future cohorts and individuals are examined.

Defining summative assessment and other terms

Surprisingly, the term summative assessment is comparatively new and Bloom et al. (1971) defined summative evaluation tests as those assessments given at the end of units, mid-term and at the end of course, which are designed to judge the extent of students' learning of the material for the purpose of grading, certification, evaluation of progress, or even for researching the effectiveness of a curriculum. The definition that tends to be used by many teachers and educators is that it is information derived from external agencies at a given point in time which defines aspects of a student's or school's performance.

Often the information derived is seen as being of little or no use to the student once it has been generated. It may, of course, have consequences for the student's future, in that they may or may not, study subjects at A-level or

Table 10.1 Framework for looking at summative assessment

Summative type	Examples	Power base and agents	Impact of derived information	Methods	Quality and technical issues
External Summative					
National testing for evaluation, monitoring and accountability	Testing at KS1, KS2, and APU	Government and their testing agencies	Educational achievement in classrooms, schools, local authorities and the *nation*	For example, all three can use, written assessments	All three are concerned with content, construct and consequential validity
National Qualification Awarding (high stakes: personal certification)	GCSE, GCE A1 A2	Examination Groups OfQUAL	Educational achievement of *individuals*, schools, local authorities and the nation	Structured, short answers, multiple choice. Practical skills and tasks	Test and marker reliability. Errors of measurement and reporting results
International testing for monitoring	PISA, TIMSS	International testing agencies	Educational achievement of the *nation* in comparison to other nations	Teacher-administered tests (e.g. reading)	
Internal Summative					
Internal purposes for review and monitoring	School exams, classroom tests	School and Teacher	The learning of *individuals* and their classes	Structured, short answers, multiple choice tests	Content and construct validity. Marker reliability
External purposes as contributions to high stakes	GCSE and GCE coursework as well as teacher assessment for national reporting	Examination Groups	Achievement of *individuals* in component of external assessment	Practical assignments	Construct validity. Marker reliability. Reporting across school moderation
		Testing Agencies	*Individual's* achievements as an alternative to national testing, National Curriculum based	Any of the above plus teacher records and observations	Content, construct and consequential validity. Marker reliability. Reporting
Individual Summative					
Cognitive	Personality, intelligence	School and Local Authority	Possible causes and problems and consequent identification of specific learning and social needs for *individual*	Written tests. Observational tasks. Specialized reports	Construct and consequential validity. Test and marker reliability. Reporting issues
Social and Educational	Attitudes, social, emotional, SEN				

go on to university. Its purpose differs from that of formative assessment (see Chapter 9 in this volume) which attempts to provide feedback to the student so that better learning can take place in the future, and also, to the teacher for better teaching and greater understanding of the pupils' learning needs. Problems occur when the functions of formative and summative assessments are not clearly delineated and this can produce tensions between the two (Black, 1993; Wiliam and Black, 1996). This tension has been particularly apparent in the English National Curriculum assessment programme where collective data on schools or educational authorities are seen as being more important than the performance of individuals within these institutions. The key difference lies in the purpose which guides the interpretation of the pupil's work, summative being for judgement, formative being for diagnosis and assistance. Thus it is, in principle, possible to use the same assessment tools for both formative and summative purposes.

The contribution of the individual student to the data is paramount. In school, each student receives an educational experience which will be represented more or less faithfully in that student's particular grades or levels of achievement when summative assessments are taken. Historically, grading pupils has undergone a number of changes. Originally, the mark out of ten or a percentage in some way characterized teachers' knowledge of testing, however, national examinations over many decades have emphasized the application of 'norms' and 'criteria' to student marks.

Applying 'norm-referencing' to marks assumes that there is some underlying pattern (the normal bell-shaped curve, for example) in the way marks or grades are distributed in a population and that this pattern is relatively stable from year to year. It also assumes that changing the educational experience will not change the performance of the class, school, education authority and nation. Clearly, this is not the case, as patterns of mark distributions do change and yet the causes for them may not be apparent without detailed analysis. On the other hand, criterion-referencing (Popham, 1978) which is associated with mastery, looks at the performance of the individual student and what they can do in defined domains, such as, biology, practical work or the microscope, etc. The collection of jewels, referred to previously, may contain some gems which satisfy specific criteria such as, high quality cut, brilliance and colour but others may have good cut but poor colour, etc. Specifying an extended list of criteria in all educational domains, and then trying to assess them, would be difficult before extensive research was carried out. Also, the interpretation of the criteria by teachers may prove difficult (Lang, 1982). Kempa and L'Odiaga (1984) suggested that it was difficult to compare grades derived from norm-referenced examinations with those obtained from criterion-referenced performances. Statistical aspects of criterion-referenced assessment were subject to debate during the 1970s and 1980s (Berk, 1980) and little progress has been made in its adoption in national testing.

Some of the technical issues associated with all types of assessment have been given by Wiliam (1993). Terms such as validity – do the tests measure what they are supposed to measure?; dependability – how much reliance can we place on the results?; and reliability – how accurate are the results? – are often misunderstood. A test can be reliable in the sense that the results obtained are repeatable or the questions correlate with total scores, but it may not be valid because it does not measure what it was intended to measure.

Views from the school, classroom and local authorities

Schools and the classroom

Each year in England, and elsewhere, headteachers, school governors and local authorities await the publication in the national press of lists of school performance defined by examinations such as the GCSE, GCE A-level and national tests. Headteachers try to account for shortfalls or improvements in their performance during the year so that the status of, and parental choice for, the school are maintained. Yet the idea that such tests may be susceptible to a range of errors and criticisms is never more than fleetingly considered. The general public's erroneous notion that a mark is a mark, and a grade is a grade, is something which has stood the test of time. Attitudes of parents to tests and ways of representing the results so that they are interpretable and useful have being examined both here, and in the USA (Desforges et al.,1996; Shepard and Bleim, 1995).

For science departments, it is important that such data are used to ask questions such as – how do the results in the department compare with others locally? What is happening over time? What can we learn from them? Moreover, what do the results hide? The patterns over time are a more effective indicator of a department's performance than those of a single year and many schools try to show this in their annual reports. The average level attained for Year 6 (age 11) pupils in the UK national tests (Key Stage 2) is about 4 (on a 6-level scale). Hence an increase in the proportion achieving these levels over time would be indicative of rising standards within the school, provided that they are not at the expense of the higher levels. The graphical analysis (Figure 10.1) shows how one school's distribution, which was above the national figures at level 4, and below the national average at level 5 for a number of years to one where it is the same.

However, even this type of analysis can be deceptive and can hide important data. For example, if the results from the pupils' test papers are re-worked into subject domains, we might find that the biology teaching is far from adequate; or that the results of one class are much worse than another, even if they have a similar ability range. If schools are to obtain maximum information from such test results, then time must be allocated for such analysis, a cursory examination is insufficient to reveal the possible richness within the data. Statistical programmes for school use are increasingly being developed and used. LA advisers are now beginning to help departments understand the data

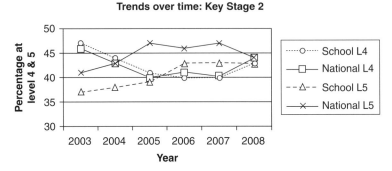

Figure 10.1 National test results for Headwood Primary School, 2003–08

more fully. Only this type of detailed analysis will allow summative information to be used in a way which helps to evaluate schemes of work, the quality of teaching, and pupil understanding in the different scientific domains. Acting on such information can then help to raise the performance of future cohorts.

Change can be a consequence of legislation but internal change can be equally effective. Taking action such as setting targets within schools and involving the teachers with this target-setting process or making effective use of national test data for curriculum design and monitoring pupil progress, can all help to raise educational standards. The government sees this as a priority and has set up websites to this end (http://www.standards.dfes.gov.uk/ts/). Consequently understanding the techniques for analysing summative assessment data and interpreting the results is becoming an increasingly important skill for teachers.

Local authorities and national data

In the UK, the role of local authorities (LA) in assessment has changed considerably during the past 20 years due, in part, to four aspects (Conner and James 1996). These are:

- the changes to the assessment orders which determine what is to be assessed by whom and how it is to be reported;
- the influence of financial controls such as grants;
- the introduction of the national tests and tasks so that any guidance on assessment that the LA gives to schools is usually directed to this area;
- the influence of the Office for Standards in Education (OfSTED) which looks at assessment and reporting as part of its framework for inspection.

LAs are therefore anxious to monitor performance of their schools and compare them with national results. These comparisons are usually distributed to schools and follow up in-service programmes are provided to try to enhance future performance.

Murphy (1997) expresses a number of legitimate concerns over the publication of league tables: (1) comparing results between years rests on an assumption that the demographic characteristics are similar, which is often unjustified; (2) comparing achievement between different subjects rests on an assumption that each subject tests similar aptitudes and abilities; and (3) comparing schools in league tables tests an assumption that all schools start with pupils of similar ability. All of these assumptions are highly questionable. For instance, research by Strand (1998), with primary school test data, revealed significant differences between schools' raw results as given in the performance tables and those which included additional measures of effectiveness in relation to the ability of their pupils. Similarly, research has shown that performance in national public examinations is underpinned by variations in socio-economic background of pupils, and Gibson and Asthana (1998) have explained how statistics which do not acknowledge the context of the performance are invalid, and that policies for school improvement must acknowledge underlying constraints. Debates over the use of published league tables will no doubt continue and research (for example, DfEE, 1995; Jesson, 1997; Schagen, 2006) is being conducted and used in value-added measures which attempt to give fairer pictures of the performance of schools. For example, it is possible to measure the progress of pupils from KS1 to KS2, or GCSE to A-levels, relative to other pupils in schools with a different intake. Examples of these contextualized value added measures (CVAs) can be seen on government websites such as http://www.dcsf.gov.uk/performancetables.

Views from the national tests

Traditionally, examinations have been developed to monitor individuals and it is only more recently that assessment has been used to monitor national or local systems. The foundations of the national assessment system introduced by the 1989 National Curriculum stemmed from a report of the Task Group on Assessment and Testing (DES, 1988a). Development of new forms of national assessment at Key Stage 3 in science, mathematics, English and technology were started in 1989. 1990 was the first year in which trials were conducted, followed by further ones in 1991 (Swain, 1991a, 1991b). Right-wing political pressure (Black, 1994, 1998a) then demanded that the style of these assessments should be changed to a 'pencil and paper' format rather than be administered in the classroom with practical elements by teachers. Thus these 'new' style tests were first used in 1992 and have remained in a similar format up until 2008 for KS3.

The standards of performance are closely monitored each year and the average level for pupils at age 11 (Key Stage 2) is set at level 4. In the UK, results between 2003 to 2008 showed that the proportion of pupils attaining level 4 showed slight variations, as did the proportion achieving level 5 (Table 10.2).

Table 10.2 The national results for Key Stage 2 Science, percentage of all children, boys and girls achieving greater than levels 4 and 5 between 2003 to 2008

	2003		2004		2005		2006		2007		2008	
Percentage achieving at or greater than	L4	L5	L4	L5	L4	L5	L4	L5	L4	L5	L4	L5
All	87	41	86	43	86	47	87	46	88	47	88	44
Boys	86	40	86	43	86	46	86	45	87	46	87	43
Girls	87	41	86	42	87	48	87	46	88	47	89	45

Source: www.standards.dfes.gov.statistics.

While the setting of the questions on these tests is criterion-referenced to the National Curriculum, the marking of the questions in the tests is not. The marking used is numerical and statistical and normative judgemental methods are used to ensure consistency of results. Looking at these and previous population results after five years of further schooling to 16+ tells a different story to one of increasing pass rates at GCSE. Ironically it seems that primary schools are failing to improve performance of their pupils in the national science tests whereas secondary schools seem to be able to do it at GCSE every year! It is likely that political pressure for improvement is more focused on potential school leavers than on primary education.

One important source of information for formative use is the annual report produced by the administrators on performance on questions and topics within papers, as they can give clear messages for teaching and learning. For example, the Qualifications and Curriculum Authority (QCA, 2005) report makes reference to areas where pupil performance has improved and also other areas where teachers could continue to improve teaching and learning. Teachers who choose to ignore these reports, and there is some evidence to suggest that they do (Swain, 1996), will be doing a disservice to future cohorts of pupils.

At age 11, the national tests are intended to assess the science teaching and learning by the student in a 1.5 hour examination period. One of the statistics used to measure the reliability of these tests is known as 'Cronbach's alpha' but it is of limited use. It is a measure of internal consistency and looks at the extent to which questions within the examination all measure the same thing. Using this simplistic statistic the national tests have been shown to have high reliability and the levels awarded are correct. However, Cronbach's alpha does not tell you what you need to know because it is first necessary to derive the standard error of measurement (SEM) and then apply this to each student's score to estimate the probability that the true score may lie on the other side of an inter-level boundary score, than the recorded score. This is then integrated over all the students in the distribution and over all the level boundaries. If this model is used, then between 20–30 per cent of students may be awarded an incorrect level (Black and Wiliam, 2006; Black et al., 2008). In addition to reliability issues, the validity may also be questionable, as the test may measure such a limited set of knowledge and competencies.

National tests provide only a limited sketch of pupil performance at a particular point in time. It is the teacher who is in a much better position to provide a more coherent picture. They see their students at work every week and they know their strengths and weaknesses in a way that the national tests cannot measure. In England, teachers are required to produce their own assessment of pupils' levels of achievement which are collected separately. However, they are not required to do this until the national test results are known, which may influence their judgement. Consequently the correlation between the national distributions of levels from the tests and the teacher assessments is unsurprisingly high (QCA 1998)! As the results of the teacher assessments are not combined with the results of national tests, there is a hidden implication that the teachers' judgements are unreliable. However, studies in Queensland in Australia (Butler, 1995), by Black (1993) and by the Assessment Reform Group (2006) suggest that teachers can provide both valid and reliable assessments. This result has been achieved by the teachers working with the State's assessment developers over a period of time and so they now have a sense of participation and ownership of the assessment.

A recent research project (Black et al., 2009) looked at how English and mathematics teachers view summative assessment systems other than externally constructed tests. There were a number of differences, for example, in their views of validity and reliability of coursework or assessing within subjects in a holistic or atomistic way. Their results also suggested that professional development focusing on assessment literacy, skills and values is essential if teachers are to develop to their potential to achieve the high standards in their own assessments.

Views of national examinations at ages 16+ (GCSE) and 18+ (GCE A-level)

National views of public examinations deserve a separate section because they have been the subject of considerable discussion and analysis. In addition, in England, there are specific assessment problems of comparability as the administration of these examinations is not conducted by a single organization, unlike the national tests, which have a single body for each Key Stage.

The numbers game and entries to 16+ examinations

Educational environments can often change quickly, something which is often reflected in summative data. During the past two decades in the UK there have been both curriculum changes and assessment changes at 16+ and the summative data show this. For example, the number of candidates taking GCSE double award science since 1989 has increased considerably. This increase in science entry has not been at the expense of other subjects such as English or mathematics but from the separate science subjects themselves. However, in more recent years, there has been an increasing trend back to the separate sciences of biology, chemistry and physics, as these sciences are thought by some schools to be a better preparation for sixth form science courses (Fairbrother and Dillon, 2009, in press). GCSE biology is a case in point; in the year 2000, the entry was about 41,000 but by 2007 it was 63,000 and chemistry and physics show similar patterns. Consequently, attempting to compare summative data over a number of years is bound to be unreliable as similar cohorts, syllabuses, question papers and grading standards do not exist.

Target setting and the publication of league tables have made the number of entries and grades obtained particularly important. In such a context, where education is now dominated by a market ideology (Ball, 1990), educational outcomes are often seen as an economic product (Apple, 1992) whose function is the production of a labour force which will sustain the economic growth of the nation and whose performance must be monitored through the use of inspections and examination results. These in turn lead to competition between schools. As a result, schools can seek to implement spurious curriculum changes that are of little benefit to many pupils, such as allowing three separate sciences, but will enhance their market position within the community. For instance, where it is possible to have three separate awards in the sciences instead of the single subject double award, there is the potential to maximize the number of top (A* and A to C) passes per student and hence, raise possible positions in league tables.

The numbers game and entries to 17+ and 18+ examinations

Advanced Subsidiary (AS) levels, usually taken at 17+, are designed to broaden the 16–19 curriculum, and are worth 0.5 of an A-level. Pupils can then go on to take A-levels (or A2) at 18+. Since their introduction, biology continues to be the most popular and physics the least popular science at both levels (Figure 10.2). There is a greater difference between the entries for AS and A-level (A2) biology than for the other two sciences, implying that AS biology is used to broaden qualifications at 17+, rather than as a necessary precursor for a specialist A-level (Bell et al., 2005).

Subject difficulty

Although carried out some time ago, research by Fitz-Gibbon and Vincent (1994, 1997) found that differences in subject difficulties at age 18 (A-level in the UK) ranged from about a third of a grade up to a grade and a quarter. In this type of study, the grades achieved by large numbers of candidates in one subject are compared with the grades achieved by the same candidates in

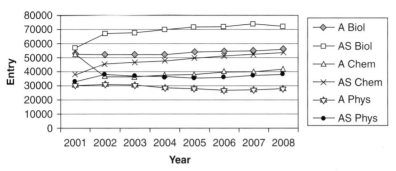

Figure 10.2 Entries to GCE A- and AS levels in the three sciences, 2001–08
Source: Joint Council for Qualifications.

another subject. These subject pairs are then compared. Table 10.3 shows the effect for physics grades relative to grades in some other subjects.

Table 10.3 shows that, on average, candidates achieved lower grades in physics than they did in their other A-levels, often by as much as one grade. Similar tables can be derived for other subjects. These types of study raise questions about what information the results provide. For example, should all subjects have the same difficulty in terms of the grades awarded or should we reduce the inherent difficulty of the syllabuses in the apparently more difficult subjects of physics and chemistry? This technique of comparing pairs of subjects to study difficulty is not without its critics and Newton (1997a) argues that, since the samples to obtain the pairs are self-selecting, it may be that one group is inherently more able than another and thus compounds the problem. This may be the case with the physics entry, which may be derived from the upper end of the ability spectrum and then paired with the whole spectrum

Table 10.3 Subject pair analysis for A-level physics and another subject

With other subject	Grade difference
Biology	+0.96
Mathematics	+0.15
Chemistry	+0.07
Business studies	+1.10
Sociology	+1.64
History	+1.01
General studies	+1.50

Note: Each number is the mean of the subject mean grades minus the physics grades.

of ability in another subject. The simple lesson here is that any conclusions from the analysis of summative data *must*, like any other data, be examined with respect to the *underlying assumptions* and not taken at face value.

The Centre for Evaluation and Monitoring (CEM) at Durham University (Hendry, 2009) looks at data collected in schools from baseline information and examination results, and makes statistical predictions of performance and including added value data. A number of acronyms apply, such as Alis, Yellis, MidYIS, and SOSCA, depending on the age of the students in the data sets. For example, the 'Advanced Level Information System' (Alis) can provide current information on subject difficulty and show that there continues to be differences in standards of grading between subjects.

Equity: gender issues

This broad topic has attracted much attention over the years and has been reviewed by Arnot et al. (1998) together with Elwood (1995) and Elwood and Comber (1995, 1996) who looked at many areas such as examination papers, coursework and entry patterns. For example, the proportion of female entries for A-level chemistry has increased by 51 per cent from 1970 to 1990. A further example shows that there are grade differences awarded between males and females. Table 10.4 shows the differences in the proportion of A–C grades awarded for boys and girls over a five-year period. Here positive values would indicate higher performance by boys and negative values by girls. As can be seen from Table 10.4, over the period 2004–08, girls achieved more grades A to C than boys in all three A-level sciences.

The differences between the girls' successes and boys' are small but significant, particularly in physics, and it would be premature to tinker with the awarding processes before looking at how subject choices interact with stereotypical beliefs about achievement and performance held by teachers and students alike. For example, an analysis of the previous decade would have shown a different pattern in which boys tended to outperform girls in all three sciences. However, at present there is an inequity which favours girls.

Table 10.4   Differences in the percentage of A–C grades awarded between boys and girls at advanced level in the three A-level Sciences, 2004–08

Subject	Difference in per cent A–C grades All GCE Groups					Mean difference
	2004	2005	2006	2007	2008	2004–08
Biology	−5.3	−3.1	−3.3	−4	−2.8	3.7
Chemistry	−3.7	−3.9	−4.3	−3.2	−3.3	3.7
Physics	−9.1	−8.6	−8.5	−7.4	−7	8.1

Note: Each number is the mean grade for boys minus the mean grade for girls.
Source: Joint Council for Qualifications, 2004–2008.

Standards

In many countries, making value judgements on the standards of achievement has become a national obsession, particularly at the times of the reporting of public examination results. Useful research evidence is difficult to obtain and Newton (1997b) suggests that such judgements are impossible, insofar as syllabuses, examination styles and teaching, change over time. Consequently studies which attempt to show changes over time must be viewed with caution. Two examples are provided to indicate some possible inferences.

The first example uses recent data to show how the grading of the UK 16+ GCSE Science Double Award examinations has changed over time (Table 10.5).

Table 10.5 shows that there have been increases in the proportion of entrants obtaining grades A*, A and B and this is particularly pronounced for grade B. This general increase appears to be at the expense of grades D to U where there is a reduction in the proportion awarded. By looking at these patterns we could make sweeping statements such as, standards are declining because more students are passing with higher grades, or that standards are rising because teaching has improved, students are better prepared and achieve higher grades. In both cases we do not know where the 'truth' lies because the evidence base is unsound. For example, the syllabuses have changed and so has the National Curriculum (Science) so again it is questionable whether like is being compared with like. Further work needs to be done here before any claims can be justified.

The second example takes another stance (SCAA, 1996) in which syllabuses, examination papers and candidates' scripts in various subjects were looked at in detail over a ten-year period. Chemistry examinations at 16+ and 18+ were chosen for the sciences. The detailed analysis that was carried out indicated that judgements of decline or improvement in performance were difficult. For example, the results from the 18+ chemistry study showed that some changes have taken place. There have been reductions in mathematical and

Table 10.5   Percentage of candidates achieving grades in Science (Double award), 2000–07

Year/grade	A*	A	B	C	D	E	F	G	U
2000	3.9	8.1	12.6	26.9	21.6	14.4	7.8	3.0	1.7
2001	4.0	8.1	12.7	27.6	21.0	14.1	7.8	3.0	1.7
2002	4.1	8.1	12.9	27.6	20.9	13.0	7.6	3.0	1.8
2003	4.0	8.5	13.1	28.2	19.5	13.1	8.1	3.4	2.1
2004	4.3	8.4	13.5	28.5	19.1	13.1	7.6	3.4	2.1
2005	4.7	9.1	14.1	28.7	19.4	12.2	6.9	3.0	0.9
2006	5.4	9.2	14.7	29.0	19.4	12.1	6.8	2.9	0.5
2007	5.2	9.5	15.0	28.9	19.5	10.4	6.3	2.6	1.6

Source: Joint Council for General Qualifications.

inorganic chemistry demands of syllabuses. There has been greater use of structured questions and candidates are now expected to use more skills such as interpreting data rather than recalling knowledge. There has been a simultaneous decline in performance in inorganic chemistry and in the use of symbolic representations of equations. A report by the Royal Society of Chemistry (1998) found that standards had declined by the equivalent of two A-level grades between 1989 and 1996. The findings were based on the results of a chemistry test given to new undergraduates which were then correlated with their A-level grade. For example, a grade A candidate in 1989 would have scored 82 on the test but would score 75 in 1996. A similar decline is shown for other grades. This research might well be usefully repeated for the first part of the millennium. However, given further evidence, the fundamental problem of comparability of standards still remains because, if the syllabus changes or the pedagogy has changed during the interim, candidates will have been exposed to a different educational experience during the period under investigation which will lead to a different performance on such an unchanged chemistry test.

The previous two examples looked at standards over time but this is just one aspect. Another is in the administration of examinations. The UK examination system is organized by a number of awarding bodies, OCR, Edexcel, AQA, WJEC, CCEA. Scotland is excluded as it operates its own system of examining and easy comparisons cannot be made. Although the awarding process has a formal structure for all of these bodies and is now overseen by OfQual (Office of the Qualifications and examinations regulator, established in April 2008), differences in the percentages of grades awarded do seem to vary both between awarding bodies and between subjects. It is usual for schools in Wales and Northern Ireland to adopt their national awarding body, that is, WJEC or CCEA, whereas in England there is much more variation and schools will often choose the awarding body which they think offers the better syllabus or the most curriculum support. Table 10.6 shows how the percentage of

Table 10.6 Variation in percentage of grades A–C and grade A for the GCE A-level Science Examinations, 2008

Awarding Bodies (number)	Percentage A–C (per cent Grade A in brackets)		
	Biology	Chemistry	Physics
England (3) AQA, Edexcel, OCR	67.0 (26.1)	76.0 (33.2)	70.6 (31.9)
Wales (1) WJEC	66.8 (23.7)	75.5 (31.7)	67.1 (25.6)
Northern Ireland (1) CCEA	79.0 (38.9)	82.3 (44.8)	77.6 (37.0)
All UK (5)	69.2 (26.7)	76.3 (33.7)	70.6 (31.8)

Source: Joint Council for General Qualifications.

A-level grades, A–C and grade A vary with awarding bodies. Clearly, Northern Ireland produces better results at A-level and Wales is less successful. However, we do not know if this reflects the quality of the entry or the teaching or the idiosyncrasies of the awarding process. Perhaps where you live can help your future! A greater transparency in the results of different boards is needed or again more research needs to be done.

National views by other means

Some countries attempt to monitor standards through systematic research. For example, in the UK, the Assessment of Performance Unit was set up in 1975 to promote the development of methods of assessing and monitoring of the achievement in schools and to identify any under-achievement (Black, 1990). Data was gathered annually from 1980 to 1984 with the focus on pupils aged 11, 13, and 15 (Johnson, 1989). The surveys used were extensive, involving typically 12,000–16,000 pupils and 300–600 schools. The assessment framework for science that was originally used was to assess students' abilities to do the following:

- Use graphical and symbolic representations.
- Use apparatus and measuring instruments.
- Make observations.
- Interpret and apply scientific knowledge.
- Plan investigations.
- Perform investigations.

There was wide use of both pencil-and-paper tests and practical tests, made up of questions derived from a bank containing many hundreds of pre-tested questions, each question carefully targeted to a specific science area and having a context defined in terms of 'everyday' or 'scientific'. Answers were analysed to see what type of response the pupils had made. Pupils' scientific achievement was found to vary considerably with the context of the question, with everyday contexts usually evoking better performance. As a result of this work, the context of the question is carefully considered and scrutinized in questions for national examinations. In addition, issues of validity and reliability, which were always in the forefront of the APU study, showed that if the assessment were to have content validity, then a hands-on practical assessment was essential to reflect the nature of science. Consequently, a novel feature was the testing of practical skills and looking at performance on planning and carrying out investigations on a national scale. This work effectively raised the status of the necessity to assess practical work at all ages for the next three decades (see, also, Chapter 6 in this volume).

Numerous APU reports were published, and the main thrust of these reports was on the performance of pupils in particular scientific areas. For example, 41 per cent of pupils knew the units of measurement of the voltmeter at age 13, and boys appeared to be better at applying chemical concepts than did girls at age 15. Perhaps one of its greatest achievements was to raise awareness of assessment issues and provide a legacy which was crucial to the development of criterion-referenced assessment frameworks such as 'The Graded Assessment in Science Project' (GASP) (Swain, 1989), where pupils were monitored on all aspects of their science during secondary schooling in order to achieve a cumulative and graded profile, rather than a norm-referenced method of assessment which has no points of reference for its final judgements on pupils. As such, this work was influential in developing the first assessment programme for the English National Curriculum (Swain, 1991a; 1991b; Taylor, 1990) and its effects still pervade current work on assessment.

International views

TIMSS surveys (Trends in International Mathematics and Science Study)

The past decade has seen assessment data move towards providing information for policy-makers. Individual countries may have their own idiosyncratic systems of education but politicians are placing an increasing emphasis on how their systems perform in comparison to the rest of the world. Whether such national indicators have a direct and immediate effect on policy is uncertain, but, nevertheless, countries will always prefer to be in the upper quartile rather than any another, which might indicate that they are far from their stated goals.

The TIMSS 2003 report is the third comparison of mathematics and science achievement carried out since 1995 by the International Association for the Evaluation of Educational Achievement (IEA) on behalf of national research organizations from the participating countries (TIMSS and PIRLS, 2004). A further round of comparisons conducted in 2007 was released in December 2008. In the 2003 survey, some 46 countries participated at either the fourth or eighth-grade level, or both. Its main objectives were: (1) to compare and analyse curricula, teaching practices and student achievement in science and mathematics in the participating countries; (2) to enable them to determine whether they were internationally competitive; (3) to examine the variety of best practices in successful schools and; (4) finally to establish worldwide benchmarks for setting and evaluating goals in mathematics and science (Murphy, 1996). Its methodology was very broad as not only were students tested in the conventional way, but teaching practices, the role of the curriculum in teaching and learning, textbooks, homework, and student attitudes were all also studied. It is from such research that we can gain an insight into how different societies and cultures with different national educational policies can influence the achievement of students within. Only the formal testing which took place in grade 8 will be discussed in this section.

Table 10.7   Scores from the TIMSS grade 8 test survey based on overall mean score for the science assessment

Country	Average scale score	Life Science	Chemistry	Physics	Earth Science	Environ Science
Highest						
Singapore	578	569	582	579	549	568
Japan	552	549	552	564	530	537
England	544	543	527	545	544	540
Netherlands	536	536	514	538	534	539
USA	527	537	513	515	532	533
Australia	527	532	506	521	531	536
Lithuania	519	517	534	519	512	507
Italy	491	498	487	470	513	497
Israel	488	491	499	484	485	486
International average	474	474	474	474	474	474
Egypt	421	425	442	414	403	430
Chile	413	427	405	401	435	436
Lowest						
South Africa	244	250	285	244	247	261

Source: TIMSS and PIRLS, 2004.

International achievement at grade 8

In these assessments, five scientific content domains were tested by means of pencil-and-paper tests with each domain containing a number of items. They were Earth Science (16 per cent), Life Science (29 per cent), Physics (24 per cent), Chemistry (16 per cent) and Environmental Science (14 per cent). Each content domain had three cognitive domains associated with it, factual knowledge (30 per cent), conceptual understanding (39 per cent), and reasoning and analysis (31 per cent). The total number of items was 189. The scores from the items were combined to produce an overall science score and then arranged in a hierarchy. In addition to the use of test items, there were questionnaires for students on their attitudes to schools and teaching and the results of these can be found in the main report. The results of the test item components for the five domains from a selection of countries are given in Table 10.7.

Singapore together with Taipei, the Republic of Korea and Hong Kong were the top performing participants and Botswana, Ghana and South Africa the lowest. England and Wales, although not first, were in the upper quartile just below Japan. Not shown in the table is Scotland which scored a total of 512.

Further information in the study reveals that there are gender differences in performance and in most countries boys had significantly higher achievement than girls. This difference was mainly due to the higher performance of boys in the earth science, chemistry and physics areas. Perhaps more surprising, from the table, is the high international performance of all countries in the life sciences and environmental science areas and the slightly lower performances on the chemistry and physics. This finding, of course, not only raises issues about the international performance in these areas but also about the validity of the questions used to assess them. However, such data do provide countries with the opportunities to re-examine their curricula and pedagogy in order to identify possible weaknesses and to implement strategies to correct these in the future, and so use the information obtained in a formative way. Indeed, a comparison of the 2003 results with those from previous surveys show an improvement in the scientific performance of young people in many countries.

The performance assessments from the 1997 study

This was the first and only time that international comparisons of practical science had been attempted and so a brief overview of this study is included here. Science is regarded as a practical subject and to ignore this domain, as the APU work showed, would be to automatically invalidate the overall assessment. Only 19 countries took part in this component (IEA, 1997) and so generalizations from these assessments to all the countries must be exercised with caution. In these performance assessments, five practical tasks (measuring your pulse, magnets, batteries, rubber band, and solutions) were used to assess the practical domain. Each task had specific performance criteria; so, for example, the 'pulse' task, where students had to look at changes of rate on exercising, assessed the presentation and quality of the data from the measured pulse rate, a description of the trend due to the increasing exercise and an explanation of the results.

The results showed that the position for England and Wales, second only to Singapore, was better in this domain than for the written components. If the standard errors are taken into account, then the two results are comparable. One likely reason for the high performance here must originate from the students' exposure to the investigative practical work in the science National Curriculum (see, also, Chapter 6 in this volume).

A fuller analysis shows that there is variation in performance across each country on each task. For example, Columbia, the lowest scoring country, produced one of the highest scores for the 'magnets' task. There was also overall variation between tasks; 'pulse', for example, was the most difficult task and 'magnets' was the easiest. This implies that students should be given experience of investigational practical work in a variety of scientific domains rather than a single one.

Simple tables of results can hide much of the richness of the data collected. For example, despite overall similarities, there are wide differences in the performance on specific skills, such as collection and presentation of results, between Singapore and England and Wales. Reasons for these differences are not clear and need further research.

The PISA surveys (Programme for International Student Achievement)

PISA is an educational survey organized by the Organization for Economic Co-operation and Development (OECD) and is usually conducted on a three-year cycle with the first being in 2000. PISA surveys assess students near the end of their schooling (age 15, year 11) on their knowledge and skills on one of three areas: reading literacy, mathematical literacy, and scientific literacy. It does not attempt to measure their mastery of school subjects taught through a national curriculum. The analysis of results is usually related to the economic development of the participating countries and so measures the yield of education systems. Drori (2000) comments on the belief that science education leads to economic development and this results in new policy from world organizations such as UNESCO and OECD and funding agencies such as the IMF and the World Bank.

Scientific literacy was the main focus of the 2006 survey conducted by means of a two-hour test and there were also student and school questionnaires (OECD, 2007). Some 57 countries participated, including all OECD members and 25 EU members, with nearly 5,000 students taking part in England. Scientific literacy was defined by PISA as the ability to use knowledge of science to identify questions, to acquire new knowledge to explain scientific phenomena and to draw evidence-based conclusions about science-related issues that students will use later in adult life. PISA defines performance in terms of six levels from a numerical scale, 500 being the mean point on the scale. The test items are classified into three broad scales:

1. Scientific processes such as identifying scientific issues, explaining phenomena scientifically and using scientific evidence.
2. Knowledge about science.
3. Knowledge of science in terms of, Earth and space, Living systems, and Physical systems.

The results for a selection of countries appear in Table 10.8 as a Science score and the additional columns give a comparison of performance on the different scales in science and indicate the extent to which they are higher or lower from the Science score.

United Kingdom students out-performed many of the OECD countries. The only two European Union countries that outperformed the UK are Finland and Estonia but outside this area we have to add Hong Kong, Canada, Japan and New Zealand. However, 13 other countries performed at levels not significantly different from that of the UK. The UK's highest scores were obtained on the 'explaining phenomena scientifically' scale but the difference between this score and those on the 'identifying scientific issues' and 'using scientific evidence' scales was small, indicating that, on average, students in

Table 10.8   Scores from the PISA 2006 test survey based on overall mean score for the science assessment

Country	science score	Identifying scientific issues	Explaining phenomena scientifically	Using scientific evidence	Knowledge about science	Knowledge of science		
						Earth & space	Living systems	Physical systems
Highest								
Finland	563	−8.4	2.8	4.1	−5.6	−9.0	−10.5	−3.6
Japan	531	−9.3	−4.1	13.0	0.2	−1.1	−5.2	−1.0
Australia	527	8.4	−6.6	4.4	6.6	3.4	−5.1	−11.8
Netherlands	525	7.7	−3.1	0.7	5.4	−6.8	−15.4	6.2
United Kingdom	515	−1.1	1.9	−1.2	1.8	−10.2	10.6	−6.4
USA	489	3.2	−2.8	−0.4	3.3	15.1	−2.1	−3.7
Lithuania	488	−11.9	6.5	−1.4	−5.6	−1.4	14.7	2.0
Italy	475	−1.2	4.1	−8.4	−3.6	−1.5	12.2	−3.0
Israel	454	3.1	−10.5	6.4	12.5	−36.9	4.5	11.3
Chile	438	5.9	−6.1	1.4	4.5	−9.9	−3.8	−5.0
Turkey	424	3.7	−0.8	−6.6	1.2	1.3	1.5	−7.7
Lowest								
Kyrgyzstan	244	−0.7	11.7	−34.0	−13.5	−7.0	7.7	27.3

Source: OECD (2007).

the UK perform in a consistent way. This may reflect the nature of the teaching as laid out in the science National Curriculum.

International comparisons attempt to give a snapshot at a particular point in time and as can be seen from Tables 10.7 and 10.8, a country's ranking can vary, even though the assessments may appear to be very similar. Researchers continue to analyse and critique the methodology used and the data that these international studies produce (Harlen, 2001; Prais, 2003; Goldstein, 2004; Murdock, 2008) and with the possible conclusion that they are not yet perfect but will have to suffice until the next attempt is made.

Some recent research on summative assessment

Research on assessment continues to capture the interests of the academic community as it has done for many decades and it seems that there is no end to the topics to explore and comment on. It would be impossible to report here on all assessment research that has taken place in the last decade. However, some recurring themes still dominate the minds of researchers and they are associated with, standards, marking, and reliability and validity. These themes will be explored briefly below.

Standards

As has been shown in previous paragraphs, differences exist in examination results in a number of ways such as, year-on-year results within subjects, between subjects, and between examination boards. Why does this variation exist? A brief answer could be that no two cohorts of pupils are the same, in that they are likely to have had different teaching and learning experiences. No two subjects are the same in terms of the knowledge, skills and processes, and no two examination organizations have the same cohorts of students taking the examinations and they also have different syllabuses, procedures, and even personnel making different judgements. Even QCA (2004) in an independent report on examination standards states, 'No examination system has found an adequate way to determine whether standards are constant across subjects.' Consequently, maintaining standards is not only about minimizing some of the differences indicated above, but also defending new standards when the old ones seem outdated because of new curricula, new criteria or examination demands. However, the manipulation of standards to endorse government policy or to increase 'market share' signifies the road to perdition for assessment unless of course it is founded on research.

Recent literature (Baird et al., 2000) on the 'gold' standard, and Newton (1997a, 1997b), indicates the problems of maintaining standards and issues of comparability and leans heavily towards the view that absolute standards do not exist and trying to prove that they do is a futile exercise. However, what is needed by government and public alike is a greater understanding of the complexity of the problem of standards and using quality data to illustrate this. Comment and research by examination boards on standards do continue: Elliot and Greatorex (2002) looked at the evolution of methods of comparability in national assessment and Black and Bramley (2008) have proposed a judgemental rank ordering method for maintaining standards on two tests.

Are the demands of questions set in, say, a GCSE biology paper, the same as the demands of questions set in other science papers? This question formed the basis of a study by QCA (2008a) on inter-subject comparability studies at GCSE, AS and A-level in the sciences. They found that at each level, chemistry was seen as the most demanding in terms of content. However, at A-level, the ability to synthesize knowledge, understanding and skills varied between the three sciences and chemistry was judged to be less demanding than physics and biology. There was also some inconsistency in the requirement for extended writing between subjects and within subjects. For example, biology tended to require more extended writing whereas physics used more short answers and calculations. Unfortunately, the study did not indicate if the demands of questions and the methods of assessment should be altered when there are differences, merely that they exist and should be monitored.

Marking

All forms of assessment, whether it be summative or formative, involves a teacher or an organization making a judgement on an individual. In summative instances this usually involves an organization, such as an examination board. They set written examination papers, standardize mark schemes and then have examiners mark them in a reliable way for outcomes for consideration at the final awarding meetings to produce judgements in which the public can have faith. Consequently, much recent research has focused on these processes. For example, Greatorex and Bell (2008) looked at the standardization of processes for marking at AS examinations and how these impacted on reliability of examiner marking. They found that standardization meetings on their own are not particularly effective for improving the reliability of experienced examiners and that experienced examiners tend to be more lenient. Combinations of interventions (meetings, personal feedback and pre-written feedback) seemed to be the more effective way of reducing marking error. However, the feedback was sometimes effective and sometimes it was not.

In another study by Suto and Nadas (2008a), the marking accuracy within GCSE mathematics and physics papers was studied: comparing the expertise in terms of two categories 'expert' (experienced examiners) and 'graduate' (newer examiners). The length of their teaching experience could vary in both categories but both had had training in marking examinations at some stage. In many public examinations now operating, expert markers are usually given the more complex answers to mark whereas graduate markers are given ones which require simple intuitive judgements. In this study, both groups were given similar questions to mark. Very few differences between expert and graduate markers were identified on a range of responses to questions. However, variations in accuracy were apparent in both groups when the questions required more complex 'reflective' thought processes. The conclusion was that, given adequate support, 'graduate' mathematics and physics markers were able to mark almost all questions as accurately as their 'expert' counterparts thus supporting a situation that had existed for many years prior to the new categorization of markers. Further work by Suto and Greatorex (2008) looked at what goes through examiners' minds when using a points-based marking scheme such as in mathematics and a level-based scheme such as in business studies using verbal protocols and semi-structured interview schedules. The study showed that examiners tended to use one of five cognitive strategies, matching, scanning, evaluating, scrutinizing or no response. Suto and Nadas (2008b) also investigated why some GSCE (mathematics and physics) examination questions are harder to mark accurately than others. They found that for both subjects marking accuracy was found to be related to various subject-specific question features, such as question difficulty for the candidate and/or apparent marking strategy complexity. There is also an extensive review of the literature on marking reliability by Meadows and Billington (2005).

Validity and reliability

Validity and reliability issues cause intense debate and the correct use of these words is fundamental to the understanding of any assessment process. The two terms are often confused, even in the educational world, and consequently if they are not correctly understood by teachers and educators, then there is little chance that meaningful debates can take place with politicians or the public. Validity is about making a judgement on the adequacy of a test for its intended purpose(s) on justifications for any inferences which may be drawn from the results. Reliability is about the consistency in arriving at a result for a student's learning outcome. Reliability can be influenced by many things, such as, question type, allowed choice, testing time and marking. It is also limited by the inevitable fact that the assessment is based on a limited sample of all the relevant things that a candidate might be able to do. The challenge here would be to ask if the student would gain the same result on a strictly parallel and comparable test; one with a different selection from all the possible questions. No test can ever achieve perfect reliability as there are always these underlying errors in the measurement and these can lead to poor inferences unless acknowledged at the time of the reporting. The inter-relationship between reliability and validity is always a difficult problem for examination design as well as for formative assessment (Stobart, 2006) and trying to improve one can undermine the other which in turn can affect the manageability of the whole and this may become an even greater issue than the other two.

Every year, examination boards are subjected to criticism in the press over administration issues, marking irregularities and declining standards. Educational measurement is both exact and inexact. It is exact in the statistical sense in that we can define its limitations with certainty but it is inexact in that it fails to produce a mark, number, or grade with absolute certainty which can be used by politicians or the public 'confidently' for whatever reason, because of the undisclosed inherent error of the measurement. Rarely do the terms or phrases, assessment purpose, consequences of assessment, validity, error or reliability, feature in any press article. Newton (2005) raised the awareness over the problem of the public understanding of measurement inaccuracy and suggested that there are a number of steps that could be taken to alter this. First, more research could be done on the validity and reliability of examinations and the results communicated to users and stakeholders. Second, there needs to be a greater transparency in the strengths and weaknesses of examination systems and the inferences that can be drawn, rather than adopting automatic defensive positions for the purposes of satisfying government policy or press concerns.

Stobart (2001) has looked at the validity of national curriculum assessment in terms of 'consequential validity' (Messick, 1989) which incorporates both conventional reliability issues and the use to which assessment is put. However, the complexity of national assessments and the variety of purposes to which they are put make evaluation difficult, as there seems to be a delicate balance between formalized external testing and continuous or periodic internal teacher assessment, using their own tests or judgements, with the latter being undermined by the need for school accountability (see also West and Pennell, 2000) and the meeting of national standards. However, teachers' own summative assessments will remain important, even if they do not replace national testing, as they are used to set and track pupils and to advise them on taking or dropping courses. The validity, including the reliability of these teacher assessments, is also very important, but receives too little attention at present (see Black et al., 2009).

In the science subject area, Fairbrother (2008) has questioned the validity of the Key Stage 3 national tests. A survey of recent tests showed that they lack validity in three ways: first, the lower emphasis on Sc1 Scientific enquiry compared with the other parts of the programme of study; second, the low levels of skills required in mathematics and writing and, third, the lack of coverage of the higher categories of skills such as analysis, evaluation or synthesis. It is suggested that these sources of invalidity could easily be rectified by including more teacher assessment for Sc1 and changing the format of examination papers to include extended answers.

Listening to evidence: a postscript

The Assessment Reform Group (ARG, formed in 1989) and others have been commenting on the UK assessment system for a number of years with a view to improving it. For example, the ARG (2002) produced a booklet, *Testing, Motivation and Learning,* which provided a review of evidence on the negative impact of high stakes assessment and testing on pupils' motivation for learning and its implications for assessment policy and practice. This detrimental effect impacted not only on the type of assessment used to help learning but also on the breadth of the curriculum and recommended action be taken by all concerned with this form of assessment. In a further useful booklet, *The Role of Teachers in the Assessment of Learning* (ARG, 2006), the group identified the pros and cons of teachers' summative assessments in terms of their validity, reliability, impact and practicability, the main conclusion being that summative assessment by teachers should use a wider variety of assessments to make judgements and also to use these to help learning.

There was also a major parliamentary investigation initiated in 2007 by the House of Commons Children, Schools and Families Committee (2008) on testing and assessment which sought to review current practice and its limitations. It took evidence from a wide range of organizations and experts working in the area. The areas of concern were found to be in two broad domains. First, the fitness for purpose, in terms of the validity and reliability, and the received public information was questioned. Second, the consequences of high stakes testing in terms of, shallow learning, teaching to the test, narrowing of the curriculum, the burden of testing and pupil stress and demotivation. The main conclusions were that the government should review the current emphasis on national tests and use a wider range of evidence for looking at school performance. In addition, the professionalism of teachers using current techniques such as classroom assessments and assessment for learning appears to have been undervalued.

In October 2008, the Secretary of State, Ed Balls, announced that the Key Stage 3 national tests for 14-year-olds were to be scrapped. It is likely that this decision was based first, on administrative and technical difficulties experienced with the KS3 2008 testing and second, the publication of the Parliamentary Report mentioned above. The national tests in English, maths and science at age 11, which are marked externally and the results of which are published nationally would remain in place. Likewise, teacher assessment of all-round development at age 5 and teacher marked national tests in English and maths at age 7, would continue.

Conclusion

The previous sections lead us to three important interrelated issues about summative assessment. The first is the concept of power within assessment and how it can determine the type used (formative or summative); the second relates to the use and purpose of summative assessment, and the third seeks a new definition for summative assessment.

Acknowledging summative assessment as an instrument of power

Assessment has always been an instrument of power. It provides a way for controlling students, people, organizations and systems; it identifies progress in them, it puts them into hierarchies, it can be used to select and decide futures, and it can be used to make decisions. It is who controls this assessment power and what is done with the information derived from it that is important and it also determines if the assessment is summative or formative. Newton (2003) has suggested that the distinctions between the two types of assessment have been over-emphasized, but clearly their functions and power base are very different. In formative assessment the intention is that the power should reside with the pupils so that they can make better decisions about their learning and progress. The teacher acts as a facilitator for this transfer of power. Summative assessment has a different locus of power. It can be the classroom teacher but, more commonly, it is an organization, such as an examination board or government legislation. It tends to serve the interests of the 'powerful' and not the interests of the students, from which the energy is derived. Unless the interests of the students are incorporated within the context of summative assessment as evaluation, then the clear distinction between formative and summative assessment will remain. It is only when we learn to use the results of summative assessment more effectively as an automatic post-summative re-flection that it will become a formative exercise. Then, intrinsic improvements in the learning experience offered to future students will take place, and the classic distinctions between summative and formative assessment might blur.

The need to clarify purpose and use in summative assessment

Those constructing summative assessments always look at the technical is-sues of the reliability, in terms of the consistency of results, and the validity, in terms of the credibility of the assessments that are given and the results produced. These are particularly important with respect to the setting of na-tional and international tests and public examinations. However, there are also socio-economic issues associated with summative assessment such as, cost, uses, time, effort, impact on staff, students, and benefits to society. This is the newer area in assessment research and is little explored or made explicit at present. However, these technical and socio-economic issues are beginning to merge and Messick's (1989) ideas on redefining validity are influential here with the notion of consequential validity which links both the purpose and use of the assessment. The purposes the test is meant to serve and the uses the results will be put to are both elements in summative assessment, but both lie outside the control of the individual student. The purposes are paramount and future policies on summative assessment should ensure that clear aims are given for its use, whether it is for the evaluation of programmes and schemes of work, teachers in science departments, student performance at various ages, or to help schools and parents with decision-making.

Towards a newer definition of summative assessment

The existing definitions of summative assessment, as used by teachers and others, seem to be limited, as they do not help us to encapsulate the potential in the data generated. It should lead, almost automatically, to questions, to analysis, and hopefully to answers, and so provide the essential ingredient in the feedback loop of teaching, learning and assessment. So far summa-tive assessment data have been under-used by teachers, even less so than by administrators and government except for political purposes. Consequently, the definition of summative assessment data needs to be re-examined in the light of its potential. A newer definition might be that, summative assessment is one which has a pre-defined purpose and will produce data on an individ-ual or individuals, at some point in time, which can then be used both to inform and to enhance the teaching and learning of future cohorts of stu-dents. The implication of this definition is that summative assessment should always have some formative function. The information component within this definition is well established, that is, students, parents, teachers, school governors, LAs, and government over time, are all made aware of such assess-ments. The actions which follow are less clear and decisions about educational interventions, teaching and course modifications, resource allocations, policy and research for the improvement of the educational system are often ignored. The full intrinsic value of summative assessment has yet to be realized.

Further reading

Black, P. J. (1993) *Testing: Friend or Foe? Theory and Practice of Assessment and Testing.* London: Falmer Press.

Gardener, J. (ed.) (2006) *Assessment and Learning.* London: Sage Publications.

Goldstein, H. and Lewis, T. (eds) (1996) *Assessment: Problems, Developments and Statistical Issues.* Chichester: John Wiley and Sons.

Pellegrino, J., Chudowsky, N. and Glaser, R. (2001) *Knowing What Students Know: the Science and Design of Educational Assessment.* Washington, DC: National Academy Press.

Thompson, B. (ed.) (2003) *Score Reliability: Contemporary Thinking on Reliability Issues.* London: Sage Publications.

11 Students' attitudes to science

Shirley Simon and Jonathan Osborne

Introduction

On a journey on the London Underground, the attention of one of the authors was drawn to a group of teenage girls who were having a heated discussion about the electrolysis of brine. They could be heard talking about 'sodium ions' and 'chlorine gas'. One girl had her science folder open on her lap and took the role of chief explainer, while three others chipped in with challenging questions and alternative ideas. The girls were totally absorbed trying to understand various terms, in what was happening at the anode and cathode, and in the movement of different ions. In short, for that 10 minutes of their lives they were engrossed in the electrolysis of brine. The train was quite crowded and soon other passengers had ceased talking and were listening to the girls' discussion. Most looked totally bemused. An elderly couple sitting opposite were staring at the girls, fascinated. Is the scenario of teenage girls being stimulated by the electrolysis of brine so strange?

A well-established aim of school science is to promote enthusiasm for the subject, not only to encourage choice of science post-16 and subsequent careers in science, but also to enhance all students' interest in scientific issues in adult life (DeBoer, 1991). Sadly, evidence shows that for many students, this aim is far from realized, for the experience of school science leaves many with the feeling that science is difficult and inaccessible. In recent years there have been a range of studies concerning students' attitudes to science, focusing on factors which influence attitudes and subject choice post-16. Though some factors are outside the influence of school, many are concerned with classroom practice. In this chapter we will review significant research which has taken place in this area, focusing on what is meant by attitudes to science; why they have been extensively researched; and what is known about such attitudes. We will then examine the major influences on attitudes to science and subject choice that have been identified, and draw some implications for classroom practice from the range of studies undertaken.

Significant research

What are attitudes?

Thirty years of research into this topic has been bedevilled by a lack of clarity about what attitudes to science are. An early contribution towards its elaboration was made by Klopfer (1971) who categorized a set of affective behaviours in science education as:

- the manifestation of favourable attitudes towards science and scientists;
- the acceptance of scientific enquiry as a way of thought;
- the adoption of 'Scientific Attitudes';
- the enjoyment of science learning experiences;
- the development of interests in science and science-related activities;
- the development of an interest in pursuing a career in science or science-related work.

Research into attitudes *towards* science is further complicated by the fact that attitudes do not consist of a single construct but rather a large number of sub-constructs, all of which contribute in varying proportions to an individual's attitudes to science. Various studies have incorporated a range of components in their measures of attitudes towards science, including:

- the perception of the science teacher;
- anxiety toward science;
- the value of science;
- self-esteem at science;
- motivation towards science;
- enjoyment of science;
- attitudes of peers and friends towards science;
- attitudes of parents towards science;
- the nature of the classroom environment;
- achievement in science;
- fear of failure on/of the course.

Ramsden (1998) draws on definitions of attitudes which include cognitive, emotional and action-tendency components – action-tendency being that which leads to particular behavioural intents. For example, that of Shaw and Wright (1968) who suggest:

> attitude is best viewed as a set of affective reactions towards the attitude object, derived from concepts of beliefs that the individual has concerning the object, and predisposing the individual to behave in a certain manner towards the object.
>
> (Ramsden, 1998, p. 13)

However, of themselves, attitudes may not necessarily be related to the behaviours a person actually exhibits (Potter and Wetherell, 1987), for example, a pupil may express interest in science but avoid publicly demonstrating it among her or his peers who regard such an expression of intellectual interest as not being the 'done thing'. In such a case, motivation to behave in a particular way may be stronger than the motivation associated with the expressed attitude, or alternatively, anticipated consequences of a behaviour may modify that behaviour so that it is inconsistent with the attitude held.

Consequently, it is behaviour rather than attitude that has become a focus of interest and which has led researchers to explore models developed from studies in social psychology. Ajzen and Fishbein's theory of reasoned action (1980) – a theory which is concerned fundamentally with predicting behaviour, is one such model. This model focuses on the distinction between attitudes towards some 'object', and attitudes towards some specific action to be performed towards that 'object', for example, between attitudes *towards* science and attitudes towards *doing* school science. Ajzen and Fishbein argue that it is the latter kind of attitude that best predicts behaviour. Their theory represents a relationship between attitude, intention and behaviour. Behaviour is seen as determined by intention, and intention is a joint product of attitude towards the behaviour and the subjective norm (that is beliefs about how other people would regard one's performance of the behaviour).

The theory of reasoned action has been applied to some attitude and behaviour studies in science education. For instance, Crawley and Coe (1990), Koballa (1988) and Oliver and Simpson (1988) have all found that social support from peers, and attitude towards enrolling for a course, are strong determinants of student choice to pursue science courses voluntarily, which suggests that the theory has at least some partial validity. Other, more recent, theories which have attempted to model the way in which students choose to study science or not are the Eccles Expectancy-Value Model (Eccles and Wigfield, 1995) and the Lent, Brown and Hackett Social Cognitive Career Theory. The main value of such theories is their value in determining salient beliefs, which can then be reinforced or downplayed to affect relevant behavioural decisions by students, such as 'girls don't do science'. Furthermore, such theories point towards the need to draw a demarcation between attitudes towards *doing* school science and attitudes towards science *in general*. It is the perception of school science, and the feelings towards undertaking a further course of study, which appear to be most significant in determining children's decisions about whether to proceed with further study of science post-16.

Why research attitudes?

The purpose of much attitude research in science education has been to identify features of an important 'problem' (Ramsden, 1998) that young people seem to be less and less interested in the study of science. This issue is most markedly shown by data emerging for the Norwegian Relevance of Science Education (ROSE) project. Using an extended questionnaire, this project has surveyed the attitudes of young people (age 15–16) towards school science in

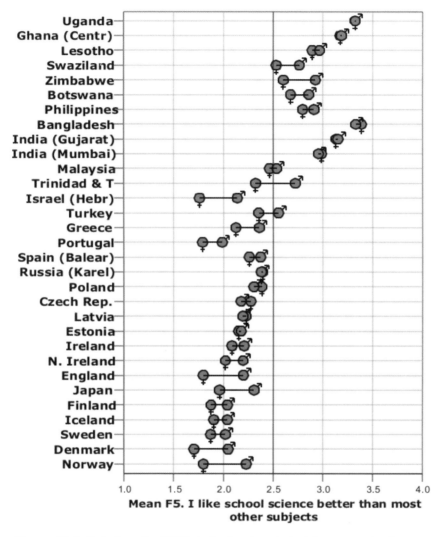

Figure 11.1 Data from the ROSE study showing students' responses to the statement 'I like school science better than most other subjects'. Percentage answering Agree plus Strongly agree, by gender

over 20 countries. Figure 11.1 shows one of the major findings of the study – students' response to the item 'I like school science better than other subjects'.

Two features stand out in such data. First, the increasingly negative response the more developed the society, suggesting that the issue of student engagement with school science is a deeply cultural phenomenon and a reflection of the values and identity of contemporary youth. Indeed, there is a

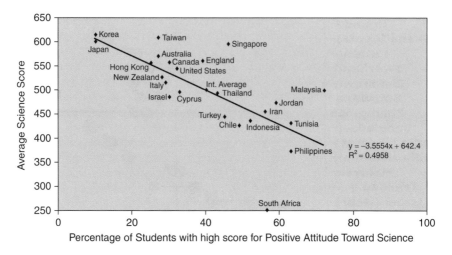

Figure 11.2 Relationship between students' achievement scores by country and their attitudes towards science

0.92 negative correlation between responses to this item and the UN Index of Human Development (Schreiner and Sjøberg, 2007). Second is the significantly more negative response of girls, raising the question of what it is about school science, and/or alternatively, what it is about girls, that leads to such a well-defined trend.

Similar findings emerge from an analysis of the 1999 data for the Third International Mathematics and Science Study (TIMSS) by Ogura (2006). He plotted the scores for average national achievement (measured by their knowledge of science concepts) against the mean of responses to various items measuring their attitudes towards science, the results of which are shown in Figure 11.2.

Again, what stands out is that those countries whose students are the most successful, and which many other countries seek to emulate, are those which offer a very traditional science education with an emphasis on learning scientific knowledge, have the students with the most negative attitudes. Such alienation is undoubtedly of concern to teachers, as their job satisfaction is likely to be strongly influenced by their students' affective responses to what is on offer in science lessons, perhaps even more than by their cognitive responses. Moreover, such data are of fundamental concern to all developed societies who perceive the lack of student interest in the study of science as a threat to their knowledge-based economies.

In one sense, such concerns about attitudes to science and the uptake of science post-16 are not new. Over thirty years ago, Ormerod and Duckworth (1975) began their review on the topic of pupils' attitudes to science with the following comment:

In 1965 a thorough inquiry began into the flow of students of science and technology in higher education. The final report (Dainton, 1968) laid particular emphasis on the phenomenon which had become known as the 'swing from science'. Several explanations were suggested for the swing, among them a lessening interest in science and a disaffection with science and technology among students. (p. 1)

However, recent years have witnessed a rising tide of concern where the issue of students' attitudes towards science has been a feature of a series of significant reports about the role of science in society, for example, the UK (Sainsbury of Turville, 2007; Roberts, 2002), Europe (European Commission, 2004), the USA (National Academy of Sciences: Committee on Science Engineering and Public Policy, 2005) and Australia (Tytler et al., 2008). However, it should be noted that all of these reports focus solely on the supply of the next generation of scientists, seeing school science as a pipeline which is leaking too much. Putting aside that this places a very instrumental function on education – making it more akin to a pre-professional training rather than an education about the major explanations it offers about the material world and the intellectual achievement it represents – the question must be asked of whether there really is the demand for more scientists. American data would suggest that there is definitely no shortages of life scientists (Teitelbaum, 2007) and the production of students with scientific PhDs is still robustly healthy in most Western countries (Jagger, 2007). Urging more students to pursue the study of science because of the potential of future scientific careers, without a careful consideration of whether such jobs might exist, is therefore morally and economically questionable.

Within the UK, where more pupils than ever are taking A-levels, part of the explanation must lie in the range of courses available for study post-16. The consequence is that, as a proportion of the cohort, fewer and fewer are taking only science and mathematics combinations (Osborne et al., 2003). The issue is not so much that science is not interesting, rather it is that science is less interesting than other subjects. For instance, a study conducted in England (Jenkins and Nelson, 2005) for the ROSE project found, using a sample of 1,277 students from 34 schools, that 61 per cent agreed with the proposition that school science is 'interesting'. And the Research Council's UK survey of public attitudes to science, which asked people whether they thought their school science was either worse than other subjects, about the same, or better (Research Councils UK, 2008), found that 1 in 5 young people (age 16–24) thought it worse, but 1 in 3 thought it better. Typical responses to the question 'I would like to work in a career involving science', among UK 15–16-year-olds, are 34 per cent agreeing or strongly agreeing (OECD, 2007) or somewhat less – 21 per cent in the Jenkins and Nelson ROSE survey. However, whether such figures should be seen as a cause for concern is debatable. After all, to have around a quarter of the school cohort interested in pursuing a career in science is about as much as could reasonably be hoped for. Rather, what is of concern is the level of negative response to students' experience of school science; the failure to realize that the three subjects which open more potential career pathways than any other are mathematics, physics and another science; and the failure to engage girls with physical sciences. Our knowledge of why such attitudes towards school science exist and the factors that have led to these attitudes are the focus of this chapter.

Research in this domain is not new. Major reviews of attitudes towards science have been conducted by Gardner (1975), Munby (1983), Schibeci (1984) and more recently by the authors (Osborne et al., 2003) drawing on over 200 studies. Since that last review, the developments in the field have been studies which have given us a better understanding of what the key issues are; a resurgence in the issue of why girls are not interested in the study of science – particularly physical science; and more development in the instruments for measuring attitudes – all aspects which are covered in this chapter, albeit briefly. However, before examining some of the findings of major studies and their implications, it is useful to look more closely at how attitudes are measured, and at some of the assumptions underlying different strategies.

Researchers have taken a number of approaches to the measurement of attitudes to science. These include subject preference studies, where pupils have been asked to rank their liking of school subjects, for example, Whitfield (1980) and Hendley et al. (1995), where attitude is inferred from relative popularity. Whitfield's analysis demonstrated that physics and chemistry were two of the least popular subjects post-14. A later study of this kind by Lightbody and Durndell (1996b) has shown boys were far more likely to report liking science than were girls. Though preference ranking is simple to use and the results easily presented and interpreted, its problem is that it is a relative scale; it is possible for a student to rank science as low, but have a more positive attitude towards it than another student who ranks it more highly. However, it can be useful if the question being asked is 'How popular is science compared to other subjects?'

More commonly, attitudes have been measured through the use of questionnaires which often consist of Likert-scale items. Here students are asked to respond to statements such as 'science is fun', 'I would enjoy being a scientist'. Likert scales include a five-point choice consisting of 'strongly agree/agree/not sure/disagree/strongly disagree'. Items on the scale have normally been derived from free-response answers generated by students. These have then been reduced to a set of usable and reliable items that have been piloted and further refined by statistical analysis.

Such scales have been widely used and extensively trialled and are the major feature of research in this domain. One well-known instrument which historically has been used frequently is the scientific attitude inventory developed by Moore and Sutman in 1970 (Moore and Sutman, 1970). However, this has been criticized by Munby (1983) for the inconsistent results it produces and its lack of reliability. Moreover, a feature of this scale is that all the attitude objects are concerned with aspects of science in society and not attitudes to science as a school subject.

The emphasis on measuring attitudes through the use of questionnaires has resulted in the development of a plethora of scales which give differing degrees of emphasis to a broader range of attitude objects. More well-known examples are the instrument developed by Simpson and Troost (1982) for their large-scale study using 4,500 students drawn equally from elementary, junior high and high schools in North Carolina, and the Attitudes toward Science Inventory (Gogolin and Swartz, 1992).

The problem of interpreting the significance of these multiple components of attitudes towards science has been clearly identified by Gardner (1975) who comments:

> An attitude instrument yields a score. If this score is to be meaningful, it should faithfully reflect the respondent's position on some well-defined continuum. For this to happen, the items within the scale must all be related to a single attitude object. A disparate collection of items, reflecting attitude towards a wide variety of attitude objects, does not constitute a scale, and cannot yield a meaningful score.
>
> (Gardner, 1975, p. 12)

If there is no single construct underlying a given scale, then there is no purpose served by adding the various ratings to produce a unitary score. The best that can be done is to ensure that the components are valid and reliable measures of the constructs they purport to measure, and then look for the significance of each of these aspects. Even so, many instruments suffer from significant problems as, statistically, a good instrument needs to be *internally consistent* and *unidimensional* (Gardner, 1995). The standard measure of internal consistency is Cronbach's alpha which measures the extent to which responses to any one item correlate with the whole set of items. By definition all items in a undimensional scale are internally consistent. However, it does not follow that internally consistent scales are unidimensional as they may consist of more than one factor which correlate well with each other. The only technique for identifying unidimensionality, therefore, is factor analysis. More fundamental than this is the issue of construct validity – whether the scale measures what it purports to measure for which there are no standard techniques to demonstrate such validity. A good discussion of these issues and an account of an instrument which has been developed to address the numerous criticisms surrounding attitude instruments can be found in Kind et al. (2007).

Another problem identified with the use of scales and inventories on a single occasion relates to the stability of attitudes (Ramsden, 1998), and the possibly erroneous assumption that attitudes are sufficiently stable to be measured at one point in time (Munby, 1983). Though, once formed, attitudes may be difficult to change, there are few studies where repeated measurements of attitudes have taken place which would reliably demonstrate that the attitudes being measured are stable.

A further extensive criticism of quantitative studies of attitudes to science has been that they provide limited understanding of the problem. Such concerns have led to studies of attitudes to science which include the use of interviews (Baker and Leary, 1995; Ebenezer and Zoller, 1993; Piburn, 1993; Woolnough, 1994) and more recently Osborne and Collins (2001). while such studies are subject to criticisms of lack of generalizability, the data do provide insights into the origins of attitudes to school science.

What do we know about attitudes to science?

Results from numerous studies of attitudes to school science (Breakwell and Beardsell, 1992; Brown, 1976; Cerini et al., 2003; Doherty and Dawe, 1988; Ebenezer and Zoller, 1993; Hadden and Johnstone, 1983; Harvey and Edwards, 1980; Haste, 2004; Havard, 1996; Jenkins and Nelson, 2005; Johnson, 1987; Murphy and Beggs, 2003; Osborne and Collins, 2001; Pell and Jarvis, 2001; Reiss, 2000; Simpson and Oliver, 1985; Sjøberg and Schreiner, 2005; Smail and Kelly, 1984) show that positive attitudes decline during the period of formal schooling by quite significant amounts. Indeed, the work of Pell and Jarvis (2001) would suggest that they decline from age 5 onwards. Even so, students still enter secondary school with a highly favourable attitude towards science and interest in science which is eroded by their experience of school science, particularly for girls (Kahle and Lakes, 1983; Murphy and Whitelegg, 2006).

Hendley et al.'s (1995) study of 4,023 Key Stage 3 pupils in Welsh schools indicates that out of the four core subjects, science, English, mathematics and technology, science is the least popular. This finding is confirmed by a smaller-scale qualitative study based on interviews with 190 pupils (Hendley et al., 1996). When asked which three subjects they liked best, science was ranked 5th out of 12 subjects. However, when asked which subjects they liked least, science emerged as the most disliked, particularly by girls. Hendley et al. conclude that science is a 'love–hate' subject which elicits strong feelings in pupils. Colley et al. (1994), in another British study, found significant gender differences among 11–13-year-old pupils, with girls favouring English and humanities and boys favouring PE and science.

In contrast to these results for attitudes to school science, many surveys show that students' attitudes to *science itself* are positive, for instance, a large-scale market research survey conducted in the UK for the Institute of Electrical Engineers (The Research Business, 1994). This study showed that students saw science as useful (68 per cent), interesting (58 per cent) and that there was no significant difference between genders. A large proportion (53 per cent) saw the relevancy of science as a reason for studying it and that it offered better employment prospects (50 per cent). Moreover, 87 per cent rated science and technology as important or very important in everyday life – findings which are supported by later studies by Jenkins and Nelson (2005) and the recent OECD PISA study (2007).

This contradiction between students' interest in science itself and their liking for school science is highlighted by the work of Ebenezer and Zoller (1993) and more recently Lyons (2006). In their study, Ebenezer and Zoller found that 72 per cent of the 1,564 16-year-olds interviewed indicated they thought science valuable, but nearly 40 per cent that they found science classes boring. Both studies suggest that this gulf is due to the message presented by school science, which situates science as a value-free, detached activity unrelated to any societal context that would give it meaning or relevance – a view which is characterized by the notion that 'science is important, but not for me'.

The relationship between attitude and achievement is another key issue permeating much of the literature over which there is some ambiguity. Gardner's (1975) review of the research evidence offered little support for any strong relationship between these two variables. Writing somewhat later, Schibeci (1984) draws a stronger link between the two, however, he also cites studies which show no relationship. Weinburgh's (1995) meta-analysis of the research suggests that there is only a moderate correlation between attitude towards science and achievement, though this correlation is stronger for high and low ability girls, indicating that for these groups 'doing well' in science is closely linked with 'liking science'. Similar findings have appeared in the major study conducted by Talton and Simpson (1990).

An exception to these findings is the research of Simpson and Oliver (1990). These authors would argue that their longitudinal study shows a strong relationship between the three affective variables – attitude towards science, motivation to achieve and the self-concept that the individual has of their own ability – and their achievement in science. In part, this may be explained by their attempt to measure 'motivation to achieve' which may be a more significant factor than attitude toward science in determining achievement. In this context, it is interesting to note that the general finding is that girls are always more motivated to achieve than boys. Some support for this theory emerges from a more recent study by Fouad et al. (2005) in a study of 1,151 students drawn from college, high school and middle school. One of the top factors correlating with the decision to study science courses or a science career was 'science interest'. The position is best summarized as seeing interest in science as one factor among several important factors which lead to engagement with and achievement in science.

Factors influencing students' attitudes to science and subject choices

Research studies have identified a number of factors influencing attitudes towards science. For the purpose of this chapter, the main factors which have implications for classroom practice and subject choice are effective teaching, perceived difficulty and gender.

Effective teaching

A considerable body of evidence now exists that identifies the quality of teaching as a major determinant of student engagement and success in all school subjects (Barber and Mourshed, 2007; Cooper and McIntyre, 1996; Darling-Hammond, 2007; Sanders et al., 1997; Strauss and Sawyer, 1986; Wayne and Youngs, 2003). For instance, in her analysis of student achievement, Darling-Hammond found that 65 per cent of the variance between schools in terms of student outcomes could be explained in terms of 'school resources' and that the two major factors within this component were teacher qualifications and the proportion of vacancies among teaching staff unfilled after nine weeks.

Within science, several studies have pointed towards the influence of classroom environment as a significant determinant of attitude (Haladyna and Shaughnessy, 1982; Myers and Fouts, 1992; Talton and Simpson, 1987). Myers and Fouts found that the most positive attitudes were associated with a high level of involvement, very high level of personal support, strong positive relationships with classmates, and the use of a variety of teaching strategies and unusual learning activities. Similar findings emerge from the work of Darby (2005) in a study of science students' perceptions of their teachers' impact on learning, which emphasizes that relational pedagogies, including *passion* toward science and teaching, providing *comfort* through friendliness and lack of threat, and *support* through encouragement and attention, are as important as instructional pedagogies which are perceived to include *explanation, discussion* and *clarification*.

Variety as a key feature in generating interest in science also comes from the work of Piburn and Baker (1993), the Scottish HMI report (HM Inspectors of Schools, 1994) *Effective Learning and Teaching in Scottish Secondary Schools,* and the work of Nolen (2003) on identifying learning environments that motivated students. Similar conclusions that 'school, particularly classroom variables, are the strongest influence on attitude toward science' were drawn by Simpson and Oliver (1990, p. 13) in their North Carolina study and from the work of Woolnough (1994) whose research showed that quality of teaching is a major factor in continuing with science education post-16. These findings were confirmed by the studies of Ebenezer and Zoller (1993) and Haladayana et al. (1982) which showed that the most important variable that affected students' attitude towards school science was the kind of science teaching they experienced. Further support for the significance of the teacher can be found in the work of Sundbergh et al. (1994) and Piburn and Baker (1993). Hendley et al.'s (1995) study of KS3 pupils' preferred subjects also found that the most common reasons given for liking or disliking the subject were teacher-related. This finding might seem to contradict the ROSE findings that the most developed countries (who have the most highly educated and qualified teachers) have the students who are least interested in science. Rather, what it suggests to us is that, while teacher quality matters, the desire to pursue the further study of science is the product of much stronger cultural factors such as perceived employment opportunities.

One well-known study into student subject choice was undertaken by Woolnough in 1994 with 1,180 A-level students who had, or had not, chosen to study science, using a mix of attitudes questionnaires and interviews. In addition, 132 heads of science completed a separate questionnaire and 108 sixth formers and 84 staff from 12 schools were interviewed. His study identified six factors which were responsible for student choice/non-choice of the sciences. Of these, the two strongest factors were the influence of students' positive experience of extra-curricular activities and the nature of in-class activities – that is the quality of their science teaching. Woolnough's work therefore supports other findings that the quality of teaching is an important determinant of attitude and subject choice. The factors Woolnough identified as contributing to such teaching included a supply of well-qualified, enthusiastic graduate science staff (including graduates in physics and engineering) who not only have a good spread of expertise across science, but who also have individual subject loyalty. Good teaching was characterized by teachers being enthusiastic about their subject, setting it in everyday contexts and running well-ordered and stimulating science lessons. Good teachers were also sympathetic and willing to spend time, both in and out of lessons, talking with the students about science, careers and individual problems. Thus the picture emerging from this body of research about what kind of teaching is required is fairly unequivocal – finding the individuals with the knowledge, skills and aptitude – particularly in the physical sciences remains an enduring problem (Osborne and Dillon, 2008; Tytler et al., 2008).

Perceived difficulty

Several studies (Crawley and Black, 1992; Fouad et al., 2007; Havard, 1996; Hendley et al., 1996) have identified students' perception of science as a difficult subject as being a determinant of subject choice. Indeed, Havard's investigation of the uptake of sciences at A-level, albeit in only four schools, points to the perceived difficulty of science as the major factor inhibiting uptake. Likewise, Tai et al.'s (2006) analysis of the US NAEP longitudinal data set shows that the probability of studying physical sciences or engineering at university is exponentially related to a student's mathematical ability. In contrast, the probability of studying a life sciences degree appears to bear little relation to mathematical ability. Further analysis of these data suggests that student *perceptions* of their mathematical ability play a significant role in their decisions to persist (Maltese, 2008).

Additional substance to the notion that physical sciences are perceived as being difficult is provided by the analysis of the data collected by the UK Department for Education and Employment on the youth cohort for 1989, 1990 and 1991 using sample sizes of approximately 14,000 students for each year (Cheng et al., 1995). These researchers found that the most significant factors correlating with uptake of *physical sciences* were the grades achieved at GCSE in science and mathematics. Likewise, another, more recent, large-scale study of 1,395, 11–16-year-old students (Spall et al., 2004) reported that students' liking for both physics and biology declined over the years. The decline in physics was more pronounced than in biology and was a result of students' perception of the increasing need for mathematics which increased the difficulty of the subject.

These studies suggest that science is only taken by students who do well, reinforcing the notion that it is for the intelligent and therefore perceived as difficult. Such perceptions have implications for students' self-image and career choice. This perception of risk does have an element of truth to it. The Centre for Evaluation and Monitoring compares student achievement in a range of A-levels using a subject pairing approach (Centre for Evaluation and Monitoring, 2008), showing that maths and science subjects were found to be between a half and whole grade more difficult than other subjects apart from foreign languages (see, also, Chapter 10 in this volume). Although these statistics support students' perceptions that they will do less well in science subjects compared to other subjects, and appear to agree with the perception held by students that the science subjects are inherently more difficult, a degree of caution must be taken when interpreting these results. Is it, for instance, that the science subjects are intrinsically difficult or rather is it that the quality of science teaching is inferior when compared with other subjects? There is no simple answer to this question suggesting that the two factors are intertwined and both contribute to student perceptions.

Gender

The most significant factor influencing attitudes towards science and subject choice is gender. As Gardner (1975) comments, 'Sex is probably the most significant variable related towards pupils' attitude to science' (p. 22). This view is supported by Schibeci's (1984) extensive review of the literature, and meta-analyses of a range of research studies by Becker (1989) and Weinburgh (1995) covering the literature between 1970 and 1991. Both the latter two papers summarize numerous research studies to show that boys have a consistently more positive attitude to science than do girls, though this effect is stronger in physics than in biology. A more recent review of the situation has been conducted by Murphy and Whitelegg (2006) which confirms this ongoing picture. Indeed, the enduring low participation of girls in the study of physical sciences (Murphy and Whitelegg, 2006), standing in stark contrast to their educational success in other domains, has led to a renewed focus in research to address the problem which has proved resistant to the many initiatives that have been taken since the early 1980s.

What is clear from an extensive literature on the subject is that girls' attitudes to science are significantly less positive than boys (Erickson and Erickson, 1984; Francis, 2000; Haste, 2004; Head, 1985; Kelly, 1981; Smail and

Kelly, 1984; Whitehead, 1996). A common thesis offered to explain this phenomenon is that it is a consequence of cultural socialization which offers girls considerably less opportunity to tinker with technological devices and use common measuring instruments (Johnson, 1987; Kahle and Lakes, 1983; Smail and Kelly, 1984; Thomas, 1986). For instance, Kahle contends that her data show there is a gap between young girls' desire to observe common scientific phenomena and their opportunities to do so. More importantly, her data show conclusively that their science education does not remediate for this lack of experience and leads her to argue that 'lack of experiences *in* science leads to a lack of understanding *of* science and contributes to negative attitudes *to* science' (Kahle and Lakes 1983, p. 135). Similarly, Johnson argues from her data, measuring a range of common childhood experiences of children, that 'early established differences in the interests and activities of boys and girls result in parallel differences in their science performances' (1987, p. 479). However, such data are contradicted by more recent findings from twin studies that there is no difference between girls' and boys' ability (Haworth et al., 2008) or interest (Pell and Jarvis, 2001).

In terms of achievement in science, Elwood and Comber (1995) have shown that the situation has reached a position where girls are doing as well, if not better than boys in biology and chemistry though boys still surpass girls at age 16 in physics. These findings suggest that gender itself may now only contribute a minor part in the attribution of success. What remains an enigma is why girls choose not to pursue science even though they are competent and do believe in their capabilities to succeed.

Blickenstaff (2005), in a useful review of the issue, notes that nine hypotheses have been advanced to explain the phenomenon. These are:

1. Biological differences between men and women.
2. Girls' lack of academic preparation for a science major/career.
3. Girls' poor attitude toward science and lack of positive experiences with science in childhood.
4. The absence of female scientists/engineers as role models.
5. Science curricula are irrelevant to many girls.
6. The pedagogy of science classes favours male students.
7. A 'chilly climate' exists for girls/women in science classes.
8. Cultural pressure on girls/women to conform to traditional gender roles.
9. An inherent masculine worldview in scientific epistemology.

Space does not permit a full discussion of all of these or their relative import here. Suffice to say that the evidence on biological differences is that there are no genetically attributable differences in ability at age 9 (Haworth et al., 2008). While the performance of woman and men does differ significantly on spatial reasoning, the difference would only predict (if spatial reasoning is an essential attribute for success in science and engineering) a ratio of two men to every woman and not the 20 to 1 ratio that is observed. The research would suggest that there is some evidence to support all of the other hypotheses. Most interesting is recent work analysing questionnaire data from samples of the youth cohort (Haste, 2004; Haste et al., 2008; Schreiner, 2006). Factor analysis of their responses have identified four or five distinct groups with different interests. Haste's work, for instance, has identified four categories of student:

> The 'Green' who are individuals with ethical concerns about the environment and scepticism about interfering with nature. This group is particularly associated with younger girls under 16 and with those who would be interested in a job related to science.
>
> The 'Techno-Investor' who links enthusiasm for investing in technology (especially space-related) and in science research, with beliefs about the beneficial effect of science, and trust in both scientists and government. This is particularly associated with boys under 16 and with young men over sixteen in the workforce.
>
> The 'Science Orientated' who is interested in science programmes on television and in science fiction, and holds a belief that a 'scientific way of thinking' can be applied widely. This is associated with boys over sixteen both in full-time education and in the workforce.
>
> The 'Alienated from Science' who is bored with science, and sceptical about its achievements. This is associated with younger girls and with young women over sixteen in the workforce who are not interested in a job related to science.
>
> (Haste, 2004, p. 11)

Her research leads her to conclude that 'girls are not so much less interested in science than boys . . . but girls focus on different things' (2004, p. 3). What kind of different things they focus on emerges from another survey (Haste et al., 2008). Their work identified four factors which distinguished the cohort which were:

1. Trust in the benefits of science.
2. Science in my life.
3. Ethical scepticism.
4. Facts and Hi-Tech Fixes.

Distinguishing the cohort into those who were interested in scientific careers and those who were not, they found that the significant distinctions between girls and boys were to be found in factors 2 and 3. Girls scored much more highly on 'Science in my life' seeing science as relevant to one's own life, wanting to know more about areas of science and engineering that affect them personally including how body organs work; holding a belief that animal experimentation is wrong and rejecting a view that in the future things will be pretty much the same as now but with a little more advanced

Table 11.1 The top five items boys would like to learn about in science and the top five for girls

Boys	Girls
Explosive chemicals	Why we dream when we are sleeping and what the dreams might mean
How it feels to be weightless in space	
How the atom bomb functions	Cancer – what we know and how we can treat it
Biological and chemical weapons and what they do to the human body	
Black holes, supernovae and other spectacular objects in outer space	How to perform first aid and use basic medical equipment
	How to exercise the body to keep fit and strong
	Sexually transmitted diseases and how to be protected against them

technology around. Likewise, girls were much more concerned about the ethics associated with the application of science (in contrast to boys) being often upset by events in the news; buying cruelty-free products; believing that the future will be worse, not better; and that science cannot solve basic human problems like poverty and unhappiness. Clearly if girls hold these values, a de-contextualized, value-free science excised of all opportunities to discuss or explore the social or ethical implications of science is unlikely to appeal. Nowhere does this come across more starkly than in the English ROSE data where respondents were asked to rank 108 items that they would like to learn about and to rate them on a 1 ('not at all') to 4 ('very interested') scale. Between English boys and girls there were 80 statistically significant differences. The top five items for boys and girls are shown in Table 11.1.

As for gender stereotyping on choice, Whitehead's (1996) research has attempted to explore its influence in more detail. She found that, although there were significant gender distinctions within pupils' perceptions of subjects, these were not significant influences on subject choice. Girls doing mainly 'feminine' subjects, who were the focus of her study, described themselves as high on the stereotypical masculine trait of competence and were highly intrinsically motivated. Boys, in contrast, taking mainly 'masculine' subjects were more likely to be extrinsically motivated for status, recognition and a highly paid job describing themselves as high on the traits of competence and aggression. In general, boys are more likely to choose sex-stereotyped careers and she suggests that this reflects a greater need to establish and strengthen their gender identity than that of girls. Hence, she suggests:

> It is not therefore that girls are under-represented in mathematics and the physical sciences, but that boys are greatly over-represented; similarly, in languages, girls appear to be over-represented in these areas only because the boys are so under-represented in them.
>
> (1996, p. 155)

Further, she comments that:

> If boys are choosing sex-appropriate subjects in order to conform to traditional notions of masculinity, then this is clearly undesirable both from the point of view of the individual, who may not necessarily be choosing those subjects at which they are most successful, and for society as a whole, as it is unlikely to gain good scientists by such a process of choice.
>
> (1996, p. 158)

Such findings would also explain why boys in boys-only schools choose more arts and humanities courses and girls in girls-only schools choose more science courses as they are under less pressure to establish and conform to their gender identity.

Evidence which supports Whitehead's findings comes from work by Pauline Lightbody in Glasgow (Lightbody and Durndell, 1996a, 1996b). In a small-scale study with 106 pupils using a novel methodology to investigate career aspirations, she found no significant difference between males and females. She explains the discrepancy between this finding and their actual career choice as a case of girls' view of science being one which is epitomized by the view 'We can, I can't', and that gender stereotyping is so deeply entrenched that it may not even be conscious. She argues that it is not so much that science and technology are perceived as masculine but more that the current focus of interest on technological matters is not of central interest to girls and that only a change in content and the style of teaching to show a greater interest in people will lead to a significant increase in the choice of physical sciences by girls.

This latter point is also supported by a small-scale study undertaken by Fielding (1998) into the reasons why academically capable girls are not choosing sciences and mathematics post-16. Fielding's study shows that girls chose not to do science because they perceived its value only as of instrumental value for a future career – in short that if they chose science they would have to be a scientist. Part of the remedy must lie in asking what might a curriculum look like that specifically addressed the interests of girls. The research of Haussler and Hoffman (2002) has shown that a curriculum which addressed these interests led to enhanced interest from girls and made no difference to the interest of the boys.

Engaging people with science

One of the contributions of research, recently, has been to identify more clearly some of the factors which lead to student engagement or interest in science. It is now clear, for instance, that by the age of 14, for the majority of students, interest in pursuing further study of science has largely been formed. In a recent analysis of data collected for the US National Educational

Longitudinal Study, Tai et al. (2006) showed that the effect was such that by age 14 students *with* expectations of science-related careers were 3.4 times more likely to earn a physical science and engineering degree than students *without* similar expectations. This effect was even more pronounced for those who demonstrated high ability in mathematics – 51 per cent being likely to undertake a STEM-related degree. Indeed Tai et al.'s analysis shows that the average mathematics achiever at age 14, with a science-related career aspiration, has a greater chance of achieving a physical science/engineering degree than a high mathematics achiever with a non-science career aspiration (34 per cent compared to 19 per cent). Further evidence that children's life-world experiences prior to 14 are the major determinant of any decision to pursue the study of science comes from a survey by the Royal Society (2006) of 1,141 SET practitioners' reasons for pursuing scientific careers. It found that just over a quarter of respondents (28 per cent) first started thinking about a career in STEM before the age of 11 and a further third (35 per cent) between the ages of 12–14. Likewise a small-scale longitudinal study conducted following 70 Swedish students from Grade 5 (age 12) to Grade 9 (age 16) (Lindahl, 2007) found that their career aspirations and interest in science was largely formed by age 13. Lindahl concluded that engaging older children in science would become progressively harder. A study of the effect of self-efficacy beliefs on the career trajectories and aspirations of 272 children with a range of ages from 11 to 15 and a mean of 12 years by Bandura et al. (2001) led these researchers to conclude:

> The findings of the current study suggest that children's career tra-jectories are getting crystallized rather early in the developmental process. Hence, efforts to reduce sociostructural biases that constrict women's career development require early intervention.
>
> (Bandura et al., 2001, p. 202)

Such data demonstrate the importance of the formation of career aspirations of young adolescents, long before the point at which many make the choice about which GCSEs to pursue, let alone A-levels. Thus, rather than plugging the leaks in the STEM science pipeline (Jacobs and Simpkins, 2006), we would contend that effort would be much more productively expended by: (1) un-derstanding what the formative influences on student career aspirations are between the ages of 10 and 14; and (2) attempting to foster and maximize the interest of this cohort of adolescents, particularly girls, in STEM-related careers.

When it comes to the issue of what the formative influences are, the most interesting research field is that which focuses on the nature of identity in late modernity and its construction. This perspective explains the lack of interest in school science as a product of the mismatch between the values communi-cated by school science, the manner in which it is taught, and the aspirations, ideals and developing identity of young adolescents. Indeed, there is a large body of work which would indicate that students' sense of self-identity is a major factor in how they respond to school subjects (Head, 1979, 1985; Schreiner and Sjøberg, 2007; Brotman and Moore, 2008). Schreiner's work provides some useful insights. Arguing from a sociological perspective, she suggests that contemporary society gives pre-eminence to the individual. Drawing on the work of Beck and Beck-Gernsheim, she argues that there is little point in re-vitalizing yesterday's concepts such as *obedience*, *conscientiousness* and *humility* as the processes of individualization at work in our society have already shaped the values of modern youth (Beck and Beck-Gernsheim, 2002). Such concepts were part of the grand narratives and traditions that shaped societies – many of which have been weakened in an era of late modernity by the dissolution of family and the increasingly reflexive nature of society (Giddens, 1990). Rather, school science needs to appeal to young people by presenting itself as the means to solve the major problems facing humanity (climate change, water and energy supply, food production) and the unique and prestigious *contribution that the individual can make*. In short, what engages modern youth is not the stepping stones by which we arrived at this point in history but rather *their* potential individual contribution to the future.

The review undertaken by Brotman and Moore (2008) focuses on gender and identity, emphasizing the need to examine the diversity of identities to be found *within* gender groupings (2008, p. 988) to avoid creating simplistic binary oppositions. They review studies by Brickhouse and colleagues (Brickhouse et al., 2000; Brickhouse and Potter, 2001), who highlight the need to support girls in viewing scientific identities as consistent with their own identities, and their findings that school experiences often serve to hinder the adoption of scientific identities. Other studies have shown how curriculum and teaching can support students, including girls, in accessing a range of scientific identities (Hughes, 2001). Identity research calls attention to deep-rooted ideas held by culture and society that need to be addressed if students, in particular girls, are to see themselves as 'the kind of people who would want to understand the world scientifically' (Brickhouse et al., 2000, p. 443).

The values emphasized by contemporary advanced societies include care for the environment, democracy, care for others, creativity and self-realization. That this is so is reflected in the fact that recruitment in Western societies into medicine, the life sciences and environmental studies is not falling and, in these areas, girls often outnumber boys. In this context, education is continuously evaluated against how it contributes to a student's self-development, asking 'What does it mean for me?' The desire, therefore, to work in an area that students find meaningful is a driving force in their choice of subjects to study. Meaning is reflected in the valuing of activities that offer the potential for self-realization; creativity and innovation, working with people and helping others; and/or earning lots of money. The problem for school science is that it is associated with building bridges, making chemicals, ever smaller mobile phones, and faster computers – very few of which comprise the values listed above. Rather, school science needs to offer a vision which shows that it is the physicist or engineer who is going to make the major contribution to providing alternative energy sources, animal- and environmentally-friendly food production, new methods of eliminating disease, and solving the challenge of global warming. In short, what is needed is a transformation of the vision offered by school science.

Havard's (1996) work suggested that a major problem lay with physics, as over 50 per cent of his sample indicated that they did not enjoy the subject at all, or very little, whereas over 60 per cent enjoyed biology a lot or quite a lot. One explanatory factor may be that physics is being taught by biology or chemistry specialists who have little enthusiasm for the subject. In such situations, teachers who lack confidence and familiarity fall back on didactic modes of teaching and the quality of teaching and learning is impoverished (Osborne and Simon, 1996).

Little research has asked what makes for effective teaching of science in the eyes of the pupil. One such revelatory study was a focus group study undertaken with 20 groups of 15–16-year-old students by Osborne and Collins (2001). This research found that students resented a curriculum that appeared to be repetitive; that frog-marched them across the scientific landscape with no time to discuss any of the issues; and which lacked contemporary relevance typified by the following comment:

> The blast furnace, so when are you going to use a blast furnace? I mean, why do you need to know about it? You're not going to come across it ever. I mean, look at the technology today, we've gone onto cloning, I mean it's a bit away off from the blast furnace now, so why do you need to know it?
>
> (2001, p. 449)

Another revealing study undertaken in the USA providing some insight on this issue is reported by Sheila Tobias (1990). The study aimed to explore why so many college students turn away from science in the course of their degree studies and involved a group of post-graduates who had successfully completed their degrees in other subjects. For a fee, the group of surrogate students were willing to revisit introductory courses in physics and chemistry in order to audit these for the research. They each enrolled for a particular course and participated in it, attending all the lectures and doing the homework assignments and examinations. They were asked to focus their attention on what might make introductory science 'hard' or even 'alienating' for students like themselves. The seven case studies in the report reveal that common problems were that the courses focused on problem-solving techniques and lacked an intellectual overview of the subject; there were too many 'how much' questions, not enough discussion of 'how' or 'why'; pedagogy was condescending and patronizing, examinations were not challenging; there was no community or discussion and the atmosphere was competitive.

Teachers need to be enthusiastic and knowledgeable about their subject, setting it in well-chosen contexts and running well-ordered and stimulating science lessons. In addition, there is now a growing body of evidence which points to the fact that it is the opportunities to engage in science outside the classroom that matter as much as that which is taught in the classroom (Jarvis and Pell, 2002; Woolnough, 1994). Or, in the words of the Head Master of Eton – a leading English private school: 'This school works because we recognise two things: pupils learn as much from each other as they do from us; and pupils learn more outside the classroom than they do inside' (Little, quoted in Eyres, 2008, p. 1).

The tendency for prescriptive national curricula to constrain science teaching at the expense of interest and depth of involvement undoubtedly has implications for the promotion of students' positive attitudes towards science beyond the experience of school. With more options open to students and less need to specialize early, it is even more crucial that enjoyment of science becomes a key factor, if students are to pursue science post-16. Thus, in this way, one would hope that the intellectual challenge and involvement experienced by the group of girls studying the electrolysis of brine with which we introduced this chapter could be sustained, reinforced and transferred beyond their study of GCSE chemistry. The decline in the study of science post-16, for all groups of students, indicates that we are failing to convince children that science is the most significant achievement of Western civilization. The message of this research is that the central question that teachers need to ask of their practice is, 'How can we make science more appealing?'

Further reading

Ajzen, I. and Fishbein, M. (1980) *Understanding Attitudes and Predicting Social Behaviour.* Englewood Cliffs, NJ: Prentice Hall.

Cooper, P. and McIntyre, D. (1996) *Effective Teaching and Learning: Teachers' and Students' Perspectives.* Buckingham: Open University Press.

Gardner, P. L. (1995) Measuring attitudes to science, *Research in Science Education,* 25(3): 283–9.

Haste, H. (2004) *Science in My Future: A Study of the Values and Beliefs in Relation to Science and Technology amongst 11–21 year olds.* Nestlé Social Research Programme.

Head, J. (1985) *The Personal Response to Science.* Cambridge: Cambridge University Press.

Murphy, C. and Beggs, J. (2003) Children's attitudes towards school science, *School Science Review,* 84(308): 109–16.

Osborne, J. F., Simon, S. and Collins, S. (2003) Attitudes towards science: a review of the literature and its implications, *International Journal of Science Education,* 25(9): 1049–79.

Schreiner, C. and Sjøberg, S. (2007) Science education and youth's identity construction – two incompatible projects? In D. Corrigan, J. Dillon and R. Gunstone (eds), *The Re-emergence of Values in the Science Curriculum* (pp. 231–47). Rotterdam: Sense Publishers.

Woolnough, B. (1994) *Effective Science Teaching.* Buckingham: Open University Press.

12 Supporting science learning in out-of-school contexts

Heather King and Melissa Glackin

Introduction

In recent years, researchers and policy-makers around the world have increasingly called for greater attention to be paid to the educational potential of out-of-school settings, citing the many benefits, and indeed the necessity, of learning in contexts other than the classroom. For example, the policy statement published by the Informal Science Education Ad Hoc Committee for the National Association for Research in Science Teaching (NARST) argued that learning 'derives from real-world experiences within a diversity of appropriate physical and social contexts' (Dierking et al., 2003, p. 109). The National Education Standards in the USA, too, recognize that science museums and science centres, in particular, 'can contribute greatly to the understanding of science and encourage students to further their interests outside of school' (NRC, 1996, p. 451). In the UK, Wellington (1998) has argued that science museums offer important teaching and learning opportunities that can contribute to the teaching and learning of science required by the National Curriculum – a view we very much share.

From a policy perspective, recent directives in the UK have been clear in their commitment to the provision of learning opportunities beyond those offered by classroom-based experiences. For example, in 2005, the UK Education and Skills Select Committee stated that:

> Education outside the classroom is of significant benefit to students. Academic fieldwork clearly enhances the teaching of science and geography, but other subjects such as history, art and design and citizenship can also be brought to life by high quality educational visits. Group activities, which may include adventurous expeditions, can develop social skills and give self-confidence. Furthermore, outdoor education has a key role to play in the social inclusion agenda offering children who may not otherwise have the opportunity the simple chance to experience the countryside, or other parts of our heritage that many others take for granted.
>
> (House of Commons, Education and Skills Select Committee, 2005, p. 7)

In November 2006, following the recommendations outlined by the Select Committee, the Department for Education and Schools (DfES) launched the *Learning Outside the Classroom Manifesto* (LoTC) (DfES, 2006). The *Manifesto* states that all children educated in England should gain direct experience of learning in different contexts. The basic premise of the *Manifesto* is that education is not only about '*what* we learn, but importantly *how* and *where* we learn' (DfES, 2006, p. 3, emphasis in the original). Further confirmation of governmental support for outdoor learning can be identified in the 2008 Key Stage 3 curriculum. For example, in the Qualification and Curriculum Authority's 'Big Picture' account of the curriculum (QCA, 2008b), learning outside the classroom is given overt prominence as a key component for the organization and implementation of learning.

In this chapter, we highlight the benefits of learning outside the classroom and offer advice based on what research has to say about how such learning may best be supported. We also discuss some of the challenges to be faced in implementing new practices. The findings we explore suggest that the benefits that we outline are universal – they apply to teachers working with all ages and across all disciplines, however, we note that the degree of challenge may vary from country to country and between different age groups, due to differing policies and curricular requirements. Given space constrictions, however, and in light of the recent policy initiatives in England, our discussions concerning the impact of various reports and polices are limited to the English context only.

A few definitions

We define opportunities for learning outside the classroom to include experiences in school grounds, streetscapes and local nature reserves. Further afield, opportunities include fieldtrips to farms, the wider countryside and sites of industry. In addition, they include visits to zoos, botanic gardens, museums, science centres, cultural sites and even fieldwork trips abroad. The timeframes for these experiences may be in the order of a single lesson, a day-trip, or a week-long residential course.

With regards to the nature of learning during such experiences, we note that the term 'informal' is often used to contrast out-of-school experiences with the 'formal' practices inherent in classrooms. Wellington (1990), for example, described formal learning as compulsory, structured, close-ended and teacher-centred. Informal learning, in contrast, was described by Wellington as voluntary, non-structured, open-ended and learner-centred. We argue, however, that such definitions create a false dichotomy and are unhelpful in exploring the ways in which the experience in one environment may complement an experience in another. Furthermore, we note that while classroom-based activities are undoubtedly constrained by timetables, space, and resources available, the learning may indeed be open-ended and learner-centred. In contrast, we have observed many school visits to museums and nature reserves that are highly structured and offer little opportunity for students to follow their own interests.

Rather than attempt to categorize the type of learning, therefore, we argue that different environments offer different types of opportunities, which together impact on the three domains of learning. Building on the original work by Bloom et al. (1956), we identify those domains as the cognitive, the affective, and the physical and behavioural. By cognitive learning, we refer to the conceptual skills of recalling facts, analysing and synthesizing information and applying knowledge. Traditionally, learning in the cognitive domain has been promoted by the school system where it has been necessary to enable students to pass exams based on retrieval and application of content knowledge. By affective learning, we refer to the way in which students come to take a personal interest in a subject and learn to express and defend opinions and values. Affective learning also encompasses attitudes towards a topic and self-perception of oneself as a learner. Finally, in referring to physical and behavioural learning, we mean the ways in which students gain skills in manipulation and planning, but also learn to work both independently and alongside others in teams. In combination, skills gained in the cognitive, affective, and physical and behavioural domains support an understanding of content, but also the application of content within everyday contexts in the wider world.

The benefits and opportunities offered by experiences outside the classroom

The importance of opportunities to learn outside the classroom is perhaps best illustrated by Figure 12.1. Figure 12.1 shows that between the ages of 5 to 18, we only spend 18.5 per cent of the 16 waking hours in formal educational contexts (Bransford, 2006)

In short, education is not something that stops at the school gate. Indeed, Winston Churchill famously quipped that 'his education was only interrupted by his schooling'. Access to information that is potentially educative has expanded considerably in the past century with the advent of radio, television, films, enhanced travel and now the Internet. For instance, it is possible to learn a lot about human anatomy from two hours spent in the popular exhibition *Bodyworks* – and moreover, possibly remember more. Increasingly, the boundaries between formal and informal contexts are dissolving, posing challenges to teachers about how they should use these new opportunities for learning. Indeed, looked at from the perspective of Figure 12.1, informal education is not something that is supplemental to formal education, rather formal education is supplemental to what is learnt in schools. In this chapter, we choose to focus very much on what it is possible for the teacher of science to exploit within the context of the school and what research has to say about how that should be best approached.

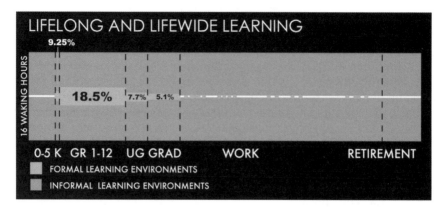

Figure 12.1 Proportion of time spent in formal and informal learning environments. K = Kindergarten; GR = Grades; UG = Undergraduates; GRAD = Graduates
Source: Bransford (2006).

Supporting science learning in the cognitive domain

Concepts in science are often abstract and complex. To help students make sense of them, Driver (1989) has argued that teachers need to present new concepts through a range of ideas and across a range of experiences. In this way, a learner's construct of a concept will be tested and refined, leading to a more secure understanding. Environments outside the classroom offer authentic and first-hand opportunities to engage with scientific concepts that are located within particular contexts and are, furthermore, addressed outside the traditional boundaries of biology, chemistry and physics. Thus, visits to sites of industry provide students with the opportunity to consider integrated industrial processes, while fieldtrips to nature reserves, countryside locations or even to local green spaces offer a resource for exploring the cross-disciplinary issues which define the environmental and geological sciences. In addition, many of the activities promoted by settings outside the classroom allow students at both primary (elementary) and secondary (high school) levels to engage in processes of data collection that are more akin to the genuine practices of science. In other words, experiments conducted and data collected in real-life settings give students an insight into the 'messiness' of science and challenge many of the myths about science propagated by the standardized experiments of school laboratories (Hodson, 1998; and see, also, Chapter 6 in this volume). While understanding the nature of experimentation in controlled laboratory conditions is important, experiments outside the laboratory, such as studying the speed of vehicles, support the development of broader and more speculative observation and interpretative skills. Similarly, when students are able to handle unique objects, from museum collections or from unfamiliar habitats, new skills of observation and categorization are afforded (Leinhardt and Crowley, 2002). Indeed, the opportunity to compare objects, artefacts or organisms presented in museum-type environments supports the identification of patterns and trends and, in turn, promotes an understanding of the way in which knowledge and our scientific culture has developed.

Finally, it has been shown that experiences gained outside the classroom actually promote long-term learning. For example, Mackenzie and White (1982), in their study of 141 Australian students in the eight and ninth grade, tested student learning and retention of facts following three different programmes: active excursion; passive excursion; and no excursion. All three programmes covered the same objectives, however, on comparing the results from students' post-test scores (immediately following the programmes) and delayed post-test scores (12 weeks later), those involved in the active excursion showed 90 per cent retention of content (where retention is expressed as percentage of the initial achievement test mean). This figure compared significantly with pupils who received a passive excursion and who showed a 58 per cent retention, and no excursion who showed a 51 per cent retention. The events involved students using a range of senses, and being active rather than passive participants in terms of generating their own data. The authors argued that this marked retention was due to the role that 'active' events have in constructing conceptual links. While it is acknowledged that teachers often include 'active' elements in their classroom-based lessons, we point to a finding by Nundy (1999) that experiences conducted outside the classroom are more effective than similar experiences conducted in class. For example, Nundy in his study of 85 upper primary students (aged 9–11), found that students studying a particular curriculum topic during a five-day residential course achieved greater cognitive gains than those studying the same topic for the same period in what was described as an 'active' classroom context. Like Mackenzie and White, Nundy attributed some of the learning gains to the novel setting, but also concluded that the students' cognitive learning had been positively impacted by gains in the affective learning domain. In short, the gains resulted from experiences afforded by the residential course that were not available to the classroom-bound pupils.

Supporting science learning in the affective domain

Learning outside the classroom automatically involves a change of scene. It may even involve an entirely new environment, and in addition, engender high levels of excitement in response to the mode of transport employed to travel to the venue. Furthermore, it is perceived to be fun: as Cerini et al. (2003) found in their review of the science curriculum for 'Science Year', students rated 'going on a science trip or excursion' to be the most enjoyable way of learning science. The consequence of novelty, fun and excitement is that student learning in the affective domain is supported, as interests are engaged and enthusiasm for a topic is enhanced.

An affective experience offered by settings outside the classroom may also support the development of positive attitudes towards science. For example, most readers will remember their sense of awe and wonder at the diversity of the natural world when they first saw a display of tropical fish in an aquarium. Others will recall their surprise and amazement at examples of technology displayed within a science museum which bear witness to the ingenuity and tenacity of scientists and engineers both today and in the past. While such information may also be presented in books, on TV or online, the sense of scale and authenticity provided by out-of-the-classroom experiences, makes them much more memorable. Indeed, as Mackenzie and White (1982) note, a memorable experience – whether it be falling over in the mud while learning about woodland fauna, or being awed by a full-sized model of the blue whale – improves long-term knowledge recall (see also Piscitelli and Anderson, 2001). Moreover, a shared memorable experience offers teachers a 'hook' upon which they may hang further experiences back in the classroom.

Lastly, experiences outside the classroom offer students an opportunity to address some of their preconceptions regarding the nature of careers in science. It has been suggested that the current decline in the uptake of post-16 science courses could be due to negative attitudes towards science and the work of scientists on the part of students (Osborne, Ratcliffe, et al., 2003; Bennett and Hogarth 2009; and see, also, Chapter 11 in this volume). Indeed, Hill and Wheeler (1991) have suggested that students do not have a well-rounded appreciation of the work that scientists undertake. As a result, it is reasonable to assume that the stereotypical view of scientists as old, White men in white coats will prevail. Thus, visits to sites of industry, to museums with resident scientists, or to nature reserves staffed by conservation officers, provide students with a unique opportunity to meet and talk with professional scientists and, in turn, gain a greater understanding of what a career in science involves and requires in terms of qualifications and training.

Supporting science learning in the physical and behavioural domain

Experiences outside the classroom provide a range of opportunities for students to engage with different structures and different sorts of social interaction than those that they are used to in school. No longer constrained by timetables, the physical space of the classroom, or even the expectation of what a lesson should entail, students and teachers can forge new ways of working. Dillon et al. (2005, p. 60), for example, note such contexts offer a 'transformative experience where new relationships form, for example, student–student, student–teacher, student–environments, student–community'. Cramp (2008), meanwhile, has noted a range of positive changes between student and teacher relationships as a result of residential experiences. In addition, researchers have highlighted the ways in which fieldwork activities develop teamwork skills and that the positive relationships built during such activities are maintained back in school. For example, in their study of

428 11–14-year-olds attending a residential science/outward-bound activity course in the UK, Amos and Reiss (2006) found that student self-esteem was boosted by the experience, and that general levels of trust in others rose significantly. In an earlier analysis of the same data set, Amos and Reiss (2004) had noted that out-of-school experiences also supported student behavioural development, with teachers reporting that behaviour was generally better than, or as good as, that in school. Finally, it should be noted that in gaining greater familiarity with contexts beyond the classroom, students will gain confidence in visiting similar settings and continue their learning outside school hours. For example, Glackin (2007) found that even short experiences conducted in the school grounds or local neighbourhood played a key in supporting students' understanding of their local environment.

Realizing the opportunities offered by contexts outside the classroom

As noted above, experiences outside the classroom include those that take place within the school grounds or local community – they do not necessarily require transport and time away from other classroom lessons. For example, the *Thinking Beyond the Urban Classroom* project (http://www.azteachscience. co.uk/projects/kings-college-london-learning-outside-the-classroom-innova tive-project.aspx) has developed a Key Stage 3 (ages 11–14) lesson on forces that can be taught in the school grounds or a local playground. The lesson involves students working in small groups to consider everyday objects in their local environment – a children's swing in the park, a basketball hoop, a tree – and then attaching arrows of different lengths and appropriate key words to indicate the types of forces acting on the object. The relative positions of all the arrows placed by the students are then discussed by the class, and then amended if necessary. The activity ends with the students sketching or photographing the objects together with their arrows in order that findings can be discussed further when back in the classroom and linked with previous or future classroom-based work.

Such an activity addresses the key content area of forces and clearly serves to illustrate the ways in which forces are interactions between objects and in turn affect an object's shape and motion. Moreover, the lesson is arguably more effective than traditional classroom-based lessons on forces in a number of ways. First, in most classrooms, the concept of forces is addressed through the use of two-dimensional diagrams or photographs. Where practical work is included, many of the examples, such as the use of large springs, are re-moved from the reality of students' everyday lives. In considering objects and phenomena outside the classroom, students are given the opportunity to see how the concept of force applies in everyday settings. As a result, students see the 'point', or real-life application, of science. The lesson also supports collaborative learning as small groups discuss and agree on the types of forces before placing their arrows. Finally, the activity supports cognitive, physical and behavioural, and also affective development. Cognitive development occurs with a practical understanding of the nature of forces; physical and behavioural development is supported by the practical activity and group work, while affective development is afforded by a richer appreciation of the local environment as the consequence of regarding it in new and different ways.

A second example of a learning opportunity beyond the classroom involves a visit to a local museum with natural history specimens, or to a national museum of natural history. Such an experience can be tailored to suit learners of all ages and begins with students observing and examining a range of natural history objects from the museum's collections and exhibitions. The students then use their skills of observation to compare specimens and to speculate on the phylogenetic (evolutionary) relationships between the specimens. They also observe the physical features of organisms and speculate on their ecology. Finally, they use the collections to answer specific questions about the natural world that they had prepared individually or in groups prior to their visit.

This activity provides an opportunity for students to obtain, analyse, evaluate and record observational data from primary sources. It also provides a context for students to develop scientific explanations based on available evidence. In focusing attention on a range of specimens, which are rarely available in school contexts, students may come to appreciate some of the similarities and differences between the diverse array of species that comprise the natural world. In addition, if museum staff are available, they may be able to offer a detailed insight into the process of collecting, classifying, and storing specimens which are used to further our understanding of the natural history of certain habitats, countries or continents. In this way, students will gain a greater understanding of the scientific discipline of natural history. Moreover, by studying various displays of natural history – from Victorian dioramas to contemporary interactive exhibits – students will gain an insight into the ways in which our knowledge of natural history, and the ways in which the discipline is presented, have changed over time. Finally, such an activity affords cognitive development with respect to the acquisition of new skills in observation and classification, together with a deeper understanding of ecology; an understanding of physical and behavioural development in that it requires team work within small groups; and affective development in that the experience provides a memorable introduction to the discipline and profession of natural history.

Addressing some key challenges to learning outside the classroom

While government documents and research findings point to the benefits of learning outside the classroom, it would appear that such opportunities are rarely taken up in practice. For example, two reports published by the

UK-based National Foundation for Educational Research (NfER) (O'Donnell et al., 2006; Kendall et al., 2006) suggest that there has been a decline in the provision and condition of outdoor learning at Key Stage 2 (age 7–11) and Key Stage 3 (age 11–14). Glackin's (2007) findings, meanwhile, from her study of the work and organization of secondary (high school) science departments across five London boroughs, indicate, similarly, that there are relatively few planned opportunities for learning outside the classroom for students at Key Stage 3 and Key Stage 4 (age 14–16). In addition, Glackin noted that where such provision did occasionally occur, it tended to focus on particular areas of the science curriculum, such as biology and ecology.

Given the learning opportunities afforded by contexts other than the classroom as outlined above, we argue that the disparity in provision has serious implications for issues of equity. All students deserve to benefit from a range of opportunities and potentially gain the knowledge, skills and experiences provided in out-of-school settings. However, we also acknowledge the enormous challenges faced by teachers in providing such opportunities. Furthermore, we note that there are many possible reasons why resources beyond the classroom are not being used. For example, O'Donnell et al. (2006) have argued that the issues of health and safety, risk management and cost are among the most significant factors in limiting out-of-school learning. Rickinson and colleagues' conclusions following a review of the literature echoes and extends this list, highlighting 'teachers' confidence and expertise in teaching and learning outdoors'; 'requirements of school and university curricula and timetables'; difficulties due to 'shortages of time, resources and support'; and more generally the susceptibility of outdoor education to the 'wider changes in the education sector and beyond' (Rickinson et al., 2004, pp. 42–44). On a more positive note, however, we note that recent changes in English policy and guidelines for practice may help to address some of the challenges and in turn create greater equity of opportunity. In the following sections we explore three key areas in which barriers to learning outside the classroom in the English school setting are being slowly, but steadily, dismantled.

Issues of health and safety in the outdoors

The 'Safety in Work' Act (1974) in Britain (excluding Northern Ireland) fundamentally changed the culture of all school visits: the new regulations meant that teachers were obliged to carry out 'risk assessments' on all student activities prior to any visit in order to minimize any health and safety risks. In addition, instances of tragic accidents highlighted by the media have made teachers very aware of their position of degree of accountability when planning outdoor activities (Jones, 1997). Indeed, the fear of accidents and the possibility of litigation are cited by the Education and Skills Committee as one of the main reasons for the decline in school visits to outdoor environments (House of Commons, 2005). Notably, the same report states that even 'with seven million pupils from schools in England going on school activities off-site or outdoors throughout the year, mishaps are rare and serious ones even more so' (House of Commons, 2005, p. 4). Nonetheless, high levels of fear and caution remain, and the situation was not helped by teaching unions advising their members 'against taking school trips because society no longer appears to accept the concept of a genuine accident' (Clare, 2004).

Fortunately, a change in attitudes towards health and safety has recently been detected. Three key events have enabled this shift. First, schools in England now have an educational visits coordinator (EVC) whose responsibility it is to ensure that schools fulfil their health and safety obligations and to liaise with local authorities regarding arrangements (DfES, 2002). In this way, a trained staff member oversees a coherent system, thus reducing the workload for individual class teachers. Second, the National Workload Agreement in England (TTA, 2003) states that teachers should not routinely undertake administrative or clerical roles. As a result, tasks associated with out-of-the-classroom visits, such as the collection of money and the production and distribution of standard letters, are now administered by support staff, leaving teachers time to plan the educational content of the activities. Finally, we note a recent initiative specifically designed to support the 2006 *Learning Outside the Classroom Manifesto*. From January 2009, providers of experiences that offer safe and high quality teaching and learning experiences outside the classroom will be able to apply for a LOtC Quality Badge. The basic premise for such a system is that teachers, schools and local authorities need a simple but trustworthy method for determining whether organizations operate recognized safety procedures and have been recognized as such. The badging system's indicators for health and safety will be informed by the comprehensive DfES Good Practice Guide (1998), and the more recent *Staying Safe Action Plan* (DCFS, 2008). Significantly, and boding well for both the badging system and learning outside the classroom in general, the NASUWT, one of the largest teaching unions, has expressed support for the initiative with Chris Keates, the Union's General Secretary, stating:

> No activity is ever risk free. However, the integrity of the Quality Badge means that providers holding the badge must be those that manage risk properly, comply with good practice and statutory provisions on health and safety, and are committed to working constructively with schools to give every pupil the best possible educational experience.
>
> (OEAP, 13 February, 2009)

The National Union of Teachers (NUT), meanwhile, has also extended its support for the Quality Badge scheme, stating:

> [We] look now to the plan to provide the basis for creating an entitlement for all children and young people to outdoor activities, and to provide the necessary protection to teachers when organising school trips.
>
> (5 February, 2008)

Teachers' confidence and expertise in teaching and learning outside the classroom

One of the most important factors determining the degree to which teachers use teaching and learning outside the classroom would seem to be the expertise of teachers (Rickinson et al., 2004; Glackin, 2007). Indeed, the schools' inspectorate, Ofsted (2004, 2008) note that the effectiveness of an outdoor learning experience varied 'according to the confidence of individual teachers' (2004, p. 9). Clearly, any deficiency in expertise, and concomitant lack in confidence, may be associated with a lack of appropriate training. After all, the English Qualified Teacher Standard (QTS) requirements do not specify that trainee teachers develop and implement opportunities for learning in out-of-school contexts. Instead, the most relevant QTS standard (Q30) simply requires trainees to '*identify* opportunities' (TDA, 2007; emphasis ours). Similarly, as Jones (1997) and Fisher (2001) have both noted, there is considerable confusion regarding what, if any, qualifications are needed to supervise and lead experiences outside the classroom.

Fortunately, a recent report for the Association of Science Education (Tilling and Dillon, 2007) has documented a series of cases in which 'effective' initial science teacher education in the areas of teaching and learning outside the classroom have been successfully implemented and thus may be copied by others. In addition, the report has proposed a minimum requirement for initial teacher education and recommends that all trainee teachers should plan and lead at least one 40-minute lesson outside the classroom. Further guidance for teacher training has recently been released in the form of the Department for Children, Schools and Families (DCSF) 'Out and About' materials (www.lotc.org.uk). This resource includes training and support materials to help teachers plan and realize opportunities outside the classroom through a set of downloadable CPD modules.

Pressures of the curriculum

The introduction of the National Curriculum in England (DfES, 1988) was seen by many to constitute an overly prescribed programme of study for science. Indeed, in order to cover all that was required, there was little time to engage in activities outside the school laboratory. Furthermore, while Braund and Reiss (2006) note that sites outside the classroom could be used for investigative work and the application of authentic process skills, the stipulated skills required by the 1988 National Curriculum were only applicable to laboratory investigations. For example, the examination boards for GCSE (age 16) and A-level (age 18) science examinations required students to control variables and to produce x–y scatter graphs of their findings. Clearly, the unpredictable results typical of fieldwork are not conducive to such requirements (Barker et al., 2002; Tilling, 2004). Moreover, while Fisher (2001) has argued that teachers could use alternative settings outside the classroom for purposes of assessment, the counter-arguments of a lack of time and the notion that pupils needed to be 'trained' in appropriate laboratory-based skills would appear to prevail.

Fortunately, the recent changes to the science curriculum in England at secondary and post-16 level have signalled a move towards a broader and more inclusive curriculum, allowing for increased flexibility and pedagogical choices. The discontinuation of the Key Stage 3 national tests; the introduction of the new diplomas and apprenticeship schemes (including the introduction of Environment and Land based studies in 2009 and Science in 2011); the opening up of different pathways for GCSE science (including applied science); and the inclusion of assessed 'Visit or Issue Reports' at A-level (for example, Biology AS level, Edexcel, 2005) all provide opportunities for the teaching of science outside the classroom. Furthermore, and in response to this new educational climate, a series of resources designed to support teachers using resources outside are being developed. For example, resources supporting the use of local green spaces have been produced by London Outdoor Science (www.field-studies-council.org/outdoorscience/), the British Ecological Society (www.britishecologicalsociety.org/articles/education/) and Thinking Beyond the Urban Classroom (http://www.azteachscience.co.uk/projects/kings-college-london-learning-outside-the-classroom-innovative-project.aspx). In addition, many museums and science centres produce resources with information about planning and conducting a visit that may be requested by schools or downloaded from the institution's web pages.

Maximizing learning outside the classroom

With the reduction of administrative duties, a more flexible curriculum, and quality ensured standards for out-of-school education providers, we are hopeful that teachers in England will make more of the opportunities offered. However, in order to do so effectively, we note, as Orion (1993) has argued, that such opportunities need to be approached from three different perspectives: in advance of the experience; during the experience; and post the experience.

In advance of an experience

In planning an activity, it is important that the teacher makes an explicit connection to the topic being studied in the classroom. This is to ensure that the learning outside the classroom is complementary to the learning that occurs inside the classroom (Hohenstein and King, 2007). Second, if the activity is to take place in a new environment, the teacher should take care to provide students with information about what to expect. As Falk et al. (1978) have shown, excessive novelty can distract learners. However, if pre-orientation to the new environment is provided, students will be better equipped to cope with the new space and in turn be stimulated by it (Anderson and Lucas, 1997; Orion and Hofstein, 1994). Pre-orientation can be provided by the provision of maps or slides, a review of the institution's website, and detailed information about the facilities at the venue and the tasks for completion. Where possible, pre-visit resource materials developed by the host organization should be used as such materials will have been developed by education staff who are highly knowledgeable about the environment and its contents. Furthermore, it is likely that such materials will have already been tested by other teachers.

In addition to considering the cognitive tasks associated with the activity, it is also important to prepare for learning in the affective, and physical and behavioural domains. Such preparation may include encouraging students to develop a set of questions based on their own interests that may then be answered during the activity (Griffin and Symington, 1997). In addition, the grouping of students should be planned in advance to allow such groups time to agree suitable rules and working arrangements to foster learning.

During the activity

Upon arrival at the new location, students may need time to orient themselves to the novel environment. Following this, it is recommended that the unique resources provided by the location – the objects within a museum, or the organisms in a natural ecosystem – constitute the primary focus rather than the completion of a worksheet. As McManus (1985) noted, by solely concentrating on a worksheet, students are likely to miss many inspiring objects. Furthermore, as Griffin and Symington (1997) have argued, the completion of worksheets promotes task-oriented behaviour rather than learning-orientated behaviour. As the latter authors note, learning-orientated behaviour stimulates greater intrinsic interest in a topic, and thus engenders both affective and cognitive development. The key role for teachers, meanwhile, should be one of facilitation and of asking questions to stimulate and develop thinking (Black et al., 2004). Where education staff or science-related professionals are available, it may be possible to team-teach, but it remains the teacher's responsibility to link the learning back to the curriculum and classroom topic.

Post activity

To ensure that the learning from the activity is maximized, it should be integrated within the classroom curriculum as soon as possible. As DeWitt and Osborne (2007) have demonstrated, photographs or film can help to prompt student recollection of their experiences. Moreover, such materials provide an appropriate 'hook' upon which to pin further content. In addition, any data that were collected during the activity should be analysed, interpreted and reported. In this way, students will realize that their experiences outside the classroom are just as significant as those that occur inside the classroom. Finally, it is important that students reflect on how any ground rules or the group structure that they themselves had established either enabled or hindered their learning. In this way, student development will also be supported in the physical and behavioural domain of learning.

Conclusion

Learning experiences outside the classroom offer students the opportunity to develop across the cognitive, affective, and physical and behavioural domains of learning. However, such experiences need to be managed by the teacher, before, during and after the event to ensure that the learning is complementary to their classroom-based instruction. While we acknowledge that teachers in England and elsewhere are undoubtedly facing a number of real challenges in planning and managing experiences outside the classroom, we argue that the recent changes to the curriculum, together with the introduction of new initiatives and guidance materials (at least in the English context) should ease the burden, making it increasingly possible to realize the valuable opportunities available for students. After all as one head of science from a London school commented following a residential field course:

> Most of the students loved it. A few hated it, but they all came away with a real sense of achievement. They will probably not do anything like it ever again in their lives. It's a real experience, and one that introduces young people to the world of science.
>
> (Teacher, quoted in Glackin, 2006)

Further reading

Bekerman, Z., Burbules, N. C. and Silberman-Keller, D. (eds) (2006) *Learning in Places: The Informal Education Reader*. New York: Peter Lang Press.

Dillon, J., Morris, M., O'Donnell, L., Reid, A., Rickinson, M. and Scott, W. (2005) *Engaging and Learning with the Outdoors: The Final Report of the Outdoor Classroom in a Rural Context Action Research Project*. Slough: National Foundation for Educational Research.

Glackin, M. (2007) Using urban green space to teach science, *School Science Review*, 89(327): 29–36.

Griffin, J. and Symington, S. (1997) Moving from task-oriented to learning-oriented strategies on school excursions to museums, *Science Education*, 81(6): 763–79.

National Academy of Science (2009) *Learning Science in Informal Environments*. Washington DC: National Academies Press.

Paris, S. (ed.) (2002) *Perspectives on Object-Centred Learning in Museums*. Mahwah, NJ: Lawrence Erlbaum Associates.

Rennie, L. (2006) Learning science outside of school. In S. Abell and N. G. Lederman (eds), *Handbook of Research on Science Education* (pp 125–70). Mahwah, NJ: Lawrence Erlbaum.

Rickinson, M., Dillon, J., Teamey, K., Morris, M., Choi, M.Y., Sanders, D. and Benefield, P. (2004) *A Review of Research on Outdoor Learning*, Shrewsbury: Field Studies Council.

Websites for resources

@ Bristol: http://www.at-bristol.org.uk/Education/default.htm
British Ecological Society: http://www.britishecologicalsociety.org/articles/
education/
London Outdoor Science: http://www.field-studies-council.org/
outdoorscience/
Thinking Beyond the Urban Classroom: http://www.azteachscience.co.uk/
projects/kings-college-london-learning-outside-the-classroom-innovative-
project.aspx
Natural History Museum: http://www.nhm.ac.uk/education/index.html
Science Museum: http://www.sciencemuseum.org.uk/educators.aspx

13 Supporting the development of effective science teachers

John K. Gilbert

The range of teachers of science

Any discussion of your development as a science teacher must be set in the context of major factors relevant to your professional life. First, what type of undergraduate degree did you take? Some teachers take 'single honours' science degrees (for example, in physics) and therefore have not systematically studied the other sciences since their schooldays (if then). Others take a 'modular' degree, where several sciences may have been studied, but perhaps none in any great depth or breadth. Still others will have studied a science alongside other subjects and the theory and practice of education. Second, to what part of the educational system are you professionally committed? This may be the 'primary' (or 'elementary') school sector, where 'science' is only one of several subjects that have to be taught. Alternatively, it could be the 'secondary' (or 'high') school and 'further education' sectors, and involve teaching one subject, perhaps a single science (biology, for example) or a more broadly conceived subject of 'science', to students of compulsory school or pre-university age. Third, at what stage of your development as a teacher are you? This may be the pre-service phase of development (Initial Teacher Training, or ITT), whether in a university-based or school-based course. Alternatively, you may be involved in continuing professional development (CPD), whether at your own volition or as suggested, or required, by your managers.

Why is teacher development important?

All countries seek a higher standard of living, which is increasingly seen to depend on the production of a 'knowledge-based economy'. Such an economy implies a wider range and greater depth of knowledge by all, the attainment of which depends on the support for learning supplied by teachers. This is especially true of the sciences and technology, where the ideas are central to the knowledge-based economy being complex and rapidly evolving. Modernizing the curriculum, adopting more effective and widely applicable teaching methods, all imply increased attention to the thorough and sustained development of teachers. This is a world wide phenomenon. As Hewson (2007) observes in respect of the USA, new curricula are systematically being introduced that imply the use of learner-centred teaching methodologies and extensive student testing. This process has been accompanied by the extensive review and expansion of high-quality provision for pre-service (Darling-Hammond, 1997) and in-service (Garet et al., 1999) science teacher development. Similar aspirations are held in the UK (House of Lords, 2000; Millar and Osborne, 2000).

In a review produced more than 10 years ago, Hsiung and Tuan (1998) noted that curriculum development in Asian countries was heavily influenced by trends in the Anglo-Saxon countries, against a background of great respect for teachers and for factual learning, that made entry into centrally managed and thorough teacher development programmes very competitive. Very recently, Coll and Taylor (2008), summing up trends in 26 countries worldwide, including most Asian countries, observed that the pace of curriculum change was very rapid but that opportunities for continuing professional development were inadequate and courses were usually short and factual in nature. In summary, there are generally high aspirations for science education but the provision of teacher development activities is more mixed in quality and quantity.

There are two core purposes for any teacher development activity. One is to be able to support the learning of science by students more effectively – to become a better teacher. The other is to improve the personal motivation of individual teachers towards their work – to increase the likelihood of them continuing to teach science.

Aims of this chapter

In the light of the interacting nature of the personal factors that underlie the development of any science teacher, this chapter has four aims. First, it presents a model for the processes of development for science teachers. Such a model will enable progression in teacher development to be represented, that is, how it takes place over an extended period of time. The model will allow such progression in that development to be discussed for individuals, since the multiplicity of relevant factors in play makes a march-in-step approach for heterogeneous groups pointless. Second, I will discuss the range of themes that may be included in developmental activities. The teaching and learning of science are a complex matter that can only be efficiently treated in any depth by considering each theme separately here, even though in classroom practice they interact in many ways. Third, I will discuss what is entailed in becoming a more effective science teacher at any stage of a professional career. Competence as a science teacher develops unevenly and idiosyncratically in the light of the response of the individual to the professional challenges faced, experiences had, and personal responses produced. However, broad facets to that development can be identified. Finally, I will present some approaches to facilitating such developments. These outlines will show effective approaches for which some research-based support is available.

A model for teacher development

One definition of a model is that it is a simplified representation of a complex set of ideas that can be used to describe economically, and then to make predictions about, the behaviour of a system to which the ideas are relevant (Gilbert et al., 1998). Teacher development is such a system and so a model is needed to grasp its complexities. Several exist, each with a different emphasis.

Fraser et al. (2007), for example, model the temporal and spatial contexts in which teacher development can take place. They differentiate, on one hand, between formal opportunities ('those explicitly established by an agent other than the teacher') as distinct from informal opportunities ('sought and established by the teacher') and, on the other hand, between planned opportunities ('pre-arranged') and incidental ('spontaneous and unpredictable') opportunities. While many invaluable opportunities are informal and incidental, this chapter will concentrate on formal and planned opportunities.

A model with a broad conception of teacher development activities and their significance has been proposed by Adey et al. (2004, pp. 155–72). They suggest that formal activities will only be successful if they meet a series of criteria. First, there must be a theoretical justification of the innovation envisaged that can be conveyed to participants, this being backed up by evidence of its effects when put into practice, and by materials that a teacher can adapt for their own use in the classroom. Second, the quality of the activity must be high: it must be long enough to be effective, intense enough so that engagement by the participants causes their ideas to change, employ teaching methods that are congruent with the nature of the innovation under consideration, and there must be coaching available to support classroom implementation of the innovation. Third, the senior management team of the school must value the innovation such that adequate time is made available for the teacher development activities and for the subsequent implementation of the innovation in the school. This will enable the innovation to be built into the permanent curriculum structure of the school. Fourth, the other teachers in the department must actively support the introduction of the innovation. At the very least, there must be a degree of collegiality such that communication about the innovation can readily take place. At best, all the teachers in the department take part in the teacher development activity and/or the introduction of the innovation (see, also, Chapter 5 in this volume).

This chapter will focus on the significance of a teacher development activity for any individual teacher engaged in it. The justification for this decision is that the readers of this book will be individuals concerned to manage their own teacher development. The model to be used here emerged from the Learning in Science (Teacher Development) Project that took place in New Zealand in the 1990s (Bell and Gilbert, 1996, 2004). Seventeen secondary school teachers met on 48 occasions over a three-year period, the sessions and their individual work being monitored throughout this period. The emphasis of this model is placed on the significance that the professional development activity has for the individual teacher concerned both as an individual and as a member of a group of similar teachers, for example, a department. It suggests that there are three elements to teacher professional development: 'personal', 'social', and 'professional'.

1. *Personal development* is the construction and critical acceptance by an individual of what it means to be a teacher of science. Individuals approach the challenge of becoming an effective teacher of science with a set of presumptions about that role and its discharge that may be strongly influenced by experience of their own teachers in their schooldays. While these presumptions may be useful bases for their own work, teachers must be critical of their relevance to the contexts of schools today. For example, the use of constructivist approaches to teaching have become widespread in the last decade or so, meaning that many new teachers, after a postgraduate period in industry, will have only personally experienced teaching as framed within behavioural principles.

2. *Social development* is the construction and critical acceptance by a teacher of acceptable ways of working with others, for example, teachers, students and parents. For many teachers, their experience of higher education was essentially a solitary one: teaching and assessment methods interpreted collaborative work and the sharing of insights as 'cheating'. However, to be effective, a science teacher must work cooperatively with individual students, to ensure that their interests and preconceptions are addressed, with other teachers, for other teachers will also have an impact on individual students, and parents, who have the longest and most intimate contact with individual students.

3. *Professional development* is the development of that repertoire of beliefs, knowledge and skills, that enable a sense of being a teacher of science to be exercised in everyday classroom practice. The personal evolution of this repertoire is what is normally seen as synonymous with 'teacher development'. In the Bell and Gilbert model it is only one element – albeit the most evident one.

These three elements of development undergo a qualitative evolution as a teacher enters the profession and gains experience. This process of evolution can, for each element, be represented in terms of three 'phases'. These phases are convenient ways of representing the changes that take place. They are not distinctive or separate within any one element. Moreover, movement within the phases in respect of any one element is not necessarily unidirectional: an individual may regress to a characteristic associated with an earlier phase when under undue stress. Equally, a particularly supportive and challenging professional environment may lead to faster than usual development taking place.

First phase

For many teachers this phase will be mainly associated with entry into initial teacher education:

1. *Personal development* involves realizing that some aspects of the practice of being a science teacher are problematic. For example, prior experience of students being silent in a lesson (except when answering a question posed by the teacher) may be found to be incompatible with the experience of many classrooms today.
2. *Social development* involves a realization by an individual that they are unable to readily communicate with other teachers – especially those of science – leading to a sense of isolation from peers and to an awareness that this is inhibiting of professional competence. Similarly, an inability to communicate effectively with individual students and their parents may be perceived to be occurring and to lead to less than desirable effectiveness as a teacher.
3. *Professional development* involves a teacher becoming prepared to entertain new ideas about teaching science and to try out new approaches to teaching albeit cautiously. Traditional ideas and practices are found to be ineffective and newer approaches are identified as being helpful.

Second phase

For many teachers, this phase will be associated with working full-time as a science teacher for the first time:

1. *Personal development* involves being able to cope with the restraints surrounding everyday teaching while, at the same time, being willing to try out new ideas/approaches. Examples of such restraints are: the need to 'cover' the curriculum; to prepare students for external assessment; and to maintain classroom discipline. At the same time, the teacher may be moving away from a total reliance on whole-class teaching to the occasional inclusion of small-group work in a professional repertoire.
2. *Social development* involves seeing the value of collaboration with colleagues, such that mutual critically supportive dialogues occur. The expression of concerns in a supportive environment can, in itself, lead to ideas about how to address those concerns, while an interlocutor may suggest new approaches. Similarly, the adoption of a 'collaborative learning environment' approach with pupils and of proactive interaction with their parents may be seen to be helpful.
3. *Professional development* involves gradually developing a philosophically coherent, reflective approach to science teaching that is consistently applied in everyday practice.

Third phase

For many teachers, this phase will be associated with the passage of several years of varied professional experience:

1. *Personal development.* Here the teacher feels empowered to take the initiative in their own further professional development. A sense of control over oneself as a professional teacher encourages the seeking out of new challenges and/or developing the will to address really complex personal concerns.
2. *Social development.* In this phase, the individual teacher will take the initiative in actively fostering collaborative ways of working with their colleagues, both within their own and other schools, and with pupils and their parents.
3. *Professional development.* In this phase, a teacher will seek out or initiate new approaches to being a science teacher that go beyond those immediately available or required. For example, they may be able to anticipate major new requirements to be included in a national curriculum and seek to develop news skills that will be needed.

The necessary characteristics of a science teacher

The material that forms the substance of professional development is the knowledge and skills that a science teacher has to possess in order to be effective, that is, to support significant learning by pupils. A typology of this knowledge and skills has been developed by Shulman and his colleagues (Abell, 2007; Shulman, 1987). This typology divides the substance of teaching into three categories, if only for the purposes of analysis. These categories are subject matter knowledge, pedagogic knowledge and pedagogic content knowledge.

Subject matter knowledge

This is the knowledge on which the science curriculum rests and it has three components. The *substantive* component is the concepts (and illustrative facts) that constitute the core of the curriculum. For example, in the National Curriculum for England and Wales, these concepts were once identified as: Energy, Particles, Forces, Life and Living (Newberry et al., 2005). Subject matter knowledge also includes the relationship sought between these concepts and the organization of their teaching over the relevant period of science education. The *syntactic* component is those rules of evidence needed to produce and justify new scientific knowledge. These rules are concerned with the use of theories to produce models of a phenomenon, with the production of predictions of behaviour from these models, with the empirical testing of those predictions, and with the critical evaluation of the outcomes of experimentation. In short, the syntactic component consists of the nature of science. The third component consists of the *beliefs* held about the nature of particular sciences and of science itself. In essence, these beliefs focus on the value that a particular science or science in general has in providing an explanation of the world in which we live. Ideas about the nature and significance of science have evolved in recent years, as Osborne and Dillon outline in Chapter 2, and these modern ideas must form part of teachers' subject matter knowledge. Equally importantly, teachers must have positive attitudes to the increased emphasis on the nature of science in science curricula: the issues involved are discussed by Simon and Osborne in Chapter 11.

Pedagogic knowledge

Pedagogic knowledge consists of general principles of instruction that are manifest in the teaching and learning of specific subjects. These general principles are concerned with the development of the student as individuals in society. They are manifest in science education by the increased emphasis in curricula on the attainment of 'scientific literacy by all'. This is an awareness of the utilitarian, economic, cultural, and democratic implications of science, as Osborne discusses in Chapter 3. Science also seeks to promote the cognitive development of students: in Chapter 5, Adey and Serret discuss the contribution that the ideas produced by the 'Cognitive Acceleration through Science Education' projects can make to this process. In the classroom, science adopts particular structures for the notion of 'lessons', not least because of the varied reasons for which practical work is undertaken, as Millar discusses in Chapter 6.

Pedagogic content knowledge (PCK)

In broad terms, PCK can be described as 'The transformation of subject matter knowledge into forms accessible to the students being taught' (Geddis, 1993, p. 675) Sandra Abell sees pedagogic content knowledge as having five aspects (Abell, 2007).

1. *The orientation taken towards the teaching of science.* That is, the reasons why science is taught to particular students. In addition to 'education for scientific literacy' (see Chapter 3), most science curricula are conflated with the purpose of providing 'education for future scientists/technologists', which makes the construction and implementation of relevant 'schemes of work' hard to attain.
2. *The nature of the science curriculum.* That is, the mandated requirements of knowledge and skills to be 'covered' in teaching a national curriculum. The nature of the science curriculum evolves gradually over time: for example, at the moment it is gradually relating more closely to the needs for environmental education (see Chapter 1). In some cases, specific teaching programmes ('schemes of work') are

followed, whether mandated by governments or the product of 'advice and guidance', and teachers need to know about these in some detail.

3. *The assessment of learning that is to take place.* To do so requires an understanding of what knowledge and skills are to be assessed, when this is to happen in relation to teaching, how is this to be done, and to what uses the outcomes are to be put (Black, 1998). This assessment can be used for formative purposes (see Black and Harrison in Chapter 9) or summative purposes (see Swain in Chapter 10).

4. *The instructional strategies that can be employed.* These might include the use of laboratory work, teacher demonstrations, the adoption of inquiry approaches, or the employment of 'teaching models' (Gilbert and Boulter, 1998). Given the width of material to be covered in initial teacher training, the integration of these strategies into a repertoire of skills takes time and effort (see Dillon and Manning in Chapter 1). Additionally, new strategies gradually emerge and need to be accommodated. To take two examples: the ever-growing use of ICT is discussed by Webb in Chapter 8; the use of out-of-school contexts for learning discussed by King and Glackin in Chapter 12. All these strategies will make extensive use of ideas about teaching the First Language that is in use: the multiple aspects of literacy; the nature and use of metaphor and analogy; the multi-semiotic construction of meaning; question types and interactive forms; the skills of argumentation (see Osborne and Evagorou in Chapter 7 and Hohenstein and Manning in Chapter 4).

5. The nature of student understanding. This will embrace broad issues of how the learning of science occurs, the nature of students' difficulties in learning science, in particular the nature of and address to the 'alternative conceptions' that students hold. Wandersee et al. (1994) have produced a comprehensive overview of this field of research and development.

The relation of experience, beliefs, and attitudes in science teaching

Now that the broad trajectory of teacher professional development has been discussed and the substance of teachers' knowledge and skills established, attention must be turned to more ephemeral, yet vital, issues. A reconsideration and expansion of the experience of being taught and teaching form the core of science teacher professional development activities. What is perceived as relevant experience and what happens as a consequence of that perception is driven by the beliefs that an individual teacher holds at a given time. Definitions are multiple in this field, but a useful attempt may be: 'A belief is information, believed to be true, that a person has about the characteristics of something (object, situation, event, individual, group)' (Jones and Martin, 2007, p. 1067). In other words, a belief is a valuation placed on a particular item or type of information. For example, one teacher may believe that science can only be successfully taught to students who have a high 'general intelligence quotient' or who can consistently think at Piaget's 'formal operations' level. Another teacher may believe that science can be successfully taught to anybody, provided the examples used and teaching methods adopted are interesting enough.

The strong holding of a belief or set of beliefs leads to a teacher displaying a particular attitude, which may be defined as a persistent disposition to respond in a consistent manner in the light of a belief. Of the two stereotypical teachers sketched above, the first might conclude that real professional effort could only be made in respect of a smallish group of 'able' students, while the second would work equally enthusiastically with all students.

A specific attitude becomes enshrined in a particular intention, where an intention is the likelihood that a person will behave in a given way when an attitude is evoked. So, when a particular piece of information is interpreted with the use of an existing belief, the associated attitude is entrained, and an intention to respond in a largely preset manner is evoked. This leads directly to a behaviour, conceptualised as a person's physical action on the world.

So, in summary, once a belief about the personal significance of a specific experience is acquired, associated attitudes, intentions and behaviours follow closely, often without conscious thought. Beliefs, the motors of behaviour, have a long-term stability. They are more labile, that is amenable to change, in young people. Such change is often needed, for the epistemological beliefs about teaching and learning of beginning teachers are based on their own experience as students at school and at university as has already been discussed. On the basis of their own experience, they will have every reason to have formed the belief that teaching in concerned with the transmission of existing knowledge from the teacher to the students (Tsai, 2002). Similarly, they will probably have acquired the belief that science involves using established and socially accepted theories to make sense of data (Brickhouse, 1990). This belief leads many to think that students should be taught pre-determined and fixed theories which should be used to interpret conveniently structured information. In short, many pre-service student teachers will start with the assumption that behaviourist approaches to teaching should be adopted to teach an inductivist view of science. This and many other such beliefs form the core focus for professional development activities.

The challenges of becoming an effective science teacher

There seems little doubt that, in respect of pre-service teachers: 'A fundamental challenge resides in the prior teaching and learning beliefs and experiences of those learning to teach' (Russell and Martin, 2007, p. 1151), a view that can be extended to most of those with many years of teaching experience.

In many ways, the two major challenges faced by those organizing pre-service courses are often fairly clear-cut. The first is to ensure that the student-teachers are satisfied that they have an understanding of the major concepts in the science(s) that they are to teach at an adequate level for that purpose. This issue is becoming increasingly important, given Dillon and Manning's report (in Chapter 1) that in 2006 only 44 per cent of biology teachers, 25 per cent of chemistry teachers, and 19 per cent of secondary physics teachers had initial degrees in those subjects in England and Wales. Improving subject knowledge can best be done by self-diagnosis, using relevant school-level tests, coupled to the availability of computer-managed remedial packages.

The second challenge is that student teachers have preconceptions about student learning that are governed by their own experience, even though their perception of those assumptions is often implicit rather than explicit. They tend to view learning from their own perspective and therefore fail to see the value of 'theories of learning', all of which emphasize the diversity of ways of and constraints on how learning takes place. They tend to believe that they can be told how to teach, for teaching is perceived as formulaic. They fail to see the need for discussion of what is involved. They cannot see that their own experience of acting as a teacher (often provided early in a pre-service course) is worth interrogating. In short, they want 'how-to-do' recipes on which to base their professional work.

The situation is inevitably more complex given the great diversity of types and length of experience of participants in teacher development activities. Those participating in such activities face a diversity of challenges. Some are in the process of changing the age-phase that they teach, this being a conse-quence of schools' change in age-profile in response to the cycles of patterns of births and immigration/emigration. Some are changing the subject that they teach, for example, the demand for the capability to teach physics seems to outstrip supply in most countries. Many are facing changes in the teaching methods that they must use, for example, the increasing use of computer-managed teaching materials.

In all these cases, issues arise in respect of individuals' subject knowledge, pedagogic knowledge and pedagogic content knowledge. Indeed, where the subject matter is entirely new to the teacher, as, for example, in enquiry-based learning, these issues will be compounded by anxiety over classroom man-agement (Roehrig and Luft, 2004). How then are these myriad and interacting issues to be addressed? How can opportunity for changes in knowledge, be-liefs, attitudes, intentions and behaviour be facilitated?

Approaches to successful professional development

The objectives of teacher development at any stage in a professional career are twofold. First, to support teachers in making changes to elements of their existing knowledge and skills. Second, to support them in changing their ex-isting beliefs about science and about teaching, where these seem needed.

Three assumptions underlie the design of teacher development activities that successfully address these objectives. These are the need for three facts to be recognized.

A recognition that teachers have alternative conceptions in respect of subject knowledge that must be addressed

There is considerable evidence that teachers in both the pre-service and in-service phases of professional development have similar alternative conceptions to those displayed by their students (Wandersee et al., 1994). It therefore seems that some, at least, of students' alternative conceptions were actually taught to them by their teachers: these can therefore be properly called 'learned misconceptions'. In a 17-year longitudinal study of science teachers' subject knowledge, Arzi and White (2008) showed that the main source of subject knowledge for teachers was the textbooks used with successive classes. If teachers learn such alternative conceptions from textbooks, it must follow that some teachers actually convey inaccurate understandings of concepts to their students. If this is so, it does suggest that more collections of clear expositions of key concepts for teachers, such as those produced by Peter Atkins (2003), are needed.

If teachers display such alternative conceptions, then opportunities to change them must be included in professional development courses. In a recent review, Duit and Treagust have brought together the major perspectives on how this has been and might be done for school students (Duit and Treagust, 2008). There seems no logical reason why these insights should not be applicable to teachers, whether pre- or in-service, an additional bonus being that the teachers will then sense what their students will undergo in similar circumstances.

Three distinctive approaches have been taken. The best known of these is the epistemological approach in which learners' grounds for belief in a particular conception are brought into question (Posner et al., 1982). The model consists of activities which successively generate dissatisfaction by an individual with their current understanding, then presents them with an alternative which they can readily understand (it is intelligible), such that it fits with their experience (it is plausible), and which can be applied in new, diverse, contexts (it is fruitful). However, although strengthened by the inclusion of bridging analogies throughout the process (Treagust et al., 1996) there seems little conclusive evidence that the approach works, a common outcome being the formation of concepts that are hybrids between the old and the new understandings (Gilbert et al., 1982).

The second, the ontological approach, seeks to bring about necessary changes in the way that knowledge is categorized (Chinn and Brewer, 1993). To take two examples, the concept of heat can be changed from that of a fluid flowing to that of kinetic energy in transit, the concept of gene can be changed from that of an inherited object to that of a biochemical process.

These changes are from material conceptions to process conceptions (Duit and Treagust, 2008). Again, this approach has been successful in particular cases (Chiu et al., 2002).

Third, the affective approach is predicated on the belief that successful conceptual change depends on the learner having a satisfactory level of self-efficacy that is manifest in a supportive social environment in pursuit of personal needs and expectations (Pintrich et al., 1993). Again, this approach has been shown to be effective (Zembylas, 2005).

Methodologies that utilize all three of these approaches seem to have distinctive merits that transcend their individual use (Tyson et al., 1997). Indeed, they have been successfully adopted for student biology teachers for a broad range of issues, including that of conceptual understanding (Hewson et al., 1999)

A recognition that teachers' pedagogic content knowledge (PCK) needs continuous development

Loughran and his colleagues point out that PCK is at the heart of good science teaching, for it focuses on aspects of subject matter found difficult to teach, is framed by reasons why particular curriculum content is important, offers ways of engaging students with that content and, above all, suggests ways that specific content can be successfully taught (Loughran et al., 2008). They suggest making the nature and development of PCK the core of initial teacher training, for by doing so the approach exemplifies the value of educational theory in science teaching,

The Loughran approach makes use of two tools for analysing curriculum content in pre-service teacher education: Content Representations (CoRes) and Professional Experience Repertoires (PaP-eRs):

> A CoRe sets out the aspects of PCK that are most closely attached to a science topic, and that most probably extend across various contexts (for example, the key content ideas, known alternative conceptions, insightful ways of testing for understanding, known points of confusion, and ways of framing ideas to support student learning). PaP-eRs characterise teacher knowledge about specific aspects of teaching the topic content by providing 'windows' into how such knowledge might inform classroom practice.
>
> (Loughran et al., 2008, p. 1305)

Early research reports suggest that the approach is found valuable by teachers-in-training (Loughran et al., 2008, pp. 1309–18).

Inevitably, teachers develop a repertoire of PCK during their early years of teaching (see Chapter 1). This has to be made explicit, modified, and amplified when a significant curriculum change takes place. Bringing about such changes is particularly challenging when no official introduction to the main facets and implications of the changes is on offer.

The recent introduction of a new science syllabus in the Netherlands offered an opportunity to see how the PCK of some of those teaching the unit 'Models of the solar system and the universe', with its emphasis on modelling rather than just learning the established models used for interpretation purposes, changed over an extended period of time without the general benefit of specific CPD (Henze et al., 2008). Nine teachers who were using the same textbook as the basis for their teaching were interviewed annually for three years. The PCK of the teachers were typified as being either of Type A, which was orientated towards teaching science as a body of knowledge and which changed over the three years to be only somewhat more sophisticated and cross-linked while remaining focused on the teaching of content, or of Type B, which was oriented towards the experience of science as a method of generating and validating scientific knowledge and which changed over the three years to show a much higher degree of cross-linkage of the elements of PCK and an emphasis on modelling. The conclusion that can be drawn from this interesting study is that, in the absence of CPD, those with the greatest 'distance to travel' make less progress towards high quality and relevant PCK than those whose initial knowledge and outlook were similar to that of the mandated change. This finding reinforces the view that the systematic development of PCK during initial teacher education is a vital precursor to its later and further elaboration.

The introduction of the same curriculum change in the Netherlands provided an opportunity to associate a small-scale research project into changes in PCK with a CPD programme designed to support that change. The work was based on the 'Interconnected Model of Teacher Professional Growth' (Clarke and Hollingsworth, 2002) which postulates that such growth draws on four sources of information: the external domain (available sources of information and stimulus), the domain of practice (the trying out of existing and new ideas), the personal domain (extant knowledge, beliefs and attitudes) and the domain of salient outcomes (the consequences of actions taken). Justi and Van Driel (2005) showed that the explicit awareness of these four domains, the extent to which they were drawn upon, and awareness of and the interconnectedness between them, evolved in respect of the teachers' PCK during and after the CPD. This study emphasizes the need for existing beliefs and new knowledge to be successfully tried out in the classroom if changes of PCK are to take place.

The cornerstone for successful change in PCK must be that new knowledge can only be successfully coupled to new actions in the classroom if a teacher's underlying beliefs are supportive of the desired change. Beliefs are the key to change.

A recognition that professionally dysfunctional beliefs must be addressed

When teachers find marked difficulty in addressing existing or new professional challenges, it is probably because they have beliefs, perhaps tacitly held, that impede the consideration and adoption of new ideas. A broad approach that has proved successful in the contexts of a wide variety of different professions is based on the idea of 'cognitive dissonance': 'Cognitive dissonance is a psychologically unpleasant state that arises when an individual holds two beliefs that are in conflict with each other. This dissonance can be reduced by changing one of the beliefs' (Festinger, 1957, p. 8). In essence, this means that an individual must have a new belief brought to their active attention such that their existing attitudes, intentions, and actions, are challenged. The tension between an existing belief and an alternative can be created in a number of ways:

1.   *Persuasive communication.* Some people can be persuaded to actively consider new beliefs by a clear, logical, and well-presented exposition of the latter that are based on evidence that has been produced by systematic research.
2.   *Active participation.* The technique here is to bring the existing belief and its desired replacement into close juxtaposition in a number of ways. Direct personal contact with somebody who holds the new belief and who can illustrate its efficacy first-hand has been found to be effective. The expert mentor, perhaps a senior science teacher, can provide this type of contact. The use of role-play, such that a person is required to pretend to hold the new belief, can be influential. The technique of role-play is widely used in the humanities, but, as yet, is not widely adopted in science education. The most extreme approach is to cause somebody to engage in counter-attitudinal behaviour, that is to actually behave in a way commensurate with the new behaviour.

Being in a state of cognitive dissonance is psychologically painful, for the two beliefs vie for acceptance by the individual concerned. A resolution of this tension can be attained by causing that individual to take a personal decision over which belief to adhere to. It can be achieved by causing that individual to consistently behave in a different manner, at the pain of the imposition of some external penalty, say, being subject to inspection in the classroom. The last approach is to engage in a disagreement over the two beliefs with another person until a resolution is reached. Whether the impact of these efforts is that the individual undergoes 'progression' or 'regression' in respect of their beliefs will depend on the individual and the beliefs in question.

Good practice in the organization of teacher development activities

By splicing together the above ideas, it is possible to identify some elements of good practice in the design of teacher development activities, building on principles put forward by Putnam and Borko (2000). These elements acknowledge five factors.

Learning must be philosophically and practically congruent with the intended purpose

Such activities should be 'in tune' with the philosophy underpinning the ideas that they advocate, for example, teaching the nature of constructivism should make use of constructivist approaches. It follows that the activities should also be internally consistent in terms of their methodology of operation, for the example given above, the whole activity must be of a 'constructivist' nature and not lapse into didactic exposition under the pressure of a shortage of time. The teaching methodology adopted should model the modified classroom procedures that are being advocated and, in particular, the beliefs that underlie those procedures. The use of cognitive dissonance techniques, where appropriate, would be useful in supporting the acquisition or reinforcement of those beliefs

Learning is a social activity

Good teacher education activities must overtly acknowledge that learning is a social activity, that it entails social cognition (Rogoff, 1994), such that 'Learning is seen as a process of enculturation, or participation in socially organised practices, through which specialised skills are developed as they engage in an apprenticeship of thinking' (Scott et al., 2007, p. 45). This apprenticeship involves participation in 'communities of practice' (Lave and Wenger, 1991), that is, in groups of people undertaking similar work. For teachers, both pre-service and in-service, their peers constitute a vital component of such a community. Rather than have individuals working on their own, better results are to be expected if they learn in groups of varying size and composition depending on the nature of the task at hand. The teachers of such groups – teacher educators – would contribute their considerable experience to such a community, but this does imply a sharp move away from any 'knowledge transmission' to a 'facilitation of learning' approach to the work by them. A third contributing group would be individual practising teachers who had expertise in the theme/problem under consideration: this group will be considered in a little more detail later.

Inevitably, all teacher education activities must necessarily include a degree of information transfer, but the amount of didactic instruction should be kept to a necessary minimum. For example, pre-service courses will have to include a considerable introduction to and appreciation of the prescribed curricula that is to be taught, but this might be done, wherever possible, by computer-managed independent-learning packages. However, even in respect of such material, work in groups is to be preferred to working alone.

Learning involves reflection

Assimilating new knowledge and accommodating it in respect of existing knowledge and experience require that individual teachers consider, reflect, upon the relationship between the two. Donald Schön conceived of the relationship being manifest in everyday professional practice in three ways. 'Reflection-in-action' involves 'thinking on one's feet', actively considering alternative lines of action and deciding to adopt one of them. 'Reflection-on-action' takes place after an action has occurred: it is much more deliberate and can lead to changes of belief. 'Knowledge-in-action', the outcome of established reflection, gives rise to action that is performed without overt consideration of it (Schön, 1983). The challenge for teacher education is to find ways of promoting reflection-on-action such that it subsequently leads to an associated reflection-in-action and, in the longer run, to the everyday display of knowledge-in-action. Bringing about that vital first stage requires recognition that:

> a problem is unlikely to be acted upon if it is not viewed as a problem; rationalisation may masquerade as reflection; experience alone does not lead to learning – reflection on experience is essential; other ways of seeing problems must be developed; articulation (of the problem) matters.
>
> (Loughran, 2006, p. 131)

Bringing about reflection-on-action requires that a teacher has an experience, either personally or indirectly (for example, by viewing a videotape of a class in action) that is an exemplar of, or relevant to, the knowledge or skill under consideration. The art of the teacher educator will be to lead the teachers to an appreciation that a problem is present and/or has been addressed.

Learning as requiring mentoring

A critical element in all these approaches is the provision of long-term school-based and/or school-focused personal support by a person or persons who is/are expert in the issues being addressed. This perspective recognizes that significant change in practice only occurs when beliefs change and that this process is not necessarily linear or rapid. While writing about pre-service teacher education, there seems no obvious reason why the in-service context should not be equally supported by what Loughran has to say about this process of mentoring:

> Mentoring is a way of helping students of teaching to study their practice (and thinking about practice with others) so that alternative perspectives and possibilities become apparent and can be acted upon. Mentoring is about creating ways of building on critical conversations so that the actions that follow might lead to concrete learning

outcomes whereby the valuing of experimentation, risk-taking and learning through experience might foster the notion that learning about teaching is a community affair.

(2006, p. 170)

Calderhead and Shorrock (1997) saw mentoring as influencing learning about teaching in six ways. First, the mentor provides an example, a model of practice, that the student teacher can observe her/him and analyse what is done. Second, the mentor provides coaching, a supportive critical commentary on the teaching of the student teacher that is augmented by ideas and suggestions. Third, the mentor engages in practice-focused discussion so that the student teachers can clarify their own perceptions of beliefs and the relation of these to actions. Fourth, the mentor structures the classroom contexts in which the student teachers will work, such that they have to face those archetypal challenges that are at the core of science teaching. Fifth, the mentor provides the student teacher with that emotional support needed to overcome the self-doubt often associated with changes in beliefs and patterns of action. Sixth, the mentor constructs tasks through which the student teacher is sensitized to the complexity of the classroom environment. Given the intellectual and psychological implications of these six forms of contribution to teacher education, it is evident that the provision of mentorship is a very demanding role. While it is possible to think of the possibilities of 'mentorship education and training', a well-developed inter-personal sensitivity coupled to varied and successful classroom teaching experience seem essential prerequisites for individuals exercising this role.

Learning as entailing action research

There is evidence that successful teacher development activities include an element of 'action research' (Elliott, 1991), otherwise known as 'practitioner-based enquiry' (Murray and Lawrence, 2000), or 'evidence-based professional development' (Simon and Harrison, 2008). Such activities involve the engagement by the student teacher with peers, teacher educators and mentors, in classroom-based research and development focused on a problem that is evident or emergent in a particular context. In broad terms, these approaches consists of the identification of a problem, the collection of relevant data, the evaluation of relevant existing educational research, the design of modified classroom procedures, their implementation and the documentation of that process, an evaluation of the action taken and, finally, a re-entry to the cycle if necessary.

These approaches have three key ingredients. First, active involvement of the student teacher in the identification of the problem. Albeit that this identification may be the subject of some guidance, it is essential if the student teacher is to become fully engaged in the enquiry. Second, the extensive use of group collaboration in the conduct and evaluation of the work which involves peers and mentors. The social learning dimension comes to the fore. Third, the introduction, at the appropriate moment, of the outcomes of prior, published, science education research. In addition to its immediate utility, such a process demonstrates that the outcomes of educational research can provide both insights and suggestions for practical actions. The ways that these principles of good practice are applied will depend on the particular phase of teacher development that is being engaged in.

Activity types relevant to the phases of teacher development

It must be re-emphasized that the 'phases' of teacher development are not distinct. However, broad themes that lie within each may be identified. For a teacher in the first phase of professional development, suitable activities will include:

- a necessarily heavy load of information about the science curriculum;
- the personal observation of actual teaching with a debriefing discussion of what has been observed;
- structured yet limited work with others, sharing experiences and perceptions;
- the introduction to new ideas, perhaps by the use of 'persuasive communication' or 'active participation' approaches to belief-change.

For a teacher in the second phase of professional development, suitable activities will include:

- a much lighter load of new information than in the first phase;
- extensive practical experience, including the introduction of new ideas into the classroom through action research;
- extended group work with peers;
- requirements to produce detailed schemes of work that include new ideas or approaches to teaching.

For a teacher in the third phase of professional development, suitable activities will include:

- very little new information;
- self-initiated action research;
- teacher-initiated professional development activities;
- a consideration by individuals of their professional futures and the skills that they will need to meet the demands of those futures.

The challenges associated with teacher development activities

While it is possible to identify which factors support professional development activities, they will be provided against a background of constraints that must be addressed if the outcomes are to be successful, that is if changes in classroom practice are to take place. Although clear policies that support teacher development are called for (Darling-Hammond and McLaughlin, 1995), there are often constraints acting on what can be done in particular contexts.

Providers

One barrier is that there will be the tension between support and assessment in respect of the participants. Providers will be seeking to provide as much support as they can for the participants yet will be responsible for the maintenance of professional standards. The resolution of this tension must involve awareness by all parties of what is entailed in both activities and of the boundary between them. A lack of knowledge about individual participants both by the provider(s) and by fellow participants is another barrier. Early and extensive opportunities for one-to-one discussions should enable this hurdle to be overcome, such that peer support and tutor support can be more personal-centred. Finally, problems arising from the stability of science staffing of schools are also barriers. In most countries, there are not enough experienced and competent science teachers. As a consequence, staff mobility among such teachers in high. This makes it difficult to assign pre-service teachers to schools with suitably expert mentors. Alas, there is no generic solution to this problem. Also, schools may be unwilling for such experts to be freed from classroom duties to themselves engage in later-phase professional development.

Participants

One of the most significant barriers is the lack of time for reflection on what has been learned in professional development activities due to a heavy course or classroom workload. This must be recognized by schools in the allocation of workloads. Second, a lack of experience of discussion, particularly by those who have recently emerged from didactic degree courses can be a barrier. The skills and protocols of discussion can be directly taught. Third, a perception of 'research' as being based on inductivism which is at variance with the hypothetico-deductive approach accepted in the philosophy of science. A more helpful perception may be produced by a combination of both direct instruction about the nature of research and by the adoption of that view in the actual teaching that takes place (for example, by associating it with action research).

The evaluation of science teacher development activities

Two definitions of evaluation are to 'form an idea of the value' of something (Soanes and Stevenson, 2008) and to engage in 'the systematic investigation of the merit or worth' of something (Guskey, 2000, p. 41). Building on the work of Smith and Glass (1987), a model for the evaluation of a teacher development activity can be designed around a series of questions: Who wanted it conducted?, Why was it conducted?, What was its scope?, What set of values underpinned it?, To what uses were the outcomes put?, Was it conducted at a suitable time relative to that at which the introduction of the innovation took place?, How was the worth of its outcomes judged? An allied model, again built around questions, has been proposed by (Guskey, 2000): What questions should the participants be asked?, What was the quality of the school's support for the introduction of the innovation?, What did the participants actually learn during the teacher development activity?, In what way and to what extent was the new knowledge utilized in the classroom?, What did the students learn after the introduction of the innovation that was not learned before the teacher development activity? These models cover a wide range of issues and would be expensive to implement in practice. Taking a somewhat simpler approach, Joyce and Showers (1995) felt that such evaluations should focus on two issues: (1) are the students experiencing the change that was the focus of the staff development activity?, and (2) is that change resulting in increased learning? In a recent review of the literature on staff development activities, specifically in science education, Hewson (2007), concluded that most evaluation studies were descriptive and focused on the activities themselves rather than on their consequences for students. The elegant model produced by Timperley and Alton-Lee (2008) refocuses attention on the processes taking place during and after an activity and on the implications for students. However, given the scant resources actually devoted to evaluation in general, a simpler model may be more pragmatically useful for everyday, small-scale, use.

Goodlad (1979) proposed a model to represent the processes of implementing a new curriculum in schools, an approach which had been built upon by Van Den Akker (1998). If a staff development activity is viewed as a new curriculum being introduced to teachers, then the model, applied in the context of science education, becomes:

- The *ideal* activity. What purposes, views of teaching and learning, underpinned its development in the eyes of the providers?
- The *formal* activity. What was actually done by the activity providers, and how?
- The *perceived* activity. What did the participating teachers understand to be the purposes of the activity? What knowledge and skills did the participating teachers believe themselves to have acquired?

- The *operational* activity. What did the teachers believe themselves to do later in their departments and classrooms as a consequence of the activity?
- The *experiential* activity. What did the students perceive to happen in their classrooms that could be traced by the evaluator to the influence of the staff development activity?
- The *attained* activity. What knowledge/skills did the students learn/acquire that could be attributed to their teacher's participation in the staff development activity?

Such a model looks at staff development activities from three perspectives: (1) those of the activity providers; (2) the participating teachers; and (3) students in school. It allows the loci of any 'identification of irrelevance' or 'decay of impact' to be pinpointed. The providers will be able to ask themselves: Was the content of the activity relevant? Was the activity effectively conducted? The teachers will be able to ask themselves: What contribution did this activity make to my personal, social, and professional development? The students will be able to ask themselves (if they are given to metacognitive speculation): Has my quality of learning improved?

The above commentary presumes that it is the needs and interests of the individual teacher that are the primary focus for staff development activities. However, given the change to top-down models of management in the educational systems of many countries, many teachers will participate in activities on behalf of their school and will be expected to disseminate the outcomes to their colleagues as part of changes that reflect departmental policy. While there have been a few studies that show teachers having initiated their own development, for example, Ritchie and Rigano (2002) – and thus being in the third phase of the Bell and Gilbert model – most professional development takes place at the behest of a school in order to be able to implement a mandated change in curriculum, teaching, or assessment. This more common context requires the teacher who has participated in a professional development activity both to implement it in classes – to take professional risks in so doing – and to disseminate the core ideas to other teachers who will have cope with the change.

Initiating and coping with change: taking professional risks

In this section, the word 'department' is used to represent both the whole staff of a primary/elementary school, where typically a 'science coordinator' leads the staff, all of whom teach science, and the staff of the science department or the separate science subject departments that are usual in secondary (high) schools.

The centrality of attitudes and beliefs is highlighted in the Kennedy (2005) framework for the intentions of teacher development activities. She differentiates between three types. 'Transmissive' activities are where expert tuition focuses on a technical aspect of teaching, the teacher is only called upon to comply with the innovation, for example, the use of the 'interactive whiteboard' in primary (elementary) schools, the formats of public examinations in secondary (high) schools. 'Transformative' activities engage attitudes and beliefs in that theories of teaching and learning are related to specific classroom practices, for example, on the place of the 'nature of science' in science education and the use of 'enquiry-based learning'. The intermediate type of 'transitional' activity is one that may or may not strongly involve attitudes and beliefs, such that mentoring/coaching plays a major role in the activity, for example, an emphasis on argumentation in science teaching. Initiating and coping with a change arising from a transmissive activity often involves little risk, provided that any associated equipment is available. The situation is more challenging in respect of the changes implied by transitional and, even more so, by transformational activities.

A teacher who has participated in a professional development activity commonly becomes the initiator of the associated change in their school. The discharge of that function is different when that teacher has a position of authority, for example, is Head of Department (HoD) and where somebody else is HoD (Fullan, 2001). For any teacher, whether the initiator or not, the introduction of an innovation poses a challenge to their professional standing with either/both pupils and colleagues. Whether the challenge is evaluated as an opportunity to be welcomed or a risk to be avoided depends on how four beliefs, the abiding 'cultural myths' of education (Tobin and McRobbie, 1996) are interpreted. Successful innovation by an individual teacher will only take place if that person holds, as a result of the professional development activity, a view about the aims, pedagogy, and content of the innovation that is congruent with the agreement or disagreement held of the following myths:

- *the transmission myth*: that teachers are the sole source of knowledge and must transmit it to the students;
- *the efficiency myth*: that teachers must have total control over classes, that time is in short supply, and that curriculum content must be covered even if it is not understood;
- *the rigour myth*: that the students must acquire as much knowledge as have previous year-groups;
- *the preparation for examination myth*: that, whether students are cognitively engaged with the work or not, they must be prepared for examinations of all kinds.

An individual teacher will show that a particular change is being coped with by complying with its requirements. However, that person may be doing so while holding beliefs, for whatever reason, that conflict with those underlying the change.

Whether the individual teachers in a department can come to share a common view of the innovation in the light of their (perhaps changed) views of the educational myths above depends on the social type of that department. Siskin (1994, pp. 99–100) identified four cardinal types:

1. the *bonded* department, where members work collaboratively with a high degree of commitment towards departmental goals;
2. the *bundled* department, where teachers share concerns but individual rather than collective aims shape decisions;
3. the *fragmented* department, where teachers act independently without commitment to shared aims;
4. the *split* department, where groups of teachers have conflicting and strongly held aims.

A general sense of successfully coping with change and of reducing risk-taking will be achieved where a department is the closest to the *bonded* model. This bonding will be achieved under *transformational leadership* (Leithwood et al., 1999) which establishes common goals, models best practice, supports individuals, has high expectations, and promotes participation in decision-taking. Such paragons of virtue do exist and should be cherished!

Overall then, and building on the ideas of Dillon (2000, p. 95), it is possible to suggest that successful whole-department change will result where there is:

- a generally-felt need for change, whether resulting from the evolution of departmental perceptions or from the (relatively) willing impositions of external requirements;
- time for the staff of the department to reflect on what is currently done, so as to identify challenges;
- a source of staff development available that is expert, both in terms of knowledge and in terms of having relevant and successful teaching strategies based on overt models of learning;
- time for colleagues to work collaboratively with the individual who has participated in the activity;
- coaching and mentoring support in respect of the change that is access to somebody who knows what effective science teaching in respect of the desired change actually is;
- a staff appraisal scheme in operation that values evidence of successful group participation in bringing about change;
- a sense of corporate ownership of any innovation and of personal growth by individuals,
- and lastly, and most importantly, active and sustained support from the Head of Department and, if relevant, the Senior Management Team of the school.

The likely success of any change and an assessment of its likely demands for coping or risk-taking can be evaluated by using these criteria as a check-list.

Finally, a cautionary note. Teaching counts itself as a profession, one of the characteristics of which is a thoughtful approach to practices that might harm its central commitments. Not all change, especially that centrally mandated, should be fully adopted uncritically, dependent on the nature of the innovation, its implications for the educational welfare of the students, and the overall culture of the school. Fullan (2001) points out that many proposed innovations (that will, by implication, be the subject of professional development activities) are driven by an excessive rationality rather than an understanding of how learning actually occurs, are inflexible in the light of the myriad variations in local educational culture that exist, and are fragmented and incomplete in their presentation. In all circumstances, teachers might ask themselves (after Fullan, 2001): Is the innovation really needed?, What is its priority where schools face 'innovation overload'?, Is it likely to benefit my students in the way suggested?, Are there adequate resources for the innovation to be carried out? Only where positive responses can be given will coping and risk-taking fall within acceptable limits for individual teachers. Partial or progressive implementation of an innovation may be in the best interests of the students. If science teaching acquires a general reputation for positive responses to such questions, then recruitment and retention of teachers will be made easier.

Recruitment and retention

The recruitment and retention of individuals with an appropriate educational background, interpersonal skills, and the ability to communicate ideas, are essential if science teaching and learning are to flourish. In those countries where the value of all teachers is recognized by high social status, a good salary, and appropriate conditions of service, the recruitment and retention of science teachers are readily and permanently achieved. In other countries, adequate numbers of really valuable people only become and remain as science teachers during times of economic recession. Research into recruitment and retention as a whole lacks continuity over time (which would show trends) and subject-specificity (which would show the situation in respect of science teaching). Overall reviews of the whole field are produced from time to time, for example, for the UK, Roberts (2002), House of Commons (2003–2004).

In a study of a single science subject (physics) Smithers and Robinson (2008, p. i) concluded for initial teacher training in the UK that:

> About four times as many biology graduates as physics graduates train to be specialist science teachers and they comprise over a third of the combined/general science trainees as against 6% from a physics background. Less than a tenth of PGCE science output in 2005–6 was

in a physics background compared with 12% in chemistry, 36% in biology and 43% in combined/general science.

Only general trends across the initial training sector have been closely studied (Edmonds et al., 2002). Trainees are most likely to withdraw during teaching practice, most commonly because of problems with personal skills (for example, timekeeping), subject knowledge, or as an overall response to the school environment. Males and older students are the most likely to withdraw. It can be inferred that failure to detect these issues beforehand is a consequence of the brevity of the selection process and the complexity of the issues involved in teaching rather than in any shortcomings in the courses provided. The availability of experienced and effective school-based mentors might be a crucial but under-researched issue.

For the in-service phase, distinction can be drawn between the *turnover* of teachers (those who move to another school) and the *wastage* of teachers (those who leave teaching) (Smithers and Robinson, 2005). In England and Wales, turnover was found to be higher in schools with poor GCSE records and higher eligibility of pupils for free school lunch (an indicator of family poverty). Both turnover and wastage were found to be higher in primary schools. The turnover of teachers under 30 years of age was about 25 per cent. The wastage rate was 9.2 per cent and 7.2 per cent for primary and secondary schools respectively, concentrated on young teachers and those approaching retirement.

A good deal can be done to support those just moving between schools and to give potential leavers pause to reconsider their decision by providing, and widely acknowledging participation in, high quality opportunities for professional development. The following suggestions for some underpinnings to such a provision are set against the multiple statements of the current problematic situation in the UK (House of Commons, 2003–2004; Edmonds et al., 2002; Roberts, 2002; Smithers and Robinson, 2008).

Teachers – including those of science – teach because they wish to work with young people, because they see teaching as providing intellectual fulfilment for themselves, and because they feel that teaching makes a worthwhile contribution to society. Leaving aside the financial aspects of personal decision taking, for these lie outside the remit of this chapter, prerequisites for effective professional development activities that would support improved recruitment and retention are:

- the belief that males have a valuable contribution to the science teaching of young children;
- efforts to overcome any particular concerns that members of ethnic minority communities may have about science teaching;
- the provision in more state schools of the support structures, including those of mentorship, that are available in many independent schools;
- opportunities to teach a science that has been most extensively studied (that is physics, chemistry, biology);

- support in teaching those sciences that have not been studied in such depth.

As structural backgrounds, attention to these issues should support the provision of high quality teacher development activities. The recruitment and retention of good science teachers should result.

Conclusion

In reading this chapter you will have become aware that your own development as a teacher can and should be modelled by you and used for your own purposes. This will be done against the background of a rapidly evolving series of opportunities to participate in staff development activities, for example, the advent in England and Wales both of the Science Learning Centres (Science Learning Centres, 2008) and of the requirement for serving teachers to take a Masters degree in 'Teaching and Learning' (TDA, 2008). Your progression through the loosely defined levels of development will be at an uneven pace, but you may see the value in aiming to participate in developmental activities so that you actually move forward through those levels over time. You will have perceived that simply aiming at professional development is not enough: it will only effectively take place if you also seek to attain personal and social development at the same time. These criteria will enable you to decide between the activities suggested to you and, in the best possible case, to design your own.

The core themes of your 'subject matter knowledge', 'pedagogic knowledge' and 'pedagogic content knowledge' frame your work. Your development as a science teacher will be manifest in the steady improvement in the range and quality of these three forms of knowledge. It will be associated with your increasingly precise awareness of the implications for your actions of teaching as being facilitative of the construction of knowledge by your students in a social context. One aim of this chapter has been to make you aware that your beliefs and attitudes shape the interpretation of the experiences that you have during teacher development activities. If you perceive yourself to have beliefs and attitudes that are dysfunctional in respect of the performance of actions that you come to see as professionally desirable, only you can personally, socially, and professionally progress by confronting these. Attaining development as a teacher certainly implies effort on your part, but that will be worthwhile for yourself, your colleagues, and, most importantly, for your students.

Further reading

Bell, B. and Gilbert, J. K. (1996) *Teacher Development: A Model from Science Education.* London: Falmer.

Fullan, M. (2001) *The New Meaning of Educational Change*, 3rd edn. London: Routledge-Falmer.

Hoban, G. (2002) *Teacher Learning for Educational Change*. Buckingham: Open University Press.

Loucks-Horsley, S., Love, N., Stiles, K. E. and Hewson, P. W. (2003) *Designing Professional Development for Teachers of Science and Mathematics*. Palo Alta, CA: Corwin Press.

Loughran, J. (2006) *Developing a Pedagogy of Teacher Education*. London: Routledge.

Bibliography

Abbott, C. (2005) Towards digital impartiality: learning from young people's online literacy practices. In C. R. Kupetz and G. Blell (eds), *Fremdsprachenlernen zwischen Medienverwahrlosung und Medienkompetenz*. Frankfurt: Peter Lang, pp. 31–41.

Abell, S. K. (2007) Research on science teacher knowledge. In S. K. Abell and N. G. Lederman (eds), *Handbook of Research on Science Education*. Mahwah, NJ: Lawrence Erlbaum, pp. 1105–49.

Abrahams, I. (2009) Does practical work really motivate? A study of the affective value of practical work in secondary school science. *International Journal of Science Education*, 31(17): 2335–54.

Abrahams, I., and Millar, R. (2008) Does practical work really work? A study of the effectiveness of practical work as a teaching and learning method in school science, *International Journal of Science Education*, 30(14): 1945–69.

Adams, J. (1995) *Risk*. London: UCL Press Ltd.

Adey, P. (ed.) (2008) *The Let's Think Handbook: A Guide to Cognitive Acceleration in the Primary School*. London: GL Assessment.

Adey, P. and Shayer, M. (1993) An exploration of long-term far-transfer effects following an extended intervention programme in the high school science curriculum, *Cognition and Instruction*, 11(1): 1–29.

Adey, P. and Shayer, M. (1994) *Really Raising Standards: Cognitive Intervention and Academic Achievement*. London: Routledge.

Adey, P. and Shayer, M. (2002) Cognitive Acceleration comes of age. In M. Shayer and P. Adey (eds), *Learning Intelligence: Cognitive Acceleration across the Curriculum*. Buckingham: Open University Press, pp. 1–17.

Adey, P., Robertson, A. and Venville, G. (2001) *Let's Think!* Windsor: NFER-Nelson.

Adey, P., Robertson, A. and Venville, G. (2002) Effects of a cognitive stimulation programme on Year 1 pupils, *British Journal of Educational Psychology*, 72(1): 1–25

Adey, P., Shayer, M. and Yates, C. (2001) *Thinking Science: The Curriculum Materials of the CASE Project*, 3rd edn. Cheltenham: Nelson Thornes.

Adey, P., Shayer, M. and Yates, C. (2003) *Thinking Science: Professional Edition*. Cheltenham: Nelson Thornes.

Adey, P., Hewitt, G., Hewitt, J. and Landau, N. (2004) *The Professional Development of Teachers: Practice and Theory*. Dordrecht: Kluwer Academic.

Adey, P., Csapo, B., Demteriou, A., Hautamäki, J. and Shayer, M. (2007) Can we be intelligent about intelligence? Why education needs the concept of plastic General Ability, *The Educational Research Review*, 2(2): 75–97.

Adey, P., Nagy, F., Robertson, A., Serret, N. and Wadsworth, P. (2003) *Let's Think Through Science*. Windsor: NFER-Nelson.

Adhami, M., Johnson, D. C. and Shayer, M. (1998) *Thinking Mathematics: The Curriculum Materials of the CAME Project*. London: Heinemann.

Advisory Group for Education for Citizenship (1998) *Education, Citizenship and the Teaching of Democracy: Final Report of the Advisory Group on Citizenship*, No. 98/155. London: Qualifications and Curriculum Authority.

Aikenhead, G. S. (1991) *Logical Reasoning in Science and Technology*. Toronto: John Wiley of Canada.

Ajzen, I. and Fishbein, M. (1980) *Understanding Attitudes and Predicting Social Behaviour*. Englewood Cliffs, NJ: Prentice Hall.

Alexander, P., Graham, S. and Harris, K. (1998) A perspective on strategy research: progress and prospects, *Educational Psychology Review*, 10: 129–53.

Alexander, R. J. (2004) *Towards Dialogic Teaching: Rethinking Classroom Talk*. York: Dialogos.

Alexander, R. J. (2008) *Essays on Pedagogy*. London: Routledge.

Alvermann, D. E. and Hynd, C. R. (1986) Effects of prior knowledge activation modes and text structure on nonscience majors' comprehension of physics. *Journal of Educational Research*, 83: 97–102.

American Chemical Society (1988) *ChemCom: Chemistry in the Community*. Dubuque, IA: Kendall/Hunt.

Amos, R. and Reiss, M. (2004) FSC London Challenge residential pilot evaluation April–July 2004, in *Research of the School of Mathematics, Science and Technology*. London: The Institute of Education. Available at: http://ioewebserver.ioe.ac.uk/ioe/cms/get.asp?cid=4381and4381_0=13511 (accessed 25/10/08).

Amos, R. and Reiss, M. (2006) What contribution can residential field courses make to the education of 11–14 year-olds? *School Science Review*, 88(322): 37–44.

Anderson, D. and Lucas, K. B. (1997) The effectiveness of orienting students to the physical features of a science museum prior to visitation, *Research in Science Education*, 27(4): 485–95.

Anderson, J. R., Reder, L. M. and Simon, H. A. (1997) Situative versus cognitive perspectives: form versus substance, *Educational Researcher*, 26(1): 18–21.

Anderson, K. E. (1950) The teachers of science in a representative sampling of Minnesota schools, *Science Education*, 34(1): 57–66.

Anderson, M. (1992) *Intelligence and Development: A Cognitive Theory*. London: Blackwell.

Andriessen, J., Baker, M. and Suthers, D. (eds) (2003) *Arguing to Learn: Confronting Cognitions in Computer-Supported Collaborative Learning Environments*. Dordrecht: Kluwer.

Apple, M. W. (1992) Educational reform and educational crisis, *Journal of Research in Science Teaching*, 29(8): 779–89.

Applebee, A. N., Langer, J. A., Nystrand, M. and Gamoran, A. (2003) Discussion based approaches to developing understanding: classroom instruction and student performance in middle and high school English, *American Educational Research Journal*, 40(3): 685–730.

Archenhold, F., Austin, R., Bell, J., Black, P., et al. (1991) *Assessment Matters No. 5: Profiles and Progression in Science Exploration*. London: School Examinations and Assessment Council.

Ardac, D. and Akaygun, S. (2004) Effectiveness of multimedia-based instruction that emphasizes molecular representations on students' understanding of chemical change, *Journal of Research in Science Teaching*, 41(4): 317–37.

Arnot, M., Gray, J., James, M., Ruddock, J. and Duveen, G. (1998) *Recent Research on Gender and Educational Performance*. London: HMSO.

Arzi, H. and White, R. (2008) Change in teachers' knowledge of subject matter: a 17 year longitudinal study. *Science Education*, 92(2): 221–51.

Assessment Reform Group (2002) *Testing, Motivation and Learning*. Cambridge: Cambridge University Press.

Assessment Reform Group. (2006) *The Role of Teachers in the Assessment of Learning*. Cambridge: Cambridge University Press.

Association for Science Education (ASE) (1979) *Alternatives for Science Education: A Consultative Document.* Hatfield: ASE.

Association for Science Education (ASE) (1981) *Education through Science.* Hatfield: ASE.

Association for Science Education (ASE) (1986) *Science and Technology in Society (SATIS).* Hatfield: Association for Science Education.

Atash, M. N. and Dawson, G. O. (1986) Some effects of the ISCS program: a meta analysis, *Journal of Research in Science Teaching,* 23: 377–85.

Atkins, P. W. (2003) *Galileo's Finger: The Ten Great Ideas of Science.* Oxford: Oxford University Press.

Atkinson, E. P. (1981) Influence of practical work on test performance, *Research in Science Education,* 11: 87–93.

Aufschnaiter, C., Erduran, S., Osborne, J. F. and Simon, S. (2007) Arguing to learn and learning to argue: case studies of how students' argumentation relates to their scientific knowledge, *Journal of Research in Science Teaching,* 45(1): 101–31.

Ausubel, D. (1968) *Educational Psychology: A Cognitive View.* London: Holt, Reinhart and Winston.

Baddeley, A. (1990) *Human Memory: Theory and Practice.* London: Lawrence Erlbaum.

Bailey, R., Wise, K. and Bolls, P. (2009) How avatar customizability affects children's arousal and subjective presence during junk food-sponsored online video games, *CyberPsychology and Behavior,* 12(3): 277–83.

Baines, E., Blatchford, P., Kutnick, P., Chowne, A., Ota, C. and Berdondini, L. (2008) *Promoting Effective Group Work in the Primary Classroom: A Handbook for Teachers and Practitioners.* London: Routledge. See also the web-site of the Social Pedagogic Research into Group-work (SPRING) project: www.spring-project.org.uk.

Baines, E., Blatchford, P. and Kutnick, P. (2009) *Promoting Effective Group Work in the Primary Classroom.* Abingdon: Routledge.

Baird, J., Cresswell, M. J. and Newton, P. (2000) Would the real gold standard please step forward? *Research Papers in Education,* 15(2): 213–29.

Baker, D. and Leary, R. (1995) Letting girls speak out about science, *Journal of Research in Science Teaching,* 32(1): 3–27.

Bakhtin, M. M. (1981) *The Dialogic Imagination,* trans. M. Holquist and C. Emerson, ed. M. Holquist. Austin, TX: University of Texas Press.

Ball, S. (1990) *Markets, Morality, and Equality in Education.* London: Tufnell Press.

Bandura, A., Barbaranelli, C., Caprara, G. V. and Pastorelli, C. (2001) Self-efficacy beliefs as shapers of children's aspirations and career trajectories, *Child Development,* 72(1): 187–206.

Barber, M. and Mourshed, M. (2007) *How the World's Best-Performing School Systems Come Out on Top.* New York: McKinsey and Company.

Barker, S., Slingsby, D. and Tilling, S. (2002) *Teaching Biology Outside the Classroom: Is it Heading for Extinction? A Report on Biology Fieldwork in the 14–19 Curriculum,* (FSC Occasional Publication 72). Shrewsbury: Field Studies Council.

Bartholomew, H., Osborne, J. F. and Ratcliffe, M. (2004) Teaching students 'Ideas-About-Science': five dimensions of effective practice, *Science Education,* 88(6): 655–82.

Barton, R. (1997) Does data-logging change the nature of children's thinking in experimental work in science? In B. Somekh and N. Davis (eds), *Using Information Technology Effectively in Teaching and Learning.* London: Routledge, pp. 63–72.

Bates, G. R. (1978) The role of the laboratory in secondary school science programs. In M. B. Rowe (ed.), *What Research Says to the Science Teacher.* Washington DC: National Science Teachers' Association, pp. 55–82.

Bauer, H. H. (1992) *Scientific Literacy and the Myth of the Scientific Method*. Chicago: University of Illinois Press.

Baxter, G. P. and Shavelson, R. J. (1994) Science performance assessments: benchmarks and surrogates, *International Journal of Educational Research*, 21: 279–98.

Beatty, J. W. and Woolnough, B. E. (1982a) Practical work in 11–13 science: the context, type and aims of current practice, *British Educational Research Journal*, 8(1): 23–31.

Beatty, J. W. and Woolnough, B. E. (1982b) Why do practical work in 11–13 science? *School Science Review*, 63(225): 768–70.

Beck, U. (1992) *Risk Society: Towards a New Modernity*. London: Sage.

Beck, U. and Beck-Gernsheim, E. (2002) *Individualization*. London: Sage.

Becker, B. J. (1989) Gender and science achievement: a reanalysis of studies from two meta-analyses, *Journal of Research in Science Teaching*, 26: 141–69.

Becta (2007) *Emerging Technologies for Learning*, vol. 2. Coventry: British Educational Communications and Technology Agency.

Bell, B. and Gilbert, J. K. (1996) *Teacher Development: A Model from Science Education*. London: Falmer.

Bell, B. and Gilbert, J. K. (2004) A model for achieving teacher development. In J. K. Gilbert (ed.), *The Routledge Falmer Reader in Science Education*. London: Routledge Falmer, pp. 258–78.

Bell, J. F., Malacova, E. and Shannon, M. (2005) The changing pattern of A level/AS uptake in England, *The Curriculum Journal*, 16(3): 391–400.

Bell, P. (2004) Promoting students' argument construction and collaborative debate in the science classroom. In M. Linn, E., Davis and P. Bell (eds), *Internet Environments for Science Education*. Mahwah, NJ: Lawrence Erlbaum, pp. 115–43.

Bell, P. and Linn, M. (2000) Scientific arguments as learning artifacts: designing for learning from the web with KIE, *International Journal of Science Education*, 22(8): 797–817.

Bencze, J. L. (1996) Correlational studies in school science: breaking the science–experiment–certainty connection, *School Science Review*, 78(282): 95–101.

Bennett, J. (2003) *Teaching and Learning Science: A Guide to Recent Research and its Applications*. London: Continuum.

Bennett, J. and Hogarth, S. (2009) Would you want to talk to a scientist at a party? High school students' attitudes to school science and to science. *International Journal of Science Education*, 31(14): 1975–98.

Bennett, J., Lubben, F., Hogarth, S. and Campbell, B. (2004) *A Systematic Review of the use of Small-Group Discussions in Science Teaching with Students Aged 11–18, and Their Effects on Students' Understanding in Science or Attitude to Science*. York: University of York, Department of Educational Studies, Research Paper 2005/05.

Ben-Zvi, R., Hofstein, A., Samuel, D. and Kempa, R. F. (1977) Modes of instruction in high school chemistry, *Journal of Research in Science Teaching*, 14(5): 431–9.

Berk, R. A. (1980) A consumer's guide to criterion-referenced test reliability, *Journal of Educational Measurement*, 17(4): 323–49.

Bhaskar, R. (1989) *Reclaiming Reality*. London: Verso.

Billig, M. (1996) *Arguing and Thinking*, 2nd edn. Cambridge: Cambridge University Press.

Binet, A. (1909) *Les idées modernes sur les enfants*. Paris: Ernest Flammarion.

Black, B. and Bramley, T. (2008) Investigating a judgemental rank-ordering method for maintaining standards in UK examinations, *Research Papers in Education*, 23(1): 1–17.

Black, P. (1990) APU Science: the past and the future, *School Science Review*, 72(258): 13–28.

Black, P. (1993) Formative and summative assessment by teachers, *Studies in Science Education*, 21: 49–97.

Black, P. (1994) Performance assessment and accountability: the experience in England and Wales, *Educational Evaluation and Policy Analysis*, 16(2): 191–203.

Black, P. (1998a) Learning, league tables and national assessment: opportunity lost or hope deferred? *Oxford Review of Education*, 24(1): 57–68.

Black, P. (1998b) *Testing: Friend or Foe?* London: RoutledgeFalmer.

Black, P. (2007) Full marks for feedback: making the grade, *Journal of the Institute of Educational Assessors*, 18–21.

Black, P., Gardener, J. and Wiliam, D. (2008) *Joint Memorandum on Reliability of Assessments Submitted to the Committee*. House of Commons, Children Schools and Families Committee: Testing and Assessment. Third Report of Session 2007–2008. Vol. II. HC169-II. Norwich: the Stationery Office. Also discussed in Vol. I, pp. 22–6.

Black, P. and Harrison, C. (2004) *Science Inside the Black Box: Assessment for Learning in the Science Classroom*. London: NFER-Nelson.

Black, P. and Wiliam, D. (1998a) Assessment and classroom learning, *Assessment in Education*, 5(1): 7–71.

Black, P. and Wiliam, D. (1998b) *Inside the Black Box: Raising Standards Through Classroom Assessment*. London: GL Assessment (also published, with minor changes and the same title, as an article in *Phi DeltaKappan*, 80(2): 139–48).

Black, P. and Wiliam, D. (2006) The reliability of assessments, in J. Gardener (ed.), *Assessment and Learning*. London: Sage, pp. 214–39.

Black, P. and Wiliam, D. (2009) Developing the theory of formative assessment, *Educational Assessment, Evaluation and Accountability,* 21(1): 5–31.

Black, P., Harrison, C., Lee, C., Marshall, B. and Wiliam, D. (2003) *Assessment for Learning: Putting it into Practice*. London: Open University Press.

Black, P., Harrison, C., Lee, C., Marshall, B. and Wiliam, D. (2004) *Working Inside the Black Box*. London: GL Assessment (also published, with minor changes and the same title, as an article in *Phi DeltaKappan*, 86(1): 8–21). (Original work published 2002)

Black, P., Harrison, C., Hodgen, J., Marshall, B. and Serret, N. (2010) Validity in teachers' summative assessments. *Assessment in Education*. In press.

Blackmore, S. (2003) *Consciousness: An Introduction*. London: Hodder and Stoughton.

Blanco, R. and Niaz, M. (1997) Epistemological beliefs of students and teachers about the nature of science: from 'Baconian inductive ascent' to the 'irrelevance' of scientific laws, *Instructional Science*, 25(3): 203–31.

Blatchford, P., Kutnick, P., Maines, E. and Gaulton, M. (2003) Toward a social pedagogy of classroom group work, *International Journal of Educational Research*, 39: 153–72.

Blickenstaff, J. C. (2005) Women and science careers: leaky pipeline or gender filter? *Gender and Education*, 17(4): 369–86.

Bloom, B., Englehart, M., Hill, W., Furst, E. and Krathwohl, D. (1956) *Taxonomy of Educational Objectives: The Classification of Educational Goals* (two vols). New York: David McKay.

Bloom, B. S., Hastings J. T. and Madhaus, G. F. (eds) (1971) *Handbook on the Formative and Summative Evaluation of Student Learning*. New York: McGraw-Hill.

Bloor, D. (1976) *Knowledge and Social Imagery*. London: Routledge and Kegan Paul.

Boaler, J. and Wiliam, D. (2001) Setting, streaming and mixed ability teaching, in J. Dillon and M. Maguire (eds), *Becoming a Teacher*. Buckingham: Open University Press.

Bodmer, W. F. (1985) *The Public Understanding of Science*. London: The Royal Society.

Bourdieu, P. (1990) *In Other Words: Essays Towards a Reflexive Sociology*, trans M. Adamson. Stanford, CA: Stanford University Press.

Brady, M. (2009) *Information Engineering and its Future*. London: Institution of Engineering and Technology.

Branigan, C. (2005) Video goes to school, *eSchool News* (April 1) Available at: http://medialit.med.sc.edu/video_goes_to_school.htm.

Bransford, J. D. (2006) Toward a 21st century learning theory: some emerging thoughts. Keynote lecture presented at the Annual Conference of the National Association for Research in Science Teaching, San Francisco, CA, 3–6 April.

Braund, M. and Reiss, M. (2006) Towards a more authentic science curriculum: the contribution of out-of-school learning, *International Journal of Science Education*, 28(12): 1373–88.

Breakwell, G. M. and Beardsell, S. (1992) Gender, parental and peer influences upon science attitudes and activities, *Public Understanding of Science*, 1(2): 183–97.

Bredderman, T. (1983) Effects of activity-based elementary science on student outcomes: a quantitative synthesis, *Review of Educational Research*, 53(4): 499–518.

Bremner, J. (1965) Observation of microscopic material by 11–12 year old pupils, *School Science Review*, 46: 385–94.

Brickhouse, N. W. (1989) The teaching of the philosophy of science in secondary classrooms: Case studies of teachers' personal theories, *International Journal of Science Education*, 11(4): 437–49.

Brickhouse, N. W. (1991) Teachers' beliefs about the nature of science and their relationship to classroom practice, *Journal of Teacher Education*, 41(3): 53–62.

Brickhouse, N. W. and Potter, J. (2001) Young women's scientific identity formation in an urban context, *Journal of Research in Science Teaching*, 38: 965–80.

Brickhouse, N. W., Lowery, P. and Schultz, K. (2000) What kind of girl does science? The construction of school science identities, *Journal of Research in Science Teaching*, 37: 441–58.

British Medical Association (1990) *The BMA Guide to Living with Risk*. London: Penguin.

Brodie, T., Gilbert, J., Hollins, M., et al. (1994) *Models and Modelling in Science Education*. London: Association for Science Education.

Brotman, J. S. and Moore, F. M. (2008) Girls and science: a review of four themes in the science education literature, *Journal of Research in Science Teaching*, 45(9): 971–1002.

Brown, A. L., Bransford, J. D., Ferrara, R. A. and Campione, J. C. (1983) Learning, remembering and understanding, in P. H. Mussen (ed.), *Handbook of Child Psychology*. New York: John Wiley.

Brown, B. (2006) It isn't no slang that can be said about this stuff: language, identity, and appropriating science discourse, *Journal of Research in Science Teaching*, 43(1): 96–126.

Brown, S. (1976) *Attitude Goals in Secondary School Science*. Stirling: University of Stirling.

Brownlie, A., Campbell, P., Cutler, M., Dillon, J. and Hulme, P. (2003) *Global Dimension in Science Guidance Booklet*. Hatfield: ASE/Development Education Association.

Bruer, J. T. (1999) In search of . . . brain-based education, *Phi Delta Kappan* (May): 649–57.

Bruner, J. (1966) *Towards a Theory of Instruction*. New York: Norton.

Brush, S. G. (1974) Should the History of Science be rated X? *Science*, 183: 1164–72.

Buckingham, D., Whiteman, N., Willett, R. and Burn, A. (2008) The impact of the media on children and young people with a particular focus on computer games and the internet. In T. Byron (ed.), *Safer Children in a Digital World: The Report of the Byron Review*. Nottingham: Department for Children, Schools and Families.

Bulgren, J., Deshler, D., Schumaker, J. and Lenz, K. (2000) The use and effectiveness of analogical instruction in diverse secondary content classrooms, *Journal of Educational Psychology*, 92(3): 426–41.

Butler, J. (1995) Teachers judging standards in senior science subjects: Fifteen years of the Queensland experiment, *Studies in Science Education*, 26: 135–57.

Butler, R. (1988) Enhancing and undermining intrinsic motivation; the effects of task-involving and ego-involving evaluation on interest and performance, *British Journal of Educational Psychology*, 58: 1–14.

Butz, W. P., Bloom, G. A., Gross, M. E., Kelly, T. K., Kofner, A. and Rippen, H. E. (2003) *Is There a Shortage of Scientists and Engineers? How Would We Know?* Santa Monica, CA: Rand Corporation.

Calderhead, J. and Shorrock, S. B. (1997) *Understanding Teacher Education: Case Studies in the Professional Development of Beginning Teachers*. London: Falmer Press.

Callaghan, V., Clarke, G. S., Colley, M. J., Hagras, H. A. K., Chin, J. S. Y. and Doctor, F. (2004) Intelligent inhabited environments, *BT Technology Journal*, 22(3): 233–47.

Capel, S. (1998) The transition from student teacher to Newly Qualified Teacher: some findings, *Journal of In-service Education*, 24(3): 393–409.

Carey, S., Evans, R., Honda, M., Jay, E., and Unger, C. (1989) 'An experiment is when you try it and see if it works': a study of grade 7 students' understanding of the construction of scientific knowledge, *International Journal of Science Education*, 11, special issue: 514–29.

Carroll, J. B. (1993) *Human Cognitive Abilities*. Cambridge: Cambridge University Press.

Carson, R. (1963) *Silent Spring*. London: Hamish Hamilton.

Case, R. (1975) Gearing the demands of instruction to the developmental capacities of the learner, *Review of Educational Research*, 45: 59–67.

Case, R., Okamoto, Y., Griffin, S., et al. (1996) The role of central conceptual structures in the development of children's thought, *Monographs of the Society for Research in Child Development*, 61.

Cassels, J. R. T. and Johnstone, A. H. (1985) *Words that Matter in Science*. London: Royal Society of Chemistry.

Cattell, R. B. (1971) *Abilities: Their Structure, Growth and Action*. Boston: Houghton Mifflin.

Cazden, C. B. (1988) *Classroom Discourse*. Portsmouth, NH: Heinemann.

Cazden, C. B. (2001) *Classroom Discourse: The Language of Teaching and Learning*. 2nd edn. Portsmouth, NH: Heinemann.

Centre for Evaluation and Monitoring (2008) *Report on A-Level Subject Difficulties*. Durham: Centre for Evaluation and Monitoring, University of Durham.

Cerini, B., Murray, I. and Reiss, M. (2003) *Student Review of the Science Curriculum: Major Findings*. London: Planet Science/Institute of Education University of London/ Science Museum. Available at: http://www.planet-science.com/sciteach/review (accessed 27 February 2007).

Chalmers, A. F. (1999) *What is This Thing Called Science?* 3rd edn. Milton Keynes: Open University Press.

Chen, Z. and Klahr, D. (1999) All other things being equal: acquisition and transfer of the control of variables strategy, *Child Development*, 70(5): 1098–120.

Cheng, Y., Payne, J. and Witherspoon, S. (1995) *Science and Mathematics in Full-Time Education After 16: England and Wales Youth Cohort Study*. Sheffield: Department for Education and Employment.

Children's Learning in Science Project (1987) *CLIS in the Classroom*. Leeds: University of Leeds Centre for Studies in Science and Maths Education.

Chinn, C. A. and Brewer, W. F. (1993) The role of anomalous data in knowledge acquisition: a theoretical framework and implications for science education, *Review of Educational Research*, 63(1): 1–49.

Chinn, C. A. and Brewer, W. F. (1998) An empirical test of a taxonomy of responses to anomalous data in science, *Journal of Research in Science Teaching*, 35(6): 623–54.

Chiu, M.-H., Chou, C.-C. and Liu, C. J. (2002) Dynamic processes of conceptual change: analysis of constructing mental models of chemical equilibrium, *Journal of Research in Science Teaching*, 39: 713–37.

CIBER (2008) *Information Behaviour of the Researcher of the Future: A CIBER Briefing Paper for the British Library and JISC*. London: University College London.

Clare, J. (2004) Union tells teachers to end all school trips, *The Daily Telegraph*, 19 February.

Clark, D. B. and Sampson, V. D. (2007) Personally-seeded discussions to scaffold online argumentation, *International Journal of Science Education*, 29(3): 253–77.

Clarke, D. and Hollingsworth, H. (2002) Elaborating a model of teacher professional growth, *Teaching and Teacher Education*, 18: 947–67.

Claxton, G. (1997) A 2020 vision of education, in R. Levinson and J. Thomas (eds), *Science Today*. London: Routledge, pp. 71–86.

Clement, J., Brown, D. E. and Zietsman, A. (1989) Not all preconceptions are misconceptions: finding 'anchoring conceptions' for grounding instruction on students' intuitions, *International Journal of Science Education*, 11(5): 554–65.

Cocker, G. (2008) *Spore*. Available at: http://m.cnet.com.au/games/339290921–2d.htm (accessed 11 August 2008).

Coffield, F., Mosely, D., Hall E. and Eccleston, K. (2004) *Learning Styles and Pedagogy in Post-16 Learning: A Systematic and Critical Review*. London: Learning Skills and Research Centre.

Cohen, I. B. (1952) The education of the public in science, *Impact of Science on Society*, 3: 67–101.

Coles, M. (1998) Science for employment and higher education, *International Journal of Science Education*, 20(5): 609–21.

Coll, R. and Taylor, N. (2008) The influence of context on science curricula: observations, conclusions and some recommendations for curriculum development and implementation, in R. Coll and N. Taylor (eds), *Science Education in Context*, Rotterdam: Sense, pp. 355–62.

Colley, A., Comber, C. and Hargreaves, D. (1994) School subject preference of pupils in single sex and co-educational secondary schools, *Educational Studies*, 20: 379–86.

Collins, H. and Pinch, T. (1993) *The Golem: What Everyone Should Know about Science*. Cambridge: Cambridge University Press.

Conner, C. and James, M. (1996) The mediating role of LEAs in the interpretation of government assessment policy at school level in England, *The Curriculum Journal*, 7(2): 153–66.

Cooper, P. and McIntyre, D. (1996) *Effective Teaching and Learning: Teachers' and Students' Perspectives*. Buckingham: Open University Press.

Corrigan, D., Dillon, J. and Gunstone, R. (eds) (2007) *The Re-emergence of Values in Science Education.* Rotterdam: Sense Publications.

Cossons, N. (1993) Let us take science into our culture, *Interdisciplinary Science Reviews,* 18(4): 337–42.

Council for Science and Technology (CST) (2000) *Science Teachers: Supporting and Developing the Profession of Science Teaching in Primary and Secondary Schools.* London: Department of Trade and Industry.

Council of Science and Technology Institutes (1993) *Occupational Mapping and Initial Functional Analysis of Occupations in Science.* London: HMSO.

Cox, M. J. and Webb, M. E. (2004) *ICT and Pedagogy: A Review of the Research Literature.* Coventry and London: British Educational Communications and Technology Agency/Department for Education and Skills.

Cox, M. J., Johnson, D. C. and Watson, D. (1993) *The Impact Report: An Evaluation of the Impact of Information Technology on Children's Achievements in Primary and Secondary Schools* (Official Research Report). London: Department for Education and King's College London, University of London.

Cox, M. J., Abbott, C., Webb, M. E., Blakeley, B., Beauchamp, T. and Rhodes, V. (2004) *ICT and Attainment: A Review of the Research Literature.* Coventry and London: British Educational Communications and Technology Agency/Department for Education and Skills.

Cramp, A. (2008) Knowing me, know you: building valuable relationships outside the classroom, *Education,* 26(2): 171–82.

Crawley, F. E. and Black, C. B. (1992) Causal modelling of secondary science students' intentions to enroll in physics, *Journal of Research in Science Teaching,* 29(6): 585–99.

Crawley, F. E. and Coe, A. E. (1990) Determinants of middle school students' intentions to enroll in a high school science course: an application of the theory of reasoned action, *Journal of Research in Science Teaching,* 27(5): 461–76.

Crook, C. (1998) Children as computer users: the case of collaborative learning, *Computers and Education,* 30(3/4): 237–47.

Dainton, F. S. (1968) *The Dainton Report: An Inquiry into the Flow of Candidates into Science and Technology.* London: HMSO.

Daniels, H. (2001) *Vygotsky and Pedagogy.* London: Routledge/Falmer.

Darby, L. (2005) Science students' perceptions of engaging pedagogy, *Research in Science Education,* 35: 425–45.

Darling-Hammond, L. (1997) *Doing What Matters Most: Investing in Quality Teaching.* New York: National Commission on Teaching and America's Future.

Darling-Hammond, L. (2007) The flat earth and education: how America's commitment to equity will determine our future, *Educational Researcher,* 36(16): 318–34.

Darling-Hammond, L. and McLaughlin, M. (1995) Policies that support professional development in an era of reform, *Phi Delta Kappan,* 76(8): 597–604.

Davies, F. and Greene, T. (1984) *Reading for Learning in the Sciences.* Edinburgh: Oliver and Boyd.

Dawes, L., Mercer, N. and Wegerif, R. (2000) *Thinking Together: A Programme of Lessons and Activities.* Birmingham: Questions Publishing.

Dawson, C. J. and Bennett, N. (1981) What do they say they want? Year 7 students' preferences in science, *Research in Science Education,* 11(1): 193–201.

Day, J. D. and Cordon, L. A. (1993) Static and dynamic measures of ability: an experimental comparison, *Journal of Educational Psychology,* 85(1): 76–82.

DeBoer, G. E. (1991) *A History of Ideas in Science Education: Implications for Practice*. New York: Teachers College Press.

Deci, E. and Ryan, R. (1985) *Intrinsic Motivation and Self-determination in Human Behavior*. New York: Plenum Press.

Department for Education and Employment (DfEE) (1995) *Value Added in Education*. London: HMSO.

Department for Education and Skills (DfES) (1998) *Health and Safety of Pupils on Educational Visits (HASPEV)*, Crown and supplement. Available at: http://www.teachernet. gov.uk/visits.

Department for Education and Skills (DfES) (2002) *Standards for LEAs for Overseeing Educational Visits*. Ref. 0564. Available at: http://www.teachernet.gov.uk/visits.

Department for Education and Skills (DfES) (2006) *Learning Outside the Classroom Manifesto*. London: DfES.

Department of Children, Families and Schools (DCFS) (2008) *Staying Safe Action Plan*. London: DCFS.

Department of Education (DoE) (1995) *Science in the National Curriculum for England and Wales*. London: HMSO.

Department of Education and Science (DES) (1978) *Primary Education in England: A Survey by HM Inspector of Schools*. London: DES.

Department of Education and Science (DES) (1979) *Aspects of Secondary Education in England: A Survey by HM Inspector of Schools*. London: DES.

Department of Education and Science (DES) (1985) *Science 5–16: A Statement of Policy*. London: HMSO.

Department of Education and Science (DES) (1988a) *National Curriculum: Task Group on Assessment and Testing: A Report*. London: Department of Education and Science and Welsh Office (with three additional Supplementary Reports).

Department of Education and Science (DES) (1988b) *Science National Curriculum*. London: DES.

Department of Education and Science/Welsh Office (DES/WO) (1989) *Science in the National Curriculum*. London: HMSO.

Desforges, C., Holden, C. and Hughes, M. (1996) Parents, teachers and the assessment of 7-year-olds, in M. Hughes (ed.), *Teaching and Learning in Changing Times*. Oxford: Blackwell.

DeWitt, J. and Osborne, J. (2007) Supporting teachers on science-focused school trips: towards an integrated framework of theory and practice, *International Journal of Science Education*, 29(6): 685–710.

Dickinson, C. and Wright, J. (1993) *Differentiation: A Practical Handbook of Classroom Strategies*. Coventry: National Council for Educational Technology.

Dierking, L. D., Falk, J. H., Rennie, L., Anderson, D. and Ellenbogen, K. (2003) Policy statement of the 'Informal Science Education' Ad hoc Committee, *Journal of Research in Science Teaching*, 40: 108–11.

Dillenbourg, P. (1999) What do you mean by collaborative learning? In P. Dillenbourg (ed.), *Collaborative Learning: Cognitive and Computational Approaches*. Oxford: Elsevier, pp. 1–19.

Dillon, J. (2000) Managing science teachers' development. In R. Millar, J. Leach and J. Osborne (eds), *Improving Science Education*. Buckingham: Open University Press.

Dillon, J. (2002) Managing teacher development: the changing role of the Head of Department in England, in P. Fraser-Abder (ed.), *Professional Development in Science Teacher Education: Local Insights with Lessons for the Global Community*. London: Taylor and Francis, pp. 172–86.

Dillon, J. T. (1994) *Using Discussion in Classrooms*. London: Open University Press.

Dillon, J. and Gill, P. (2001) Risk, environment and health: aspects of policy and practice, *School Science Review*, 83(303): 65–73.

Dillon, J., Morris, M., O'Donnell, L., Reid, A., Rickinson, M and Scott, W. (2005) *Engaging and Learning with the Outdoors: The Final Report of the Outdoor Classroom in a Rural Context Action Research Project*. Slough: National Foundation for Educational Research.

Dillon, J. and Osborne, J. (1999) Unpublished tender document. London: King's College London.

Dillon, J. and Scott, W. (eds) (2002) *International Journal in Science Education*, 24(11) (Special Issue: Perspectives on Environmental Education-related Research in Science Education).

Dillon, J., Rickinson, M., Teamey, K., Morris, M., Choi, M., Sanders, D., and Benefield, P. (2006) The value of outdoor learning: evidence from research in the UK and elsewhere, *School Science Review*, 87(320): 107–11.

Doherty, J. and Dawe, J. (1988) The relationship between development maturity and attitude to school science, *Educational Studies*, 11: 93–107.

Donaldson, M. (1978) *Children's Minds*. Glasgow: Fontana.

Donnelly, J. F. (1987) Fifteen-year-old pupils' variable handling performance in the context of scientific investigations, *Research in Science and Technological Education*, 5(2): 135–47.

Donnelly, J. F. (1998) The place of the laboratory in secondary science teaching, *International Journal of Science Education*, 20(5): 585–96.

Donnelly, J. F. (1999) Interpreting differences: the educational aims of teachers of science and history, and their implications, *Journal of Curriculum Studies*, 31(1): 17–41.

Donnelly, J. F., Buchan, A., Jenkins, E., Laws, P. and Welford, G. (1996) *Investigations by Order: Policy, Curriculum and Science Teachers' Work under the Education Reform Act*. Nafferton: Studies in Education.

Donnelly, J. F. and Jenkins, E. W. (1999) *Science Teaching in Secondary School under the National Curriculum*. Leeds: Centre for Studies in Science and Mathematics Education, University of Leeds.

Donnelly, J. F. and Jenkins, E. W. (2001) *Science Education, Policy, Professionalism and Change*. London: Paul Chapman.

Dori, Y. J. and Barak, M. (2001) Virtual and physical molecular modeling: fostering model perception and spatial understanding, *Educational Technology and Society*, 4(1): 61–74.

Dori, Y. J., Barak, M. and Adir, N. (2003) A web-based chemistry course as a means to foster freshmen learning, *Journal of Chemical Education*, 80(9): 1084–92.

Driver, R. (1975) The name of the game, *School Science Review*, 56(197): 800–5.

Driver, R. (1983) *The Pupil as Scientist*. Milton Keynes: Open University Press.

Driver, R. (1985) Pupils' alternative frameworks in science, in B. Hodgson and E. Scanlon (eds), *Approaching Primary Science*. Milton Keynes: Open University Press.

Driver, R. (1989) Students' conceptions and the learning of Science, *International Journal of Science Education*, 11(5): 481–90.

Driver, R. (1995) Constructivist approaches to science teaching, in L. Steffe and J. Gale (eds), *Constructivism in Education*. Hillsdale, NJ: Lawrence Erlbaum, pp. 385–400.

Driver, R., Asoko, H., Leach, J., Mortimer, E. and Scott, P. (1994) Constructing scientific knowledge in the classroom, *Educational Researcher*, 23(7): 5–12.

Driver, R., Leach, J., Millar, R. and Scott, P. (1996) *Young People's Images of Science*. Buckingham: Open University Press.

Driver, R., Squires, A., Rushworth, P. and Wood-Robinson, V. (1994) *Making Sense of Secondary Science: Research into Children's Idea.* Oxford: Taylor and Francis.

Driver, R., Newton, P. and Osborne, J. F. (2000) Establishing the norms of scientific argumentation in classrooms, *Science Education*, 84(3): 287–312.

Drori, G. S. (2000) Science education and economic development: trends, relationships and research agenda, *Studies in Science Education*, 35: 27–58.

Duit, R. and Treagust, D. F. (2003) Conceptual change: a powerful framework for improving science teaching and learning, *International Journal of Science Education*, 25(6): 671–88.

Duit, R. and Treagust, D. F. (2008) Teaching science for conceptual change: theory and practice, in S. Vosniadou (ed.), *International Handbook of Research on Conceptual Change*. New York: Routledge, pp. 629–46.

Dunbar, K. (1995) How scientists really reason: Scientific reasoning in real-world laboratories, in R. Sternberg and J. Davidson (eds), *The Nature of Insight*. Cambridge, MA: MIT Press.

Dunbar, K. and Klahr, D. (1989) Developmental differences in scientific discovery strategies, in D. Klahr and K. Kotovsky (eds), *Complex Information Processing: The Impact of Herbert A. Simon*. Hillsdale, NJ: Lawrence Erlbaum, pp. 109–43.

Dunn, R. and Dunn, K. (1992) *Teaching Secondary Students Through their Individual Learning Styles*. Boston: Allyn and Bacon.

Durant, J. R., Evans, G. A. and Thomas, G. P. (1989) The public understanding of science, *Nature*, 340: 11–14.

Duschl, R. A. (1990) *Restructuring Science Education: The Importance of Theories and Their Development*. New York: Teachers College Press.

Duschl, R. A. (2007) Science education in three-part harmony: balancing conceptual, epistemic and social learning goals, *Review of Research in Education*, 32: 268–91.

Duschl, R. A. and Gitomer, D. H. (1997) Strategies and challenges to changing the focus of assessment and instruction in science classrooms, *Educational Assessment*, 4(1): 37–73.

Duschl, R. A. and Wright, E. (1989) A case study of high school teachers' decision making models for planning and teaching science, *Journal of Research in Science Teaching*, 26(6): 467–501.

Dweck, C. S. (2000) *Self-theories: Their Role in Motivation, Personality and Development*. Philadelphia, PA: Psychology Press.

Dweck, C. S. and Leggett, E. (1988) A social-cognitive approach to motivation and personality, *Psychological Review*, 95(2): 256–73.

Ebare, S. (2004) Digital music and subculture: sharing files sharing style, *First Monday e-journal*, 9(2), Available at: http://firstmonday.org/htbin/cgiwrap/bin/ojs/index.php/fm/article/view/1459/1374.

Ebenezer, J. V. and Zoller, U. (1993) Grade 10 students' perceptions of and attitudes toward science teaching and school science, *Journal of Research in Science Teaching*, 30(2): 175–86.

Eccles, J. S. and Wigfield, A. (1995) In the mind of the actor: the structure of adolescents' achievement task values and expectancy-related beliefs, *Personality and Social Psychology Bulletin*, 21: 215–25.

Eddington, A. (1928) *The Nature of the Physical World*. Cambridge: Cambridge University Press.

Edelman, G.M. (1987) *Neural Darwinism: The Theory of Neuronal Group Selection*. New York: Basic Books.

Edexcel (2005) Edexcel Advanced Subsidiary GCE in Biology (Salters-Nuffield), in Edexcel. Available at: http://www.edexcel.org.uk/quals/gce/biology/adv/9048/(cdxcel) (accessed 25 Oct. 2008).

Edmonds, S., Sharp, C. and Benefield, P. (2002) *Recruitment and Retention in ITT: A Systematic Review*. Slough: NFER.

Elawar, M.C. and Corno, L. (1985) A factorial experiment in teachers' written feedback on student homework: changing teacher behaviour a little rather than a lot, *Journal of Educational Psychology*, 77(2): 162–73.

Elliott, G. and Greatorex, J. (2002) A fair comparison? The evolution of methods of comparability in national assessment, *Educational Studies*, 28(3): 253–64.

Elliott, J. (1991) *Action Research for Educational Change*. Milton Keynes: Open University Press.

Elman, J., Bates, E., Johnson, M., Karmiloff-Smith, A., Parisi, D., and Plunkett, K. (1996) *Rethinking Innateness: A Connectionist Perspective on Development*. Cambridge, MA: MIT Press.

Elwood, J. (1995) Undermining gender stereotypes: examination and coursework performance in the UK at 16, *Assessment in Education*, 2(3): 283–304.

Elwood, J., and Comber, C. (1995) Gender differences in 'A' level examinations: the reinforcement of stereotypes. Paper presented as part of the symposium,A New ERA? New Contexts for Gender Equality, BERA conference.

Elwood, J. and Comber, C. (1996) Gender differences in A-level examinations: new complexities or old stereotypes? *British Journal of Curriculum and Assessment*, 6(2): 24–8.

Ergazaki, M., Komis, V. and Zogza, V. (2005) High-school students' reasoning while constructing plant growth models in a computer-supported educational environment, *International Journal of Science Education*, 27(8): 909–33.

Erickson, G. and Erickson, L. (1984) Females and science achievement: evidence, explanations and implications, *Science Education*, 68: 63–89.

Eshet-Alkalai, Y. (2004) Digital literacy: a conceptual framework for survival skills in the digital era, *Journal of Educational Multimedia and Hypermedia*, 13(1): 93–106.

European Commission (1995) *White Paper on Education and Training: Teaching and Learning – Towards the Learning Society*. Luxembourg: Office for Official Publications in European Countries.

European Commission (2004) *Europe Needs More Scientists: Report by the High Level Group on Increasing Human Resources for Science and Technology*. Brussels: European Commission.

European Commission (2005) *Europeans, Science and Technology*. Brussels: Directorate General Research.

Evans, W. A., Krippendorf, M., Yoon, J. H., Posluszny and Thomas, S. (1990) Science in the prestige and national tabloid presses, *Social Science Quarterly*, 71: 105–17.

Eyres, H. (2008) Bold Etonians, *Financial* Times, 23 May, p. 1.

Facer, K. (2003) *Computer Games and Learning: Why Do We Think It's Worth Talking about Computer Games and Learning in the Same Breath? A Discussion Paper*. Bristol: Futurelab.

Fairbrother, R. (2008) The validity of the Key Stage 3 science tests, *School Science Review*, 89(329): 107–13.

Fairbrother, R. and Dillon, J. (2009) Triple science back on the agenda. *School Science Review*, 91(334): 65–9.

Falk, J. H., Martin, W. W. and Balling, J. D. (1978) The novel field-trip phenomenon: adjustment to novel settings interferes with task learning, *Journal of Research in Science Teaching*, 15(2): 127–34.

Farrell, M. P. and Ventura, F. (1998) Words and understanding in physics, *Language and Education*, 12(4): 243–53.

Fay, A. L. and Mayer, R. E. (1994) Benefits of teaching design skills before teaching LOGO computer programming: evidence for syntax-independent learning, *Journal of Educational Computing Research*, 11(3): 187–210.

Fensham, P. (2004) Engagement with science: an international issue that goes beyond knowledge. Paper presented at the SMEC Conference, Curtin University of Science and Technology, 23/24 September. Available at: http://www.dcu.ie/smec/plenary/Fensham,%20Peter.pdf (accessed 7 December 2008).

Festinger, L. (1957) *A Theory of Cognitive Dissonance*. Evanston, IL: Row-Peterson.

Fielding, H. (1998) The undesirable choices? Unpublished undergraduate dissertation, King's College London.

Finkelstein, N. D., Adams, W. K., Keller, C. J., Kohl, P. B., Perkins, K. K., Podolefsky, N. S. and Reid, S. (2005) When learning about the real world is better done virtually: a study of substituting computer simulations for laboratory equipment, *Physical Review Special Topics – Physics Education Research*, 1, 010103: 1–8.

Fisher, J. A. (2001) The demise of fieldwork as an integral part of science education in United Kingdom schools: a victim of cultural change and political pressure? *Pedagogy, Culture and Society*, 8(1): 75–96.

Fisher, R. (2005) *Teaching Children to Learn*, 2nd edn. Cheltenham: Nelson Thornes.

Fitz-Gibbon, C. T. and Vincent, L. (1994) *Candidates' Performance in Public Examinations in Mathematics and Science: A Report for SCAA*. Newcastle: University of Newcastle upon Tyne.

Fitz-Gibbon, C. T. and Vincent, L. (1997) Difficulties regarding subject difficulties: developing reasonable explanations for observable data, *Oxford Review of Education*, 23(3): 291–8.

Flexer, R. J., Cumbo, K., Borko, H., Mayfield, V. and Marion, S. (1995) *How 'Messing About' with Performance Assessment in Mathematics Affects What Happens in Classrooms*. Technical Report 396. Los Angeles: Center for Research on Evaluation, Standards and Students Testing (CRESST).

Ford, M. (2008) Disciplinary authority and accountability in scientific practice and learning, *Science Education*, 92(3): 404–23.

Fouad, N., Byars-Winston, A. and Angela, M. (2005) Cultural context of career choice: meta-analysis of race/ethnicity differences, *Career Development Quarterly*, 53(3): 223–33.

Fouad, N., Hackett, G., Haag, S., Kantamneni, N. and Fitzpatrick, M. E. (2007) Career choice barriers: environmental influences on women's career choices. Paper presented at the Annual Meeting of the American Psychological Association Convention, San Francisco, CA, August.

Foulds, K. and Gott, R. (1988) Structuring investigations in the science curriculum, *Physics Education*, 23: 347–51.

Foulds, K., Gott, R. and Feasey, R. (1992) *Investigative Work in Science: Report for the National Curriculum Council*. Durham: University of Durham School of Education.

Francis, B. (2000) The gendered subject: students' subject preferences and discussions of gender and subject ability, *Oxford Review of Education*, 26(1): 35–48.

Francis, R. (2006) Towards a pedagogy for game-based learning. *JISC Online Conference: Innovating with e-Learning 2006.* Available at: www.jisc.ac.uk/elp_conference06. html: Cheltenham: Direct Learn Services Ltd.

Fraser, C., Kennedy, A., Reid, L. and McKinney, S. (2007) Teachers' continuing professional development: contested concepts, understandings and models, *Journal of In-Service Education*, 33(2): 153–69.

Fullan, M. (2001) *The New Meaning of Educational Change*, 3rd edn. New York: Teachers College Press.

Fullan, M. and Stiegelbauer, S. (1991) *The New Meaning of Educational Change.* London: Cassell.

Fuller, S. (1997) *Science.* Buckingham: Open University Press.

Fullick, P. and Ratcliffe, M. (1996) *Teaching Ethical Aspects of Science.* Southampton: Bassett Press.

Gallagher, J. J. (1991) Prospective and practicing secondary school teachers' knowledge and beliefs about the philosophy of science, *Science Education*, 75(1): 121–33.

Gallas, K. (1995) *Talking their Way into Science.* New York: Teachers College Press.

Gamble, R., Davey, A., Gott, R. and Welford, G. (1985) *Science at Age 15: A Report on the Findings of the Age 15 APU Science Surveys: Assessment of Performance Unit. Science Report for Teachers: 5.* London: DES/WO/DENI.

Gardner, H. (1993) *Frames of Mind*, 2nd edn. New York: Basic Books.

Gardner, H., Kornhaber, M. and Wake, W. (1996) *Intelligence: Multiple Perspectives.* Fort Worth, TX: Harcourt Brace.

Gardner, P. and Gauld, C. (1990) Labwork and students' attitudes. In E. Hegarty-Hazel (ed.), *The Student Laboratory and the Science Curriculum.* London: Routledge, pp. 132–56.

Gardner, P. L. (1975a) Attitudes to science, *Studies in Science Education*, 2: 1–41.

Gardner, P. L. (1975b) Logical connectives in science: a summary of the findings, *Research in Science Education*, 7: 9–24.

Gardner, P. L. (1995) Measuring attitudes to science, *Research in Science Education*, 25(3): 283–9.

Garet, M. S., Birman, B. F., Porter, A. C., Desimone, L. and Herman, R. (1999) *Designing Effective Professional Development: Lessons from the Eisenhower Program.* Washington DC: US Department of Education.

Garrett, R. M. and Roberts, I. F. (1982) Demonstration versus small group practical work in science education: a critical review of studies since 1900, *Studies in Science Education*, 9: 109–46.

Gauld, C. (1989) A study of pupils' responses to empirical evidence, in R. Millar (ed.), *Doing Science: Images of Science in Science Education*, London: Falmer Press, pp. 62–82.

Geddis, A. N. (1993) Transforming subject-matter knowledge: the role of pedagogic content knowledge in learning to reflect on teaching, *International Journal of Science Education*, 15: 673–83.

Gee, J. (1996) *Social Linguistics and Literacies*, 2nd edn. London: Taylor and Francis.

Geison, J. (1995) *The Private Science of Louis Pasteur.* Princeton, NJ: Princeton University Press.

Gentner, D. (1983) Structure mapping: a theoretical framework for analogy, *Cognitive Science*, 7(2): 155–70.

Gentner, D., Lowenstein, J. and Thompson, L. (2003) Learning and transfer: a general role for analogical encoding, *Journal of Educational Psychology*, 95(2): 393–408.

Gewirtz, S. (2002) *The Managerial School: Post-welfarism and Social Justice in Education.* London: Routledge.

Gibson, A. and Asthana, A. (1998) School, pupils and examination results: contextualising school 'performance', *British Educational Research Journal*, 24(3): 269–82.

Gibson, J. J. (1979) *The Ecological Approach to Visual Perception.* Boston: Houghton Mifflin.

Giddens, A. (1990) *The Consequences of Modernity.* Cambridge: Polity Press.

Giere, R. (2006) *Understanding Scientific Reasoning*, 5th edn. Fort Worth, TX: Holt, Rinehart and Winston.

Gilbert, J. K. (2004) Models and modelling: routes to more authentic science education, *International Journal of Science and Mathematics Education*, 2(2): 115–30.

Gilbert, J. K. (2005) *Catching the Knowledge Wave? The Knowledge Society and the Future of Education.* Wellington, New Zealand: NZCER Press.

Gilbert, J. K. and Boulter, C. (1998) Learning science through models and modelling, in B. Fraser and K. Tobin (eds), *International Handbook of Science Education*, Vol. 2. Dordrecht: Kluwer, pp. 53–66.

Gilbert, J. K. and Boulter, C. (eds) (2000) *Developing Models in Science Education.* Dordrecht: Kluwer.

Gilbert, J. K., Osborne, R. J. and Fensham, P. J. (1982) Children's science and its consequences for teaching, *Science Education*, 66(4): 623–33.

Gilbert, J. K., Boulter, C. and Rutherford, M. (1998) Models in explanations, Part 1: horses for courses, *International Journal of Science Education*, 20(1): 83–97.

Glackin, M. (2006) Fieldwork; Can it Be Aided? Unpublished MA dissertation: King's College London.

Glackin, M. (2007) Using urban green space to teach science, *School Science Review*, 89(327): 29–36.

Glazer, E., and Hannafin, M. J. (2006) The Collaborative Apprenticeship model: situated professional development within school settings, *Teaching and Teacher Education*, 22(2): 179–93.

Gogolin, L. and Swartz, F. (1992) A quantitative and qualitative inquiry into the attitudes toward science of nonscience college majors, *Journal of Research in Science Teaching*, 29(5): 487–504.

Goldstein, H. (2004) International comparisons of student attainment: some issues arising from the PISA study, *Assessment in Education*, 11(3): 319–30.

Goldsworthy, A., Watson, R. and Wood-Robinson, V. (2000) *Investigations: Developing Understanding.* Hatfield: Association for Science Education.

Goodlad, J. (1979) *Curriculum Enquiry: The Study of Curriculum Practice.* New York: McGraw-Hill.

Goodson, I. F. (ed.) (1985) *Social Histories of the Secondary Curriculum.* Lewes: Falmer Press.

Goswami, U. (2006) Neuroscience and education: from research to practice? *Nature Reviews Neuroscience*, 7: 406–13.

Gott, R. and Duggan, S. (1995) *Investigative Work in the Science Curriculum.* Buckingham: Open University Press.

Gott, R. and Murphy, P. (1987) *Assessment of Performance Unit: Science Report for Teachers: 9. Assessing Investigations at Ages 13 and 15.* London: Department of Education and Science, Welsh Office, Department of Education for Northern Ireland.

Gott, R., Welford, D. and Foulds, K. (1988) *The Assessment of Practical Work in Science.* Oxford: Blackwell.

Gouge, K. and Yates, C. (2008) *Let's Think through Literacy!* London: NFER-Nelson.

Grant, H. and Dweck, C. (2003) Clarifying achievement goals and their impact, *Journal of Personality and Social Psychology*, 85(3): 541–53.

Greatorex, J. and Bell, J. F. (2008) What makes AS marking reliable? An experiment with some stages from the standardization process. *Research Papers in Education*, 23(3); 333–55.

Green, H. and Hannon, C. (2007) *Their Space, Education for a Digital Generation.* New York: Demos.

Greenfield, S. (1995) *Journey to the Centers of the Mind.* New York: W. H. Freeman.

Greenfield, S. (1998) *The Human Brain: A Guided Tour.* London: Phoenix.

Greenhough, W. T., Black, J. E., and Wallace, C. S. (1987) Experience and brain development, *Child Development*, 58: 539–59.

Gregory, J. and Miller, S. (1998) *Science in Public: Communication, Culture and Credibility.* New York: Plenum Press.

Griffin, J. and Symington, S. (1997) Moving from task-oriented to learning-oriented strategies on school excursions to museums, *Science Education*, 81(6): 763–79.

Gunstone, R. (1991) Reconstructing theory from practical experience, in B. E. Woolnough (ed.), *Practical Science.* Milton Keynes: Open University Press, pp. 67–77.

Guskey, T. R. (2000) *Evaluating Professional Development.* Thousand Oaks, CA: Corwin Press.

Guzetti, B., Williams, W. O., Skeels, S. A. and Ming Wu, S. (1997) Influence of text structure on learning counterintuitive physics concepts, *Journal of Research in Science Teaching*, 34(7): 701–19.

Hacking, I. (1983) *Representing and Intervening.* Cambridge: Cambridge University Press.

Hadden, R. A. and Johnstone, A. H. (1983) Secondary school pupils' attitudes to science: the year of erosion, *European Journal of Science Education*, 5: 309–18.

Hainsworth, M. D. (1956) The effect of previous knowledge on observation, *School Science Review*, 37: 234–42.

Haladyna, T. and Shaughnessy, J. (1982) Attitudes toward science: a quantitative synthesis, *Science Education*, 66(4): 547–63.

Haladyna, T., Olsen, R. and Shaughnessy, J. (1982) Relations of student, teacher, and learning environment variables to attitudes to science, *Science Education*, 66(5): 671–87.

Hallam, S., Kirton, A., Pfeffers, J., Robertson, P. and Stobart, G. (2004) *Evaluation of Programme One of the Assessment Development programme: Support for Professional Practice in Formative Assessment.* London: Institute of Education.

Halliday, M. A. K. (1998) Things and relations: regrammaticising experience as technical knowledge, in J. R. Martin and R. Veel (eds), *Reading Science.* London: Routledge. pp. 185–235.

Halliday, M. A. K. and Martin, J. R. (1993) *Writing Science: Literacy and Discursive Power.* London: Falmer Press.

Hand, B. (2008) Introducing the science writing heuristic approach, in B. Hand (ed.), *Science Inquiry, Argument and Language.* Rotterdam: Sense Publishers.

Hanson, N. R. (1958) *Patterns of Discovery.* Cambridge: Cambridge University Press.

Haraway, D. (1989) *Primate Visions: Gender, Race and Nature in the World of Modern Science.* New York: Routledge.

Harding, S. (1991) *Whose Science? Whose Knowledge?* Ithaca, NY: Cornell University Press.

Harlen, W. (2001) The assessment of scientific literacy in the OEDC/PISA Project, *Studies in Science Education*, 36(1): 79–103.

Harlen, W. and Deakin-Crick, R. (2002) *Testing, Motivation and Learning*. Cambridge: The Assessment Reform Group.

Harré, R. (1984) *The Philosophies of Science: An Introductory Survey*, 2nd edn. Oxford: Oxford University Press.

Harré, R. (1986) *Varieties of Realism: A Rationale for the Natural Sciences*. Oxford: Basil Blackwell.

Harrison, A. and Treagust, D. (2000) Learning about atoms, molecule, and chemical bonds: a case study of multiple-model use in grade 11 chemistry, *Science Education*, 84(3): 352–81.

Harrison, C. (2006) Banishing the quiet classroom, *Education Review*, 19(2): 67–77.

Harrison, C. and Howard, S. (2009) *Inside the Primary Black Box*. London: GL Assessment.

Harrison, C., Simon, S. and Watson, R. (2001) Progression and differentiation, in J. Osborne and M. Monk (eds), *Good Practice in Science Teaching; What Research Has to Say*, 1st edn. Buckingham: Open University Press.

Harrison, C., Comber, C., Fisher, T., Haw, K., Lewin, C., Lunzer, E., et al. (2002) *ImpaCT2: The Impact of Information and Communication Technologies on Pupil Learning and Attainment* (No. 7). Coventry: British Educational Communications and Technology Agency.

Harrison, C., Eric, A., Lunzer, P., Tymms, C., Taylor Fitz-Gibbon, J. and Restorick, J. (2004) Use of ICT and its relationship with performance in examinations: a comparison of the ImpaCT2 project's research findings using pupil-level, school-level and multilevel modelling data, *Journal of Computer Assisted Learning*, 20(5): 319–37.

Hart, C., Mulhall, P., Berry, A. Loughran, J. and Gunstone, R. (2000) What is the purpose of this experiment? Or can students learn something from doing experiments? *Journal of Research in Science Teaching*, 37: 655–75.

Harvey, T. J. and Edwards, P. (1980) Children's expectations and realisations of science, *British Journal of Educational Psychology*, 50: 74–6.

Haste, H. (2004) *Science in My Future: A Study of the Values and Beliefs in Relation to Science and Technology Amongst 11–21 Year Olds*: Nestlé Social Research Programme.

Haste, H., Muldoon, C., Hogan, A. and Brosnan, M. (2008) If girls like ethics in their science and boys like gadgets, can we get science education right? Paper presented at the Annual Conference of the British Association for the Advancement of Science, Liverpool, 11 Sept.

Hatano, G. and Inagaki, K. (1991) Sharing cognition through collective comprehension activity, in L. Resnick, J. M. Levine and S. D. Teasley (eds), *Perspectives on Socially Shared Cognition*, Washington DC: American Psychological Association, pp. 331–48.

Hatano, G. and Inagaki, K. (1993) Desituating cognition through the construction of conceptual knowledge, in G. Salomon (ed.), *Distributed Cognitions*. New York: Cambridge University Press.

Haussler, P. and Hoffmann, L. (2002) An intervention study to enhance girls' interest, self-concept, and achievement in physics classes, *Journal of Research in Science Teaching*, 39(9): 870–88.

Havard, N. (1996) Student attitudes to studying A-level sciences, *Public Understanding of Science*, 5(4): 321–30.

Haworth, C. M. A., Dale, P. and Plomin, R. (2008) A twin study into the genetic and environmental influences on academic performance in science in nine-year-old boys and girls, *International Journal of Science Education*, 30(8): 1003–25.

Head, J. (1979) Personality and the pursuit of science, *Studies in Science Education*, 6: 23–44.

Head, J. (1982) What can psychology contribute to science education? *School Science Review*, 63(225): 631–42.

Head, J. (1985) *The Personal Response to Science*. Cambridge: Cambridge University Press.

Hebb, D. O. (1949) *The Organization of Behaviour*. New York: John Wiley.

Heeter, C. (2003) Reflections on real presence by a virtual person, *Presence: Teleoperators and Virtual Environments*, 12(4): 335–45.

Helsby, G. and Knight, P. (1997) Continuing professional development and the National Curriculum, in G. Helsby and G. McCulloch (eds), *Teachers and the National Curriculum*. London: Cassell, pp. 145–62.

Hendley, D., Parkinson, J., Stables, A. and Tanner, H. (1995) Gender differences in pupil attitudes to the National Curriculum Foundation subjects of English, Mathematics, Science and Technology in Key Stage 3 in South Wales, *Educational Studies*, 21(1): 85–97.

Hendley, D., Stables, S. and Stables, A. (1996) Pupils' subject preferences at Key Stage 3 in South Wales, *Educational Studies*, 22(2): 177–87.

Hendry, P. (2009) *Understanding and Using CEM Data*. Durham: University of Durham.

Hennessy, S., Deaney, R. and Ruthven, K. (2005) Emerging teacher strategies for mediating 'Technology-integrated Instructional Conversations': a socio-cultural perspective, *Curriculum Journal*, 16(3): 265–92.

Hennessy, S., Wishart, J., Whitelock, D., Deaney, R., Brawn, R., La Velle, L., et al. (2007) Pedagogical approaches for technology-integrated science teaching, *Computers and Education*, 48(1): 137–52.

Henze, I., Van Driel, J. H. and Verloop, N. (2008) Development of experienced science teachers' pedagogical content knowledge of models of the solar system and the universe, *International Journal of Science Education*, 30(10): 1321–42.

HESA (Higher Education Statistics Agency) (2009) Students and Qualifier Data Tables. Available at: http://www.hesa.ac.uk/index.php/component/option,com_datatables/Itemid,121/task,show_category/catdex,3/#subject (accessed 12 June 2009).

Hewson, P. W. (2007) Teacher professional development in science, in S. K. Abell and N. G. Lederman (eds), *Handbook of Research on Science Education*, Mahwah, NJ: Lawrence Erlbaum, pp. 1177–202.

Hewson, P. W., Tabachnick, B. R., Zeichner, K. M. and Lemberger, J. (1999) Educating prospective teachers of biology: findings, limitations, and recommendations, *Science Education*, 83: 373–84.

High Level Group on Science Education (2007) *Science Now: A Renewed Pedagogy for the Future of Europe*. Brussels: European Union.

Hill, C. (2008) The post-scientific society. *Issues in Science and Technology*, Summer.

Hill, D. and Wheeler, A. (1991) Towards a clearer understanding of students' ideas about science and technology: an exploratory study, *Research in Science and Technological Education*, 9(2): 127–37.

Hinkle, G. and Elliot, W. R. (1989) Science coverage in three newspapers and three supermarket tabloids, *Journalism Quarterly*, 66: 353–8.

Hipkins, R., Bolstad, R., Baker, R., Jones, A., Barker, M., Bell, B., et al. (2002) *Curriculum, Learning and Effective Pedagogy: A Literature Review in Science Education*. Auckland: New Zealand: Ministry of Education.

Hirsch, E. D. (1987) *Cultural Literacy: What Every American Needs to Know*. Boston: Houghton Mifflin.

HM Inspectors of Schools (1994) *Effective Learning and Teaching in Scottish Secondary Schools: The Sciences*. Edinburgh: The Scottish Office Education Department.

Hobbes, T. ([1651] 1968) *Leviathan*. Harmondsworth: Penguin.

Hodgen, J. and Marshall, B. (2005) Assessment for learning in mathematics and English: contrasts and resemblances, *The Curriculum Journal*, 16(2): 153–76.

Hodson, D. (1990) A critical look at practical work in school science, *School Science Review*, 71(256): 33–40.

Hodson, D. (1991) Practical work in science: time for a reappraisal, *Studies in Science Education*, 19: 175–84.

Hodson, D. (1992) Redefining and reorienting practical work in school science, *School Science Review*, 73(264): 65–78.

Hodson, D. (1993a) Philosophic stance of secondary school science teachers, curriculum experiences, and children's understanding of science, *Interchange*, 24(1 and 2): 41–52.

Hodson, D. (1993b) Re-thinking old ways: towards a more critical approach to practical work in school science, *Studies in Science Education*, 22: 85–142.

Hodson, D. (1998) Is this really what scientists do? Seeking a more authentic science in and beyond the school laboratory, in J. Wellington (ed.), *Practical Work in School Science: Which Way Now?* London: Routledge, pp. 93–108.

Hoffman, J. L., Wu, H.-K., Krajcik, J. S. and Soloway, E. (2003) The nature of middle school learners' science content understandings with the use of on-line resources, *Journal of Research in Science Teaching*, 40(3): 323–46.

Hofstein, A. and Lunetta, V. N. (1982) The role of the laboratory in science teaching: neglected aspects of research, *Review of Educational Research*, 52(2): 201–17.

Hofstein, A. and Lunetta, V. N. (2004) The laboratory in science education: foundations for the twenty-first century, *Science Education*, 88(1): 28–54.

Hogarth, S., Bennett, J., Lubben, F., Campbell, B. and Robinson, A. (2006) *ICT in Science Teaching: The Effect of ICT Teaching Activities in Science Lessons on Students' Understanding of Science Ideas. Technical Report*. London: EPPI-Centre, Social Science Research Unit, Institute of Education, University of London.

Hohenstein, J. and King, H. (2007) Learning in and outside of the classroom, in J. Dillon and M. Maguire (eds), *Becoming a Teacher: Issues in Secondary Teaching*, 3rd edn. Buckingham: Open University Press, pp. 127–38.

Hollow, R. P. (2000) The student as scientist: secondary student research projects in astronomy, *Publications of the Astronomical Society of Australia*, 17(2): 162–7.

Holton, G. and Brush. (1996) *Physics, the Human Adventure: From Copernicus to Einstein and Beyond*. New Jersey: Rutgers University Press.

Horton, R. (1971) African traditional thought and Western science, in M. D. Young (ed.), *Knowledge and Control*. London: Collier-Macmillan, pp. 208–66.

House of Commons (2003–2004) *Secondary Education: Teacher Retention and Recruitment* (No. HC 1057–1). London: House of Commons Education and Skills Committee.

House of Commons, Children, Schools and Families Committee (2008) *Testing and Assessment: Third Report of Session 2007–08*, Vols I and II. Norwich: The Stationery Office.

House of Commons, Education and Skills Committee (2005) *Education Outside the Classroom: Second Report of Session 2004–05. Report, Together with Formal Minutes, Oral and Written Evidence (HC 120)*. London: The Stationery Office.

House of Lords (2000) *Science and Society: Third Report of the Select Committee on Science and Society*. London: House of Lords.

House of Lords, Science and Technology Committee (2006) *Tenth Report of Session 2005–06 Science Teaching in Schools*. Available at: http://www.publications.parliament.uk/pa/ld200506/ldselect/ldsctech/257/25706.htm#a12 (accessed 20 January 2008).

House of Lords, Select Committee on Science and Technology (2001) *Science in Schools*. London: HMSO.

Howe, C. J., Rodgers, C. and Tolmie, T. (1989) Physics in the primary school: peer interaction and understanding of floating and sinking, *European Journal of Psychology of Education*, 5(4): 459–75.

Howe, C. J., Tolmie, A. and Rodgers, C. (1992) The acquisition of conceptual knowledge in science by primary school children: group interaction and the understanding of motion down an inclined plane, *British Journal of Developmental Psychology*, 10: 113–30.

Howe, C. J., Tolmie, A., Duchak-Tanner, V. and Rattray, C. (2000) Hypothesis testing in science: group consensus and the acquisition of conceptual and procedural knowledge, *Learning and Instruction*, 10: 361–91.

Hsiung, C.-T. and Tuan, H.-L. (1998) Science teacher education in selected countries in Asia, in B. Fraser and K. G. Tobin (eds), *International Handbook of Science Education*, Vol. 2. Dordrecht: Kluwer, pp. 733–44.

Hughes, G. (2001) Exploring the availability of student scientist identities within curriculum discourse: an anti-essentialist approach to gender-inclusive science, *Gender and Education*, 13: 275–90.

Hunt, A. and Millar, R. (eds) (2000) *Science for Public Understanding*. London: Heinemann Educational.

Huppert, J., Lomask, M. S. and Lazarowitz, R. (2002) Computer simulations in the high school: students' cognitive stages, science process skills and academic achievement in microbiology, *International Journal of Science Education*, 24(8): 803–21.

Hurd, P. D. (1997) *Inventing Science Education for the New Millennium*. New York: Teachers College Press.

Hynd, C. and Alvermann, D. E. (1986) The role of refutation text in overcoming difficulty with science concepts, *Journal of Reading*, 29(5): 440–6.

Independent (1999) Editorial: the real challenges of the next century are scientific, *The Independent*, January 2, p. 3.

Inhelder, B., and Piaget, J. (1958) *The Growth of Logical Thinking*. London: Routledge & Kegan Paul.

Inhelder, B., Sinclair, H. and Bovet, M. (1974) *Learning and Cognitive Development*. Cambridge, MA: Harvard University Press.

International Association for the Evaluation of Educational Achievement (IEA) (TIMSS). (1997) Harmon, M., Smith, T., Martin, M., et al. (eds), *Performance Assessment in IEA's Third International Mathematics and Science Study*. Centre for the Study of Testing, Evaluation and Educational Policy.

Irwin, A. (1995) *Citizen Science*. London: Routledge.

Irwin, A. and Wynne, B. (eds) (1996) *Misunderstanding Science: The Public Reconstruction of Science and Technology*. Cambridge: Cambridge University Press.

Isaacs, W. (1999) *Dialogue and the Art of Thinking Together*. New York: Doubleday

Ito, M. (2003) Mobile phones, Japanese youth, and the re-placement of social context, in R. Ling and P. Pedersen (eds), *Mobile Communications: Re-negotiation of the Social Sphere*. Dordrecht: Springer, pp. 131–66.

Ito, M., Horst, H. A., Bittanti, M., et al. (2008) *Living and Learning with New Media: Summary of Findings from the Digital Youth Project*. Chicago: The John D. and Catherine T. MacArthur Foundation.

Jaakkola, T. and Nurmi, S. (2008) Fostering elementary school students' understanding of simple electricity by combining simulation and laboratory activities, *Journal of Computer Assisted Learning*, 24(4): 271–83.

Jacobs, J. E. and Simpkins, S. D. (eds) (2006) *Leaks in the Pipeline to Math, Science, and Technology Careers: New Directions for Child and Adolescent Development.* New York: Wiley.

Jagger, N. (2007) Internationalising doctoral careers. Paper presented at the The National Value of Science Education, September

Jarman, R. and McClune, B. (2007) *Developing Scientific Literacy.* Maidenhead: Open University Press.

Jarvis, T. and Pell, A. (2002) Effect of the Challenger experience on children's attitudes to science, *Journal of Research in Science Teaching*, 39(10): 979–1000.

Jenkins, E. (1998) *Scientific and Technological Literacy for Citizenship: What Can We Learn from the Research and Other Evidence?* Available at: http://www.leeds.ac.uk/educol/documents/000000447.doc.

Jenkins, E. and Nelson, N. W. (2005) Important but not for me: students' attitudes toward secondary school science in England, *Research in Science and Technological Education*, 23(1): 41–57.

Jenkins E. J. and. Pell R. G. (2006) *The Relevance of Science Education Project (ROSE) in England: A Summary of Findings.* Leeds: Centre for Studies in Science and Mathematics Education, University of Leeds.

Jenkins, E. W. (1992) School science education: towards a reconstruction, *Journal of Curriculum Studies*, 24(3): 229–46.

Jenkins, E. W. (2004) From option to compulsion: school science teaching, 1954–2004, *School Science Review*, 85(313): 33–40.

Jenkins, H., Clinton, K., Purushotma, R., Robison, A. J. and Weigel, M. (2006) *Confronting the Challenges of Participatory Culture: Media Education for the 21st Century.* Chicago: The John D. and Catherine T. MacArthur Foundation.

Jennings, A. (1992) *National Curriculum Science: So Near and Yet So Far.* London: Tufnell Press.

Jesson, D. (1997) *Value Added Measures of School GCSE Performance.* London: DFEE.

Jevons, F. R. (1969) *The Teaching of Science: Education, Science and Society.* London: George Allen and Unwin.

Jimoyiannis, A. and Komis, V. (2001) Computer simulations in physics teaching and learning: a case study on students' understanding of trajectory motion, *Computers and Education*, 36(2): 183–204.

John, P. and Baggott La Velle, L. (2004) Devices and desires: subject subcultures, pedagogical identity and the challenge of information and communications technology, *Technology, Pedagogy and Education*, 13(3): 102–7.

Johnson, D. W., Johnson, R. T. and Stanne, M. B. (2000) *Co-operative Learning Methods: A Meta-Analysis.* Minneapolis: University of Minnesota Press.

Johnson, D. W., Johnson, R. T. and Johnson-Houlbec, E. (2002) *Circles of Learning: Co-operation in the Classroom*, 5th edn. Minnesota: Interaction Book Company.

Johnson, M. H. (1997) *Developmental Cognitive Neuroscience.* Oxford: Blackwell.

Johnson, S. (1987) Gender differences in science: parallels in interest, experience and performance, *International Journal of Science Education*, 9(4): 467–81.

Johnson, S. (1989) *National Assessment: The APU Science Approach.* London: Her Majesty's Stationery Office.

Johnstone, A. H. and El-Banna, H. (1986) Capacities, demands, and processes: a predictive model for science education, *Education in Chemistry*, 23(3): 80–4.

Johnstone, A. H. and Wham, A. J. B. (1982) The demands of practical work, *Education in Chemistry*, 19(3): 71–3.

Jones, A. and Issroff, K. (2005) Learning technologies: affective and social issues in computer-supported collaborative learning, *Computers and Education*, 44(4): 395 408.

Jones, A. T., Simon, S. A., Black, P. J., Fairbrother, R. W. and Watson, J. R. (1992) *Open Work in Science: Development of Investigations in Schools*. Hatfield: Association for Science Education.

Jones, M. G. and Martin, A. K. (2007) Science teacher attitudes and beliefs, in S. Abell and N. G. Lederman (eds), *Handbook of Research on Science Education*. Mahweh, NJ: Erlbaum, pp. 1067–104.

Jones, R. L. (1997) Some implications of an increasing drive towards aspects of safety, accountability, and teacher competency, within fieldwork, *Teaching Earth Science*, 22(3): 83–7.

Joyce, B. and Showers, B. (1988) *Student Achievement through Staff Development*. New York: Longman.

Joyce, B. and Showers, B. (1995) *Student Achievement Through Staff Development*, 2nd edn. White Plains, NY: Longman.

Justi, R. and Van Driel, J. H. (2005) The development of science teachers' knowledge on models and modelling: promoting, characterising and understanding the process. *International Journal of Science Education*, 27(5): 549–73.

Kahle, J. B. and Lakes, M. K. (1983) The myth of equality in science classrooms, *Journal of Research in Science Teaching*, 20: 131–40.

Kanari, Z. and Millar, R. (2004) Reasoning from data: how students collect and interpret data in scientific investigations, *Journal of Research in Science Teaching*, 41(7): 748–69.

Kang, S., Scharmann, L. C., and Noh, T. (2005) Examining students' views on the nature of science: results from Korean 6th, 8th, and 10th graders. *Science Education*, 89(2): 314–34.

Kapenda, H. M., Kandjeo-Marenga, H. U., Kasanda, C. D. and Lubben, F. (2002) Characteristics of practical work in science classrooms in Namibia, *Research in Science and Technological Education*, 20(1): 53–65.

Kelly, A. (ed.) (1981) *The Missing Half: Girls and Science Education*. Manchester: Manchester University Press.

Kempa, R. and Dias, M. (1990) Students' motivational traits and preferences for different instructional modes in science education: Part 2, *International Journal of Science Education*, 12(2): 205–16.

Kempa, R. F. and L'Odiaga, J. (1984) Criterion-referenced interpretation of examination grades, *Educational Research*, 26(1): 56–64.

Kendall, S., Murfield, J., Dillon, J. and Wilkin, A. (2006) *Education Outside the Classroom: Research to Identify What Training Is Offered by Initial Teacher Training Institutions*, DfES Research Report 802. London: DfES.

Kennedy, A. (2005) Models for continuing professional development (CPD): a framework for analysis, *Journal of In-Service Education*, 31(2): 235–50.

Kent, N. and Facer, K. (2004) Different worlds? A comparison of young people's home and school ICT use, *Journal of Computer Assisted Learning*, 20(6): 440–55.

Keogh, B. and Naylor, S. (1999) Concept cartoons, teaching and learning in science: an evaluation, *International Journal of Science Education*, 21(4): 431–46.

Keohane, K. W. (1986) Foreword, in M. Lyth (ed.), *Nuffield Science 11 to 13: Teachers' Guide 1. How Scientists Work*. Harlow: Longman.

Kerr, J. F. (1958–59) Some sources for the history of the teaching of science in England, *British Journal of Educational Studies*, VII: 149–60.

Kerr, J. F. (1963) *Practical Work in School Science: An Enquiry into the Nature and Purpose of Practical Work in School Science in England and Wales*. Leicester: Leicester University Press.

Keys, C. W. (1994) The development of scientific reasoning skills in conjunction with collaborative writing assignment: an interpretive study of six ninth-grade students, *Journal of Research in Science Teaching*, 31(9): 1003–22.

Keys, C. W. (1999) Revitalising instruction in scientific genres: connecting knowledge production with writing to learn in science, *Science Education*, 83(2): 115–30.

Keys, W. (1987) *Aspects of Science Education in English Schools* (International Studies in Pupil Performance Series). Windsor: NFER-Nelson.

Khisfe, R. (2008) The development of seventh graders' views of the nature of science, *Journal of Research in Science Teaching*, 45(4): 470–96.

Khisfe, R. and Abd-El-Khalick, F. (2002) Influence of explicit and reflective views versus implicit 'inquiry orientated' instruction on sixth graders' views of the nature of science, *Journal of Research in Science Teaching*, 39(7): 551–78.

Kim, G. and Shin, W. (2001) Tuning the Level of Presence (LOP), paper presented at Fourth International Workshop on Presence, Temple, PA.

Kinchin, I. and Hay, D. (2000) How a qualitative approach to concept map analysis can be used to aid learning by illustrating patterns of conceptual development, *Educational Research*, 42(1): 43–57.

Kind, P. M., Jones, K. and Barmby, P. (2007) Developing attitudes towards science measure, *International Journal of Science Education*, 29(7): 871–93.

King, A. (1994) Guiding knowledge construction in the classroom: effects of teaching children how to question and how to explain, *American Education Research Journal*, 31(2): 338–68.

King, B. B. (1991) Beginning teachers' knowledge of and attitudes toward history and philosophy of science, *Science Education*, 75(1): 135–41.

King, S. D. (2007) Meeting contemporary challenges. Paper presented at the Annual Meeting of the Association for Science Education, January.

Klahr, D. and Dunbar, K. (1988) Dual search space during scientific reasoning, *Cognitive Science*, 12; 1–48.

Klahr, D. and Nigam, M. (2004) The equivalence of learning paths in early science instruction: effects of direct instruction and discovery learning, *Psychological Science*, 15(10): 661–7.

Klahr, D., Chen, Z. and Toth, E. E. (2001) Cognitive development and science education: ships that pass in the night or beacons of mutual illumination? in S. M. Carter and D. Klahr (eds), *Cognition and Instruction: Twenty-five Years of Progress*. Mahwah, NJ: Lawrence Erlbaum, pp. 75–119.

Klahr, D., Triona, L. M. and Williams, C. (2007) Hands on what? The relative effectiveness of physical versus virtual materials in an engineering design project by middle school children, *Journal of Research in Science Teaching*, 44(1): 183–203.

Klainin, S. (1988) Practical work and science education, in P. J. Fensham (ed.), *Development and Dilemmas in Science Education*. Lewes: Falmer Press, pp. 174–82.

Klopfer, L. E. (1971) Evaluation of learning in science, in B. S. Bloom, J. T. Hastings and G. F. Madaus (eds), *Handbook of Formative and Summative Evaluation of Student Learning*. London: McGraw-Hill Book Company.

Kluger, A. N. and DeNisi, A. (1996) The effects of feedback interventions on performance: a historical review, a meta-analysis, and a preliminary feedback intervention theory, *Psychological Bulletin*, 119(2): 254–84.

Koballa Jr., T. R. (1988) The determinants of female junior high school students' intentions to enroll in elective physical science courses in high school: testing the applicability of the theory of reasoned action, *Journal of Research in Science Teaching*, 25(6): 479–92.

Koehler, M. J. and Mishra, P. (2005) What happens when teachers design educational technology? The development of technological pedagogical content knowledge, *Journal of Educational Computing Research*, 32(2); 131–52.

Kolstoe, S. D. (2001) Scientific literacy for citizenship: tools for dealing with the science dimension of controversial socioscientific issues, *Science Education*, 85(3); 291–310.

Koslowski, B. (1996) *Theory and Evidence: The Development of Scientific Reasoning*. Cambridge, MA: MIT Press.

Kouladis, V. and Ogborn, J. (1989) Philosophy of science: an empirical study of teachers' views, *International Journal of Science Education*, 11(2): 173–84.

Kozma, R. B. E. (ed.) (2003) *Technology, Innovation, and Educational Change: A Global Perspective*. Eugene, OR: International Society for Educational Technology (ISTE).

Krange, I. and Ludvigsen, S. (2008) What does it mean? Students' procedural and conceptual problem solving in a CSCL environment designed within the field of science education, *Computer-Supported Collaborative Learning*, 3(1): 25–51.

Kress, G., Jewitt, C., Ogborn, J. and Tsatsarelis, C. (2001) *Multimodal Teaching and Learning: The Rhetorics of the Science Classroom*. London: Continuum Books.

Kuhn, D. (1991) *The Skills of Argument*. Cambridge: Cambridge University Press.

Kuhn, D. (1993) Science as argument: implications for teaching and learning scientific thinking, *Science Education*, 77(3): 319–37.

Kuhn, D. and Angelev, J. (1976) An experimental study of the development of formal operational thought, *Child Development*, 47(3): 697–706.

Kuhn, D. and Dean, D., Jr. (2005) Is developing scientific thinking all about learning to control variables? *Psychological Science*, 16(11): 866–70.

Kuhn, D., Shaw, V. and Felton, M. (1997) Effects of dyadic interaction on argumentative reasoning, *Cognition and Instruction*, 15(3): 287–315.

Kuhn, D., Amsel, E. and O'Loughlin, M. (1988) *The Development of Scientific Thinking Skills*. San Diego, CA: Academic Press.

Kuhn, T. E. (1962) *The Structure of Scientific Revolutions*. Chicago: University of Chicago Press.

Kumpalainen, K., Vasama, S. and Kangassalo, M. (2003) The intertextuality of children's explanations in a technology-enriched early years science classroom, *International Journal of Educational Research*, 39(8): 793–805.

Labour Party (2001) *The Best Place to Do Business: Labour Party Business Manifesto*. London: Labour Party. Available at http://www/labour.org/uk/index.php?id= businessmanifesto2001 (accessed 30 March 2005).

Lampert, M., Rittenhouse P., et al. (1996). Agreeing to disagree: developing sociable mathematical discourse, in D. O. N. Torrance (ed.), *The Handbook of Education and Human Development*. Malden, MA: Blackwell, pp. 731–64.

Lang, H. G. (1982) Criterion-referenced tests in science: an investigation of reliability, validity, and standards-setting, *Journal of Research in Science Teaching*, 19(8): 665–74.

Larkin, S. (2001) Creating metacognitive experiences for 5- and 6- year old children, in M. Shayer and P. Adey (eds), *Learning Intelligence*. Buckingham: Open University Press.

Latour, B. and Woolgar, S. (1986) *Laboratory Life: The Construction of Scientific Facts*, 2nd edn. Princeton, NJ: Princeton University Press.

Lave, J. and Wenger, E. (1991) *Situated Learning: Legitimate Peripheral Participation*. Cambridge: Cambridge University Press.

Lawson, A. E. (2003) The nature and development of hypothetico-predictive argumentation with implications for science teaching, *International Journal of Science Education*, 25(11): 1387–408.

Layton, D. (1973) *Science for the People: The Origins of the School Science Curriculum in England*. London: Allen and Unwin.

Layton, D., Jenkins, E. W., McGill, S. and Davey, A. (1993) *Inarticulate Science? Perspectives on the Public Understanding of Science*. Driffield, Nafferton: Studies in Education.

Lazarowitz, R. and Tamir, P. (1994) Research on using laboratory instruction in science, in D.L. Gabel (ed.), *Handbook of Research on Science Teaching and Learning*. New York: Macmillan, pp. 94–128.

Leach, J. and Scott, P. (2000) Children's thinking, learning, teaching and constructivism, in M. Monk and J. Osborne (eds), *Good Practice in Science Teaching: What Research Has to Say*. Buckingham: Open University Press.

Leach, J., Hind, A. and Ryder, J. (2003) Designing and evaluating short teaching interventions about the epistemology of science in high school classrooms, *Science Education*, 87(6): 831–48.

Learning Outside the Classroom Quality Badge. See www.lotcqualitybadge.org.uk (accessed 9 Feb. 2009).

Leat, D. and Higgins, S. (2002) The role of powerful pedagogical strategies in curriculum development, *Curriculum Journal*, 13(1): 71–85.

Lederman, N. G. (1992) Students' and teachers' conceptions of the nature of science: a review of the research, *Journal of Research in Science Teaching*, 29: 331–59.

Lederman, N. G. (2006) Nature of science: past, present and future, in S. Abell and N. G. Lederman (eds), *Handbook of Research on Science Education*, Mawah, NJ: Lawrence Erlbaum, pp. 831–79.

Lederman, N. G. and Abd-el-Khalick, F. (1998) Avoiding de-natured science: activities that promote understandings of the nature of science, in W. F. McComas (ed.), *The Nature of Science in Science Education: Rationales and Strategies*. Dordrecht: Kluwer Academic Publishers pp. 83–126.

Lederman, N. G. and O'Malley, M. (1990) Students' perceptions of tentativeness in science: development, use, and sources of change, *Science Education*, 74: 225–39.

Lederman, N. G. and Zeidler, D. L. (1987) Science teachers' conceptions of the nature of science: do they really influence teaching behaviour? *Science Education*, 71: 721–34.

Lederman, N. G., Gess-Newsome, J. and Katz, M. S. (1994) The nature and development of preservice science teachers' conceptions of subject matter and pedagogy, *Journal of Research in Science Teaching*, 31(2): 129–46.

Lee, M. and Thompson, A. (1997) Guided instruction in LOGO programming and the development of cognitive monitoring strategies among college students, *Journal of Educational Computing Research*, 16: 125–44.

Leinhardt, G. and Crowley, K. (2002) Objects of learning, objects of talk: changing minds in museums, in S. Paris (ed.), *Perspectives on Object-centred Learning in Museums*. Mahwah, NJ: Lawrence Erlbaum Associates, pp. 301–4.

Leithwood, K., Jantzi, D. and Steinbach, R. (1999) *Changing Leadership for Changing Times*. Buckingham: Open University Press.

Lemke, J. (1990) *Talking Science: Language, Learning and Values*. Norwood, NJ: Ablex Publishing.

Lemke, J. (1998) *Teaching All the Languages of Science: Words, Symbols, Images and Actions.* Available at: http://academic.brooklyn.cuny.edu/education/jlemke/papers/barcelon.htm.

Lightbody, P. and Durndell, A. (1996a) Gendered career choice: is sex-stereotyping the cause or the consequence? *Educational Studies,* 22(2): 133–46.

Lightbody, P. and Durndell, A. (1996b) The masculine image of careers in science and technology – fact or fantasy? *British Journal of Educational Psychology,* 66(2): 231–46.

Lindahl, B. (2007) A longitudinal study of students' attitudes towards science and choice of career. Paper presented at the 80th NARST International Conference New Orleans, Louisiana.

Linn, M. C. (2000) Designing the knowledge integration environment, *International Journal of Science Education,* 22(8): 781–96.

Linn, M. C. and Hsi, S. (2000) *Computers, Teachers, Peers: Science Learning Partners.* London: Erlbaum.

Linn, M. C. and Petersen, A. C. (1985) Emergence and characterization of sex differences in spatial ability: a meta-analysis, *Child Development,* 56(6): 1479–98.

Linn, M. C., Davis, E. A. and Bell, P. L. (2004) *Internet Environments for Science Education.* Mahwah, NJ: Lawrence Erlbaum Associates

Lock, R. (1990) Assessment of practical skills, Part 2: Context dependency and construct validity, *Research in Science and Technological Education,* 8(1): 35–52.

Lohman, D. F., Hagen, E. P. and Thorndike, R. L (2001) *Cognitive Abilities Test.* London: GL Assessment.

Longino, H. (1990) *Science as Social Knowledge.* Princeton, NJ: Princeton University Press.

Loughran, J. (2006) *Developing a Pedagogy of Teacher Education.* London: Routledge.

Loughran, J., Mulhall, P. and Berry, A. (2008) Exploring pedagogical content knowledge in science teacher education, *International Journal of Science Education,* 30(10): 1301–20.

Lubben, F. and Millar, R. (1996) Children's ideas about the reliability of experimental data, *International Journal of Science Education,* 18(8): 955–68.

Luft, J. A. and Cox, W. (1998) *Final Report: A Report on Preservice and Mentoring Programs in Arizona for Mathematics and Science Teachers.* Phoenix, AZ: Arizona Board of Regents: Eisenhower Mathematics and Science Program.

Lunetta, V. N. and Tamir, P. (1981) An analysis of laboratory activities: project physics and PSSC, *School Science and Mathematics,* 81: 635–42.

Lunetta, V. N., Hofstein, A. and Clough, M. P. (2007) Teaching and learning in the school science laboratory: an analysis of research, theory, and practice, in S. K. Abell and N. G. Lederman (eds), *Handbook of Research on Science Education.* Mahwah, NJ: Lawrence Erlbaum, pp. 393–431.

Lunzer, E. and Gardner, K. (1979) *The Effective Use of Reading.* London: Heinemann Educational.

Lynn, L. and Salzman, H. (2006) Collaborative advantage: new horizons for a flat world, *Issues in Science and Technology,* Winter: 74–81.

Lyons, T. (2006) The puzzle of falling enrolments in physics and chemistry courses: putting some pieces together, *Research in Science Education,* 36(3): 285–311.

Mackenzie, A. A. and White, R. T. (1982) Fieldwork in geography and long-term memory structures, *American Educational Research Journal,* 19(4): 623–32.

Maltese, A. (2008) Persistence in STEM: an investigation of the relationship between high school experiences in science and mathematics and college degree completion in STEM fields. Unpublished Doctor of Philosophy thesis, University of Virginia, Charlotteville.

Marshall, B. and Wiliam, D. (2006) *English Inside the Black Box: Assessment for Learning in the English Classroom*. London: GL Assessment.

Marshall, G. and Cox, M. J. (2008) Research methods; their design, applicability and reliability, in J. Voogt and G. Knezek (eds), *International Handbook of Information Technology in Primary and Secondary Education*, Berlin: Springer, pp. 965–88.

Martin, J. R. (1998) Discourses of science, in J. R. Martin and R. Veel (eds), *Reading Science*. London: Routledge, pp. 3–14.

Martin, K. and Miller, E. (1988) Storytelling and science, *Language Arts*, 65(3): 255–9.

Masnick, A. M. and Klahr, D. (2003) Error matters: an initial exploration of elementary school children's understanding of experimental error, *Journal of Cognition and Development*, 4(1): 67–98.

Matthews, M. R. (1994) *Science Teaching: The Role of History and Philosophy of Science*. New York: Routledge.

Mayer, R. (2004) Should there be a three-strikes rule against pure discovery learning? The case for guided methods of instruction, *American Psychologist*, 59(1): 14–19.

McComas, W. F. and Olson, J. K. (1998) The nature of science in international science education standards documents, in W. F. McComas (ed.), *The Nature of Science in Science Education: Rationales and Strategies*, Dordrecht: Kluwer, pp. 41–52.

McManus, P. (1985) Worksheet induced behaviour in the British Museum, *Journal of Biological Education*, 19(3): 237–42.

McRobbie, C., Roth, W.-M. and Lucas, K. B. (1997) Multiple learning environments in a physics classroom, *International Journal of Science Education*, 27: 333–42.

Mead, M. and Métraux, R. (1957) Image of the scientist among high-school students, *Science*, 126: 384–90.

Meadows, M. and Billington, L. (2005) *A Review of the Literature on Marking Reliability*. London: AQA for the National Assessment Agency.

Mehan, H. (1979) *Learning Lessons: Social Organizations in the Classroom*. Cambridge, MA: Harvard University Press.

Mellado, V. (1998) Preservice teachers' classroom practice and their conceptions of the nature of science, in B. J. Fraser and K. G. Tobin (eds), *International Handbook of Science Education*. Dordrecht: Kluwer.

Mercer, N. (1996a) Sociocultural perspectives and the study of classroom discourse, in C. Coll and D. Edwards (eds), *Discourse and Learning in the Classroom*. Madrid: Infancia and Aprendizaje, pp. 13–23.

Mercer, N. (1996b) The quality of talk in children's collaborative activity in the classroom, *Learning and Instruction*, 6(4): 359–75.

Mercer, N. (2002) Developing dialogues, in G. Wells and G. Claxton (eds), *Learning for Life in the 21st Century*. Oxford: Blackwell Publishers, pp. 141–53.

Mercer, N. and Littleton, K. (2007) *Dialogue and the Development of Children's Thinking*. London: Routledge.

Mercer, N., Dawes, L., Wegerif, R. and Sams, C. (2004) Reasoning as a scientist: ways of helping children to use language to learn science, *British Educational Research Journal*, 30(3): 359–77.

Merron, S. and Lock, R. (1998) Does knowledge about a balanced diet influence eating behaviour? *School Science Review*, 80(290): 43–8.

Merton, R. K. (ed.) (1973) *The Sociology of Science: Theoretical and Empirical Investigations*. Chicago: University of Chicago Press.

Merzyn, G. (1987) The language of school science, *International Journal of Science Education*, 9(4): 483–9.

Messick, S. (1989) Validity, in R. L. Linn (ed.), *Educational Measurement*, 3rd edn. New York and London: Macmillan and American Council on Education.

Midgley, C., Kaplan, A. and Middleton, M. (2001) Performance-approach goals: good for what, for whom, under what circumstances, and at what cost? *Journal of Educational Psychology*, 93(1): 77–86.

Millar, R. (1989) What is scientific method and can it be taught? In J. J. Wellington (ed.), *Skills and Processes in Science Education: A Critical Analysis*. London: Routledge, pp. 47–62.

Millar, R. (1996) Towards a science curriculum for public understanding, *School Science Review*, 77(280): 7–18.

Millar, R. (1998a) Rhetoric and reality: what practical work in science education is *really* for, in J. Wellington (ed.), *Practical Work in School Science: Which Way Now?* London: Routledge, pp. 16–31.

Millar, R. (1998b) Review of B. Koslowski (1996) 'Theory and evidence: The development of scientific reasoning' (Cambridge, MA: MIT Press), *British Journal of Educational Psychology*, 68(3): 467–9.

Millar, R. (2006) Twenty first century science: insights from the design and implementation of a scientific literacy approach in school science, *International Journal of Science Education*, 28(13): 1499–521.

Millar, R. and Driver, R. (1987) Beyond processes, *Studies in Science Education*, 14: 33–62.

Millar, R. and Osborne, J. (1998) *Beyond 2000: Science Education for the Future*. London: King's College.

Millar, R., Lubben, F., Gott, R. and Duggan, S. (1994) Investigating in the school science laboratory: conceptual and procedural knowledge and their influence on performance, *Research Papers in Education*, 9(2): 207–49.

Millar, R., Gott, R., Lubben, F. and Duggan, S. (1996) Children's performance of investigative tasks in science: a framework for considering progression, in M. Hughes (ed.), *Progression in Learning*. Clevedon: Multilingual Matters, pp. 82–108.

Millar, R., Tiberghien, A. and Le Maréchal, J.-F. (2002) Varieties of labwork: a way of profiling labwork tasks, in D. Psillos and H. Niedderer (eds), *Teaching and Learning in the Science Laboratory*. Dordrecht: Kluwer, pp. 9–20.

Miller, J. D. (1997) Civic scientific literacy in the United States: a developmental analysis from middle-school through adulthood, in W. Gräber and C. Bolte (eds), *Scientific Literacy*. Kiel: Institut für die Pädogogik Naturwissenschaften an der Universität Kiel, pp. 121–42.

Miller, J. D. (1998) The measurement of civic scientific literacy, *Public Understanding of Science*, 7: 203–23.

Miller, J. D. (2006) Civic Scientific Literacy in Europe and the United States. Paper presented at the World Association for Public Opinion Research, Montreal, Canada.

Moje, E. B., Collazo, T., Carrillo, R. and Marx, R. W. (2001) "Maestro, what is ls 'quality'?": Language, literacy, and discourse in project-based science, *Journal of Research in Science Teaching*, 38(4): 469–98.

Monk, M. (2001) Learning in the classroom, in J. Dillon and M. Maguire (eds), *Becoming a Teacher*. Buckingham: Open University Press.

Monk, M. and Dillon, J. (1995) From telling to selling: one historical perspective on consultancy in science education, *Journal of Education Policy*, 10(3): 317–23.

Monk, M. and Dillon, J. (2000) The nature of scientific knowledge, in M. Monk and J. Osborne (eds), *Good Practice in Science Teaching: What Research Has to Say*. Milton Keynes: Open University Press, pp. 72–87.

Monk, M. and Osborne, J. F. (1997) Placing the history and philosophy of science on the curriculum: a model for the development of pedagogy, *Science Education*, 81(4): 405–24.

Monk, M., Fairbrother, B. and Dillon, J. (1994) Notes on the re-integration of practical work into science education. Unpublished paper. King's College London.

Montgomery, S. L. (1996) *The Scientific Voice*. New York: Guilford Press.

Montgomery, S. L. (2003) *The Chicago Guide to Communicating Science*. Chicago: University of Chicago Press.

Moor, H., Jones, M., Johnson, F., Martin, K., Cowell, E. and Bojke, C. (2006) *The Deployment of Teachers and Support Staff to Deliver the Curriculum*. London: Department for Education and Skills.

Moore, R. W. and Sutman, F. X. (1970) The development, field test and validation of an inventory of scientific attitudes, *Journal of Research in Science Teaching*, 7: 85–94.

Mortimer, E. and Scott, P. (2003) *Meaning Making in Secondary Science Classrooms*. Maidenhead: Open University Press.

Mulholland, J. and Wallace, J. (1999) Learning and teaching elementary science in the transition from preservice to inservice teaching. Paper presented at the Annual Meeting of the American Educational Research Association (AERA), Montreal, Canada, April.

Munby, H. (1983) Thirty studies involving 'Scientific Attitude Inventory': what confidence can we have in this instrument? *Journal of Research in Science Teaching*, 20(2): 141–62.

Murdock, J. (2008) Comparison of curricular breadth, depth, and recurrence and physics achievement of TIMSS Population 3 Countries, *International Journal of Science Education*, 30(9): 1135–57.

Murphy, C. (2003) *Literature Review in ICT and Primary Science*. Bristol: NESTA Futurelab.

Murphy, C. and Beggs, J. (2003) Children's attitudes towards school science, *School Science Review*, 84(308): 109–16.

Murphy, P. (1991) Gender differences in pupils' reactions to practical work, in B. E. Woolnough (ed.), *Practical Science*, Milton Keynes: Open University Press, pp. 112–22.

Murphy, P. (1996) The IEA assessment of science achievement, *Assessment in Education: Principles Policy and Practice*, 3(2): 129–41.

Murphy, P. and Whitelegg, E. (2006) *Girls in the Physics Classroom: A Review of Research of Participation of Girls in Physics*. London: Institute of Physics.

Murphy, R. (1997) Drawing outrageous conclusions from national assessment results: where will it all end? *British Journal of Curriculum and Assessment*, 7(2): 27–39.

Murray, L. and Lawrence, B. (2000) *Practitioner-based Enquiry: Principles for Postgraduate Research*. London: Falmer Press.

Myers, R. E. and Fouts, J. T. (1992) A cluster analysis of high school science classroom environments and attitude toward science, *Journal of Research in Science Teaching*, 29(9): 929–37.

National Academy of Science (1995) *National Science Education Standards*. Washington DC: National Academy Press.

National Academy of Science, Committee on Science Engineering and Public Policy (2005) *Rising Above the Gathering Storm: Energizing and Employing America for a Brighter Economic Future*. Washington DC: National Academy Sciences.

National Endowment for Science, Technology and the Arts (NESTA) (2005) *Science Teachers Survey*. Bristol: NESTA.

National Research Council (1996) *National Science Education Standards*. Washington DC: National Academy Press.

National Research Council (2008) *Research on Future Skill Demands*. Washington DC: National Academy Press.

National Science Board (2008) *Science and Engineering Indicators*. Arlington, VA: National Science Foundation.

Naylor, S. and Keogh, B. (2000) *Concept Cartoons in Education*. Sandbach: Millgate House Publishers.

Nelkin, D. and Lindee, S. (1995) *The DNA Mystique: The Gene as a Cultural Icon*. New York: W. H. Freeman.

Newberry, M., Hardcastle, D. and Gilbert, J. K. (2005) Visualizing progression through the science curriculum in order to raise standards, *School Science Review*, 86(316): 87–96.

Newman, D., Griffin, P. and Cole, M. (1989) *The Construction Zone: Working for Cognitive Change in School*. Cambridge: Cambridge University Press.

Newmann, F. M., Bryk, A. S. and Nagaoka, J. K. (2001) *Authentic Intellectual Work and Standardized Tests: Conflict or Coexistence?* Chicago: Consortium on Chicago School Research.

Newton, P. E. (1997a) Measuring comparability of standards between subjects: why our statistical techniques do not make the grade, *British Educational Research Journal*, 23(4): 433–49.

Newton, P. E. (1997b) Examining standards over time, *Research Papers in Education*, 12(3): 227–48.

Newton, P. E. (2003) The defensibility of National Curriculum assessment in England, *Research Papers in Education*, 18(2): 101–27.

Newton, P. E. (2005) The public understanding of measurement inaccuracy, *British Educational Research Journal*, 31(4): 419–42.

Newton, P. E., Driver, R. and Osborne, J. (1999) The place of argumentation in the pedagogy of school science, *International Journal of Science Education*, 21(5): 553–76.

Nisan, M. (1992) Beyond intrinsic motivation: cultivating a 'sense of the desirable', in F. Oser, A. Dick, and J. Patry (eds), *Effective and Responsible Teaching: The New Synthesis*. San Francisco: Jossey-Bass.

Nolen, S. B. (2003) Learning environment, motivation and achievement in high school science, *Journal of Research in Science Teaching*, 40(4): 347–68.

Norris, S. (1997) Intellectual independence for nonscientists and other content-transcendent goals of science education, *Science Education*, 81(2): 239–58.

Norris, S. and Phillips, L. (1994) Interpreting pragmatic meaning when reading popular reports of science. *Journal of Research in Science Teaching*, 31(9): 947–67.

Norris, S. and Phillips, L. (2003) How literacy in its fundamental sense is central to scientific literacy, *Science Education*, 87: 224–40.

Nott, M. and Smith, R. (1995) 'Talking your way out of it', 'rigging' and 'conjuring': what science teachers do when practicals go wrong, *International Journal of Science Education*, 17(3): 399–410.

Nott, M. and Wellington, J. J. (1993) Your Nature of Science profile: an activity for science teachers. *School Science Review*, 75(270

Nott, M. and Wellington, J. J. (1996) When the black box springs open: practical work in school science and the nature of science, *International Journal of Science Education*, 18(7): 807–18.

Novak, J. D. (1990) Concept mapping: a useful tool for science education. *Journal of Research in Science Teaching*, 27(10): 937–49.

Novak, J. D. (2002) Meaningful learning: the essential factor for conceptual change in limited or inappropriate propositional hierarchies leading to empowerment of learners, *Science Education*, 8(4): 548–71.

Nuffield Science 11 to 13 (1986) *Teachers' Guide 1: How Scientists Work*. Harlow: Longman.

Nundy, S. (1999) The fieldwork effect: the role and impact of fieldwork in upper primary school, *International Research in Geography and Environmental Education*, 8(2): 181–9.

Nussbaum, E. M., Hartley, K., Sinatra, G. M., Reynolds, R. E. and Bendixen, L. D. (2004) Personality interactions and scaffolding in on-line discussions, *Journal of Educational Computing Research*, 30(1 and 2): 113–37.

NUT (2008) *Staying Safe Action Plan*. Press release: Pr1008.

Nuthall, G. and Alton-Lee, A. (1995) Assessing classroom learning: how students use their knowledge and experience to answer classroom achievement test questions in science and social studies, *American Educational Research Journal*, 32(1): 185–223.

Nyquist, J. B. (2003) The benefits of reconstruing feedback as a larger system of formative assessment: a meta-analysis. Unpublished Master of Science thesis, Vanderbilt University, USA.

Nystrand, M., Wu, L. L., Gamoran, A., Zeiser, S. and Long, D. A. (2003) Questions in time: structure and dynamics of unfolding classroom discourse, *Discourse Processes*, 35(2): 135–98.

O'Donnell, L., Morris, M. and Wilson, R. (2006) *Education Outside the Classroom: An Assessment of Activity and Practice in Schools and Local Authorities*, DfES Research Report 803. London: DfES.

OEAP (Outdoor Education Advisor's Panel). Available at: http://www.oeap.info/news/display/BALLS_CALLS_TIME_ON_RED_TAPE_AROUND_SCHOOL_TRIPS_740/ (accessed 31 March 2009).

Ofcom (2006) *Media Literacy Audit: Report on Media Literacy Amongst Children*. London: Ofcom.

Office for Standards in Education (Ofsted) (1998) *Secondary Education 1993–7: A Review of Secondary Schools in England*. London: HMSO.

Office for Standards in Education (Ofsted) (2004) *Outdoor Education: Aspects of Good Practice*. London: HMSO.

Office for Standards in Education (Ofsted) (2007) *Annual Report of Her Majesty's Chief Inspector 2006–2007*. London: HMSO.

Office for Standards in Education (Ofsted) (2008) *Learning Outside the Classroom: How Far Should You Go?* London: Ofsted, Ref: 070219.

Ogborn, J., Kress, G., Martins, I. and McGillicuddy, K. (1996) *Explaining Science in the Classroom*. Buckingham: Open University Press.

Ogura, Y. (2006) Graph of student attitude v student attainment. Based on data from Martin, M.O. *et al.* (2000) *TIMSS 1999 International Science Report: Findings from IEA's Repeat of the Third International Mathematics and Science Study at the Eighth Grade*. Chestnut Hill, MA: Boston College, Tokyo: National Institute for Educational Research.

Oliver, J. S. and Simpson, R. D. (1988) Influences of attitude toward science, achievement motivation, and science self concept on achievement in science: a longitudinal study, *Science Education*, 72(2): 143–55.

Organisation for Economic Co-operation and Development (OECD) (2007) *PISA 2006: Science Competencies for Tomorrow's World: Vol. 1: Analysis*. Paris: OECD.

Orion, N. (1993) A model for the development and implementation of field trips as an integral part of the science curriculum, *School Science and Mathematics*, 93(6): 325–31.

Orion, N. and Hofstein, A. (1994) Factors that influence learning during a scientific field trip in a natural environment, *Journal of Research in Science Teaching*, 31(10): 1097–119.

Ormerod, M. B. and Duckworth, D. (1975) *Pupils' Attitudes to Science*. Slough: NFER.

Osborne, J. (1993) Alternatives to practical work, *School Science Review*, 75(271): 117–23.

Osborne, J. (1996) Beyond constructivism, *Science Education*, 80(1): 53–82.

Osborne, J. (1998a) Science education without a laboratory? In J. J. Wellington (ed.), *Practical Work in School Science: Which Way Now?* London: Routledge, pp. 156–73.

Osborne, J. (1998b) Learning and teaching about the nature of science, in M. Ratcliffe (ed.), *ASE Guide to Secondary Science Education*. Cheltenham: Stanley Thornes, pp. 100–8.

Osborne, J. and Collins, S. (2000) *Pupils' and Parents' Views of the School Science Curriculum: A Study Funded by the Wellcome Trust*. London: King's College London.

Osborne, J. and Collins, S. (2001) Pupils' views of the role and value of the science curriculum: a focus-group study, *International Journal of Science Education*, 23(5): 441–68.

Osborne, J. and Dillon, J. (2008) *Science Education in Europe: Critical Reflections*. London: Nuffield Foundation.

Osborne, J. and Simon, S. (1996) Primary science: past and future directions, *Studies in Science Education*, 27: 99–147.

Osborne, J., Ratcliffe, M., Collins, S., Millar, R. and Duschl, R. (2003) What 'ideas-about-science' should be taught in school science? A Delphi study of the 'Expert' community, *Journal of Research in Science Teaching*, 40(7): 692–720.

Osborne, J., Simon, S. and Collins, S. (2003) Attitudes towards science: a review of the literature and its implications, *International Journal of Science Education*, 25(9): 1049–79.

Osborne, J., Erduran, S. and Simon, S. (2004) *Ideas, Evidence and Argument in Science Education: A CPD Pack*. London: King's College London.

Oulton, C., Day, V., Dillon, J. and Grace, M. (2004) Controversial issues – teachers' attitudes and practices in the context of citizenship education, *Oxford Review of Education*, 30(4): 489–507.

Oulton, C., Dillon, J. and Grace, M. (2004) Reconceptualizing the teaching of controversial issues, *International Journal of Science Education*, 26(4): 411–23.

Out and About (2008) Available at: http://www.lotc.org.uk/Out-and-about-guidance/ Introduction (accessed 9 Feb. 2009).

Palincsar, A.S. and Brown, A.L. (1994) Reciprocal teaching of comprehension: fostering and comprehension-monitoring activities. *Cognition and Instruction*, 1(2): 117–75.

Paris, S. and Paris, A. (2001) Classroom applications of research on self-regulated learning, *Educational Psychologist*, 36(2): 89–101.

Pascual-Leone, J. (1976) On learning and development, Piagetian style, *Canadian Psychological Review*, 17(4): 270–97.

Pascual-Leone, J. (1984) Attention, dialectic and mental effort: towards an organismic theory of life stages, in M. Commons, F. Richards and C. Armon (eds) *Beyond Formal Operations: Late Adolescent and Adult Cognitive Development*. New York: Praeger.

Patronis, T., Potari, D. and Spiliotopoulou, V. (1999) Students' argumentation in decision-making on a socio-scientific issue: implications for teaching, *International Journal of Science Education*, 21(7): 745–54.

Pavlov, I. (1927) *Conditioned Reflexes*. New York: Dover.

Pea, R. D. and Kurland, D. M. (1984) On the cognitive effects of learning computer programming, *New Ideas in Psychology*, 2(2): 137–68.

Pedretti, J. E., Mayer-Smith, J. and Woodrow, J. (1998) Technology, text, and talk: students' perspectives on teaching and learning in a technology-enhanced secondary science classroom, *Science Education*, 82(5): 569–90.

Pell, T. and Jarvis, T. (2001) Developing attitude to science scales for use with children of ages from five to eleven years, *International Journal of Science Education*, 23(8): 847–62.

Pellechia, M. (1997) Trends in science coverage: a content analysis of three US newspapers, *Public Understanding of Science*, 6: 49–68.

Pena-Shaff, J. B. and Nicholls, C. (2004) Analyzing student interactions and meaning construction in computer bulletin board discussions, *Computers and Education*, 42(3): 243–65.

Perkins, D. (1995) *Outsmarting IQ*. New York: The Free Press.

Perkins, D. N. and Saloman, G. (1989) Are cognitive skills context bound?, *Educational Researcher*, 18(1): 16–25.

Perlman, D. (1974) Science and the mass media, *Daedalus*, 103: 207–22.

Perrenoud, P. (1998) From formative assessment to a controlled regulation of learning processes: towards a wider conceptual field, *Assessment in Education*, 5(1): 85–102.

Perry, D. (1992) Designing exhibits that motivate, *ASTC Newsletter*, 20(2): 9–10.

Phillips, D. (1997) How, why, what, when, and where: Perspectives on constructivism in psychology and education, *Issues in Education*, 3(2): 151–94.

Phillips, L. (2002) Making new and making do: epistemological, normative and pragmatic bases of literacy, in D. R. Olson, D. Kamawar and J. Brockmeier (eds), *Literacy and Conceptions of Language and Mind*. Cambridge: Cambridge University Press, pp. 283–300.

Piaget, J. (1950) *The Psychology of Intelligence*. London: Routledge & Kegan Paul.

Piaget, J. (1952) *Origins of Intelligence in Children*. New York: International Universities Press.

Piaget, J. and Inhelder, B. (1974) *The Child's Construction of Quantities*. London: Routledge & Kegan Paul.

Piburn, M. (1993) If I were the teacher . . . qualitative study of attitude toward science, *Science Education*, 77(4): 393–406.

Piburn, M., Reynolds, S., McAuliffe, C., Leedy, D., Birk, J. and Johnson, J. (2005) The role of visualization in learning from computer-based images, *International Journal of Science Education*, 27(5): 513–27.

Pickering, A. (1984) *Constructing Quarks*. Edinburgh: Edinburgh University Press.

Pickering, A. (1995) *The Mangle of Practice: Time, Agency and Science*. Chicago: University of Chicago Press.

Pickersgill, S. and Lock, R. (1991) Students' understanding of selected non-technical words in science, *Research in Science and Technological Education*, 9(1): 71–9.

Pintrich, P. R., Marx, R. W. and Boyle, R. A. (1993) Beyond cold conceptual change: the role of motivational beliefs and classroom contextual factors in the process of conceptual change, *Review of Educational Research*, 6: 167–99.

Piscitelli, B. and Anderson, D. (2001) Young children's perspectives of museums' settings and experiences, *Museum Management and Curatorship*, 19(3): 269–82.

Popham, J. W. (1978) *Criterion Referenced Measurement*. Englewood Cliffs, NJ: Prentice-Hall.

Popper, K. (1963) *Conjectures and Refutations: The Growth of Scientific Knowledge*. London: Routledge & Kegan Paul.

Posner, G. J., Strike, K. A., Hewson, P. W. and Gertzog, W. A. (1982) Accommodation of a scientific conception: towards a theory of conceptual change, *Science Education*, 66: 211–27.

Potter, J. and Wetherell, M. (1987) *Discourse and Social Psychology: Beyond Attitudes and Behaviour*. London: Sage Publications.

Prain, V. and Hand, B. (1996) Writing for learning in secondary science: rethinking practices, *Teaching and Teacher Education*, 12: 609–26.

Prais, S. J. (2003) Cautions on OECD's recent educational survey, *Oxford Review of Education*, 29(2): 139–63.

Prenksy, M. (2001) Digital natives, digital immigrants. *On the Horizon*, 9(5): 1–6.

Puntambekar, S. and Hubscher, R. (2005) Tools for scaffolding students in a complex learning environment: what have we gained and what have we missed? *Educational Psychologist*, 40(1): 1–12.

Putnam, H. (1975) *Mind, Language and Reality*. Cambridge: Cambridge University Press.

Putnam, H. (2004) *The Collapse of the Fact/Value Dichotomy and Other Essays*. Cambridge, MA: Harvard University Press.

Putnam, R. T. and Borko, H. (2000) What do new views of knowledge and thinking have to say about research on teacher learning? *Educational Researcher*, 29(1): 4–15.

Qualifications and Curriculum Authority (QCA) (1998) *Standards at Key Stage 3: Science: A Report on the 1997 National Curriculum Assessments for 14 Year Olds*. London: QCA.

Qualifications and Curriculum Authority (QCA) (2004) *Examination Standards: Report of the Independent Committee to QCA*. London: QCA.

Qualifications and Curriculum Authority (QCA) (2005) *Implications for Teaching and Learning from the 2005 National Curriculum Tests*. London: QCA.

Qualifications and Curriculum Authority (QCA) (2007) *Assessment for Learning*. Available at http://www.qca.org.uk/7658.html (accessed 23 January 2007).

Qualifications and Curriculum Authority (QCA) (2008a) *Inter-subject comparability studies, Study 1b: GCSE, AS and A level Sciences*. London: QCA.

Qualifications and Curriculum Authority (QCA) (2008b) The Big Picture. Available at: http://www.qca.org.uk/qca_5856.aspx (accessed 26 Sept. 2008).

Qualifications and Curriculum Authority (QCA) (2008c) *Science National Curriculum*, in *National Curriculum Online*, London: HMSO. Available at: http://curriculum.qca.org.uk/key-stages-3-and-4/subjects/science/index.aspx (accessed 25 October 2008).

Quinn, P. C. and Eimas, P. D. (1997) A reexamination of the perceptual-to-conceptual shift in mental representations, *Review of General Psychology*, 1(3): 271–87.

Ramsden, J. M. (1998) Mission Impossible? Can anything be done about attitudes to science? *International Journal of Science Education*, 9(5): 505–18.

Ratcliffe, M. and Grace, M. (2003) *Science Education for Citizenship*. Buckingham: Open University Press.

Raven, J. C. (1960) *Guide to the Standard Progressive Matrices Set A, B, C, D, E*. London: H. K. Lewis.

Reddy, M. (1979) The conduit metaphor, in A. Ortony (ed.), *Metaphor and Thought*. New York: Cambridge University Press.

Reid, D. J., Zhang, J. and Chen, Q. (2003) Supporting scientific discovery learning in a simulation environment, *Journal of Computer Assisted Learning*, 19(1): 9–20.

Reiss, M. (1993) *Science Education for a Pluralist Society*. Buckingham: Open University Press.

Reiss, M. (2000) *Understanding Science Lessons: Five Years of Science Teaching*. Buckingham: Open University Press.

Research Councils UK (2008) *Public Attitudes to Science 2008: A Survey*. London: Department for Innovation, Universities and Skills.

Rickinson, M., Dillon, J., Teamey, K., Morris, M., Choi, M.Y., Sanders, D. and Benefield, P. (2004) *A Review of Research on Outdoor Learning*. Shrewsbury: Field Studies Council.

Ridgway, J., McCusker, S. and Nicholson, J. (2008) 'Alcohol and a mash-up: understanding student understanding'. Paper presented at EARLI/Northumbria Conference: Challenging Assessment, 27–29 August.

Ritchie, S. M. and Rigano, D. L. (2002) Discourses about a teacher's self-initiated change in praxis: storylines of care and support, *International Journal of Science Education*, 24(10): 1079–94.

Rivard, L. P. (1994) A review of writing to learn in science: implications for practice and research, *Journal of Research in Science Teaching*, 31(9): 969–83.

Rivard, L.P. (2004) Are language-based activities in science effective for all students, including low achievers? *Science Education*, 88: 420–42.

Rivard, L. P. and Straw, S., B. (2000) The effect of talking and writing on learning science: an exploratory study, *Science Education*, 84(5): 566–93.

Roberts, D. A. (2007a) Scientific literacy/science literacy, in S. Abell and N. G. Lederman (eds), *Handbook of Research on Science Education*. Mahwah, NJ: Lawrence Erlbaum, pp. 729–80.

Roberts, D. A. (2007b) Opening remarks, in C. Linder, L. Östman, and P.-O. Wickman, (eds), Promoting scientific literacy: science education research in transaction, in *Proceedings of the Linnaeus Tercentenary Symposium*. Uppsala: Uppsala University, pp. 9–17.

Roberts, G. (2002) *SET for Success: The Supply of People with Science, Technology, Engineering and Mathematics Skills*. London: HM Treasury.

Roberts, R. and Gott, R. (2004) A written test for procedural understanding: a way forward for assessment in the UK science curriculum? *Research in Science and Technological Education*, 22(1): 5–21.

Roberts, R. and Gott, R. (2006) Assessment of performance in practical science and pupil attributes, *Assessment in Education*, 13(1): 45–67.

Roehrig, G. and Luft, J. (2004) Constraints experienced by beginning secondary science teachers in implementing scientific enquiry lessons, *International Journal of Science Education*, 26(1): 3–24.

Rogers, L. and Finlayson, H. (2003) Does ICT in science really work in the classroom? Part 1, The individual teacher experience, *School Science Review*, 84(309): 105–11.

Rogers, L. and Finlayson, H. (2004) Developing successful pedagogy with information and communications technology: how are science teachers meeting the challenge? *Technology, Pedagogy and Education*, 13(3): 287–305.

Rogoff, B. (1994) Developing understanding of the idea of communities of learners, *Mind, Culture and Activity*, 1: 209–29.

Rogoff, B. (2003) *The Cultural Nature of Human Development*. Oxford: Oxford University Press.

Roth, W. M., McRobbie, C. J., Lucas, K. B., and Boutonné, S. (1997) The local production of order in traditional science laboratories: a phenomenological analysis, *Learning and Instruction*, 7: 107–36.

Rowe, M. B. (1974) Wait time and rewards as instructional variables, their influence on language, logic and fate control, *Journal of Research in Science Teaching*, 11: 81–94.

Royal Society (1982) *Science Education in England and Wales.* London: The Royal Society.

Royal Society (1997) *Science Teaching Resources: 11–16 Year Olds: A Report by a Working Group of the Education Committee of the Royal Society.* London: The Royal Society.

Royal Society (2006) *Taking a Leading Role.* London: The Royal Society.

Royal Society of Chemistry (RSC) (1998) *Research in Assessment XIII (An Updated Report on the Skills Test Survey of Chemistry Degree Course Entrants).* London: RSC.

Rummelhart, D. and McClelland, J. (eds) (1986) Parallel distributed processing: explorations in the microstructure of cognition. Vol. 2, in *Psychological and Biological Models.* Cambridge, MA: MIT Press.

Russell, D. W., Lucas, K. B. and McRobbie, C. J. (2004) Role of the microcomputer-based laboratory display in supporting the construction of new understandings in thermal physics, *Journal of Research in Science Teaching,* 41(2): 165–85.

Russell, M. and Martin, A. M. (2007) Learning to teach science, in S. K. Abell and N. G. Lederman (eds), *Handbook of Research on Science Teaching.* Mahwah, NJ: Erlbaum, pp. 1151–78.

Ruthven, K. (2005) *Eliciting Situated Expertise in ICT-integrated Mathematics and Science Teaching: End of Award Report*: London: ESRC.

Ruthven, K., Hennessy, S. and Brindley, S. (2004) Teacher representations of the successful use of computer-based tools and resources in secondary-school English, mathematics and science, *Teaching and Teacher Education,* 20(3): 259–75.

Ruthven, K., Hennessy, S. and Deaney, R. (2004) Incorporating Internet resources into classroom practice: pedagogical perspectives and strategies of secondary-school subject teachers, *Computers and Education,* 44(1): 1–34.

Ryder, J. (2001) Identifying science understanding for functional scientific literacy, *Studies in Science Education,* 36: 1–44.

Sainsbury of Turville (2007) *The Race to the Top: A Review of Government's Science and Innovation Policies.* London: HM Treasury.

Sakonidis, H. (1994) Representations and representation systems, in H. Mellar, J. Bliss, R. Boohan, J. Ogborn, and C. Tompsett (eds), *Learning with Artificial Worlds: Computer Based Modelling in the Curriculum.* London: Falmer Press, pp. 39–46.

Sanders, W., Wright, S. P. and Horn, S. (1997) Teacher and classroom context effects on student achievement: implications for teacher evaluation, *Journal of Personnel Evaluation in Education,* 11(1): 57–67.

Scanlon, E., Jones, A. and Waycott, J. (2005) Mobile technologies: prospects for their use in learning in informal science settings, *Journal of Interactive Media in Education,* 25. Available from http://jime.open.ac.uk/2005/25/scanlon-2005-25-t.html.

Schagen, I. (2006) The use of standardised residuals to derive value-added measures of school performance, *Educational Studies,* 32(2): 119–32.

Schibeci, R. A. (1984) Attitudes to science: an update, *Studies in Science Education,* 11: 26–59.

Schome-community (2007) *TheSschomeNAGTY Teen Second Life Pilot Final Report.* Milton Keynes: Open University Press. Available at: http://kn.open.ac.uk/public/getfile.cfm?documentfileid=11344.

Schön, D. (1983) *The Reflective Practitioner.* London: Temple Smith.

School Curriculum and Assessment Authority (SCAA) (1996) *Standards in Public Examinations 1975 to 1995.* London: SCAA.

Schreiner, C. (2006) EXPLORING A ROSE-GARDEN: Norwegian youth's orientations towards science – seen as signs of late modern identities. Thesis submitted for Doctor Scientarium, Oslo, Faculty of Education.

Schreiner, C. and Sjøberg, S. (2007) Science education and youth's identity construction – two incompatible projects? In D. Corrigan, J. Dillon and R. Gunstone (eds), *The Re-emergence of Values in the Science Curriculum*. Rotterdam: Sense Publishers, pp. 231–47.

Schwab, J. J. (1962) *The Teaching of Science as Enquiry*. Cambridge, MA: Harvard University Press.

Science Learning Centres (2008) *Homepage for Science Learning Centres*. Available at: http://www.sciencelearningcentres.org.uk.

SCORE (Science Community Representing Education) (2008) *Practical Work in Science: A Report and Proposal for a Strategic Framework*. London: SCORE. Available at: http://www.score-education.org (accessed 27 February 2009).

Scott, P. and Leach, J. (1998) Learning science concepts in the secondary science classroom, in M. Ratcliffe (ed.), *ASE Guide to Secondary Science Education*. Cheltenham: Stanley Thornes, pp. 59–66.

Scott, P., Asoko, H. and Leach, J. (2007) Student conceptions and conceptual learning in science, in S. A. Abel and N. G. Lederman (eds), *Handbook of Research on Science Education*, Mahwah, NJ: Erlbaum, pp. 31–56.

Scott, P. H., Mortimer, E. F. and Aguiar, O. G. (2006) The tension between authoritative and dialogic discourse: a fundamental characteristic of meaning making interactions in high school science lessons, *Science Education*, 90(4): 605–31.

Screen, P. (1986) The Warwick Process Science course, *School Science Review*, 68(242): 12–16.

Sefton-Green, J. (2007) Youth, technology, and media culture, *Review of Research in Education*, 30(1): 279–306.

Seidenberg, M. and Elman, J. (1999) Networks are not 'hidden rules', *Trends in Cognitive Sciences*, 3(8): 288–9.

Shaw, M. E. and Wright, J. M. (1968) *Scales of Measurement of Attitude*. New York: McGraw-Hill.

Shayer, M. (1999) Cognitive Acceleration through science education II: its effects and scope, *International Journal of Science Education*, 21(8): 883–92.

Shayer, M. (2008) Intelligence for Education: As *described* by Piaget and *measured* by psychometrics, *British Journal of Educational Psychology*, 78(1): 1–29.

Shayer, M. and Adey, P. (1981) *Towards a Science of Science Teaching*. London: Heinemann.

Shayer, M. and Wylam, H. (1978) The distribution of Piagetian stages of thinking in the British middle and secondary school children. II: 14–16 year-olds and sex differentials, *British Journal of Educational Psychology*, 48: 62–70.

Shayer, M., Coe, R. and Ginsburg, D. (2007) 30 years on – a large anti-'Flynn effect'?, the Piagetian test Volume and Heaviness norms 1975–2003, *British Journal of Educational Psychology*, 77(1): 25–41.

Shell, D. F., Husman, J., Turner, J. E., Cliffel, D. M., Nath, I. and Sweany, N. (2005) The impact of computer supported collaborative learning communities on high school students' knowledge building, strategic learning, and perceptions of the classroom, *Journal of Educational Computing Research*, 33(3): 327–49.

Shepard, L. A. and Bleim, C. L. (1995) Parents' thinking about standardised tests and performance assessments, *Educational Researcher*, 24(8): 25–32.

Shepardson, D. P. and Moje, E. B. (1999) The role of anomalous data in restructuring fourth graders' frameworks for understanding electric circuits, *International Journal of Science Education*, 21(1): 77–94.

Shulman, L. (1987) Knowledge and teaching: foundations of the new reform, *Harvard Educational Review*, 57(1): 1–22.

Shymansky, J. A., Kyle, W. C., Jr. and Alport, J. M. (1983) The effects of new science curricula on student performance, *Journal of Research in Science Teaching*, 20: 387–404.

Shymansky, J. A., Yore, L. D., Treagust, D. F., et al. (1997) Examining the construction process: a study of changes in Level 10 students' understanding of classical mechanics, *Journal of Research in Science Teaching*, 34(6): 571–93.

Siegel, H. (1989) The rationality of science, critical thinking and science education, *Synthese*, 80(1): 9–42.

Siegler, R. S. and Liebert, R. M. (1975) Acquisition of formal scientific reasoning by 10- and 13-year-olds: designing a factorial experiment, *Developmental Psychology*, 11: 401–2.

Simon, S. and Harrison, C. (2008) Evidence-based professional development of for science teachers: collaboration and evaluation in two countries, *International Journal of Science Education*, 30(5): 575.

Simpson, G., Hoyles, C. and Noss, R. (2005) Designing a programming-based approach for modelling scientific phenomena, *Journal of Computer Assisted Learning*, 21(2): 143–58.

Simpson, R. D. and Oliver, J. S. (1985) Attitude toward science and achievement motivation profiles of male and female science students in grades six through ten, *Science Education*, 69(4): 511–26.

Simpson, R. D. and Oliver, J. S. (1990) A summary of the major influences on attitude toward and achievement in science among adolescent students, *Science Education*, 74(1): 1–18.

Simpson, R. D. and Troost, K. M. (1982) Influences of committment to and learning of science among adolescent students, *Science Education*, 69(1): 19–24.

Sinclair, J., Ironside, M. and Seifert, R. (1996) Classroom struggle? Market oriented education reforms and their impact on the teacher labour process, *Work, Employment and Society*, 10(4): 641–61.

Siskin, L. S. (1994) *Realms of Knowledge: Academic Departments in Secondary Schools*. Washington DC: Falmer Press.

Sjøberg, S. and Schreiner, C. (2005) How do learners in different cultures relate to science and technology? Results and perspectives from the project ROSE, *Asia Pacific Forum on Science Learning and Teaching*, 6(2): 1–16.

Skinner, B. F. (1974) *About Behaviorism*. New York: Alfred A. Knopf.

Smail, B. and Kelly, A. (1984) Sex differences in science and technology among 11 year old schoolchildren: II – Affective, *Research in Science and Technology Education*, 2: 87–106.

Smith, F., Hardman, F., Wall, K. and Mroz, M. (2004) Interactive whole class teaching in the National Literacy and Numeracy Strategies, *British Educational Research Journal*, 30(3): 395–411.

Smith, M. K., Wood, W. B., Adams, W. K., Wieman, C., Knight, J. K., Guild, N. and Su, T. T. (2009) Why peer discussion improves student performance on in-class concept questions, *Science*, 323(5910): 122–4.

Smith, M. L. and Glass, G. V. (1987) *Research and Evaluation in Education and the Social Sciences*. Englewood Cliffs, NJ: Prentice-Hall.

Smithers, A. and Robinson, P. (2005) *Teacher Turnover, Wastage and Destinations* (No. RB 553). London: Department for Education and Skills.

Smithers, A. and Robinson, P. (2008) *Physics in Schools IV: Supply and Retention of Teachers*. London: The Gatsby Charitable Foundation.

Snir, J., Smith, C. L. and Raz, G. (2003) Linking phenomena with competing underlying models: a software tool for introducing students to the particulate model of matter, *Science Education*, 87(6): 794–830.

Snow, C. P. (1959) *The Two Cultures*. Cambridge: Cambridge University Press.

Soanes, C. and Stevenson, A. (eds) (2008) *Concise Oxford English Dictionary* (11th, revised ed.). Oxford: Oxford University Press.

Soderberg, P. and Price, F. (2003) An examination of problem-based teaching and learning in population genetics and evolution using EVOLVE, a computer simulation, *International Journal of Science Education*, 25(1): 35–55.

Sokal, A. and Bricmont, J. (1998) *Intellectual Impostures: Postmodern Philosophers' Abuse of Science*. London: Profile Books.

Solomon, J. (1983) *Science in a Social Context (SISCON)-in-Schools*. Oxford: Basil Blackwell.

Solomon, J. (1991a) *Exploring the Nature of Science: Key Stage 3*. Glasgow: Blackie.

Solomon, J. (1991b) School laboratory life, in B. E. Woolnough (ed.), *Practical Science*. Milton Keynes: Open University Press, pp. 101–11.

Solomon, J. (1992) The classroom discussion of science-based social issues presented on television: knowledge, attitudes and values, *International Journal of Science Education*, 14(4): 431–44.

Solomon, J. (1994) The rise and fall of constructivism, *Studies in Science Education*, 23: 1–19.

Solomon, J., Duveen, J. and Scott, L. (1992) *Exploring the Nature of Science: Key Stage 4*. Hatfield: Association for Science Education.

Sorby, S. A. (2009) Educational research in developing 3-D spatial skills for engineering students, *International Journal of Science Education*, 31(3,4): 459–80.

SPACE Reports (1990–1992) Liverpool: Liverpool University Press.

Spall, K., Stanisstreet, M., Dickson, D. and Boyes, E. (2004) The development of students' construction of biology and physics, *International Journal of Science Education*, 26(7): 787–803.

Spearman, C. (1927) 'General Intelligence', objectively determined and measured, *American Journal of Psychology*, 15: 201–93.

Spelke, E. and Kinzler, K. (2007) Core knowledge, *Developmental Science*, 10(1): 89–96.

Stahl, G., Koschmann, T. and Suthers, D. (2006) Computer-supported collaborative learning: an historical perspective, in R. K. Sawyer (ed.), *The Cambridge Handbook of the Learning Sciences, Washington University, St Louis*. New York: Cambridge University Press, pp. 409–26.

Stobart, G. (2001) The validity of National Curriculum assessment, *British Journal of Educational Studies*, 49(1): 26–39.

Stobart, G. (2006) The validity of formative assessment,in J. Gardener (ed.) *Assessment and Learning*. London: Sage, pp. 133–46.

Stohr-Hunt, P. M. (1996) An analysis of the frequency of hands-on experience and science achievement, *Journal of Research in Science Teaching*, 33(1): 101–9.

Strand, S. (1998) A 'value added' analysis of the 1996 primary school performance tables, *Educational Research*, 40(2): 123–37.

Strang, J., Daniels, S. and Bell, J. (1991) *Assessment Matters No. 6: Planning and Carrying out Investigations*. London: School Examinations and Assessment Council.

Strauss, R. P. and Sawyer, E. A. (1986) Some new evidence on teacher and student competencies, *Economics of Education Review*, 5(1): 41–8.

Strauss, S. and Shilony, T. (1994) Teachers' models of children's minds and learning, in L. A. Hirschfied and S. A. Gelman (eds), *Mapping the Mind: Domain Specificity in Cognition and Culture*. Cambridge: Cambridge University Press, pp. 455–73.

Street, B. (2006) *Literacy as Text: Multimodality and Multiliteracies, EFA Global Monitoring Report 2006*. New York: UNESCO.

Sundberg, M. D., Dini, M. L. and Li, E. (1994) Decreasing course content improves student comprehension of science and attitudes toward science in freshman biology, *Journal of Research in Science Teaching*, 31(6): 679–93.

Suto, W. M. I. and Greatorex, J. (2008) What goes through an examiner's mind? Using verbal protocols to gain insights into the GCSE marking process, *British Educational Research Journal*, 34(2): 213–33.

Suto, W. M. I. and Nadas, R. (2008a) What determines GCSE marking accuracy? An exploration of expertise among maths and physics markers, *Research Papers in Education*, 23(4): 1–21.

Suto, W. M. I. and Nadas, R. (2008b) Why are some GCSE examination questions harder to mark accurately than others? Using Kelly's Repertory Grid technique to identify relevant question features, *Research Papers in Education*, 23(2): 1–42.

Sutton, C. (1998) New perspectives on language learning, in B. Fraser and K. Tobin (eds), *The International Handbook of Science Education*. London: Kluwer, pp. 27–38.

Swain, J. R. L. (1989) The development of a framework for the assessment of process skills in a Graded Assessments in Science Project, *International Journal of Science Education*, 11(3): 251–9.

Swain, J. R. L. (1991a) Standard assessment tasks in science at Key Stage 3: initial development to the 1990 trial, *British Journal of Curriculum and Assessment*, 1(2): 26–8.

Swain, J. R. L. (1991b) Standard assessment tasks in science at Key Stage 3: the 1991 Pilot, *British Journal of Curriculum and Assessment*, 2(1): 19–20.

Swain, J. R. L. (1996) The impact and effect of Key Stage 3 science tests, *School Science Review*, 78(283): 79–90.

Swain, J. R. L., Monk, M. and Johnson, S. (1999) A comparative study of attitudes to the aims of practical work in science education in Egypt, Korea and the UK, *International Journal of Science Education*, 21(12): 1311–23.

Swain, J. R. L., Monk, M. and Johnson, S. (2000) Developments in science teachers' attitudes to aims for practical work: continuity and change, *Teacher Development*, 4(2): 281–92.

Tai, R. H., Qi Liu, C., Maltese, A. V. and Fan, X. (2006) Planning early for careers in science, *Science*, 312: 1143–5.

Talton, E. L. and Simpson, R. D. (1987) Relationships of attitude toward classroom environment with attitude toward and achievement in science among tenth grade biology students, *Journal of Research in Science Teaching*, 24(6): 507–25.

Talton, E. L. and Simpson, R.D. (1990) A summary of major influences on attitude toward and achievement in science among adolescent students, *Science Education*, 74(1): 1–18.

Tao, P.-K. (2004) Developing understanding of image formation by lenses through collaborative learning mediated by multimedia computer-assisted learning programs, *International Journal of Science Education*, 26(10): 1171–97.

Tao, P.-K. and Gunstone, R. F. (1999) Conceptual change in science through collaborative learning at the computer, *International Journal of Science Education*, 21(1): 39–57.

Taylor, C. (1996) *Defining Science: A Rhetoric of Demarcation*. Madison: WI: University of Wisconsin Press.

Taylor, R. M. (1990) The National Curriculum: a study to compare levels of attainment with data from APU science surveys (1980–4), *School Science Review*, 72(258): 31–7.

Teachernet (2005) *Health and Safety*. Available at: http://www.teachernet.gov.uk/teachinginengland/detail.cfm?id=336 (accessed 6 March 2005).

Teacher Training Agency (TTA) (1997) *Consultation on Standards for the Award of Qualified Teacher Status*. London: TTA.

Teacher Training Agency (TTA) (1998) *Initial Teacher Training: National Curriculum*. London: Teacher Training Agency.

Teacher Training Agency (TTA) (2003) Raising standards and tackling workload: a national agreement. Available at: http://www.tda.gov.uk/upload/resources/pdf/n/na_standards_workload.pdf (accessed 25 Oct. 2008).

Teitelbaum, M. (2007) Do we need more scientists and engineers? Paper presented at the Conference on the National Value of Science Education, University of York, September.

The Research Business (1994) *Views of Science Among Students, Teachers and Parents*. London: Institution of Electrical Engineers.

Thijs, G. D. and Bosch, G.M. (1995) Cognitive effects of science experiments focusing on students' preconceptions of force: a comparison of demonstrations and small-group practicals, *International Journal of Science Education*, 17(3): 311–23.

Thomas, G. and Durant, J. (1987) Why should we promote the public understanding of science. In *Science Literacy Papers*. Oxford: University of Oxford, Department of Educational Studies, pp. 1–14.

Thomas, G. E. (1986) Cultivating the interest of women and minorities in high school mathematics and science, *Science Education*, 73(3): 243–9.

Thompson, J. and Soyibo, K. (2002) Effects of lecture, teacher demonstration, discussion and practical work on 10th graders' attitudes to chemistry and understanding of electrolysis, *Research in Science and Technological Education*, 20(1): 25–35.

Thompson, J. J. (ed.) (1975) *Practical Work in Sixthform Science*. Oxford: Department of Educational Studies, University of Oxford.

Thorndike, R. L., Hagen, E. P. and Sattler, J. M. (1986) *Stanford-Binet Intelligence Scale*, 4th edn. Riverside: DLM Teaching Resources.

Tiberghien, A. (2000) Designing teaching situations in the secondary school, in R. Millar, J. Leach, and J. Osborne (eds), *Improving Science Education: The Contribution of Research*. Buckingham: Open University Press, pp. 27–47.

Tiberghien, A., Veillard, L., Le Maréchal, J.-F., Buty, C. and Millar, R. (2001) An analysis of labwork tasks used in science teaching at upper secondary school and university levels in several European countries, *Science Education*, 85(5): 483–508.

Tilling, S. (2004) Fieldwork in UK secondary schools: influences and provision, *Journal of Biological Education*, 38(2): 54–8.

Tilling, S. and Dillon, J. (2007) *Initial Teacher Education and the Outdoor Classroom: Standards for the Future*. Shrewsbury: ASE and FSC.

Timperley, H. and Alton-Lee, A. (2008) Reframing teacher professional development: an alternative policy approach to strengthened values outcomes for diverse learners, *Review of Educational Research*, 32: 328–69.

TIMSS and PIRLS (2004) *TIMSS 2003 International Science Report*, by Michael O. Martin, Ina V.S. Mullis, Eugenio J. Gonzalez, Steven J. Chrostowski. Boston: TIMSS & PIRLS International Study Center, Boston College.

Tobias, S. (1990) *They're Not Dumb, They're Different: Stalking the Second Tier*. Tucson, AZ: Research Corporation.

Tobin, K. and McRobbie, C. (1996) Cultural myths as constraints to the enacted science curriculum, *Science Education*, 80(2): 223–41.

Tobin, K. and McRobbie, C. (1997) Beliefs about the nature of science and the enacted science curriculum, *Science and Education*, 6(4): 331–54.

Towse, J., Hitch, G. and Hutton, U. (1998) A re-evaluation of working memory capacity in children, *Journal of Memory and Language*, 39: 195–217.

Training and Development Agency for Schools (TDA) (2007) *Professional Standards for Qualified Teacher Status and Requirements for Initial Teacher Training.* London: Training and Development Agency.

Training and Development Agency for Schools (TDA) (2008) *Masters in Teaching and Learning*, from http://www.tda.gov.uk.

Traweek, S. (1988) *Beamtimes and Lifetimes: The World of High Energy Physicists.* Cambridge, MA: Harvard University Press.

Treagust, D. F., Harrison, A. G., Venville, G. J. and Dagher, Z. (1996) Using an analogical teaching approach to engender conceptual change, *International Journal of Science Education*, 18(2); 213–29.

Tsai, C. (2002) Nested epistemologies: science teachers' beliefs of teaching, learning and science, *International Journal of Science Education*, 24; 771–83.

Turner, D. M. (1927) *History of Science Teaching in England.* London: Chapman and Hall.

Turner, S. (2008) School science and its controversies; or, whatever happened to scientific literacy? *Public Understanding of Science*, 17: 55–72.

Tversky, B., Morrison, J. B. and Betrancourt, M. (2002) Animation: does it facilitate? *International Journal of Human-Computer Studies*, 57(4): 247–62.

Tyson, L. M., Venville, G., Harrison, A. G. and Treagust, D. F. (1997) A multidimensional framework for interpreting conceptual change in the classroom, *Science Education*, 81: 387–404.

Tytler, R., Osborne, J., Williams, G., et al. (2008) *Opening Up Pathways: Engagement in STEM across the Primary-Secondary School Transition: A Review of the Literature Concerning Supports and Barriers to Science, Technology, Engineering and Mathematics Engagement at Primary-Secondary Transition. Commissioned by the Australian Department of Education, Employment and Workplace Relations.* Melbourne: Deakin University.

Van den Akker, J. (1998) The science curriculum: between ideals and outcomes, in B. J. Fraser and K. G. Tobin (eds), *International Handbook of Science Education*, Vol. 1. Dordrecht: Kluwer, pp. 421–48.

Van Lier, L. (1996) *Interaction in the Language Curriculum.* New York: Longman.

Van Praagh, G. (2003) *A Fire to be Kindled: The Global Influence of Christ's Hospital on Science Education.* Bury St Edmunds: St Edmundsbury Press.

Van Zee, E. H., Iwasyk, M., Kurose, A., Simpson, D. and Wild, J. (2001) Student and teacher questioning during conversations about science. *Journal of Research in Science Teaching*, 38(2): 159–90.

Von Glaserfeld, E. (1989) An exposition of constructivism: why some like it radical, in R. Davis, C. Maher and N. Noddings (eds), *Constructivist Views on the Teaching and Learning of Mathematics.* Reston, VA: National Council of Teachers of Mathematics.

Vosniadou, S. and Ortony, A. (1989) *Similarity and Analogical Reasoning.* Cambridge: Cambridge University Press.

Vygotsky, L. S. (1978) *Mind in Society: The Development of Higher Psychological Processes.* Cambridge, MA: Harvard University Press.

Vygotsky, L. S. (1986) *Thought and Language.* A. Kozulin (ed. and trans.) Cambridge, MA: MIT Press.

Wandersee, J. H., Mintzes, J. J. and Novak, J. D. (1994) Research on alternative conceptions in science, in D. L. Gabel (ed.), *Handbook of Research on Science Teaching and Learning*. New York: Macmillan, pp. 177–210.

Waring, M. R. H. (1979) *Social Pressures and Curriculum Innovation*. London: Routledge.

Watson, J. R., Goldsworthy, A. and Wood-Robinson, V. (1999a) What is not fair with investigations? *School Science Review*, 80(292): 101–6.

Watson, J. R., Goldsworthy, A. and Wood-Robinson, V. (1999b) One hundred and twenty hours of practical science investigations: a report of teachers' work with pupils aged 7 to 14, in K. Neilsen and A. C. Paulsen (eds), *Practical Work in Science Education: The Face of Science in Schools*. Copenhagen: Royal Danish School of Educational Studies, pp. 112–21.

Watson, J. R., Prieto, T. and Dillon, J. (1995) The effect of practical work on students' understanding of combustion, *Journal of Research in Science Teaching*, 32(5): 487–502.

Watson, J. R., Swain, J. R. L. and McRobbie, C. (2004) Students' discussions in practical scientific inquiries. *International Journal of Science Education*, 26(1): 25–46.

Watson, J. R., Wood-Robinson, V. and Nikolaou, L. (2006) Better scientific enquiries, in V. Wood-Robinson (ed.), *ASE Guide to Secondary Science Education*. Hatfield: Association for Science Education, pp. 196–204.

Wayne, A. and Youngs, P. (2003) Teacher characteristics and student achievement gains: a review, *Review of Educational Research*, 73(1): 89–122.

Webb, M. E. (2005) Affordances of ICT in science learning; implications for an integrated pedagogy, *International Journal of Science Education*, 27(6); 705–35.

Webb, M. E. and Cox, M. J. (2004) A review of pedagogy related to ICT, *Technology, Pedagogy and Education*, 13(3): 235–86.

Webb, N. (2009) The teacher's role in promoting collaborative dialogue in the classroom, *British Journal of Educational Psychology*, 79(1): 1–28.

Wechsler, D. (1958) *The Measurement and Appraisal of Adult Intelligence*, 5th edn. Baltimore, MD: Williams and Wilkins.

Weinburgh, M. (1995) Gender differences in student attitudes toward science: a meta-analysis of the literature from 1970 to 1991, *Journal of Research in Science Teaching*, 32(4): 387–98.

Wellington, J. (1981) What's supposed to happen, Sir? Some problems with Discovery Learning, *School Science Review*, 63: 167–73.

Wellington, J. (1990) Formal and informal learning in science: the role of interactive science centres, *Physics Education*, 25(5): 247–52.

Wellington, J. (1991) Newspaper science, school science: friends or enemies? *International Journal of Science Education*, 13(4): 363–72.

Wellington, J. (1998) *Interactive Science Centres and Science Education*. Croner's Heads of Science Bulletin. (Issue 16). Kingston-upon-Thames: Croner Publications.

Wellington, J. and Osborne, J. F. (2001) *Language and Literacy in Science Education*. Buckingham: Open University Press.

Wells, G. (1999) *Dialogic Inquiry: Toward a Sociocultural Practice and Theory of Education*. Cambridge: Cambridge University Press.

Wells, G. and Arauz, R. M. (2006) Dialogue in the classroom, *The Journal of the Learning Sciences*, 15(3): 379–428.

West, A. and Pennell, H. (2000) Publishing school examination results in England: incentives and consequences, *Educational Studies*, 26(4): 423–36.

White, B. Y. and Frederiksen, J. R. (1998) Inquiry, modeling, and metacognition: making science accessible to all students, *Cognition and Instruction*, 16(1): 3–118.

White, R. T. and Gunstone, R. F. (1992) *Probing Understanding*. London: Falmer Press.

Whitehead, J. M. (1996) Sex stereotypes, gender identity and subject choice at A level, *Educational Research*, 38(2): 147–60.

Whitfield, R. C. (1980) Educational research and science teaching, *School Science Review*, 60: 411–30.

Wiliam, D. (1993) Validity, dependability and reliability in National Curriculum assessment, *The Curriculum Journal*, 4(3): 335–50.

Wiliam, D. (1998) Making international comparisons: the third international mathematics and science study, *British Journal of Curriculum & Assessment*, 8(3): 33–8.

Wiliam, D. and Black, P. (1996) Meanings and consequences: a basis for distinguishing formative and summative functions of assessment, *British Educational Research Journal*, 22(5): 537–48.

Wiliam, D., Lee, C., Harrison, C. and Black, P. (2004) Teachers developing assessment for learning: impact on student achievement, *Assessment in Education*, 11(1): 49–65.

Wilkinson, J. and Ward, M. (1997) A comparative study of students' and their teacher's perceptions of laboratory work in secondary schools, *Research in Science Education*, 27(4): 599–610.

Willard, C. (1985) The science of values and the values of science, in J. Cox, M. Sillars and G. Walker (eds), *Argument and Social Practice: The Fourth SCA/AFA Summer Conference on Argumentation*. Annadale, VA: Speech Communication Association, pp. 435–44.

Wilson, J. (2001) Putting life back into biology coursework, *School Science Review*, 83(302): 98–100.

Wittgenstein, L. (1961) *Tracatus Logico-Philosophicus*. London: Routledge.

Wood, D. J., Bruner, J.S. and Ross, G. (1976) The role of tutoring in problem solving, *Journal of Child Psychology and Psychiatry*, 17(2): 89–100.

Wood, R., Griffiths, D. M., Chappel , D. and Davies, N. O. M. (2004) The structural characteristics of video games: a psycho-structural analysis, *CyberPsychology and Behaviour*, 7(1): 1–10.

Woolnough, B. E. (1994) *Effective Science Teaching*. Buckingham: Open University Press.

Woolnough, B. E. and Alsop, T. (1985) *Practical Work in Science*. Cambridge: Cambridge University Press.

Wray, D. and Lewis, M. (1997) *Extending Literacy: Children Reading and Writing Non-fiction*. London: Routledge.

Yager, R. E., Engen, H. B. and Snider, B. C. F. (1969) Effects of the laboratory and demonstration methods upon the outcomes of instruction in secondary biology, *Journal of Research in Science Teaching*, 6: 76–86.

Yore, L., Bisanz, G. L. and Hand, B. M. (2003) Examining the literacy component of science literacy, *International Journal of Science Education*, 25(6): 689–725.

Zacharia, Z. C. (2007) Comparing and combining real and virtual experimentation: an effort to enhance students' conceptual understanding of electric circuits, *Journal of Computer Assisted Learning*, 23(2): 120–32.

Zacharia, Z. C. and Anderson, O. R. (2003) The effects of an interactive computer-based simulation prior to performing a laboratory inquiry-based experiment on students' conceptual understanding of physics, *American Journal of Physics*, 71(6): 618–29.

Zacharia, Z. C. and Constantinou, C. P. (2008) Comparing the influence of physical and virtual manipulatives in the context of the Physics by Enquiry curriculum: the case of undergraduate students' conceptual understanding of heat and temperature, *American Journal of Physics*, 76(4/5): 425–30.

Zacharia, Z. C., Olympiou, G., and Papaevripidou, M. (2008) Effects of experimenting with physical and virtual manipulatives on students' conceptual understanding in heat and temperature, *Journal of Research in Science Teaching*, 45(9): 1021–35.

Zembylas, M. (2005) Three perspectives on linking the cognitive and emotional in science learning: conceptual change, socio-constructivism, and post-structuralism, *Studies in Science Education*, 41: 91–116.

Zhang, J., Chen, Q., Sun, Y. and Reid, D. J. (2004) Triple scheme of learning support design for scientific discovery learning based on computer simulation: experimental research, *Journal of Computer Assisted Learning*, 20(4): 269–82.

Zhao, Y. and Rop, S. (2001) A critical review of the literature on electronic networks as reflective discourse communities for inservice teachers, *Education and Information Technologies*, 6(2); 81–94.

Ziman, J. (1979) *Reliable Knowledge*. Cambridge: Cambridge University Press.

Ziman, J. (2000) *Real Science: What it Is and What it Means*. Cambridge: Cambridge University Press.

Zimmerman, C. (2000) The development of scientific reasoning skills, *Developmental Review*, 20: 99–149.

Zimmerman, C. (2007) The development of scientific thinking skills in elementary and middle school, *Developmental Review*, 27: 172–223.

Zimmerman, C., Bisanz, G. L., Bisanz, J., Klein, J. S. and Klein, P. (2001) Science at the supermarket: a comparison of what appears in the popular press, experts' advice to readers, and what students want to know, *Public Understanding of Science*, 10(1): 37–58.

Zion, M., Michalsky, T. and Mevarech, Z. (2005) The effects of metacognitive instruction embedded within an asynchronous learning network on scientific inquiry skills, *International Journal of Science Education*, 27(8): 957–83.

Zohar, A. (2004) *Higher Order Thinking in Science Classrooms: Students' Learning and Teachers Professional Development*. Dordrecht: Kluwer.

Zohar, A. and Nemet, F. (2002) Fostering students' knowledge and argumentation skills through dilemmas in human genetics, *Journal of Research in Science Teaching*, 39(1): 35–62.

Index

DEVELOPING SCIENTIFIC LITERACY

Using News Media in the Classroom

Ruth Jarman; Billy McClune

"Throughout the book, all the ideas, content, suggestions and arguments are supported by in-depth research and solid referencing, making this an authoritative, yet eminently readable, reference volume for current and would-be secondary science teachers."

School Science Review

Science-related news stories have great potential as a resource for teaching and learning about science and its impact on society. By demonstrating the relevance of the subject in everyday life, they can form a valuable bridge between the school classroom and the 'real world'.

Worldwide, those advocating science education reforms stress the need to promote 'scientific literacy' among young people and typically this includes equipping students to critically engage with science reports in the media.

However, very little guidance exists for those who wish to do so. *Developing Scientific Literacy* addresses this gap, offering a much-needed framework for teachers wishing to explore 'science in the media' in secondary schools or colleges.

This timely book is a source of valuable ideas and insights for all secondary science teachers. It will also be of interest to those with responsibilities for initial teacher training and continuing professional development.

Contents: *Scientific literacy and science in the news - What is news? What is science news? - News production, science news production - News reception, science news reception - What research tells us about news and science education - Thinking about aims, articles and activities - Using the news to teach about science 'content' and 'enquiry' - Using the news to teach about science and society - Teaching about science in the news - Working together to ensure 'science in the news' a place in the curriculum - References and further reading - Index*

2007   232pp

978-0-335-21795-3 (Paperback)
978-0-335-21796-0 (Hardback)

LEARNING SCIENCE TEACHING

Developing a Professional Knowledge Base

Keith Bishop; Paul Denley

"Bishop and Denley in Learning Science Teaching have focused as much on good pedagogy as on the peculiarities of science teaching. It is for this reason that their book will be of value not only to trainees in education, but also to a range of professionals working in schools, Higher Education and, in particular, to those responsible for planning and delivering CPD. It is far more than a test for trainee teachers."

Science Teacher Education

- What do you need to know to be a successful science teacher?
- How do you develop or acquire that knowledge?

If you are just embarking on your learning journey as a science teacher, or are involved in supporting beginning and early career teachers on their way, then this book is written for you.

The authors show how the route to success involves the development of a personal, yet distinctive and complex set of inter-related professional knowledge bases. Throughout the book, the classroom practice of a group of highly accomplished science teachers is analysed to reveal the knowledge bases that they have acquired, which the reader can then reflect upon. In addition, students provide penetrating insights into the kinds of science teaching that engages them.

The book argues that highly accomplished science teachers are also continually learning science teachers. It stresses the importance of learning through others, by participation in communities of science practitioners, as well as individual learning through classroom research. Whether you are a beginning teacher or a more experienced teacher looking to support beginning and early career teachers, this book offers a rich source of experiences, ideas and insights to support you on your journey to becoming a successful science teacher.

Contents: *Preface - Acknowledgements Professional knowledge of the science teacher: a worldwide perspective - Transforming science knowledge - Physics - Biology - Chemistry - The nature of science - The student voice - Professional learning - Professional knowledge in context- Appendix References - Index*

2007   240pp

978-0-335-22235-3 (Paperback)   978-0-335-21510-2 (Hardback)